Teaching Learners with Mild Disabilities

Integrating Research and Practice

Teaching Learners with Mild Disabilities

Integrating Research and Practice

Ruth Lyn Meese
Longwood College

with contributions by
Terry Overton and Patty Whitfield

Brooks/Cole Publishing Company
Pacific Grove, California

The trademark ITP is used under license.

Brooks/Cole Publishing Company

A Division of Wadsworth, Inc.

© 1994 by Wadsworth, Inc., Belmont, California 94002.

Printed in the United States of America.

10   9   8   7   6   5   4   3   2   1

Library of Congress Cataloging-in-Publication Data

Meese, Ruth Lyn.
    Teaching learners with mild disabilities : integrating research and practice / Ruth Lyn Meese.
        p.   cm.
    Includes bibliographical references and indexes.
    ISBN 0-534-21102-X
    1. Handicapped children—Education—United States—Case studies.   2. Special education—Study and teaching—United States.   I. Title.
    LC4031.M44   1993
    371.91′0973—dc20   93-28274
                                                                                                      CIP

Sponsoring Editor: Vicki Knight
Marketing Representative: Bob Podstepney
Editorial Assistant: Lauri Banks-Wothe
Production Coordinator: Kirk Bomont
Production: Johnstone Associates
Manuscript Editor: Ann Mirels
Permissions Editor: Roxane Buck Ezcurra
Interior Design: Detta Penna
Cover Design: Susan Haberkorn
Cover Artist: Judith Larzelere
Cover Photo: Jan Bindas Studio, Boston
Interior Illustration: Hal Keith, K & S Graphics
Photo Researcher: Lindsay Kefauver
Typesetting: TCSystems, Inc.
Printing and Binding: Arcata Graphics/Fairfield

Credits continue on page 452.

To James W. Windle,
my husband, who cooked the meals, washed the clothes,
and gave me abundant encouragement throughout this project,
and to all those who teach children with mild disabilities—thank you.

Preface

One particularly thorny problem my colleagues and I have faced every day is how to help the preservice teacher apply theoretical principles to daily classroom activities. Having had only limited classroom experience, the teacher-to-be is often unable to relate topics covered in college "methods" courses to the "real-world" situations in which teachers are involved throughout the school day. Although our students participate in early supervised field experiences and related classroom discussions, each assigned field placement is unique. Naive learners can easily become confused about their observations.

In an attempt to integrate theory and research with practice in my methods courses, I developed numerous activities, examples, and scenarios for our classroom discussions. However, this practical material lacked the cohesive framework it needed to put it in perspective. In addition, although case approaches encourage reflective discussion, I've found that my preservice teachers first must acquire some fundamental information if they are to profit from these discussions.

This book, then, was born of necessity. To unify activities, examples, and cases for classroom discussion, I developed a set of hypothetical schools, students, and teachers with whom my preservice teachers could identify. These fictional students and their teachers have become the framework for relevant on-campus instruction in theory, research, and related practice. In the college classroom, for example, we can discuss decisions made by Ms. Kirk, a fourth-grade teacher, and Ms. Lopez, a special educator, both of whom are responsible for the instruction of Travis and Joey, two fourth-graders with mild disabilities. We can assume the role of Mr. Abel, a secondary-level special educator, or that of Mr. McNally, a geography teacher, and conduct collaborative planning and teaching role plays in our classroom. In addition, we can plan lessons and activities appropriate for sixth-graders Travis and Joey and ninth-graders Susan and Robert, also identified as having mild disabilities. Moreover, because many students with learning and behavioral problems are never identified for special education programs but nonetheless present instructional challenges for their regular classroom teachers, I have included students without mild disabilities—Celie, Kevin, Leon, and Marcus—in our instructional framework.

This book, therefore, is most appropriate for the preservice teacher of students with mild disabilities—both the classroom teacher and the special educator. Inservice teachers new to the field of special education may also find the book helpful in meeting their needs. Throughout the text, I have attempted to present not only research-based instructional methods, but also those proven effective by teachers through reflective practice.

Part One provides some basic foundations for instruction. In Chapter 1 we introduce our fictional schools, teachers, and students. These teachers and students then become the basis for examples, feature boxes, and application exercises in subsequent chapters. Although adequate introductory information about these students and teachers is presented in Chapter 1, with details provided in Appendix A for the four students with mild disabilities, I would encourage the instructor who uses this text to personalize the hypothetical students and teachers to reflect local or regional needs of the schools he or she serves. Chapters 2 and 3 also provide foundations for instruction. Chapter 2 centers on the characteristics of learners with mild disabilities, while the focus of Chapter 3 is on historical and current approaches to teaching these learners.

In Part Two, "Organizing for Instruction," we discuss the importance of communicating for student success in Chapter 4 and managing the classroom environment in Chapter 5. Chapter 6, "Assessing Student Progress," and Chapter 7, "Planning for Successful Instruction," offer beginning teachers the means for linking the knowledge gained about students with relevant instructional objectives and lesson plans.

The content of Part Three, "Providing Instruction," is sufficiently detailed to be of immediate practical classroom use. Effective teacher behaviors are the focus of Chapter 8, and techniques to promote student-mediated learning are introduced in Chapter 9. Chapters 10 through 14 provide the classroom teacher with effective methods for reading instruction, language arts instruction, mathematics instruction, content instruction in the regular classroom, and instruction in social and independent living skills, respectively. Again, examples, boxed material, and application exercises throughout these chapters feature the students and teachers introduced in Chapter 1, whom the reader by now has come to "know."

I owe a debt of gratitude to the many indispensable people who have made a project of this magnitude possible. My colleagues, Terry Overton and Patty Whitfield, made significant contributions to the manuscript through their initial drafts of Chapters 4, 5, 6, 7, and 9, as well as through their ongoing support and helpful suggestions. My graduate assistant, Lisa McVey Reid, spent many hours obtaining permissions, proofreading, and constructing the index. Fran Hughes, a talented artist, created the sketches of my hypothetical students. Vicki Knight, my sponsoring editor at Brooks/Cole, offered her usual invaluable editorial advice and support. Finally, the following reviewers gave generously of their time to provide thoughtful comments and suggestions that strengthened each draft of the manuscript: Lyman W. Boomer, Western Illinois University; Kathy Boyle-Gast, University of Georgia; Steven Daley, Idaho State University; Darcy Miller, Washington State University; Lewis Putnam, University of Wisconsin, Milwaukee; and Deborah Bott Slaton, University of Kentucky. To each of you, and to the many others who have contributed to the production of this text, I extend my sincerest thank-you.

Ruth Lyn Meese

Brief Contents

Contents

13   Content Instruction in the Regular Classroom   325

Part One

Foundations for Instruction

The Learners and Their Teachers

Chapter 1

Focus

As you read, think about the following questions:

How do schools reflect today's society?

What is America 2000 and how will it affect programs for students with special educational needs?

What special programs are currently operating to help children with low achievement become successful in school?

How does compensatory education differ from special education?

✎ For some students, learning is relatively easy and exciting. Yet, for many youngsters who are performing below grade level, learning is a difficult process and school is a constant struggle. Some children who are having problems are enrolled in special education programs for students with disabilities. Most of these students spend a portion of their school day mainstreamed in the regular classroom. Those who do not qualify for special education are taught solely by the regular classroom teacher. Whether in a special education program or in the regular classroom, children who struggle to learn challenge the skills of their teachers.

This book is primarily about students with mild disabilities. The term *mild disabilities* encompasses learning disabilities, emotional/behavioral disorders, and mild mental retardation. Students with mild disabilities share certain characteristics and have similar instructional needs (Hallahan & Kauffman, 1977). Despite the term *mild*, they all have significant problems with learning and behavior that interfere with their progress in school, and they all require special assistance from their teachers.

Although this text is intended for teachers of students with mild disabilities, we believe that other children who are performing below grade level but who are not in special education programs can also benefit from the instructional strategies we will describe. As you read, please bear this in mind, along with the following additional beliefs that guide our thinking:

- All children and youth can learn when appropriate goals are set for them.

- All children and youth deserve the best instruction their schools can offer, regardless of the setting in which that instruction is delivered.

- Effective teaching strategies for students with mild disabilities are likely to be similar, regardless of the categorical label assigned.

- Effective teaching strategies for students with mild disabilities include those in published research studies as well as those "proven" in practice by professionals observing "what works" in specific school settings.

- Special education and regular classroom teachers must collaborate to improve instruction for *all* students who struggle to learn.

This text is arranged in three parts. In Part One, "Foundations for Instruction," the three chapters include an introduction to today's schools, to learners with mild disabilities, and to teaching approaches designed for these learners. Part Two, "Organizing for Instruction," includes four chapters examining methods used by teachers to enhance communication, manage the classroom environment, assess student progress, and plan instruction. In Part Three, "Providing Instruction," we focus on effective teacher behaviors, strategies to enhance student-mediated learning, reading and language-arts instruction, mathematics instruction, methods for teaching social studies and science in the regular classroom, and techniques to promote social skills and independent living skills.

In the balance of this introductory chapter, we will take a look at what's happening in our schools as we approach the twenty-first century. Following a brief overview of the special programs currently underway in the public schools, we will introduce you to some very special learners and their teachers.

✎ Schools, Society, and Achievement

During the 1980s, several national reports emphasized problems in America's schools (Carnegie Council on Adolescent Development, 1989; National Commission on Excellence in Education, 1983; National Governor's Association, 1986). Chief among the concerns were poor school achievement, substandard schools, lack of good teachers, and unmet needs of students at risk for dropping out of school. In 1985, for example, almost 25% of 17-year-olds still in school did not have the skills necessary to read simple magazines, and only 50% had the skills to read popular novels and newspaper stories (National Assessment of Educational Progress, 1985). According to a more recent assessment, only 42% of America's 17-year-olds were able to read at the highest levels, and very few students were proficient in writing, mathematics, or science (National Center for Education Statistics, 1990).

Moreover, in 1990, according to the National Center for Education Statistics (1991), 4.1% of the 15- to 21-year-olds in grades 10 through 12 (i.e., approximately 347,000 students) dropped out of school. In addition, 12.1% of all individuals from 16 to 24 years of age (an astonishing 3.8 million people) had failed to complete high school and were not enrolled in school. These figures were even higher for youth in the inner cities and for young people of Hispanic background. Apparently, for many youngsters, school is not a satisfying venture.

Today's teachers also believe that societal problems hamper school performance. According to a poll conducted by Harris and Associates (1989), absenteeism is viewed as a serious problem by 53% of all teachers of kindergarten through grade 12. Among teachers of grades 7 through 12, 81% report alcohol abuse and 70% report drug use as significant problems for their students. Furthermore, a startling 76% of all teachers believe that many children attending their school are ''latchkey kids''—youngsters left alone after school hours. In fact, approximately 3 million children ranging in age from 5 to 13 are without adult supervision after school (Eitzen, 1992).

Absenteeism, alcohol and drug use, and the latchkey phenomenon are all related to a changing economy and changing family structure. Eitzen (1992) presents some alarming statistics, including a 14% decline in real wages between 1973 and 1986. By 1990, 13.5% of the U.S. population was living below the poverty level and many people were unemployed. Approximately 70% of mothers of 6- to 17-year-olds now work outside the home, and over half of today's 5-year-olds will live in a single-parent family by the age of 18. Less fortunate youngsters—an estimated 450,000 children and youth—are homeless (National Law Center on Homelessness and Poverty, 1990).

Poverty and poor adult supervision are related to low achievement and high dropout rates (Eitzen, 1992). Even more alarming, however, is the increasing level of violence that characterizes today's schools. For example, according to one recent study, 38% of the urban children surveyed reported that they often worry that someone on drugs may hurt them; moreover 40% of their parents worry that their children might be shot (National Commission on Children, 1991). And according to findings of the National Center for Education (1990), over 40% of students in public schools are concerned about high levels of classroom disruption that interfere with learning. Schools, after all, are social institutions and, clearly, problems in our society are reflected in our schools through student behavior and academic performance. In addition, children from increasingly diverse cultural and ethnic backgrounds are attending today's schools. By 1995, about 40% of our students will be African-, Hispanic-, Asian-, or Native-American young people (Ramirez, 1988).

To address these societal changes, President Bush met with the governors from the 50 states in 1989 at an "education summit" held in Charlottesville, Virginia. The governors and the president agreed on six national education goals for America's schools in a plan called America 2000 (U.S. Department of Education, 1991a). These goals state that by the year 2000:

1. All children in America will start school ready to learn.

2. The high school graduation rate will rise to at least 90%.

3. American students will leave grades 4, 8, and 12 having demonstrated competency in challenging subject matter including English, mathematics, science, history, and geography; moreover, every school in America will see to it that all students learn to use their minds well in preparation for responsible citizenship, further learning, and productive employment.

4. American students will be first in the world in science and mathematics achievement.

5. Every adult American will be literate and possess the knowledge and skills necessary to compete in a global economy and exercise the rights and responsibilities of citizenship.

6. Every school in America will be free of drugs and violence and will offer a disciplined environment conducive to learning.

Certainly the National Education Goals are admirable in their intent, but the impact they will have on special education programs is as yet unclear. Only in the first goal are children with disabilities specifically included. Some authorities also worry that pressure for increased competency testing and performance in challenging subject matter may actually force students with mild disabilities out of the mainstream unless special educators assume a leadership role in the reforms of America 2000 (Sindelar, Watanabe, McCray, & Hornsby, 1992).

We agree with Sindelar and his colleagues that special educators have much to offer regular education. We firmly believe that *all* children can learn when appropriate goals are set for them, and that special educators and regular classroom teachers must collaborate in order to assist *all* students experiencing difficulty in school. Given proper instruction, most children will attain important skills necessary for success in school and in later life. Fortunately, those instructional techniques that are effective for students with mild disabilities can be as effective for other children with learning or behavioral problems who are in regular classrooms or in compensatory education programs (Slavin, Karweit, & Madden, 1989; Ysseldyke & Algozzine, 1982). Indeed, it is for this reason that we include children with learning problems who are not in special education programs in our discussions throughout the text.

✎ Special Programs

Some children having difficulty in school may receive part or all of their instruction through special programs. These programs, which typically receive federal funding, include compensatory education programs and special education programs.

Compensatory Education Programs

Compensatory education programs are federal efforts designed to help low-achieving, disadvantaged youngsters. Chapter 1, previously known as Title 1, is the largest of these programs, serving almost 5 million children in the areas of reading, language arts, and mathematics. Schools receive Chapter 1 funds based on the number of low-income students they serve, and they must use these funds to supplement instruction for those students scoring below a certain cutoff point on standardized tests of achievement.

Most Chapter 1 students are in elementary schools and receive remedial instruction in reading and/or mathematics from a Chapter 1 teacher. This instruction most often occurs in a "pull-out" setting in which children leave the regular classroom for periods of remedial help. To date, research indicates that students receiving Chapter 1 services experience only very limited academic gains—perhaps two to three percentile points on standardized tests of achievement (Slavin, Karweit, & Madden, 1989).

Special Education Programs

Special education programs are designed to serve children with disabilities that impair their performance in school. Since the passage of Public Law 94-142 in 1975—the Education for All Handicapped Children Act now renamed the Individuals with Disabilities Education Act (PL 101-476)—public schools have served millions of youngsters in special education programs. According to recent figures reported to Congress on the implementation of PL 94-142, for the 1989–90 school year approximately 6.9% of children and youth from 3 to 21 years of age received special education and related services (U.S. Department of Education, 1991b). Across the states, the percentage of youngsters of ages 6–17 served under PL 94-142 varied from a high of 15% to a low of only 6.2%, with the vast majority of these children enrolled in programs for students with mild disabilities.

For example, of those children of ages 6–21 in special education, most

(48.5%) were in programs for students with learning disabilities. Another 13.3% were in programs for children with mental retardation, and 9% were in programs for youngsters with emotional disturbance. An overwhelming majority (93%) of students between the ages of 3 and 21 received their special education in regular public school buildings. Of these youngsters, 31% were in regular classroom placements, spending under 21% of the school day in special education classrooms. Another 37% received resource-room services, spending over 21%, but under 60%, of the school day in special education classes. Only 24% of all children of ages 3–21 receiving special education services spent over 60% of their school day in separate special education classrooms, and very few were in separate facilities. (U.S. Department of Education, 1991b). (For a more detailed discussion of special education services, see Chapter 3.)

Now that we have briefly reviewed some of the special programs in todays schools, let's turn our attention to some special students and their teachers.

✎ Special Students: Their Schools and Teachers

The students, schools, and teachers described in this section are entirely fictitious. Yet, they strongly resemble actual students, schools, and teachers throughout the United States. Please acquaint yourself with these special students and their teachers. We will refer to them in vignettes throughout the text and in application exercises at the end of each chapter. Although only basic information about each youngster is given here, details are included in Appendix A for the students who receive special educational programs.

Oak Hill Elementary School

Oak Hill Elementary School is located in the northern section of Byrd County, which is a large, primarily suburban, public school district near a city of approximately 500,000 people. The school system is rapidly growing and presently serves just over 55,000 youngsters. Some low-income families live in the southern and eastern portions of the county; however, the northern and western ends of the county are home to primarily middle- to upper-income professional people. Approximately 60% of the children attending school in Byrd County are Anglo-American and 27% are African-American. In recent years, many Hispanic- and Asian-American families have made Byrd County their home.

Oak Hill Elementary is an attractive, modern school facility serving over 600 youngsters in kindergarten through grade 5. The school has full-time art, music, and physical education teachers and a staffed computer lab. Housed within the school are self-contained classrooms for preschoolers with disabilities and for children with severe/profound mental retardation. The school also serves 41 children with learning disabilities and 15 children with serious emotional disturbances/behavior disorders.

Ms. Lopez is a special education teacher at Oak Hill Elementary. She is in her third year of teaching. Certified in the fields of learning disabilities and emotional disturbance, she serves as an LD/ED teacher in a cross-categorical program for children with mild disabilities. Ms. Lopez's classroom is located in the fourth-grade wing of the building, although she works closely with members of the third-, fourth-, and fifth-grade–level teams.

Ms. Kirk, with twelve years of classroom experience, is the fourth-grade lead teacher at Oak Hill Elementary School. This year, she has 27 students in her class. The walls within and immediately outside of Ms. Kirk's classroom are decorated with student work samples and projects, and the student desks and chairs are arranged in clusters of five or six. Although Ms. Kirk proudly speaks of all of her students as individuals with unique needs and abilities, four children in her class are of special concern to her.

Travis. Travis is an attractive nine-year-old who was identified last year as a student with a learning disability. He lives with his mother, a registered nurse, and two older sisters in a comfortable, modest home about a mile from Oak Hill Elementary. Travis is of above-average intelligence, yet he reads at only the beginning second-grade level. He has difficulty decoding unknown words and reads with little comprehension. His manuscript and cursive writing are almost illegible. Although Travis can readily recall the basic addition and subtraction facts, he has problems with place value and with copying and aligning numbers. He has not yet mastered multiplication. According to his previous teachers, Travis seems to have trouble paying attention and he often "tunes out" during lessons and seatwork. They state that he knows something one day and "forgets" it the next, but quickly add that he is a very polite, well-behaved child. Travis enjoys science activities and hopes someday to become a geologist. Ms. Lopez works with Travis for approximately 2 hours daily to improve his reading and math skills. In addition, she assists Ms. Kirk in maintaining Travis in the regular classroom for science, social studies, and health.

Joey. Joey is a small, ten-year-old boy who was retained one year in kindergarten because of poor social skills. While in the first grade, Joey continued to experience significant interpersonal problems with his peers and teachers. Following a comprehensive evaluation, Joey began to receive special education services for children with emotional disturbance/behavior disorders. Joey is constantly "on the move"—out of his seat and disrupting others. When corrected by his teachers or confronted by his peers, Joey lashes out, alternately fighting, crying, and calling them names. He is not well liked by his classmates. His papers, desk, and "personal space" are messy, and he frequently forgets or misplaces his books, homework, pencils, and other important items, which he then must "borrow" from those nearby. Joey also has difficulty with his schoolwork. Although he is of average intelligence, he functions approximately 2 years below grade level in all academic skills. When Joey was 3 years old, his older brother died in an automobile accident. Now Joey is the only child in the family. His mother works at a local convenience store and his father works the evening shift at a factory across town. Both parents express frustration at their inability to control Joey's temper tantrums at home. Joey sees Ms. Lopez daily for help with reading, math, and social skills.

Celie. Celie is a new nine-year-old at Oak Hill Elementary. Her parents recently relocated to a large apartment complex in Byrd County. Celie has one younger sister and one younger brother at home. She cares for her brother and sister after school while her mother goes to a part-time job. Celie is a pretty, well-mannered child. She is of average intelligence, but there are wide gaps in her learning. Her father is a laborer in the construction industry; therefore, the family has moved frequently to be near his work. Celie reads at the third-grade level, but math is particularly troublesome for her. She uses her fingers for basic addition, and is confused by place value. Her written sentences are marked by many misspelled words and faulty punctuation. Celie dislikes reading and math; however, she enjoys art—an area in which she shows a strong talent. Celie is not in a special educational program.

Kevin.   Kevin is a large ten-year-old boy. Like Joey, he was retained one year in kindergarten. Kevin, however, is of below-average intelligence and he functions about 2 years below grade level in all academic areas. Kevin is easily frustrated with his schoolwork. He sometimes cries when he can't do his assignments or when the other children tease him. He is the "main target" for Joey, who tries to provoke Kevin's tears. Kevin's second-grade teacher referred him for testing to determine whether he qualified to receive special education services. The eligibility committee decided that he did not qualify. Kevin lives with his mother, a beautician. His grandmother lives with them. He does not know where his father lives, nor has he seen him for several years.

Apple County Middle School and Apple County High School

The Apple County Public School District serves approximately 2,700 children in grades K–12. Within the school system are three elementary schools, one middle school, and one high school. Apple County is primarily rural, although a few light industries have located there. Apple County Middle School enrolls about 650 children in grades 6–8. Apple County High School serves almost 600 students in grades 9–12. In both schools, the student body is approximately 60% African-American, 35% Anglo-American, and 5% Hispanic- and Asian-American.

Mr. Abel is an itinerant resource teacher for Apple County Middle and Apple County High School. He grew up in Apple County and attended a nearby college to become certified as a teacher of children with mild mental retardation. After teaching in a self-contained special education classroom for 7 years, he returned to the college to earn his master's degree, adding certification for learning disabilities to his teaching credentials. He now divides his time between the middle school and the high school, serving a total of 18 students in a cross-categorical special education program. Although most of his students are youngsters with learning disabilities, his caseload also includes three students with mild mental retardation.

Mr. Abel considers his position demanding, but he knows his students, their parents, and the community well. In addition, he works closely with several teachers at the middle school, including Ms. Booker, the sixth-grade English teacher, and Mr. Mathis, a mathematics teacher. Mr. Abel is also extremely proud of his working relationship with several teachers at the high school, including the ninth-grade earth science teacher, Ms. Stone, and the geography teacher, Mr. McNally. These teachers work hard to help all their students succeed. For four of their students, however, they have "gone the extra mile."

Susan.   Susan is an overweight, 13-year-old sixth-grader with mild mental retardation. Her appearance is often unkempt. She lives in an old farmhouse with her grandmother, her 29-year-old mother, and an uncle and his wife and their three young children. Susan is performing 3 to 4 years below grade level in all academic areas. She lacks confidence in her ability to complete her assignments, often asking her teachers, "Is that right?" after each item. When she makes errors, she becomes frustrated and cries. Susan is shy, soft-spoken, and rarely interacts with her peers. At Apple County Middle School, Mr. Abel helps her in her mainstreamed classes, particularly in language arts with Ms. Booker and in general math with Mr. Mathis.

Leon.   Leon is an eleven-year-old sixth-grader attending Apple County Middle School in Ms. Booker's language arts class and in Mr. Mathis's general math class. Although Leon is of average intelligence, he is failing both classes. He is not eligible for special education services, however. Leon constantly "tests" his teachers. He is late to class; rarely prepared with books, homework, or other necessities; and disrespectful when addressing his teachers. Attempts to contact Leon's parents are usually unsuccessful because his mother works the evening shift at a local plant, sleeping during the day, and his father works from 7 A.M. to 3 P.M. at the plant before going to a second part-time job. Leon returns to an empty home after school each day.

Robert.   Robert is a 15-year-old ninth-grader at Apple County High School. He has been in a program for students with learning disabilities since the third grade. Robert reads at about the fifth-grade level and performs mathematics at approximately the sixth-grade level. He has trouble with the language and organizational structure of his textbooks. Robert's spelling and handwriting are poor; consequently, he often cannot read the notes he takes in his classes. His written paragraphs are short and poorly organized, and he is a poor test-taker. Robert is earning D's and low C's in most subject areas. He sees Mr. Abel for assistance with study skills and learning strategies. In addition, Mr. Abel helps Ms. Stone, Robert's earth science teacher, and Mr. McNally, Robert's geography teacher, to adapt tests, lectures, and assignments to meet Robert's needs. Robert is hoping to enter the program for heating and refrigeration at the local technical school. Although he is often frustrated with his schoolwork, he is a likeable young man with a good sense of humor and supportive parents. His mother is a teacher at one of the county's elementary schools and his father owns a large orchard in the county.

Marcus.   Marcus is a slightly built, 14-year-old ninth-grader at Apple County High School. He receives Chapter 1 reading services for one period each day, but he is failing most of his classes and is often absent from school. When he is in attendance, Marcus frequently puts his head down on his desk during class discussions and rarely participates. Marcus does not complete his homework; he cannot read the assigned textbooks. When asked what he would like to do after graduation, he responds, ''I'm gonna get outta this place and work at my uncle's garage.'' Marcus lives with his grandmother; his parents are divorced. His father, a truck driver, is often away from home for weeks at a time. Marcus is of low to average intelligence. He has earth science with Ms. Stone and geography with Mr. McNally.

✎ Summary

According to several national reports, America's schools fail to help many students attain adequate achievement levels. Today's schools reflect societal problems, including poverty, drug use, and escalating violence. Educational reforms are directed at eliminating these problems and enhancing school achievement.

Millions of children struggle and fail to achieve in school. Some receive help in the form of special education programs for students with mild disabilities. Others receive compensatory education programs. Still others receive only the assistance provided by teachers in regular classrooms.

Given proper instruction and appropriate goals, all children can learn. Techniques likely to be effective with students with mild disabilities are also likely to work for children who are poor achievers but who have not been assigned to a special education program.

At Oak Hill Elementary School, Travis, Joey, Celie, and Kevin are students in Ms. Kirk's fourth-grade class. Travis and Joey receive special services from Ms. Lopez, their resource teacher. Celie and Kevin remain in the regular classroom and receive no special services.

In Apple County, Mr. Abel is an itinerant resource teacher serving the middle school and the high school. At Apple County Middle School, he works closely with the English teacher, Ms. Booker, and the mathematics teacher, Mr. Mathis. Susan and Leon, sixth-graders, are in the same English and general math classes, but only Susan reports to Mr. Abel for special education. Ms. Stone is an earth science teacher, and Mr. McNally is a geography teacher at Apple County High School. Both have Robert, a student with learning disabilities, and Marcus, a student with learning problems, in their classes. However, only Robert receives special education services from Mr. Abel.

✎ Application Exercises

1. Interview a regular classroom teacher at either the elementary or secondary level. Find out if this teacher perceives absenteeism, the dropout rate, substance abuse, or low achievement to be a problem at his or her school. Next, interview a special education teacher at the same grade level. Are there similarities or differences in perceived problems by these teachers?

2. Arrange to spend a day observing in an elementary- or secondary-level classroom. Count the number of boys and the number of girls in the class and compute the percentage of each. Also, compute the percentage of minority children in the class. Next, spend a day observing in a special education class for children with mild disabilities. Compute the percentage of boys, girls, and minorities for this class. Are there differences in the student populations of these two classrooms?

3. Describe the types of special education services (e.g., resource room, team teaching, self-contained classroom, consultation) provided by the school in which you observed.

Learners with Mild Disabilities

Chapter 2

Focus

As you read, think about the following questions:

Do children with mild disabilities differ from their low-achieving peers?

What are the major cognitive, academic, and social-emotional characteristics shared by children with mild disabilities?

How does knowledge of the characteristics of children with mild disabilities help teachers make decisions about curriculum or instruction?

✎ Learners with mild disabilities exhibit a wide variety of characteristics. Accordingly, it should be kept in mind that not all of the characteristics discussed in this chapter will apply to every child having difficulty in school. Moreover, each characteristic may affect a child's performance to varying degrees. When planning instruction, however, the teacher may find it helpful to keep in mind those characteristics representative of many children who have mild disabilities, as well as those children with low achievement who are not so labeled. Consider, for example, the following conversation between Ms. Kirk and Ms. Lopez:

Ms. Kirk: *I'm concerned about Travis—particularly his inability to pay attention. He takes such a long time to get started and to finish his work. I'm afraid he might fall even further behind the other children in my classroom. I do have other children, though, who have at least as much difficulty keeping up as Travis.*

Ms. Lopez: *I noticed that the desks in your classroom are arranged in groups. Is there another child in the group who could be paired with Travis to help get him started and to answer his questions?*

Ms. Kirk: *That's not a bad idea. I have another child who has trouble staying on task, and a buddy system helped him. You know, that student isn't in any type of special education program; yet, he's a lot like Travis in several ways. Often, I don't see the difference between a child like Travis and my other boy. Anyway, the same teaching methods seem to help them both. So, what's the difference?*

Special education teachers often hear similar comments and questions from the regular classroom teacher: "She does better than several of the other children not in special eduction." "What's the difference?" Let's examine the issues surrounding this situation.

✎ Labels and Children with Mild Disabilities

The vast majority of children in special education programs are considered to have mild disabilities and are placed for most of the school day in either the regular classroom or a combination of the regular classroom and the special education resource room (U.S. Department of Education, 1991b). Typically, these are children with learning disabilities, mild mental retardation, or behavioral disorders. (See Box 2.1 for the current PL 94-142 definitions for each of these categories.)

Labeling a child may not accomplish very much. In fact, it may do little more than grant that child access to a special education program. These labels tell the teacher very little about the child's instructional needs. A child with a learning disability may, for example, have difficulty in certain academic areas but no attendant behavioral problems. Another child with a learning disability may exhibit severe attentional and behavioral problems in addition to academic deficits, necessitating more intensive educational programming (McKinney,

Box 2.1   Current Definitions

The most widely accepted definitions for mental retardation, learning disabilities, and emotional disturbance are those entered into the regulations accompanying Public Law 94-142. Although each has been criticized for various reasons, these are the definitions currently governing most services and programs for children with mild disabilities.

Mental Retardation

"Mental retardation refers to significantly subaverage intellectual functioning resulting in or associated with impairments in adaptive behavior and manifested during the developmental period." (From: Grossman, 1983, p. 11.) Recently the American Association on Mental Retardation (1993) published a new definition placing greater emphasis on behavioral competence than the Grossman definition: "Mental retardation refers to substantial limitations in present functioning. It is characterized by significantly subaverage intellectual functioning, existing concurrently with related limitations in two or more of the following applicable adaptive skill areas: communication, self-care, home living, social skills, community use, self-direction, health and safety, functional academics, leisure, and work. Mental retardation manifests before age 18."

Learning Disabilities

"Specific learning disability means a disorder in one or more of the basic psychological processes involved in understanding or in using language, spoken or written, which may manifest itself in an imperfect ability to listen, think, speak, read, write, spell, or to do mathematical calculations. The term includes such conditions as perceptual handicaps, brain injury, minimal brain dysfunction, dyslexia, and developmental aphasia. The term does not include children who have learning problems which are primarily the result of visual, hearing, or motor handicaps, of mental retardation, of emotional disturbance, or of environmental, cultural, or economic disadvantage." (From: *Federal Register*, 1977, De-

cember 29, p. 65083.) The interested reader is referred also to Hammill (1990) and to Hammill, Leigh, McNutt, and Larsen (1981) for a discussion of issues surrounding the federal definition of learning disabilities and for an alternative definition proposed by the National Joint Committee on Learning Disabilities.

Seriously Emotionally Disturbed

(i) The term means a condition exhibiting one or more of the following characteristics over a long period of time and to a marked extent, which adversely affects educational performance:
   (A) an inability to learn that cannot be explained by intellectual, sensory, or health factors;
   (B) an inability to build or maintain satisfactory relationships with peers and teachers;
   (C) inappropriate types of behavior or feelings under normal circumstances;
   (D) a general pervasive mood of unhappiness or depression; or
   (E) a tendency to develop physical symptoms or fears associated with personal or school problems.

(ii) The term includes children who are schizophrenic. The term does not include children who are socially maladjusted, unless it is determined that they are seriously emotionally disturbed.

(Adapted from: *Federal Register,* 1977, August 23, p. 42478.) The interested reader is referred also to Kauffman (1989) for a discussion of the issues surrounding the federal definition of emotional disturbances and its origin. In addition, the reader may wish to consult the February 1991 newsletter of the Council for Children with Behavior Disorders, available from the Council for Exceptional Children in Reston, Virginia, for a new definition of emotional disturbance/ behavioral disorders proposed by the National Mental Health and Special Education Coalition.

1987). Children within a categorical area of special education may differ from one another as much as they differ from those youngsters in other categories.

According to Hallahan and Kauffman (1977), the categories of learning disabilities, mild mental retardation, and emotional disturbance overlap considerably. Some authorities argue that children within these three groups cannot be reliably distinguished from one another using the present federal definitions and psychometric testing practices (Ysseldyke, 1987). Moreover, assigning a child to a particular category of special education does not mean that the youngster will receive instruction that is vastly different from that received by children bearing other diagnostic labels. Despite many years of study, researchers are unable to prescribe teaching approaches that differ substantially from one another based solely on the labels assigned to students in different special education categories (Christenson, Thurlow, & Ysseldyke, 1987; Gardner, 1982, Lloyd 1984).

Although they have been the focus of considerable research, children with learning disabilities are also difficult to distinguish from other low-achieving children not placed in special education programs (Algozzine & Korinek, 1985). Moreover, effective teaching methods for children with mild disabilities do not differ from those that help youngsters who are having difficulty in school but who are not placed in special education (Christenson, Ysseldyke, & Thurlow, 1989; Slavin, Karweit, & Madden, 1989). Some authorities do argue, however, that the *curriculum* may need to be altered for some students having mild disabilities, even though the teaching methods may not differ (Patton, Beirne-Smith, & Payne, 1990). That is, for some students, the ''mild disability'' represents a significant problem affecting all aspects of the child's life, requiring a more functional orientation to the curriculum than that typically found in the regular classroom. In particular, those students with mild mental retardation may need greater emphasis on daily living skills or social skills within the curriculum (Patton, Beirne-Smith, & Payne, 1990).

Nevertheless, for most students with mild disabilities, instruction takes place primarily in the regular classroom, within the regular education curriculum. Therefore, the special and regular education teachers must work together to provide the most powerful teaching techniques available to assist all students having difficulty. In this regard, knowledge of shared characteristics may enable teachers to make better instructional decisions for students with mild disabilities as well as for other children who are having trouble.

Let's now consider the nature of those cognitive, academic, and social-emotional characteristics that youngsters with mild disabilities often have in common.

✎ Cognitive Characteristics

Cognition generally refers to processes involved in thinking. Students with mild disabilities may have below-average intellectual ability, and they may have trouble maintaining or focusing attention and/or retrieving information from memory. Although each of these problems may affect the child to varying degrees, all of them may result in less efficient learning for the youngster with learning disabilities, behavioral disorders, or mild mental retardation.

Intellectual Ability

Children with mild disabilities may vary widely with respect to intellectual ability. By definition (Grossman, 1983), children with mental retardation are substantially below average in general intellectual functioning and have difficulty adapting their behavior in order to function competently in their environment. More specifically, these youngsters usually score near or below 70 IQ points on a standardized test of intelligence. Students with learning disabilities, on the other hand, are generally thought to have intellectual ability within the average, or even above average, range (i.e., an IQ score of 85 or above on a standardized test of intelligence). Despite adequate intelligence, however, youngsters with learning disabilities do not do well in many academic areas. Authorities debate how (or even whether) to measure this discrepancy between IQ and achievement as a defining characteristic of learning disabilities (Bateman, 1992), and some refute the notion that learning disabilities and mental retardation cannot occur concomitantly (Hammill, 1990; Hammill, Leigh, McNutt, & Larsen, 1981; National Joint Committee on Learning Disabilities, 1988). Finally, children with emotional disturbances/behavior disorders demonstrate an inability to learn that cannot be explained by intellectual factors (Bower, 1981). Thus, for children having ''mild'' behavior disorders, adequate intellectual ability is implied within the definition.

In practice, however, there is considerable overlap in intellectual ability across these three special education categories. For example, children with IQ scores in the below-average range may sometimes be considered for identification as learning disabled if they exhibit no impairments in their adaptive behavior but show a discrepancy between their ability and their actual achievement (Frankenberger & Fronzaglio, 1991). Furthermore, children with mild to moderate emotional disturbances score anywhere in intelligence from mentally retarded to gifted, with the majority having tested IQs in the slightly below average range (Kauffman, 1989).

The teacher must be careful not to limit the child with a relatively low IQ score by automatically assuming that the child has a reduced capacity to learn. Simply knowing an IQ score tells the teacher very little about *how* or *what* a child may learn. Nevertheless, because IQ tests are correlated with academic achievement, children scoring in the below-average range of intelligence often experience more academic failure than those who score higher.

Attentional Deficits

Children with mild disabilities often exhibit attentional deficits that affect their progress in the classroom. For example, many youngsters with attentional problems are also hyperactive. Attention-deficit hyperactivity disorder is characterized by behaviors detrimental to classroom adjustment and school achievement (American Psychiatric Association, 1987). Some children may experience difficulty coming to attention and focusing on the task at hand. Others may respond impulsively, not considering all the alternatives to a problem, or they may have trouble paying attention long enough to complete a given task (Hallahan & Kauffman, 1991). (See Box 2.2.) Consequently, children with mild disabilities may make errors on assignments, or find themselves in troublesome situations

Box 2.2

According to his teachers, Travis often has difficulty "paying attention." He "tunes out" during lessons and has trouble maintaining his attention when completing seatwork. Let's observe Travis while he is working on a math assignment in his fourth-grade class.

Ms. Kirk: *Let's do the first problem on the practice sheet together. Now,*
$1/7 + 3/7 =$ _____ . *What's the first thing to do . . . Tammy? Right! Check the denominators. They are both seven. So, what do I do next . . . Travis?* [Noticing Travis has been rubbing his pencil eraser with his finger and examining the pieces of rubber] *Travis, please put your pencil down. Now, look at the problem.* [Pointing] *The denominators are both the same, seven. So, what do I do next?*

Travis: *You add the top numbers together and leave the bottom the same.*

Ms. Kirk: *Good job. One plus three equals four. So the answer is four-sevenths* [Writing 4/7]. *Now, you do the rest. You have 10 minutes before we get ready for lunch.*

Travis: [Looks at his paper and fills in all of the denominators across the first row of five problems. When Peter, at Travis's cluster of tables, begins to erase a problem, Travis looks up watching Peter. He then examines his own eraser and begins to erase marks off the top of his desk.]

Ms. Kirk: [Noticing Travis playing with his eraser again, Ms. Kirk moves to Travis's desk and touches his paper.] *Travis, you need to finish the practice sheet before lunch. Look at the second problem* [Pointing]. *You have the correct denominator. Now, what is the numerator?* [Travis writes the correct answer.] *Good job, Travis. Now, do the next problem and keep on working. Let's see if you can do the first two rows before I come back.* [Ms. Kirk moves on to another student.]

Travis: [Writes answers quickly to the next five problems. However, when he lays his pencil down to get a tissue from his pocket, the pencil rolls off his desk. He crawls under his chair to get the pencil, finds the point now broken, and is off to the pencil sharpener . . .]

in the classroom, more frequently than their peers. Finally, some youngsters with mild disabilities, particularly those with mild mental retardation, may have difficulty attending to more than one part of a task at a time (Brooks & McCauley, 1984). For example, the student who is devoting a lot of attention to decoding words on a page may have little attention left to remember and comprehend what was read. Therefore, teachers must construct tasks so that relevant features are emphasized, and they must reward their students for paying attention.

Memory Deficits

Paying attention is only the first step in learning. Students must also organize information in meaningful ways so that it can be stored in short-term and then long-term memory to be recalled when needed. Children with mild disabilities often have considerable difficulty organizing and retrieving information in a purposeful manner.

According to Torgesen and Kail (1990), many youngsters with mild disabilities are not aware of the strategies their peers often use to help organize and remember important information. For example, they do not spontaneously use such techniques as verbal rehearsal (repeating to oneself, aloud or silently, something to be remembered), or clustering (organizing material into small chunks containing similar items). When taught to use such strategies, however, the memory performance of many children with mild disabilities improves significantly (Hallahan, Kauffman, & Lloyd, 1985; Patton et al., 1990).

A related factor contributing to the memory deficits of youngsters with mild disabilities is metacognition (Flavell, 1979). Metacognition means knowledge about one's own thought processes and learning. It involves not only an awareness of the strategies and skills necessary to accomplish a task effectively, but also the ability to monitor one's performance while completing the task. For example, as you read this paragraph, you may monitor your own comprehension and reread certain sentences when you encounter new words or difficult concepts. Although many children with mild disabilities do not spontaneously use metacognitive processes to direct and monitor their learning, they can be taught to employ these skills. Teachers must model effective problem-solving and/or memory strategies during lessons, explicitly show students how and where to use these strategies, and reward students for using them appropriately (Deshler & Schumaker, 1988). (See Box 2.3.)

✎ Academic Characteristics

The most widely shared characteristic of students with mild disabilities is academic difficulty. Although some children have deficits in only one or two specific academic areas, other youngsters have significant and pervasive difficulty in all areas of academic endeavor, particularly in reading, the language arts, and mathematics.

Box 2.3

Mr. McNally is distressed about Robert's most recent test grade in geography. He asked Mr. Abel to work with Robert on test-taking skills. Let's listen to Mr. Abel's conversation with Robert about the test score.

Mr. Abel: *Robert, I know you're not pleased with this test grade of F. Based on Mr. McNally's comments about your participation in class, I believe you know more than this test grade shows.*

Robert: *I studied for the test. I'm just not good at multiple-choice tests.*

Mr. Abel: *Let's look at how you studied for the test. First, Mr. McNally said the test would be 30 multiple-choice items, and he gave you a study guide listing terms to know. Everyone filled out the study guide in class. Did you use it to study from?*

Robert: *No, I couldn't find it when I went to my locker after school.*

Mr. Abel: *Could you have asked Mr. McNally for another one?*

Robert: *I guess so, but I was kind of in a hurry.*

Mr. Abel: *So, what did you do to study for the test?*

Robert: *Well, I looked over Chapter 2 that the test was going to be on.*

Mr. Abel: *What did you do when you were "looking over" the chapter? Did you make up questions or say the terms out loud to practice them? What exactly did you do to study the chapter?*

Robert: *No, I didn't do that stuff. I just, you know, looked it over . . .*

Reading

Without a doubt, the academic area in which children with mild disabilities most often encounter failure is reading. Their reading difficulties include phonological, syntactic, and semantic problems that hinder their ability to become fluent readers. For example, students with phonological difficulties, which involve the inability to detect sounds in spoken language, exhibit weak segmentation and sound-blending skills (Samuels, 1988). Other youngsters have syntactic deficits, involving an inability to cluster words into meaningful phrases on the basis of sentence structure (Wiig, 1990). For other children, semantic problems, such as not being able to remember new vocabulary or to understand the use of figurative language, reduce comprehension of what is read. In addition, some students experience difficulty when asked to determine sentence and/or paragraph relationships, especially when this information must be inferred. They are hard-pressed to identify main ideas or themes and supporting details. Moreover, these deficits in reading affect performance in all other academic areas, particularly as students in the secondary grades are expected to read expository text for content (Stanovich, 1986a).

Special educators must provide systematic and repeated practice in the basic decoding and comprehension skills, coordinated with instruction in the regular classroom, if their students are to be successfully mainstreamed. In addition, teachers must take care not to penalize students with poor reading skills by basing content-area instruction primarily on textbook reading assignments.

Language Arts

In addition to reading, the language arts include listening, speaking, spelling, handwriting, and composing skills. Children with mild disabilities experience more difficulty with oral expression and listening comprehension than do non-disabled peers (Wiig, 1990). Although the writing abilities of children with mild disabilities have not been as well-researched as their abilities in other academic areas, these students are likely to have numerous problems with written expression. These include illegible handwriting and/or a slow writing speed; difficulty remembering the written equivalents for sounds or using phonetic rules to spell words correctly (Carpenter, 1983); frequent punctuation, capitalization, and word-usage errors; and difficulty generating content, planning written products, and producing and revising written text (Graham, Harris, & Sawyer, 1987).

Children with mild disabilities need frequent, real-life writing experiences with many opportunities to plan, revise, and edit their work. They also need direct instruction in specific writing skills and strategies. Teachers must, of course, provide alternatives to written assignments when the goal of instruction is not writing skill, but rather content-area knowledge.

Mathematics

Many students with mild disabilities also have trouble with math. Among the difficulties these youngsters experience in mathematics are problems remembering basic arithmetic facts and the meaning of mathematical symbols, understanding place value, performing operations using fractions and decimals, and following the steps in complicated math tasks like long division (Wallace & McLoughlin, 1988). In addition, children with mild disabilities are likely to have problems with arithmetic word problems and concepts of time and money (Cawley & Parmar, 1992; Horton, Lovitt, & White, 1992). Teachers must provide sequenced instruction, frequent practice opportunities, and explicit strategies for problem-solving if their special education students are to master mathematics skills. In addition, teachers must show their students where and when to apply mathematics skills, monitor student progress, and reward youngsters for using new skills appropriately (Lloyd & Keller, 1989).

✎ Social-Emotional Characteristics

Children with mild disabilities may not be able to interact appropriately with their peers and teachers. For example, some youngsters with learning disabilities may misinterpret social cues or the feelings of others (Weiss, 1984). Consequently, they may violate social norms or respond inappropriately to those around them. Children with behavioral disorders, too, have difficulty building and maintaining interpersonal relationships, exhibiting extreme behavioral excesses and deficiencies when compared with their peers (Kauffman, 1989). In addition, some children with mild disabilities tend to be less task-oriented, more distractible, and less independent than their nondisabled counterparts (McKinney, 1989). Such "off-task" behaviors are problematic in the classroom and are often considered disruptive and intolerable by the regular classroom teacher (Ysseldyke, Algozzine, & Thurlow, 1992). Special educators must prepare students to handle not only the academic expectations of the regular classroom but also the social expectations if their mainstreaming efforts are to be successful (Downing, Simpson, & Myles, 1990).

Youngsters with mild disabilities may also hold maladaptive beliefs about themselves and their abilities. For example, many students in special education programs suffer from low self-esteem. They question their academic competence and depend on others for help on tasks they are capable of performing independently (Bryan, 1986). (See Box 2.4.) Some children with mild disabilities have an external locus of control, believing situations in their lives to be the result of such uncontrollable forces as chance. Children having an external locus of control do not take responsibility for their successes, but they often ascribe their failures to lack of ability (Bryan, 1986). Such youngsters exhibit "learned helplessness" (Abramson, Seligman, & Teasdale, 1978), giving up easily in the face of even small difficulties in the belief that no amount of effort will circumvent their failure. Many students with mild disabilities are at risk to enter a vicious cycle of failure: doubt regarding their ability to succeed, lack of effort when faced with a task perceived to be difficult, subsequent failure "confirming" their lack of ability, and increased expectancy of failure in the future (Licht, 1984). Therefore, teachers must construct tasks to demonstrate that success is attainable, and they must reward students for accomplishments resulting from appropriate effort.

✎ Individualizing Instruction

The teacher must remember that each student is a unique individual, including the student with mild disabilities. As we mentioned early in the chapter, knowl-

---

Box 2.4

Susan lacks confidence in her ability. She is very dependent on others for help, even when she is capable of performing a task on her own. In general math class, with Mr. Mathis, Susan is afraid she will make errors.

Mr. Mathis: [Pointing to the overhead projector he has been using during his lesson] *Okay, everyone. You've done a good job helping me fill out these checks. Now, it's your turn to fill out a check. Look at the first check on your worksheet. What goes on the first line . . . Bob? Yes, today's date. Write in the date, everybody.*

Susan: [Raising her hand] *I don't understand.*

Mr. Mathis: [Pointing] *We write today's date on this line. What is today's date?*

Susan: *October 25, 1993.*

Mr. Mathis: *That's right. It's written on the board. Now, you write it on your check.*

Susan: [Copies the date from the board and raises her hand.] *Is this right?*

Mr. Mathis: [Looks at Susan and nods his head.] *Now, everyone, let's make this check out to the Surprise Shop.* [Writes it on the board.] *Write "Surprise Shop" next to "Pay to the order of" on your check.*

Susan: [Looking around at the others and then at the board, she begins to copy "Surprise Shop" on her check. Halfway through her copying, she looks up, looks around at the others, and then raises her hand.] *Is this right?*

---

edge of a student's special education label gives the teacher very little information regarding how best to teach that child. However, a basic understanding of the major cognitive, academic, and social-emotional characteristics often displayed by problem learners can provide a starting point for anticipating the kind of instruction that might be required. The teacher must then consider the skills, abilities, and behaviors demonstrated by the individual child and design instruction tailored to that youngster's unique set of characteristics and needs. For some students with mild disabilities, the curriculum and instruction received in the regular classroom will suffice with only minor adjustments. For those who are experiencing significant behavioral, motivational, or academic difficulties, however, the curriculum must be altered to emphasize daily living and social skills. For each student, joint planning and instruction by the regular and special educator will be necessary to keep the child in the regular classroom as much as possible. Such individualized instruction is essential for mainstreamed students with mild disabilities, and it is equally helpful for other youngsters with low achievement not placed in any special education program.

This does not mean, however, that every child in the regular or special education classroom must be provided with one-on-one instruction. For example, children having the same skill levels may be grouped for instruction in a particular area of need, regardless of a categorical label. Similarly, the student with a mild disability, or the nondisabled learner with special needs, may be paired with another child for assistance or placed in a cooperative learning group in which all students share responsibility for helping one another to succeed (Slavin et al., 1989). Teachers can also adapt instruction to accommodate the unique needs of their students with mild disabilities or low achievement. For example, the teacher may give students a dittoed outline of a lesson for them to fill in while he or she completes an identical outline on the overhead projector. Or they can modify assignments, perhaps by altering the number of problems for practice in mathematics. Teachers must begin by using those instructional techniques likely to be successful with most students with mild disabilities and then adjust the instruction to suit the individual child.

✎ Summary

Children with mild disabilities exhibit numerous cognitive, academic, and social-emotional characteristics. Some students with mild disabilities have below-average intellectual ability, while others have average or above-average intelligence. Many children with learning disabilities, emotional disturbances, or mild mental retardation exhibit memory deficits or attentional problems. These students may not focus on the task at hand, or they may fail to make use of problem-solving strategies that come naturally to their peers. Almost all students with mild disabilities have academic deficits in reading, the language arts, and/or mathematics. Such difficulties range from only minor problems in one academic area to significant and pervasive deficiencies in all academic areas, often in combination with attentional or behavioral troubles. Many youngsters with mild disabilities suffer from low self-esteem. They may find it difficult to build and maintain satisfying interpersonal relationships with peers and teachers.

Knowledge of shared characteristics among children with mild disabilities represents only a starting point for instructional planning. Students in special educational programs differ from one another as much as they differ from their nondisabled peers. Teachers must design instruction to meet the individual needs of each learner, regardless of whether the child has a disability. In addition, teachers must consistently focus on the whole child as an individual with interests and strengths that can be used to enhance learning.

✎ Application Exercises

1. Interview a regular classroom teacher at a chosen grade level who has at least one child with a mild disability mainstreamed in his or her class. What are the major cognitive, academic, and social-emotional needs of the special student(s)? Be certain not to use names or identifying information when presenting your answers to this question. (Note: PL 94-142 requires that information about children in special education programs remain confidential.) What differences, if any, does this teacher see between the student(s) with mild disabilities and other children with low achievement in the classroom?

2. What are some common characteristics shared by Travis, Joey, Celie, and Kevin? How might these shared characteristics serve as a starting point for instructional planning?

3. What are the identification criteria used by your local public school district for determining eligibility for special education services for students with learning disabilities, emotional disturbance/behavioral disorders, or mild mental retardation?

Approaches to Teaching Learners with Mild Disabilities

Chapter 3

Focus

As you read, think about the following questions:

How are services, curriculum, and instructional methods interrelated?

Which approaches to teaching learners with mild disabilities are supported by research?

Which approaches to teaching learners with mild disabilities are not supported by research?

What are some of the current issues surrounding the provision of special education services and instruction to students with mild disabilities?

✎ Over the years, numerous approaches to teaching learners with mild disabilities have become popular, only to fall out of favor after a relatively short time. Although not supported by research, some approaches were intuitively appealing to teachers who believed strongly that they would improve the academic performance of their students with special needs. Vestiges of these approaches are still apparent in special and regular education classrooms today. Other teaching methods have survived the tests of time and research, continuing to improve the academic achievement and behavior of many children with mild disabilities. Consider, for example, the following exchange between Ms. Lopez and Joey, her student.

Ms. Lopez: *Joey, your first reading assignment is on page 34 today. Please turn to page 34.*

Joey: [Turns to page 34 and slips a paper out of his reading folder.] *I read this one yesterday and I bet I read it better today! I'm gonna smash my record!*

Ms. Lopez: [Looking at Joey's graph on the paper in his reading folder] *Yes, you read at a rate of 75 words per minute yesterday with only six errors. I bet you can reach your goal today! What's the goal?*

Joey: *Eighty-five words a minute and only five errors.*

Ms. Lopez: *Are you ready?* [She has a stopwatch ready to time Joey and a photocopy of the reading passage in front of her. At a nod from Joey, she starts the stopwatch.] *Begin!*

Joey: [He reads the passage as Ms. Lopez follows along on her page. When he finishes, Ms. Lopez stops the watch.] *How did I do?*

Ms. Lopez: [Counting] *Ninety words per minute, Joey, and four errors! Super job!*

Joey: [Smiles and pulls out his pencil to plot the information on his graph.] *See. I told you I was gonna smash that goal today!*

Procedures derived from the principles of applied behavior analysis, such as the direct, repeated measurement and recording of a specific targeted behavior as described in the preceding scenario, are among the most effective techniques known to teachers of students with special educational needs (Wolery, Bailey, & Sugai, 1988). What other instructional methods are supported by the research literature? Where, what, and how should students in special education be taught?

In this chapter, we will first examine the interrelated nature of special education services, curriculum, and instruction. Next, we will discuss current research-supported approaches to teaching learners with mild disabilities, as well as some historical approaches whose effectiveness has not been empirically confirmed. Finally, we will explore some of the current issues concerning the provision of special education services and instruction to students with mild disabilities.

✎ Services, Curriculum, and Instruction

Teachers must make decisions regarding services, curriculum, and instructional methods for their students with mild disabilities. These three aspects of special education are interrelated and vitally important to special learners.

Services

The term *services* is generally used with reference to the setting in which instruction takes place, and consequently to the role assumed by the special education teacher. Frequently, for youngsters with learning disabilities, mild mental retardation, or behavioral disorders, this setting is the regular classroom, often with the special educator providing resource-room assistance to the student and/or consultation services to the regular classroom teacher (U.S. Department of Education, 1991b). Increasingly, too, regular and special educators are sharing instructional responsibility within the regular classroom for mainstreamed students with disabilities and for other children achieving below grade level through collaborative or team-teaching arrangements (Morsink, Thomas, & Correa, 1991).

Teachers should not automatically assume, however, that the regular classroom and the resource room are the only services appropriate for students with mild disabilities. For some students, "mild" disabilities represent significant impairments that require self-contained classrooms, or even special schools. Public Law 94-142, now called the Individuals with Disabilities Education Act (PL 101-476), requires that a range of services be available to meet the unique needs of individual students in special education programs. Special education services, goals, and objectives are specified on a student's Individualized Education Program (IEP). (See Chapter 7 for a discussion of the IEP and Table 3.1 for a description of special education services.)

Curriculum

Although the question of where to educate students with mild disabilities is an important one, the related question of what the students are taught is even more important. Teachers must carefully address curricular issues in a manner consistent with the mandate that students receive an appropriate education in the least restrictive environment. By *least restrictive environment* is meant that environment in which opportunities for integration with nondisabled peers are maximized, at the same time providing the child with an appropriate education. For many students with learning disabilities or behavioral disorders, college or technical school might be a likely outcome upon graduation. These students must progress through the regular school curriculum, perhaps with additional instruction in learning strategies or social skills provided by the special education teacher, or accommodations to circumvent specific skill deficits offered by the regular classroom teacher. Students receiving the regular education curriculum are often taught, for the most part, in the regular classroom.

On the other hand, some students with learning disabilities, behavioral disorders, or mild mental retardation may need a modified curriculum emphasizing functional academics (e.g., learning to read in order to follow a recipe or

Table 3.1   Special Education Services for Students with Mild Disabilities

Service	Description	Role of Special Teacher
Regular class	Student is in the regular classroom all day.	Consults with regular teacher to adapt materials/instruction. May engage in team or collaborative teaching with regular teacher.
Resource room	Student is in the regular classroom for most of the day, but spends some time (e.g., 50–60 minutes) with the resource teacher daily or weekly, depending upon individual student needs.	Provides instruction in basic academic/social skills and/or learning strategies. Consults with regular teacher to adapt materials and/or instruction. May also engage in team or collaborative teaching with regular teacher for part of the day.
Self-contained classroom (part-time and full-time)	*Part-time*: Student is in a special education class for all instruction in one or more academic areas daily, but receives art/music/P.E., etc., in the regular classroom. *Full-time*: Student receives all instruction in the special class.	Provides instruction in academic subject areas. May consult with regular teacher to adapt materials and/or instruction in regular classroom. Integrates learning through community-based instruction.
Special day school	Student attends a special school for all instruction.	Provides instruction in all subject areas and integrates learning with community-based instruction.
Residential school	Student lives in the facility and receives all instruction there.	Provides instruction in all subject areas. May integrate learning with community-based experiences.

learning to count money and make change) and social skills. Such a curriculum should provide these youngsters with the skills necessary for getting and keeping a job and for living productive, independent lives as future adults (see Chapter 14). This curriculum, however, might entail placement in self-contained classrooms for most of the school day, or even placement in special school settings.

Instruction

Whereas services and curriculum refer to where and what students are taught, instruction refers to how teachers provide appropriate learning experiences for their students. Teachers must provide quality instruction to learners with mild disabilities, regardless of the setting or the curriculum. In fact, Slavin et al. (1989) maintain that the setting for special and remedial education is not as important as the quality of instruction received. They suggest that effective programs for students who have mild disabilities and others who are low achievers include the following five elements:

1. instruction designed to accommodate individual needs;

2. instruction based on frequent assessment of student progress;

3. immediate and intensive direct instruction to strengthen skills and prevent small deficits from becoming larger ones;

4. collaboration between the regular and special education teachers and consistency in the teaching methods used in various settings; and

5. teaching behaviors that provide students with high levels of on-task time, support, and success.

These essential elements of effective instruction are embodied in the teaching approaches we will now consider.

✎ Research-Based Approaches

Among the more recent approaches to teaching learners with mild disabilities are applied behavior analysis, direct instruction, strategy training, peer tutoring, and cooperative learning arrangements. Each has a growing research base and increasing popularity in both regular and special education classrooms. Although these approaches will be discussed in greater depth in the coming chapters, the following brief descriptions serve as an introduction.

Applied Behavior Analysis

Without a doubt, applied behavior analysis has been used successfully to improve the overt behaviors and academic performance of many children with mild disabilities. Like behavior modification, this approach relies on the direct, repeated measurement and recording of observable behaviors targeted for change. Environmental events preceding and following these targets are arranged to increase appropriate behaviors and decrease inappropriate behaviors. You might recall, for example, how Ms. Lopez measured Joey's oral reading rate by timing him with a stopwatch and how Joey eagerly recorded his performance on a graph. (For excellent reviews of applied behavior analysis with exceptional students, the interested reader may wish to consult Jenson, Sloane, & Young, 1988; or Wolery et al., 1988).

Direct Instruction

Like applied behavior analysis, direct instruction emphasizes direct measurement and careful sequencing of the component skills necessary to perform a specific task. Direct instruction, too, focuses on the teaching process, offering special educators powerful techniques for improving the academic achievement of their students with mild disabilities (Lloyd, 1988).

Direct instruction grew out of the work of Bereiter and Engelmann (1966), who advocated the use of a highly structured repetitive approach to teaching basic skills to disadvantaged preschoolers. Teachers using direct instruction present clear, well-sequenced, highly-focused, fast-paced lessons; elicit frequent responses from students taught in small groups; and provide immediate corrective feedback. Direct instruction emphasizes mastery of critical concepts and skills. Although teachers can use direct instructional techniques when teaching within the regular curriculum (Carnine, Silbert, & Kameenui, 1990), direct instructional materials with demonstrated effectiveness are also available commercially. These include *Corrective Reading* (Engelmann, Carnine, Johnson, & Meyers, 1988); *Reading Mastery: DISTAR Reading* (Engelmann & Bruner, 1984); and *Corrective Mathematics* (Carnine & Engelmann, 1981).

The term *direct instruction* first entered the wider educational sphere through the work of Rosenshine (1976), who used the terminology with reference to certain teacher behaviors correlated with the academic achievement of their students. Demonstration, guided practice, and feedback also became the hallmarks of mastery teaching, or the Instructional Theory into Practice (ITIP) model, popularized by Hunter (1982) during the 1980s in regular classrooms across the United States. According to Englert (1984), similar patterns of teacher behaviors also correlate with the academic achievement of students in special education classrooms. (See Chapter 8 for a detailed discussion of direct instruction and effective teacher behaviors in special education.)

Strategy Instruction

Unless explicitly taught to do so, students with mild disabilities often fail to transfer the skills and behaviors learned in the classroom to new situations (Gerber, 1988; Stokes & Baer, 1977). Also, students with learning disabilities, mild mental retardation, and behavioral disorders often fail to take an active role in their own learning and fail to devise strategies that could help them accomplish tasks efficiently (Torgesen, 1982).

Teachers want their students to become independent and self-directed. They want their students to take responsibility both for their own learning and for their own behaviors. Strategy instruction—also called cognitive behavior modification (Meichenbaum, 1977); learning strategy instruction (Deshler & Schumaker, 1986); and metacognitive strategy instruction (Flavell, 1979)— offers promise for helping students with mild disabilities to set goals, devise or select effective ways to approach a task, and monitor their own performance.

Strategy instruction combines the powerful teaching technologies of applied behavior analysis and direct instruction with concern for cognitive processes (i.e., those thoughts and feelings children have about themselves and about their learning). Through strategy training, students are taught how to improve important behaviors, including attending to seatwork tasks (Hallahan, Lloyd, & Stoller, 1982); comprehending reading passages (Palincsar, 1986); or memorizing content-area information (Mastropieri & Scruggs, 1989c). In addition to providing teachers with important instructional methods, strategy instruction is now the focus of an entire curriculum for secondary-level students with learning disabilities—the Learning Strategies Curriculum developed by Donald Deshler and Jean Schumaker and their colleagues at the University of Kansas Institute for Research on Learning Disabilities (Deshler & Schumaker, 1986).

Peer Tutoring

In an attempt to maximize the time spent by learners with mild disabilities on academic tasks, teachers at both the elementary and secondary levels have involved other students as instructional aides. Often, children without disabilities serve as tutors for their counterparts in special education programs; however, students with mild disabilities can also serve as tutors for younger peers. In order for peer-tutoring programs to be successful, though, the teacher must remain actively involved. Teachers must plan structured lessons for tutors to follow, train tutors to use important interpersonal behaviors that will facilitate learning, and monitor the performance of both tutors and tutees (Jenkins & Jenkins, 1988). Although peer-tutoring programs can improve the academic achievement of learners with mild disabilities, they do not necessarily improve the self-concept of these learners (Scruggs & Richter, 1985).

Cooperative Learning

In a recent effort to improve the academic achievement and social acceptance of mainstreamed students with mild disabilities, as well as other students with low achievement, teachers have arranged students in cooperative learning groups. Rather than competing against one another for grades, group members share the responsibility for helping one another learn. Although groups may compete against one another, the emphasis within each group is on cooperation and shared responsibility.

Johnson and Johnson (1987), for example, describe a tournament arrangement in which students from mixed-ability learning groups assist one another to learn and then compete with students of similar ability from other groups. Slavin (1990) discusses a similar arrangement, whereby students from mixed-ability teams called STADs (Student Teams Achievement Divisions) attempt to ensure that each team member will improve previous scores on quizzes covering the material learned. Other cooperative learning groups use jigsaw arrangements (Aronson, Blaney, Stephan, Sikes, & Snapp, 1978), in which each group member makes a specific and essential contribution toward a final group product, or classwide peer-tutoring teams (Maheady & Harper, 1987; Maheady, Sacca, & Harper, 1988).

Although research on cooperative learning arrangements is mixed, most of the research appears promising. Johnson and Johnson (1986) report that non-disabled peers have more positive attitudes toward mainstreamed students with disabilities as a result of cooperative learning groups. Moreover, Slavin et al. (1989) suggest that some cooperative learning arrangements may also enhance the academic achievement of these students. To be effective, however, these researchers believe that cooperative learning must include both group incentives and individual accountability. All group members must participate equally in order for the group to be successful. (See Chapter 9 for a detailed discussion of cooperative learning arrangements, peer tutoring, and strategy instruction.)

Cooperative learning arrangements promote increased academic achievement for students with mild disabilities in mainstreamed classrooms.

✎ Traditional Teaching Approaches

Despite the accumulating research evidence to support the effectiveness of applied behavior analysis, direct instruction, strategy instruction, peer tutoring, and cooperative learning arrangements, some teachers cling to more "traditional" instructional approaches. Many of these are outgrowths of the early work of such pioneers in the field of mental retardation as Alfred Strauss, Heinz Werner, and Laura Lehtinen (Hallahan & Cruickshank, 1973; Strauss & Lehtinen, 1947). Although not all traditional approaches to instruction have been supported by current research, some are still commonly accepted and widely used by special education teachers. These include stimulus-reduction procedures, multisensory approaches, modality-based instruction, and diet/drug therapies.

Stimulus Reduction

Strauss and Lehtinen (1947) first recommended the use of structure and reduced environmental stimulation when teaching the "brain-injured mentally retarded child." William Cruickshank and his colleagues later took a similar approach to the education of children with attentional problems and hyperactivity—children who today are often thought to have learning disabilities or emotional disturbance (Cruickshank, Bentzen, Ratzeburg, & Tannhauser, 1961). Stimulus-reduction techniques are applied in carefully structured, teacher-directed programs that attempt to minimize distracting elements of the child's surroundings. All irrelevant environmental stimuli are reduced and important instructional materials are highlighted in some way. For example, study carrels or cubicles are often used as individual work areas for pupils, and unused materials are put away so that they do not distract the child from his or her work. Assignments are often presented by giving only one item at a time or by using color to enhance the stimulus value of the material to be learned.

Although these procedures are still advocated by some special education teachers, research regarding their effectiveness has been mixed. In 1975, Cruickshank reported improved attention to task but no gains in academic achievement for those children in his experimental program. Other studies (for example, Gorton, 1972; Jenkins, Gorrafa & Griffiths, 1972; Rost & Charles, 1967; Shores & Haubrich, 1969; Sommervill, Warnberg, & Bost, 1973) have yielded similar findings; however, these studies have been criticized for numerous methodological flaws (Hallahan & Kauffman, 1975). Although stimulus-reduction procedures may help some children with attentional deficits, teachers

Research on the effectiveness of stimulus reduction has been mixed. These procedures may help some students pay attention, but they do not result in automatic gains in academic achievement.

should not rely solely on these techniques to improve academic achievement for their students with mild disabilities.

Multisensory Approaches and Modality-Based Instruction

Fernald's (1943) VAKT (visual, auditory, kinesthetic, tactile) technique exemplifies a multisensory instructional approach. For example, when learning to read new words, students first dictate a story. The teacher, writes each new word on a card, and subsequently holds up the cards for the students to see. As each card is viewed, the teacher pronounces the word clearly. Students then repeat each new word while looking at it, trace the word with their fingers as they say it, and then copy the word. Throughout instruction, teachers emphasize to students that this is a new and different way to learn.

Fernald originally used this multisensory approach to motivate and instruct delinquent, disabled readers, and today, numerous programs are purportedly based on her methods (for example, Gillingham & Stillman, 1956). In addition, teachers often encourage their students to see, hear, touch, and feel words, letters, or numbers by having them trace letters made from sandpaper or write words in trays filled with sand. Although the effectiveness of these techniques is not supported by a substantial body of research, many teachers strongly believe that they help pupils who are experiencing difficulty learning to read, write, or spell. One interesting research question that remains unexplored is whether the purported effectiveness of multisensory approaches is due to the use of the senses in combination or to the structure and repetition that characterize the technique.

A related approach is to determine the child's preferred sensory channel for learning. Proponents of this approach assume that in order for special education children to learn, instruction must be adjusted to match the sensory channel that is strongest for the individual child (Carbo, 1983, 1987, 1988; Carbo, Dunn, & Dunn, 1986; Dunn, 1988). Teachers advocating such methods believe that some children, for example, may learn best through the visual modality. For others, auditory channels may be preferred. A teacher using this approach might teach the visual learner to read by presenting sight words, while teaching letter-sound associations to an auditory learner.

Matching instruction to a student's preferred learning modality, however, is another approach whose effectiveness has not been empirically confirmed (Kavale & Forness, 1987). Although some teachers still believe that students with mild disabilities can be best taught through preferred sensory channels, no evidence exists for such an aptitude-treatment interaction (Lloyd, 1984). When teaching through learning modalities, teachers should use common sense: What they say they should also show, and what they show they should also say. That is, instruction should incorporate both oral and visual presentations by the teacher and active involvement by the student.

Modality-based instruction, however, should not be confused with accommodation strategies. Accommodation strategies offer students alternative ways to learn new information or to complete assignments. Rather than assuming that learning-modality preferences can be identified and that instruction can be matched to these strengths, the teacher using accommodation techniques attempts to circumvent deficiencies in specific academic skills. Accommodating deficits in basic skills in order to meet individual learning needs is a time-honored tradition among both special and regular classroom teachers. For example, Robert, with severe handwriting problems, might use a word processor to complete written work in Mr. McNally's geography class. Similarly, Travis might use a calculator when solving mathematical word problems in order to circumvent his difficulty in remembering the addition and subtraction facts.

Diet/Drug Therapies

Teachers often encounter children with attentional problems or hyperactivity who are taking Ritalin, Cylert, or other medication prescribed by a physician. Although these drugs can be quite effective in improving the behavior of many children for whom they are prescribed, teachers must remember that drugs are not a panacea. They are only one part of a total educational program in which teachers must provide for the individual instructional needs of their students. In addition, teachers must be aware of potential side-effects of these drugs. Common side-effects of psychostimulants include insomnia, weight loss, nausea, skin rashes, and dizziness (Forness & Kavale, 1988). Teachers should be prepared to carefully monitor the behavior of students taking any medication and, if necessary, report their observations to the child's parents and/or physician. Finally, teachers should refrain from suggesting to parents or other teachers that a child might require drug therapy. (See Box 3.1 for a detailed listing of cautions related to the use of psychostimulant drugs.)

A similar approach to treatment of attentional problems and hyperactivity involves careful control of the child's diet. In the Feingold (1976) diet, for example, children are prohibited from eating foods containing additives. Sugar, too, has often been implicated as the culprit in precipitating hyperactivity. To date, however, the results of well-conducted research studies fail to support any relationship between hyperactivity and the ingestion of food additives or sugar (Whalen, 1989). In short, teachers must evaluate their instructional methods rather than the child's diet when explaining or treating inattentive behavior.

A Summary of Traditional Approaches

Not all of the traditional approaches for teaching children with mild disabilities have research support. Clearly, evidence of the effectiveness of modality-based instruction and diet therapy is lacking. Stimulus reduction and drug therapy may increase a child's attention span, but not necessarily improve his or her academic achievement. Multisensory approaches have the support of practitioners in the field but lack research support. Teachers should choose instructional methods supported by research and best practice, rather than relying on familiar techniques presumed to be helpful.

The use of research-based instructional practices is, however, only one issue affecting special education teachers today. In the balance of this chapter, we will explore some other important issues surrounding special education programs.

Box 3.1   The Use and Misuse of Drugs for Hyperactivity: What the Research Tells Us

1. Psychostimulants produce inconsistent effects on intelligence and achievement test scores—some studies have found gains, others have not.

2. Possibly related to the first point is the conclusion that drugs do not appear to have much, if any, effect on the child's acquisition of new skills but do influence academic productivity—the child's ability to produce more of the kind of academic work with which he or she is already familiar.

3. The time course for many of these drugs is relatively brief, meaning that optimal response to the medication may last only a few hours.

4. Side effects are common. The most frequent are a decrease in appetite and an increase in sleeplessness.

5. Psychostimulants do not affect all children in the same way. Some experience side effects; others do not. Researchers estimate that around 60 to 70 percent who receive psychostimulants show improvement on teacher's ratings of their behavior. The remainder either do not improve or actually get worse.

6. There are few data to support the long-term benefits of psychostimulant use. Although some have speculated that there may be a causal relationship between psychostimulant use in childhood and later substance abuse, researchers have not yet conducted definitive studies on this possibility.

7. There is the possibility that the taking of medication leads to undesirable motivational changes. Children may come to rely on the medicine rather than themselves to change their behavior.

8. The medication of children may also lead to motivational changes on the part of adults. It may be that in some cases drugs are too effective in the sense that they appear to offer an apparently quick and easy solution to a problem that needs to be approached on a variety of fronts. Drugs may, for example, afford an easy excuse for teachers to shirk their duties.

9. Teachers need to be aware that dosage levels that lead to a lessening of motor activity may be so high as to lead to impaired performance on cognitive tasks. The result can be a situation in which, although the child's behavior seems better to the teacher, he or she is actually on too high a dosage level to gain any benefits in academic performance.

10. Medication alone is rarely, if ever, enough. A child whose behavioral problems are severe enough to warrant the administration of psychostimulants will almost always need to be provided with strong educational programming.

From Daniel P. Hallahan and James M. Kaufman, *Exceptional Children: Introduction to Special Education*, Fifth Edition. Copyright © 1991. Reprinted with permission of Allyn & Bacon.

✎ Issues Regarding Special Education Services and Instruction

During the 1980s, special education programs began to draw criticism. Although earlier self-contained classrooms for students with mild disabilities had largely been replaced with resource room and regular classroom programs, these efforts at mainstreaming were not resulting in consistently improved social status for children with disabilities (Sabornie, 1985); moreover, students with learning problems were not consistently demonstrating improved academic achievement as a result of their special education programs (Anderson & Pellicer, 1990; Slavin, 1988). Some authorities charge that students who are pulled out of the regular classroom for remedial help may actually spend less time on appropriate learning tasks than their counterparts who remain in the regular classroom (Slavin et al., 1989). These critics also suggest that students in pullout programs may miss essential instruction and activities in the regular classroom and that they may become confused if the materials, methods, or expectations of their special education teachers differ from those of their regular classroom teachers.

Moreover, Ysseldyke and Algozzine (1982) argue that students with low achievement levels who are placed in special education programs cannot be reliably distinguished from others with similar problems but who are not receiving these special services. Furthermore, they question whether special education programs are the appropriate response in all cases involving low achievement. In fact, some authorities even point to the Individualized Education Program (IEP) mandated by PL 94-142 as a document that fails to ensure specially designed and appropriate (i.e., effective) instruction for youngsters with disabilities (Smith, 1990).

These criticisms are currently fueling arguments against pullout special education and other remedial programs. Such arguments are motivated by the desire to reform special education and return all students with mild disabilities to the regular classroom. The reader must remember, however, that the quality of instruction received, not the physical setting in which it is delivered, is the important element in determining student success. We will now briefly examine two calls for reform in special education: the Regular Education Initiative and supportive/preventative special education services.

The Regular Education Initiative

As the public schools implemented PL 94-142, it became evident that some students who were in need of support services, but who did not meet federal eligibility criteria, would not be served. For example, students who were achieving just below average, who lacked motivation, who were abused and neglected, or who were from dysfunctional families were not necessarily eligible for special education services (Reynolds, Wang, & Walberg, 1987). As stated by Madeleine Will, assistant secretary for the Office of Special Education and Rehabilitative Services of the U.S. Department of Education, Public Law 94-142 provides services for students who are already experiencing failure in their learning environment rather than providing preventative services for students to eliminate learning difficulties prior to failure (Will, 1986).

Such problems with the implementation of PL 94-142 have resulted in a call for significant changes in the delivery of services for those who experience learning problems. The Regular Education Initiative (REI) issued by Will cited the following problems with the current system of special education:

- Special education pullout services have not proven to be effective, although this is the common method of providing support services.

- Special education services, as well as other services for students at risk (e.g., Chapter 1) are fragmented and segregated.

- Special education is provided in a categorical fashion, but not all students fit into categories.

- Services are not preventative in nature.

- Parents are not considered to be active participants in the special education process.

Will (1986) suggested that regular and special educators and administrators be empowered to design and implement school-based alternative strategies and approaches for educating students who have learning problems. These approaches should focus on early intervention and prevention of learning problems in the regular classroom rather than on categorical pullout programs. Further, Will argued that needed reforms in special education must include the integration of special and regular education resources, the provision of special services without labeling of students, and greater support in regular education. Regular educators, therefore, should be involved cooperatively throughout the process.

Reynolds et al. (1987) also strongly supported a major restructuring of special education. They argued for "rights without labels" to ensure that screening, assessment, and appropriate programs would be provided for all students with special needs. A *complete* merger of regular and special education services was called for by Stainback, Stainback, and Bunch (1989). Others argued that some students were often labeled so as to receive support services, even when their disabilities were not significant (Wilson, 1991).

Although there are numerous arguments for changing the current system of delivery of special education services, there are others who argue against radical changes (for example, Davis, 1988; Hallahan, Keller, McKinney, Lloyd, & Bryan, 1988; Kauffman, 1989; Kauffman, Gerber, & Semmel, 1988; Schumaker & Deshler, 1988). Among the criticisms of the REI are the following:

- Regular educators and other consumers, especially at the local level, have not been sufficiently involved in the debate over proposed changes.

- The REI debate has largely involved faculty in higher education, specifically faculty in special education, rather than faculty in elementary and secondary education (Davis, 1988).

- There is danger that the student-deficit model will be replaced with a teacher-deficit model.

- Increasing the number of difficult-to-teach students in the regular classroom and adding to the variety of students within each class will not result in the progress of students unless there are increased resources (Kauffman, Gerber, & Semmel, 1988).

- A sufficient variety of services may not be available for those students who need them.

- Efficacy research on new teaching methods should be undertaken prior to implementing sweeping changes (Hallahan et al., 1988).
- The REI lacks specificity on how to restructure special education and implement proposed mergers (Kauffman, 1989).

Research regarding the regular classroom teacher's perception of the REI has just started to appear in the literature (Coates, 1989; Semmel, Abernathy, Butera, & Lesar, 1991). Practicing teachers believe that traditional service-delivery systems in special education, particularly pullout programs, do serve the needs of their students. Semmel et al. (1991) found that both regular and special education teachers prefer pullout programs, yet these teachers also believe that students with mild disabilities have a basic right to education in the regular classroom. Many teachers, however, believe that a redistribution of special education resources to the regular classroom would reduce their instructional load (Semmel et al., 1991).

Although we support some of the changes advocated by REI proponents, particularly cooperation and collaboration among special and regular educators in order to assist teachers with problem learners in the regular classroom and to prevent unnecessary special education referrals, we do not advocate acceptance of the REI unless extensive research demonstrating positive effects is forthcoming. Clearly, such extensive research into new teaching methods and strategies is needed before implementation of any proposal as broad as the Regular Education Initiative.

Supportive/Preventative Services

The current reform movement in regular and special education emphasizes support for the at-risk learner and the prevention of significant learning problems within the regular classroom (Pianta, 1990). Teachers are increasingly forming flexible problem-solving groups called teacher assistance teams (Chalfant, Pysh, & Moultrie, 1979), or student support teams (Glickman, 1990; Ramey & Robbins, 1989), or mainstream assistance teams (Fuchs, Fuchs, & Bahr, 1990), in order to help one another maintain students with special needs in the regular classroom. Team membership may include regular classroom teachers, special education teachers, principals, school psychologists, and guidance counselors. When teachers are experiencing difficulty with instructional or behavioral needs of students in their classrooms, they may solicit help from the team. Team members work together as equal partners to address the teachers' concerns and to coach them in solving problems. Teacher assistance teams result in fewer referrals by classroom teachers of troublesome students for special education evaluation and placement (Chalfant et al., 1979).

Consultation and collaboration or collaborative team teaching are two additional strategies designed to assist problem learners. Although both have varying definitions among professionals (see, for example, Johnson, Pugach, & Hammittee, 1988; Morsink et al., 1991; Phillips & McCullough, 1990), in this text we define the terms in the following manner:

Consultation—The sharing of information or expertise through explanation or demonstration by one person to another (Morsink et al., 1991).

Collaboration—A type of consultation in which all people involved are viewed as having unique areas of expertise and who interact equally to resolve problems (Villa, Thousand, Paolucci-Whitcomb, & Nevin, 1990).

The consultation model.   The consultant is an expert who provides information and advice to others. The consultation process may involve school psychologists, special education teachers, counselors, principals, or regular education teachers (Phillips & McCullough, 1990). The consultant plays an indirect, rather than direct, role in providing services to students. For example, a school psychologist may provide suggestions to the special educator on how to handle the acting-out behavior of a young student who has recently learned that his parents are separating, or a special education teacher may give a regular classroom teacher ideas about how to reduce distractors in the environment for a mainstreamed student with attention problems.

The collaborative team teaching model.   Collaborative team teaching, or collaboration, implies an equal partnership among professionals. There are numerous examples of collaboration used in teaching both regular and special education students (see, for example Affleck, Madge, Adams, & Lowenbraun, 1988; Self, Benning, Marston, & Magnusson, 1991; Wiedmeyer & Lehman, 1991). These collaborative models may be called integrated classroom models or adapted learning environments. The common factor, however, is the shared responsibility by regular and special educators for teaching students with special needs within the regular classroom. (See Table 3.2 for a summary of collaborative teaching arrangements.)

Through collaboration, special educators and regular classroom teachers work cooperatively as partners to plan and provide instruction for all students

---

Table 3.2   Collaborative Teaching Arrangements

The following collaborative teaching arrangements are described in the special education literature:

The Adaptive Learning Environment Model	Instructional teaming is used to adapt the regular educational environment to meet the needs of special, regular, and at-risk learners. Systematic teaching and multiaged grouping to meet student needs is encouraged (Wang & Birch, 1984).
The Integrated Classroom Model	A teacher trained in special education is assigned to a regular classroom of about 24 students. Of the children in the class, approximately two-thirds are regular education students and one-third are students with mild disabilities. The special educator shares responsibility for planning and instruction with the regular classroom teacher (Affleck, Madge, Adams, & Lowenbraun, 1988). In some school districts this model may also be referred to as co-teaching.

in the class. For example, the special education teacher may share information regarding curriculum design or behavior management and the regular classroom teacher may contribute information and instructional methods specific to a particular content area. Because both professionals work together as a team, the pupil-to-teacher ratio is reduced and instructional resources are pooled (Thousand & Villa, 1989). Furthermore, the number of special education referrals and placements may be reduced as a result of collaborative efforts (Chalfant et al., 1979; Self et al., 1991). (See Table 3.3 for a description of collaborative teaching activities.)

Table 3.3   Collaborative Teaching Activities

In collaborative teaching, the following activities generally take place:

Sharing Responsibility for Planning and Delivering Instruction	Ms. Lopez and Ms. Kirk work together daily to plan and team-teach social studies in Ms. Kirk's fourth-grade classroom. Both teachers share ideas for how instruction and materials might be adapted to meet the needs of each student in the class. Ms. Lopez suggests techniques to incorporate learning strategies and social skills into the present social studies unit and Ms. Kirk provides expertise on the fourth-grade social studies curriculum. Ms. Lopez coteaches social studies lessons with Ms. Kirk, answering questions, assisting students, adapting tests, and checking assignments.
Monitoring Academic Progress and Student Behavior	This year, Mr. Abel and Mr. McNally are piloting a collaborative teaching arrangement in the ninth-grade geography class for one period per day. In addition to planning and teaching cooperatively, Mr. Abel will monitor the academic progress and behaviors of students with mild disabilities who have been mainstreamed into Mr. McNally's class. For example, on a daily basis, Mr. Abel checks to be sure that Robert is taking notes and using in-class study time wisely. In addition, he checks to be sure that Robert understands important concepts and makes note of those areas that will require reteaching and/or reinforcement during Robert's resource-room period.

✎ Summary

Students with mild disabilities are already behind their peers academically. They have many needs, but only limited time. Therefore, the teacher's ability to make appropriate decisions regarding instructional services, content, and methodology for special learners is critical. Special education teachers must base their decisions about service and curricular options on careful assessment of individual student need rather than on current availability of programs or materials. A range of service options, from the regular classroom to segregated placement, is necessary in order to meet the needs of all students with mild disabilities.

Similarly, teachers must use the most powerful instructional techniques possible. Effective approaches to teaching children with mild disabilities include applied behavior analysis, direct instruction, strategy instruction, peer tutoring, and cooperative learning arrangements. Research evidence suggests that these methods enhance the academic achievement of many students in special education programs, and that each holds promise for future usefulness.

The teacher must remember, however, that even approaches that have been tested and proven effective for most students may not work for a particular student. Teachers must carefully observe the individual child's response to a given instructional approach. If that approach is not leading to academic gains or to increased social acceptance for the youngster, the teacher must choose a different method of instruction for that child.

Teachers must begin with intensive, direct instruction of essential academic and social skills identified through daily assessment of student performance. As these skills are mastered, strategies related to specific content-area knowledge or to particular environmental or task demands can also be taught explicitly. To be most effective, strategy instruction must be integrated with direct instruction of relevant skills and content, rather than treated as a separate curricular offering (Pressley et al., 1990). As students master strategies and skills, teachers can arrange peer-tutoring or cooperative learning groups to facilitate integration into the regular classroom and to enhance instructional time. Similarly, applied behavior analysis can be used to build appropriate behaviors in the special education setting and to maintain these behaviors within the regular classroom. (We will return to these critical areas repeatedly in the coming chapters.)

Although teachers may use traditional methods when teaching students with mild disabilities, not all of these are supported by research. Modality-based instruction and diet therapy, for example, lack research evidence of effectiveness. On the other hand, stimulus reduction and the careful use of drug therapy appear to improve the child's attention to task, but not necessarily academic achievement. Although teachers believe that modality-based and multisensory approaches have positive outcomes for many youngsters with mild disabilities, research does not fully support this claim.

Service, curriculum, and instruction refer to three interrelated ideas—the where, what, and how of teaching. Special education teachers must make many decisions regarding the appropriate setting and curriculum for youngsters with mild disabilities. However, it is important to remember that quality instruction must take place, regardless of the setting, if students in special education are to master the chosen curricular option. The responsibility for wise decisions and quality instruction rests squarely with the teacher.

✎ Application Exercises

1. Contact a local school system. Describe the range of services provided to students in special education programs in that school district.

2. Interview two or three special education teachers at both the elementary and the secondary level from local school districts. What curricular options are available for students at each level? Which instructional methods are most often used by these teachers?

3. Interview two or three regular classroom teachers at both the elementary and the secondary level from local school districts. Which instructional methods are most often used by these teachers? Are there differences in the approaches most often used by the regular classroom teachers and by the special education teachers you interviewed in Question 2? Why or why not?

4. Ask two or three special and regular education teachers in your local school system if they are familiar with the REI. Summarize their answers in one or two short paragraphs.

5. Contact a local elementary or secondary school. Are teacher assistance teams or student support teams or mainstream assistance teams used in these schools? If so, how do these teams function?

Part Two

Organizing for Instruction

Communicating
for Student Success

Chapter 4

Focus

As you read, think about the following questions:

What skills are essential for successful consultation and collaboration?

How can teachers communicate with other professionals in the school?

How can teachers communicate with parents and guardians of students with mild disabilities?

How can teachers coordinate the activities of paraprofessionals and volunteers?

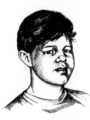

✎ Recall from Chapter 3 the range of service options necessary to provide an appropriate education for students with mild disabilities. Those models involving student placement in the regular classroom for all or part of the school day (the resource room, for example), require ongoing communication between regular and special educators if students are to be successful in their mainstreamed classes. In addition, consultation models and collaborative or team-teaching arrangements depend on skilled communications and cooperative efforts among professionals. This point is illustrated by the activities of Ms. Lopez.

Ms. Lopez team-teaches each Tuesday and Thursday afternoon in Ms. Kirk's fourth-grade social studies class. At the moment, Ms. Lopez is assisting Celie and Kevin with a group project in social studies. Although Celie and Kevin are not eligible for special education services, both are "at risk." Both are likely to experience academic failure unless they receive special help. The teachers at Oak Hill Elementary School hope to maintain Celie and Kevin in their regular class and to strengthen their academic performance through this collaborative, team-teaching arrangement.

As soon as Ms. Lopez helps Kevin locate a word in the dictionary, she notices that Travis is staring out the window. He is not interacting with his group nor is he working on his contribution to the group's social studies project. Ms. Lopez moves toward Travis, and he immediately resumes his task. Ms. Lopez surveys the classroom and is pleased to see that all of the students are attending to their social studies projects. Joey is using colored pencils to decorate the cover of a booklet about colonial life that he and other members of his group wrote together.

The social studies period passes quickly. As Ms. Lopez looks at her watch, she notices that in 5 minutes she must attend a meeting of the teacher-assistance team. A third-grade teacher has asked for help in solving the academic problems of one of the children in her classroom. Ms. Lopez also remembers that she has an appointment at 3:30 with the school psychologist. This time Ms. Lopez will be the consultee, seeking information about a behavioral intervention to help Joey generalize appropriate social skills in both his regular and special education classes. At 4:00, Ms. Lopez will attend a parent–teacher conference with Travis's mother to discuss ways to increase the time Travis spends working on his homework.

Busy teachers like Ms. Lopez must possess superb communications and human-relations skills in order to assume their many roles. In this chapter, we will first examine the communication skills required of consultants and collaborators and suggest ideas to facilitate successful consultation and collaborative teaching. Next, we will explore ways to communicate with parents and enhance their involvement in educational programming for their children with special needs. Finally, we will present methods by which to communicate with paraprofessionals and volunteers who perform many essential duties in special education classrooms.

✎ Consulting and Collaborating

Consultation and collaboration require an extensive knowledge base, including curriculum design, instructional methods, cognitive and developmental theory, and behavior management. In addition, positive human relationships and effective communication skills are essential to successful consultation and collaboration. Gutkin and Curtis (1990), for example, suggest that consultation can be facilitated through the following behaviors:

1. Setting the Proper Tone: The consultant is sincere and respectful during interactions with others.

2. Listening and Encouraging: The consultant listens attentively and encourages others to talk.

3. Demonstrating Empathy: The consultant responds in an understanding and nonjudgmental manner.

4. Paraphrasing: The consultant rephrases to ensure that both parties clearly understand what has been said.

5. Summarizing and Previewing: The consultant sums up progress and helps to set the agenda for the next meeting.

Knoff, McKenna, and Riser (1991) identify several additional behaviors of effective consultants. These include practicing in an ethical manner, maintaining confidentiality, respecting the consultee, and being approachable. On the other hand, behaving in an authorative or aggressive manner, attempting to be colorful or funny, exhibiting a deferential attitude, and self-disclosing during consultation can lead to negative outcomes according to these authors.

Apparently, an essential characteristic of skilled consultants and collaborators is the ability to build and maintain an open and trusting rapport with others. Such rapport is based on mutual respect and clearly communicates that all parties are viewed as equals (Gutkin & Curtis, 1990). Trust, respect, and rapport, of course, are built through many positive communications with professionals and parents over the course of the school year. (See Box 4.1 for an illustration of one form of ongoing positive communication.)

Communication Skills

Skillful communication depends on attention to both nonverbal and verbal behavior. Whereas verbal behavior is what we say, nonverbal behavior is how we say it. If we are not careful, our words might send one message and our actions another. Say, for example, Ms. Lopez approaches Ms. Kirk and states, "You said Joey had a problem in class today. Do you want to talk about it?" At the same time, Ms. Lopez is looking at her watch, scowling, and tapping her foot. In this instance, Ms. Kirk would not be likely to sit down and talk about Joey!

Body posture, facial expressions, gestures, and eye contact may send messages that are either intimidating or encouraging. For example, crossed arms and a "nose-to-nose and toe-to-toe" body posture are threatening to most people. Teachers should maintain a relaxed body posture when talking with others, standing or sitting slightly off to one side with arms down and visible. Whereas eye contact in Anglo-American culture is generally seen as positive, in Native-American, Asian-American, and African-American cultures, eye contact with authority figures is sometimes seen as a sign of disrespect (Chan, 1987;

Box 4.1   A Newsletter from Special Education Teachers

The following newsletter illustrates one way to improve communication and positive relationships among professionals in schools. In this newsletter, Mr. Abel wrote a "Teacher Feature" to highlight the contributions of regular classroom teachers to the success of his students mainstreamed into their classes.

Special-needs students often comment on how very special their mainstream teachers are. To let classroom teachers know about these comments and to reward students for putting their thoughts down on paper, a writing contest was held. These paragraphs come to you straight from the pens of our students.

First Place Winners

My Favoite Teacher is *Mrs. Scott.* She is very nice to people. Also, if you have a problem with your work in class she will help you with it. And if you have a sersious problem about your family she will sit down and talk about the problem.

Also she is nice about letting people in class room go a minute early to lunch if we are good. She let's us talk silent in class. She is very understandable about things that go on in class or out of class.

By T.

I like *Mr. O'Brien* because he is very fair in class and in gym. He is a health and gym teacher. The reason he is my favorite teacher is because he is one of the most understanding, nice, polite, kind, and sweet teachers. He explains his subject well and makes me feel confident in his own way.

He also has a family of his own. He has two little boys and a wife. He talks about them in class alot. He is also an open person and he cares about his students.

By M.

My best teacher is *Mr. Childress.* We can work at air own place. We do not have to work together. He crakes jokes everyday and he smiles at us a lot. He dose not yell at us that much, he just talkes to us. The work is real easy and I do not have to rack my brean.

By R.

Teacher Feature

Apple County High School mainstream teachers are to be commended for continually making accommodations in their classrooms for special-needs students. The support they offer the Special Education Department is outstanding.

Carol Knott and *Wayne Meher* review basic math, algebra, and geometry concepts for the L.D. and E.D. teachers. Using this mini-refresher course enables special education teachers to teach their students more effectively.

(continued)

Box 4.1   *(Continued)*

The Math Department generously supplies supplemental worksheets and tests for use in Special Education resource classes.

Pat Brashears changes the seating arrangement of her English classes every two weeks, allowing each student to have a front-row seat sometime during the grading period.

Denise Dunn provides her math students with a monthly planning sheet, noting assignments, page numbers, due dates, and quiz days. This computerized sheet is extremely helpful to special-needs students who have difficulty with organizational skills. (She often adds a personal touch with comments like "Have a great holiday!" or "Enjoy your break!")

Evelyn Parker has a learning disabled student in her algebra class who does well on daily work, but who has difficulty passing tests and quizzes. Mrs. Parker has discovered that if she waits for a week and gives a second quiz on the same material, this student's grade improves. Mrs. Parker also offers after-school study sessions to students who need extra assistance in completing her math assignments.

Adapted from "A Newsletter from Special Education Teachers," by Clover Hill High School Special Education Department, 1987, Learning, *June, pp. 1–2. Adapted by permission of Chesterfield County Schools, Chesterfield, VA.*

Gilliam & Van Den Berg, 1980; Simpson, 1982). Also, the tone, volume, and rhythm of the spoken message may communicate confidence and respect or distrust and fear.

Turnbull and Turnbull (1986) suggest that teachers practice several techniques to improve communication. For example, they can ask open-ended questions that encourage elaborated responses (e.g., "What behaviors did Joey exhibit in class today?"), or they can paraphrase what the other person has said. For example, if Ms. Kirk answers the question about Joey's behavior by saying, "Joey was constantly pushing and hitting the other children today," Ms. Lopez might respond by saying, "Joey was quite aggressive with the other children today." By paraphrasing, the teacher can check whether or not he or she has correctly understood what was said. In addition, paraphrasing allows the initial speaker to hear the message from a slightly different perspective.

Active listening also enables teachers to check their understanding of a message and helps the speaker feel that he or she has been understood and accepted (Turnbull & Turnbull, 1986). Active listening responds to the feelings behind a message as well as to the message itself. For example, suppose Ms. Kirk responded to the question about Joey's behavior by saying, "Joey was out of his seat constantly. He was pushing and hitting the other children, and I couldn't seem to get him to stop no matter what I said or did." Ms. Lopez might convey empathy by responding, "It's frightening when Joey behaves so aggressively and it's frustrating when he won't listen." When teachers use active listening, they demonstrate a sincere interest in the feelings of others, encouraging openness and honesty.

Occasionally, parents or colleagues become upset during consultative or collaborative meetings. At these times, teachers must remain calm and attend to their nonverbal communications. Usually, when individuals are upset, they need to know that someone is listening to them. Active listening, paraphrasing, and open-ended questions will often de-escalate the situation as the distraught individual realizes that he or she is being heard and understood (Turnbull & Turnbull, 1986). In addition, although it is difficult, teachers must not take personally what is said during emotional outbursts. When consulting or collaborating with others, the teacher must maintain a professional manner.

Consultation

Consultation involves the sharing of information by professionals engaged in problem-solving activities. Pugach and Johnson (1989) suggest that consultation is most effective when consultants shed their expert or specialist roles and become partners with teachers and parents. At the same time, consultants must structure interactions and communicate that structure to others. As listed in Table 4.1, Morsink et al. (1991) identify eight steps to structure the consultation process.

Once the relationship has been established, the next step is to gather information. Sources of information include the student's parents, other teachers,

---

Table 4.1   The Consultation Process

According to Morsink, Thomas, and Correa (1991), the consultation process involves the following eight stages:

1. Establishing the relationship: Meet and establish rapport with the consultee.

2. Gathering information: Check a variety of sources to get background information about the problem.

3. Identifying the problem: Determine the history and frequency of the problem and define it in measureable terms.

4. Stating the target behavior: Consider whether the behavior must be increased or decreased and determine the criteria by which to evaluate progress.

5. Generating interventions: Discuss options to consider and select alternatives to try.

6. Implementing the interventions: Put the interventions into effect and collect data on their success or failure.

7. Evaluating the interventions: Determine whether the desired outcomes have been achieved and modify the interventions if necessary.

8. Withdrawing from the consultation relationship: End the process when the goal has been reached or when an agreement has been made to discontinue.

Reprinted with permission of Macmillan Publishing Company from Interactive Teaming: Consultation and Collaboration in Special Programs, *p. 45, by Catherine V. Morsink, Carol Chase Thomas and Vivian I. Correa. Copyright © 1991 by Macmillan Publishing Company.*

the principal, the school nurse, guidance counselors, and school records. Collecting information from many different sources enables the consultant to determine the settings in which the child is likely to display problem behavior; the intensity, duration, and frequency of the behavior; and the expectations of those who are objecting to the behavior (Polsgrove & McNeil, 1989). Consultants must ensure that the information on which they will base their decisions and recommendations is, indeed, objective.

Next, the consultant identifies the problem. In this critical step, the problem behavior is pinpointed and clarified. For example, after speaking with Travis's mother, Ms. Lopez determines that Travis must increase the amount of time he spends on homework from 15 minutes to 1 hour each evening. Following identification and clarification of the problem, the consultant and parent must analyze the forces impinging on the problem; in this case, the amount of time Travis spends watching television after school and the time he is unsupervised before his mother returns home from work. They then brainstorm alternative strategies and choose from among the alternatives. For example, they may decide on the strategy of setting aside a specific time and place for homework. Ms. Lopez will be responsible for giving Travis a daily homework sheet to be signed by his mother and returned the next day. Travis' mother and Ms. Lopez together will then evaluate the effectiveness of the chosen intervention (Gutkin & Curtis, 1990). Throughout the process, Ms. Lopez must be sure to specify clearly who will do what and when, and she must set aside a time and place to meet to conduct follow-up discussions in order to evaluate and readjust the agreed-upon intervention. (See Box 4.2 for an illustration of the consultation process.)

Although consultation is an important role of special educators, special education teachers actually spend very little time in consultation activities (Idol-Maestas & Ritter, 1985). Johnson et al. (1988) cite insufficient time, large numbers of students, limited resources, and lack of administrative support as barriers to effective consultation in the schools. In addition, they suggest that classroom teachers may believe that special educators do not appreciate the demands of the regular classroom. Therefore, problem-solving strategies offered by special education teachers who assume an expert role may not be perceived as feasible by regular educators.

Collaboration

The most effective form of consultation is one in which all parties are viewed as having equal expertise (Gutkin & Curtis, 1990; Pugach & Johnson, 1989). Consultation that involves contributions by all parties and that considers all parties to be experts is known as collaborative consulting, or simply, collaboration. When collaborating, teachers, parents, and other professionals generate viable educational interventions (Donaldson & Christiansen, 1990) during interactions characterized by mutual respect, open communication, and consensual decision making (West, 1990).

Collaboration is taking place, for example, when a special educator and a regular classroom teacher (e.g., Ms. Lopez and Ms. Kirk) work together on a social studies curriculum for students who are reading four levels below grade expectancy. Collaboration also is taking place when a teacher and the school

Box 4.2   The Consultation Process

Mr. McNally has requested a consultation with Mr. Abel regarding Marcus's performance in geography class. Marcus has not performed well during the current grading period, and Mr. McNally is concerned that he will fail. Some of the strategies for successful consultation offered by Gutkin and Curtis (1982) and by Morsink, Thomas, and Correa (1991) are shown in parentheses. Let's listen to the conversation.

Mr. Abel: *Hi. How are you doing? (Establishing rapport)*

Mr. McNally: *Okay. You?*

Mr. Abel: *Fine, thanks. Did you see the game Friday night? That was a great game!*

Mr. McNally: *Yeah. The kids played really well.*

Mr. Abel: *I understand that you want to talk about Marcus. I know he's been having difficulty in class. (Reviewing the information)*

Mr. McNally: *Yeah. I'm afraid I need to do something fast. He just doesn't seem to be doing his work.*

Mr. Abel: *Tell me how he works in class. (Defining and clarifying the problem)*

Mr. McNally: *He doesn't. He doesn't listen. He stares out the window or he just puts his head down on the desk and sleeps.*

Mr. Abel: *So he doesn't pay attention or participate in class. (Paraphrasing)*

Mr. McNally: *No, when he's there, he doesn't participate at all.*

Mr. Abel: *How many assignments has he completed?*

Mr. McNally: *Let me look in my grade book. Let's see. He turned in 5, no, 6 of the 12 class assignments since the grading period started the week before last, and he made an F on the quiz Friday.*

Mr. Abel: *Marcus needs to turn in his assignments. (Stating the target behavior) Do you know of anything that might be going on at home or school that could be affecting his work? (Analyzing forces impinging on the problem)*

Mr. McNally: *Well, a couple weeks ago, Marcus told me his mother started working the evening shift. I think he's got a younger brother or sister at home that he babysits.*

Mr. Abel: *So Marcus may not be able to get his work done if he's watching his brother or sister. Maybe he's tired from staying up later, too.*

Mr. McNally: *He told me about his mother when I asked him about his map project just after the grading period started. He finally turned it in, but it was late.*

Mr. Abel: *Let's think about what we could try to help Marcus get his assignments done. What does he need to turn in in order to pass this grading period? (Listing strategies to improve performance. Determining criteria for judging success)*

Mr. McNally: *I think he said his mother leaves at five o'clock. Maybe he could come back to my room after school to get his work done. I think he walks. Anyway, he'll need to have at least 75% of his work completed correctly to pass.*

Mr. Abel: *Okay. That means he needs to complete two more of the assignments correctly and then keep up with the rest. (Establishing criteria for evaluation)*

Mr. McNally: *I'll ask Marcus tomorrow if he walks and if he'd like to stay after school. Maybe that will get him on the right track.*

Mr. Abel: *All right. I'll check with you tomorrow afternoon to see what Marcus said. Do you need any special materials for Marcus? (Specifying responsibilities and follow-up)*

Mr. McNally: *No, but thanks.*

Mr. Abel: *Okay. You let me know tomorrow if you need anything. I'll see you tomorrow afternoon. (Closing the consultation contact)*

Mr. McNally: *Thanks. See you tomorrow.*

psychologist design a behavior-management plan across the entire school day for a student, like Joey, who has been unable to follow classroom rules. Or, when a teacher meets with a speech-language therapist and a parent to design a home–school language-intervention program, the three are involved in a collaborative process.

Collaboration is a problem-solving method that draws on the professional expertise of two or more individuals who work together to achieve a common goal. However, according to Phillips anbd McCullough (1990), for collaboration to take place in schools, certain central tenets must be acknowledged by professionals engaging in the process:

1. There must be joint responsibility for problems (i.e., all professionals share responsibility and concern for students).

2. There must be joint accountability and recognition for problem resolution.

3. There must be a shared belief that pooling talents and resources is mutually advantageous, with the following benefits:

   (a) a wide range of solutions generated;

   (b) diversity of expertise and resources available;

   (c) superiority and originality of solutions generated.

4. There must be a belief that teacher or student problem resolution merits expenditure of time, energy, and resources.

5. There must be a belief that correlates of collaboration are important and desirable (e.g., group morale, group cohesion, increased knowledge of problem-solving processes and specific alternative classroom interventions).

It should be noted, however, that joint responsibility and accountability do not preclude designating one member of the collaborative group as a case manager to facilitate the group's activities. The case manager might coordinate services needed by the student and his or her family, delegate responsibilities, and ensure follow-up activities (Morsink et al., 1991).

Coordinating services.   Coordinating needed services might, for example, entail obtaining appropriate curricular materials needed to implement IEP objectives for Travis, or it may mean referring Joey's family for services provided in a community mental-health center. The case manager acts as the clearinghouse for locating materials and services and for obtaining access to these.

Delegating responsibilities.   Members of collaborative teams must function together as a group, each contributing equally to the problem-solving effort. The case manager may choose to delegate specific responsibilities to each team member in order to facilitate the problem-solving process. Delegating responsibilities will be more easily accomplished if the case manager follows the guidelines suggested by Morsink et al. (1991) as listed in Table 4.2

Table 4.2   Delegating Responsibility

Teachers may need to delegate responsibilities to members of a collaborative team. These may include other teachers and professionals, parents, and paraprofessionals. The following suggestions will help teachers ensure that delegated responsibilities are performed correctly:

1. State the task clearly and objectively.

2. Tell the person why the task is important.

3. Give "permission." Unless others know who has been delegated authority to accomplish the task, they may not cooperate fully.

4. Clarify the results that are expected. It is important to tell designees *what* to accomplish but not how to do the job.

5. Allow for interaction. Make certain that the task and its results are clear by asking the designee to restate what is to be done. Also allow time for questions or clarification.

6. Agree on follow-up. Set a time and place to meet after the task has been completed in order to evaluate the results. It is not adequate to say, "Let's get together sometime and talk about it some more."

Ensuring follow-up.   Follow-up activities are critical if goals are to be met. Follow-up must be conducted in a systematic manner so that all parties involved know when and how the follow-up activities will occur. For example, the case manager should establish the next meeting date, time, and place before the group adjourns, and he or she should provide the means for regular communication in order to monitor progress. Figure 4.1 illustrates a communication form used by Mr. Abel to provide systematic follow-up to monitor Robert's progress in his mainstreamed classes.

Collaboration can be an effective way to provide educational services to a variety of students within the same school or classroom. According to Thousand and Villa (1989), "school personnel who effectively collaborate will agree that each teacher, left alone, is limited in the instructional responses he or she can conceptualize or deliver. However, when a school staff pool their conceptual, material, technical, and human resources, students and staff benefit from the collective wisdom" (pp. 99–100). In order to benefit from collective wisdom, teachers must keep the child as the focal point and seek out others who have information, materials, and strategies necessary to meet the child's needs (Johnson, Pugach, & Devlin, 1990).

Figure 4.1   Mainstreaming Checklist

Mr. Abel uses a mainstreaming checklist to monitor Robert's performance in his regular classes. The checklist goes to teachers once each week. By using two identical columns, Mr. Abel saves paper. Classroom teachers circle problem areas and make comments. When problems are noted, Mr. Abel documents the action he takes.

CHECKLIST FOR MAINSTREAMED STUDENTS

STUDENT: _____   TEACHER: _____
SUBJECT: _____   SP. ED. TEACHER: _____

I would appreciate your response to the items below so that I may better evaluate this student's progress and modify my instructional program with the student as needed. Please circle the appropriate responses and drop the completed form in my box by the due date indicated. Thank you!

Confidential or Nonconfidential

Grading Period____ Due Date_____

I. PREPARATION   *Problem   No Problem*
   Circle problem areas if they exist:
   • tardy to class
   • unprepared with paper, pencil, and book(s)
   • does not complete homework (List assignments under "Comments.")
   • other: _____

II. CLASS PARTICIPATION *Problem No Problem*
   Circle problem areas if they exist:
   • does not complete assignments (List missing assignments under "Comments.")
   • does not appear to listen to instructions
   • does not take notes in class
   • does not ask teacher questions
   • does not answer questions
   • does not participate in class discussions
   • does not have a good attitude toward class
   • other: _____

III. BEHAVIOR   *Problem   No Problem*
   Circle problem areas if they exist:
   • does not work quiety
   • distracts other students
   • uses inappropriate language and tone of voice
   • does not attend to task
   • interacts inappropriately with other students
   • other: _____

Grading Period ____ Due Date_____

I. PREPARATION   *Problem   No Problem*
   Circle problem areas if they exist:
   • tardy to class
   • unprepared with paper, pencil, and book(s)
   • does not complete homework (List assignments under "Comments.")
   • other: _____

II. CLASS PARTICIPATION *Problem No Problem*
   Circle problem areas if they exist:
   • does not complete assignments (List missing assignments under "Comments.")
   • does not appear to listen to instructions
   • does not take notes in class
   • does not ask teacher questions
   • does not answer questions
   • does not participate in class discussions
   • does not have a good attitude toward class
   • Other: _____

III. BEHAVIOR   *Problem   No Problem*
   Circle problem areas if they exist:
   • does not work quietly
   • distracts other students
   • uses inappropriate language and tone of voice
   • does not attend to task
   • interacts inappropriately with other students
   • other: _____

(continued)

Figure 4.1   *(Continued)*

IV. ACHIEVEMENT	IV. ACHIEVEMENT
Estimated Grade at Present _____	Estimated Grade at Present _____
Do you desire a conference with the LD teacher? __ yes __ no	Do you desire a conference with the LD teacher? __ yes __no
If so, when is a convenient time to meet? _____	If so, when is a convenient time to meet? _____
Grading Period ____ *Due Date*_____	*Grading Period* ____ *Due Date* _____
V. COMMENTS	V. COMMENTS
Note specific skills or concepts with which the student is having difficulty. Include names of texts, specific pages, etc. Please also note upcoming work needs and/or missing assignments.	Note specific skills or concepts with which the student is having difficulty. Include names of texts, specific pages, etc. Please also note upcoming work needs and/or missing assignments.
_____	_____
Action Taken	Action Taken

Reprinted by permission of Chesterfield County Schools, Chesterfield, VA.

Johnson et al. (1990) offer several suggestions to move teachers toward collaboration:

1. Collaborative efforts should be sanctioned at the administrative level. Teachers need support and freedom to engage in mutual problem solving.

2. Teachers should be given assistance with clerical work and other noninstructional tasks to leave them more time to interact with each other. Teacher aides, parents, volunteers, or student helpers might be used to serve this purpose.

3. Teachers should be encouraged to organize meeting times for the purpose of mutual problem solving. Prearranged after-school meetings or meetings scheduled during mutual planning periods would provide a set time for teachers to discuss the problems they are facing.

4. Specialists and classroom teachers should be given opportunities to coteach. This could enhance mutual understanding of the unique expertise each has to offer.

5. The use of specialized terminology should be avoided. Using jargon that others do not understand can imply an expert-to-novice relationship. Hierarchical relationships are rarely conducive to collaboration.

6. Faculty or inservice meetings could be reserved for collaborative problem solving.

Pugach and Johnson (1988) also offer some excellent ideas to provide teachers with the time they need for collaborative activities. These include use of floating substitutes to cover classes for teachers engaged in collaborative problem solving; coordination of activities like art, music, and physical education, so that peer pairs can meet; and use of principals as substitute instructors.

Educators who have been involved in collaborative efforts have reported success in resolving instructional and planning problems (Everson, 1990; Meyers, Gelzheiser, & Yelich, 1991). Thousand and Villa (1989) urge teachers to make every effort to seek out all potential members of a collaborative team, including the student with a disability and his or her parents.

✎ Parents as Partners

In the best collaborative arrangements, parents are considered to be equal participating partners (Morsink et al., 1991; Thousand & Villa, 1989). Public Law 94-142 mandates involvement by parents in planning and decision making, and parents should be encouraged to take an active role in both processes. All too often, however, parents are perceived by teachers as adversarial and responsible for their child's problems (Sonnenschein, 1981). Parents who are rushed or who believe that their opinions are not valued by professionals may feel that they are not respected by teachers and may choose to withdraw from the process (Turnbull & Turnbull, 1986). In fact, the majority of parents prefer to have only limited involvement in educational programming for their children (Winton & Turnbull, 1981).

Parent preference for only limited participation does not obviate the need for teachers to solicit their involvement, however. Beale and Beers (1982) identify three types of approaches used by school staff when interacting with parents:

✎ **Category 1:**   Teach them what they need to know. This approach focuses on parent education and training and emphasizes the expert role of educators. Ms. Lopez, for example, might teach Travis's mother to monitor his behavior at home when he is completing homework assignments, or she might demonstrate a specific method to help Travis rehearse material orally when studying for a test.

✎ **Category 2:**   Bring them in and put them to work. This approach uses parents as volunteers and increases parental involvement in the school. Ms. Kirk might use parents of the children in her classroom as helpers or as chaperones on field trips.

✎ **Category 3:**   I talk, you talk, we talk. This approach stresses honest communication and collaboration between parents and teachers and requires effective communication skills and respect for parents as equal partners in the education process.

The key element to a successful partnership with parents is regular and open communication. Too often, parents hear from the child's teacher or school only when a behavioral or learning problem surfaces. In order to establish and maintain a positive relationship with parents, communication must be ongoing and offer a nonthreatening avenue for parents to express concerns and ask questions (deBettencourt, 1987). Notes sent home on a regular basis, telephone calls to discuss progress, home visits, or invitations to visit the classroom are all ways of keeping the communication lines open. Shea and Bauer (1991) suggest the following strategies to facilitate teacher/parent communication:

- daily or periodic written reports on progress sent home with students;

- telephone calls or recorded telephone messages;

- praise notes or positive letters; for example, the note sent by Ms. Lopez to Joey's parents regarding his improvements in behavior (Figure 4.2);

- two-way notebooks, in which teachers and parents write questions and comments to each other;

- behavioral or achievement awards; and,

- monthly calendars, notices, or newsletters about class and student activities.

Notes, Letters, and Two-Way Notebooks

Notes and letters sent home to parents should provide good news more often than bad. Parents are busy people; therefore, notes and letters should be concise and to the point. When requesting a school visit, teachers should express a clear reason for the request. For example, when teachers arrange for a visit by parents for the IEP meeting, they should remind parents of the agreed-upon meeting place, date, and time and ask the parents to think about goals for their child for

---

Figure 4.2   A Note from Ms. Lopez to Joey's Parents

December 13, 1992

Dear Mr. and Mrs. Greenhill,
Joey has successfully completed his work contract for the week of December 9! He completed 5/5 class assignments, kept his assignment sheet up to date all week long, and kept his desk neat. He has earned a ticket to the class coke party on Friday. He is also excited about the pizza that you promised him as a part of his reward!

Joey's work contract for next week will be the same, with the addition of the following: Joey will keep his weekly homework notebook neat, with all of his assignments in the correct order.

Please call me if you have any questions.

Sincerely yours,
Susan Lopez
Ms. Lopez

---

the school year. Marion (1979) cautions that teachers must guard against a condescending tone or use of educational jargon. Also, a sign-off portion for parents, when appropriate, may ensure that they received the message.

Although personal notes and letters are excellent ways to maintain communication with individual parents, weekly, biweekly, or monthly class or school letters and newsletters are another important means for keeping parents informed. Many teachers send an introductory letter home to all parents at the start of each school year. These letters might welcome the child and the parents to the classroom, list supplies and materials required by the child for the school year, and emphasize the importance of the parents to the child's educational activities. Shea and Bauer (1985) suggest several additional items that might be included in letters or newsletters:

- a list of the year's scheduled subjects, activities, or special events;

- an invitation to parents to visit the classroom or the school;

- an invitation to parents to participate in the class as volunteers;

- a list of special classroom rules and procedures;

- the teacher's telephone number; and

- suggestions for parents wishing to help at home.

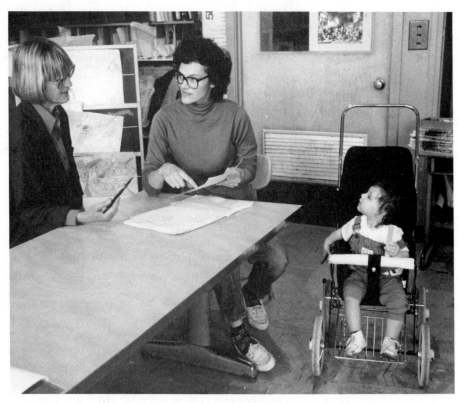

Parents are equal partners in the best collaborative arrangements, particularly when teachers encourage regular and open communication.

Two-way notebooks, sometimes called "passports" (Runge, Walker, & Shea, 1975), are spiral-bound notebooks that children carry with them during the school day. Teachers, bus drivers, other school personnel, and parents, make comments in the notebook regarding the child's academic or behavioral progress. To encourage children to carry this notebook, teachers may assign points to be exchanged for a reward. Shea and Bauer (1985) suggest that comments written in the two-way notebook be brief and positive, honest, and responsive. It is also important to be consistent in using this system of communication and to guard against use of jargon. Furthermore, the worries and aggravations of a bad day should not be projected onto the child or his or her parents.

Telephone Calls

Although telephone calls from school may be threatening to some parents, teachers can help to eliminate this threat by calling parents at the start of the school year to introduce themselves and by periodically calling parents to deliver positive comments. Teachers should refrain from making numerous phone calls home regarding a child's behavior at school. Some teachers maintain a calendar to ensure periodic phone calls to parents. Of course, any time the teacher attempts to contact the child's parents, whether by telephone or by letter or note home, he or she should document the contact on a log sheet, including the date, time, and method of contact; the name of the person contacted; and a brief summary of the conversation. (See Figure 4.3 for a sample contact log.)

Marion (1979) points out that teachers must show courtesy and respect in their phone conversations with parents. Using a polite and respectful tone of voice and addressing parents as "Mr./Mrs." (or, when appropriate, "Ms.") may make the difference between a positive or a negative contact. In addition, teachers should call parents in the evening, if possible, rather than interrupting them at work.

Parent–Teacher Conferences

Parents have a legal right under PL 94-142 to be provided with all available information about their child and his or her progress; therefore, teachers will be involved in numerous parent–teacher conferences throughout the school year. Parent–teacher conferences are conducted for planning the IEP, for reporting pupil progress, and for problem solving. Although these conferences can be intimidating for both parents and educators, careful planning can help to alleviate anxiety for everyone.

DeBettencourt (1987) suggests that prior to the conference teachers prepare an outline of all information they wish to share or collect. In addition, she encourages teachers to prepare an agenda for the meeting and to give parents a copy of the agenda before the meeting begins. (See Figure 4.4 for an agenda used during Ms. Lopez's conference with Travis's mother.) Other ideas for parent–teacher conferences offered by deBettencourt include (a) stating objectives in clear terms that parents can understand, (b) holding the conference in a small room free from distractions, (c) starting on time and keeping to the scheduled time limit, (d) arranging chairs so that parents and teachers can see each other

---

Figure 4.3   A Contact Log

Ms. Lopez documents all letters, notes, phone calls, and meetings with parents. Shown below is part of her contact log for Travis.

Contact Log for: Travis Johnson

Date	Time	Type of Contact	Person Contacted	Content
9-1-92	8:05 A.M.	Phone call	Mrs. Johnson	Invited Mrs. Johnson to meet to talk about Travis completing homework.
9-3-92	4:00 P.M.	Conference at school	Mrs. Johnson	Planned ways to encourage Travis to do homework. Ms. Lopez to provide an assignment sheet. Mrs. Johnson to sign sheet & schedule a time/place for homework 1 hour per night before supper.
9-9-92	9:03 A.M.	Phone call	From Mrs. Johnson	Mrs. Johnson says Travis is doing his homework.

---

without obstacles, and (e) presenting all information clearly, using jargon-free language. Additional suggestions for successful parent–teacher conferences are presented in Table 4.3.

Shea and Bauer (1985) recommend use of a letter or newsletter at the start of the school year offering conference tips. (see Figure 4.5). They also recommend several excellent do's and don'ts for teachers conducting parent–teacher conferences. These suggestions are presented in Figure 4.6.

✎ Paraprofessionals and Volunteers

Paraprofessionals and volunteers play an extremely important role in the education of students with mild disabilities. Paraprofessionals, sometimes called teacher aides or teacher assistants, are salaried, full-time or part-time members of the school staff. According to Fimian, Fafard, and Howell (1984), paraprofessionals may or may not be certified in special education, although they usually have designated classroom duties. Volunteers, on the other hand, are parents, college students, senior citizens, or others who donate their time in order to help out during the school day.

Paraprofessionals may assume a number of duties in the classroom. In special education classes, for example, they may provide instructional support by supervising independent work, reinforcing concepts taught by the teacher,

---

Figure 4.4   A Meeting Agenda for a Parent–Teacher Conference

---

Ms. Lopez planned an agenda for the parent–teacher conference she held with Travis's mother, Mrs. Johnson. Shown below is the agenda she used during the conference.

   I. Welcome & Preview Meeting
  II. Share samples of Travis's work
 III. Discuss homework assignments completed
 IV. Discuss homework assignments not completed
  V. Discuss ways to increase homework completed by Travis
 VI. Summarize

Ms. Lopez gave Mrs. Johnson a copy of the agenda when she arrived. Mrs. Johnson wrote her own comments and questions on the agenda as the discussion proceeded.

---

making materials, or listening to students read or reading to them. They may offer behavior-management support by praising students for appropriate behaviors and they may offer diagnostic support by correcting and grading papers or observing and recording academic or social behaviors (McKenzie & Houk, 1986). Paraprofessionals also prepare bulletin boards or instructional games, locate materials or supplies, type and duplicate written materials, take attendance, record grades, and supervise students during lunch or recess. Marozas and May (1988) report that paraprofessionals are increasingly assuming responsibility for such critical duties as planning and delivering instruction and testing students. Paraprofessionals from culturally or linguistically diverse backgrounds may also serve as essential team members, assisting teachers to communicate with students and their parents (Miramontes, 1990). Yet, little research exists to document the efficacy of paraprofessionals assuming these duties or their preparation to do so (Jones & Bender, 1993).

Volunteers may help teachers make instructional materials, games, or bulletin boards. They may listen to children read, read to children, or help as tutors. In addition, volunteers may have special skills or talents to draw upon in providing enriching activities for students with mild disabilities and their peers. Volunteer room mothers or fathers are also invaluable sources of help for classroom parties and for such special events as field trips or field days.

The benefits of using paraprofessionals or volunteers in the classroom are numerous. Marozas and May (1986) and Boomer (1980, 1982) cite the following benefits of using paraprofessionals:

1. The student-to-teacher ratio is decreased, thereby increasing individual attention for each child (Marozas & May, 1986).

2. Paraprofessionals enable alternative classroom arrangements to provide small-group and one-on-one activities with supervision (Boomer, 1980).

Table 4.3   Suggestions for Successful Parent–Teacher Conferences

---

1. Establish communication with parents *before* problems arise.

2. Communicate with parents in a positive manner.

3. Schedule conferences regularly and frequently to discuss student progress rather than scheduling them only for problem resolution.

4. Schedule conferences at mutually agreed-upon times and places. Consider the parents' work schedules and child-care concerns. Provide help with child care and transportation arrangements if possible.

5. Plan your conference. Provide a written list of student achievements and progress, as well as concerns about the student.

6. Schedule the conference in an inviting environment rather than in a conference room or office if possible. If the conference must be in the classroom, arrange the table and chairs so as to avoid obstructions between you and the parents. Be sure parents have adult-sized chairs. Place flowers, refreshments, or other items on the table to enhance the environment and parental comfort.

7. Have student work samples available for parents to review. These samples can exhibit strengths as well as weaknesses.

8. Provide objective documentation of problems or concerns. Refrain from making negative statements or subjective comments.

9. Make positive comments about student performance and behavior, emphasizing student strengths, before discussing problem areas.

10. Listen to the parent's concerns and questions. Provide adequate time for parents to reflect on information and to ask questions.

11. Answer questions asked by parents clearly and honestly.

12. Monitor parental understanding of the information you provide by questioning and paraphrasing.

13. Review and summarize statements made by teachers and parents during the conference at the end.

14. Before the meeting is concluded, be sure that all parties understand the next steps to be taken; for example, who is responsible for particular activities and how follow-up communication will take place.

15. Set a time, place, and date for the next meeting if appropriate.

---

3. Paraprofessionals contribute strengths and talents that the teacher may not have (Marozas & May, 1986).

4. Paraprofessionals help teachers form a more complete and accurate picture of a student through ongoing feedback and mutual problem

---

Figure 4.5   A Conference Handout for Parents

Shea and Bauer (1985) suggest that teachers can encourage parental participation in conferences by giving them a handout at the start of the school year. Following is a sample of such a handout.

Before the Conference

1. Make arrangements for your other children if necessary. Conferences are for you and your child's teacher. Small children can be distracting and take time away from the discussion.

2. Jot down any questions you may have for the teacher; for example:
    - How is my child progressing in reading, math, and other subjects?
    - Does he or she get along well with other students?
    - Does he or she get along well with teachers?
    - What do the tests say about my child?

3. Talk to your child about the conference. Find out whether he or she wants you to ask any questions or voice concerns.

4. Collect any records or information that might help the teacher. Try to anticipate questions and gather materials.

At the Conference

1. Please be prompt and stay only for your scheduled time. Please feel free to schedule another conference if we do not cover all the necessary information in the allotted time.

2. Discuss only the child at issue. He or she is the focus of this conference.

3. Ask questions about your child's education. Please advocate for your child. Know your rights and those of your child.

4. Volunteer information that may help the teacher plan programming for your child.

5. Feel free to take notes during the conference.

After the Conference

Please feel free to contact your child's teacher for further clarification or information at_____.

Adapted from T.M. Shea and A.M. Bauer, Parents and Teachers of Exceptional Students: A Handbook for Involvement. *Copyright © 1985. Adapted with permission of Allyn & Bacon.*

---

solving, resulting in better decision making and enhanced instructional creativity (Boomer, 1982).

5. The relationship between the teacher and the paraprofessional facilitates emotional support and meaningful dialogue throughout the school day (Marozas & May, 1986).

Figure 4.6 Do's and Don'ts for Parent–Teacher Conferences

Parent–teacher conferences will proceed more smoothly if teachers keep in mind several "Do's" and "Don'ts" when meeting with parents.

1. Don't make parents defensive by criticizing them, their children, or their lifestyle.

2. Don't argue. Teachers are not always right, nor do they have all the answers.

3. Don't belittle students, the school, the administration, or the school system.

4. Don't talk or gossip about other children or parents. Maintain confidentiality.

5. Don't become overly personal. Avoid embarrassing the parents.

6. Don't assume that the parents are "problem parents," or that they need, want, or will accept your help or advice.

7. Don't dwell on negatives. Seek the positive and remain positive throughout the conference.

8. Don't promise things that are not deliverable.

9. Don't assume full responsibility for the child. Share responsibility with the parents and with other teachers.

10. Don't take yourself too seriously. Teachers are human and they do make mistakes.

11. Don't avoid difficult topics because of your own anxiety. Everyone is nervous but gets over it with success and experience.

12. Do listen to parents. They can provide you with valuable information.

13. Do listen to parents. Be friendly, relaxed, and empathetic.

14. Do listen to parents. Let them speak or think without interruption.

15. Do prepare for the conference by gathering materials and making an outline beforehand.

16. Do emphasize the positive.

Adapted from T.M. Shea and A.M. Bauer, Parents and Teachers of Exceptional Students: A Handbook for Involvement. *Copyright © 1985. Adapted with permission of Allyn & Bacon.*

---

6. Paraprofessionals act as liaisons between the teacher and other staff members (Boomer, 1982).

7. Paraprofessionals provide partial relief for teachers from noninstructional duties, such as taking attendance or collecting lunch money (Marozas & May, 1986).

Using paraprofessionals and volunteers to greatest advantage, however, requires careful planning and communication (Boomer, 1981). McKenzie and

Houk (1986) suggest that assistants should be matched with teachers according to their particular skills. Ms. Lopez, for example, might require an assistant to give her instructional support by reviewing new vocabulary with Travis. She may also need help in monitoring and rewarding Joey for appropriate social skills. Mr. Abel, on the other hand, may require assistance with making and duplicating materials for his students.

Regardless of the tasks to be performed, teachers must clearly communicate responsibilities and expectations to paraprofessionals and volunteers. The teacher also must monitor the performance of assistants, giving them feedback and recognizing their efforts. The following procedures are recommended when utilizing paraprofessionals and volunteers:

- Orient assistants to the school. Orientation sessions can be conducted for a group when more than one assistant is new to the school. However, whether conducted individually or with a group, assistants will require a tour of the school; introductions to principals and other professionals, as well as to one another; and information regarding school schedules, policies, and procedures. When appropriate, they should be provided with a copy of the faculty/student handbook. In addition, assistants may be trained as a group to operate the school copier or audiovisual equipment.

- Orient assistants to the classroom. Provide name tags or a seating chart for identifying students. Introduce the assistant to the children and show the assistant where materials are located in the classroom. Provide a personal space for the assistant, including a table or desk, a chair, and a place to secure his or her belongings.

- Plan responsibilities for assistants. Although the teacher assistant may be involved in the planning process, the teacher is still responsible for all activities within the classroom.

- Prepare and post a written schedule of duties for assistants. The schedule might include specific daily responsibilities in addition to ongoing duties. As the needs of the classroom change, the duties of the assistants should change as well.

- Clearly tell assistants what they are to do and demonstrate tasks for them whenever possible. If, for example, Ms. Lopez asks her assistant to make multiplication flashcards for Travis, she will need to specify exactly which facts are to be included. She may also want to show the assistant a sample flashcard. Ask assistants specific questions to be sure they understand directions, and provide them with the opportunity to ask for clarification.

- Schedule daily conferences with assistants to plan and evaluate their responsibilities, give specific feedback, and offer praise for their accomplishments.

✏ Summary

Good communication skills are a must for teachers of students with mild disabilities. Consultation and collaboration require teachers to communicate clearly and honestly in order to maximize success for their students with learning and behavioral problems. Clear and honest communication requires attention to both verbal and nonverbal behaviors.

Contact with parents also requires skillful communication. Teachers may communicate with parents through telephone calls, written notes or letters, or parent–teacher conferences. Clear, concise, ongoing communication will help teachers enlist the support of parents as partners in the education of their children with mild disabilities.

Paraprofessionals and volunteers provide important assistance for students with special needs. Careful planning and clear communication of responsibilities and expectations will increase the likelihood that classroom assistants will contribute to student success.

✏ Application Exercises

1. Interview a practicing special education teacher in a local school system. Ask this teacher to suggest useful techniques for systematic communication with regular classroom teachers and with parents.

2. Contact teachers or administrators in a local school division. Are consultation and collaboration used in this school system? If so, how are these models implemented?

3. Interview a special education teacher in a local school system. What methods does this teacher use to plan, schedule, and conduct parent–teacher conferences?

4. Create a file for parental communication. From the professional literature, gather sample notes, progress reports, newsletters, and so forth, for communicating with parents.

5. Interview a paraprofessional in a local school system. Ask this person to explain his or her duties in the special education classroom. What assistance does this person appreciate from the supervising teacher?

6. Pair up with a regular educator. List important skills that characterize regular classroom teachers and special educators. Are there similarities? What are some important skills that special educators can learn from regular classroom teachers?

7. Ms. Booker states, "Susan is constantly asking me for help when I know she can do her work. She wants my help every step of the way, and I think the other children resent her trying to get all my attention. She takes a lot of my time. . . ." Assume you are Mr. Abel. Paraphrase Ms. Booker's comment. Now, frame an active-listening response reflecting the emotion as well as the content of Ms. Booker's message.

Managing the
Classroom Environment

Chapter 5

Focus

As you read, think about the following questions:

What do the terms *classroom management* and *discipline* really mean?

What can the teacher do to create a classroom atmosphere conducive to efficient learning and appropriate behavior?

How can the teacher maintain a positive classroom environment?

What can the teacher do to maximize the amount of time for planning and instruction?

✎ Whether a teacher is a novice, preparing for his or her first year in the classroom, or a veteran of several years of teaching, managing the classroom environment—particularly managing the behavior of students—can be a frightening prospect. An organized and sequential approach to classroom management will reduce the stress that teachers frequently experience as they plan for the new school year.

For example, Ms. Kirk knows that there will be several students with special needs in her classroom this year. She has learned that the best way to create a positive atmosphere in her class is to begin the school year well prepared. Before the school year begins, she plans the physical arrangement of her classroom. She also considers instructional objectives and materials for her students. At the beginning of the school year, she sets aside some time each day to instruct her students in the rules, routines, and procedures. Her students know what is expected of them regarding behavior and achievement.

Mr. Abel knows that the "general attitude" of the students in his resource room can sometimes become negative. To counter this negativism, he considers several sources of reinforcement that may motivate his students. He determines which reinforcers are likely to be readily available and which will be the most helpful in terms of the age and interests of each student. Then, he introduces a behavior-management program to his students.

Ms. Lopez sometimes becomes so bogged down in the mechanics of running a classroom that she finds little time for planning. Interruptions, correspondence, and record keeping are eating away at her time. An inservice course on microcomputers, through which she learns of a software package to use with her class, and a few suggestions from a more experienced teacher on how to maximize time in the classroom, keep Ms. Lopez from becoming discouraged.

In this chapter, we will examine classroom-management techniques for teachers. First, we will explore ways in which teachers can manage the physical environment and promote a positive climate in the classroom. Next, we will discuss the teacher's management of time. Finally, we will introduce the reader to reinforcement—a particularly important principle for teachers of students with mild disabilities to understand.

✎ Classroom Management and Discipline

As described by O'Melia and Rosenberg (1989), classroom management frequently invokes "images of docile students, tyrannical teachers, and sterile settings, where academic achievement takes a back seat to compliance with rules and procedures. Rarely does the phrase invoke scenes of talented teachers and scholarly students engaged in educationally effective endeavors" (p.23). Classroom management, however, when properly designed and implemented, can make the difference for students between meaningful experiences and merely putting in time. Successful classroom management can also be the deciding factor between a rewarding career and utter frustration for teachers.

Classroom management has been defined as "the positive manipulation of the learning environment to promote successful behavior and skill acquisition" (O'Melia & Rosenberg, 1989, p. 23). Specifically, classroom management involves the manipulation of the physical environment, the emotional climate, the time allocated to various activities, and, of course, classroom discipline.

Discipline, too, is a commonly misunderstood term. To many, discipline equals punishment. Punishment, however, is only a small part of discipline. Effective discipline involves teaching students rules and proper conduct, and then giving them the opportunity to practice these appropriate actions and to receive rewards for doing so.

Gartland (1990) identifies three kinds of discipline: (a) *preventive discipline* (taking measures to avoid inappropriate behavior), (b) *supportive discipline* (assisting students when they first show signs of inappropriate behavior), and (c) *corrective discipline* (suppressing and redirecting misbehavior when it occurs). The third type, corrective discipline, is unfortunately overused by many teachers. The successful teacher will integrate preventive, supportive, and corrective discipline into a well-coordinated program that is implemented consistently. Discipline that emphasizes prevention of inappropriate behaviors increases the amount of time available for instruction. The more effort that is expended in preventive discipline, the less a teacher will need supportive or corrective discipline, according to Gartland.

Sabatino (1987) defines preventive discipline as "the teacher's realization that discipline begins with a positive attitude that nurtures students' learning of personal, social, and academic skills. It is the realization that discipline is as much a teaching/learning interaction as is any academic subject matter. It is the realization that special educators must have control, that they are in charge, and that discipline is required, especially with handicapped audiences" (pp. 8–9). With this definition in mind, we offer suggestions to the teacher that will enhance the behavior and learning of students in the special education and/or regular classroom.

The primary focus of this chapter, then, will be on preventive discipline—proactive strategies and activities that will minimize the need for supportive or corrective discipline, both of which are essentially reactive. Proactive strategies include managing the physical environment, rules and procedures, and time in a way that promotes a positive atmosphere conducive to learning and appropriate behavior. In addition, the teacher may use reinforcement or punishment to maintain a positive classroom atmosphere.

✎ Promoting a Positive Atmosphere

Classroom management begins long before the students enter the classroom on the first day of school. It involves careful planning in several different areas: the physical environment, the classroom climate, rules and operating procedures, and the use of time.

The Physical Environment

Clearly, the physical structure or arrangement of the classroom contributes to learning and classroom behavior (Minner & Prater, 1989; O'Connor, 1988; Stainback, Stainback, & Froyen, 1987). Aspects of physical structure include:

(a) teacher proximity and view, (b) separation of space, (c) traffic patterns, (d) extraneous stimuli, and (e) seating arrangements. Each can play an important role in determining behavior and academic achievement.

Teacher proximity and view.   A teacher's presence in the classroom keeps youngsters on-task and improves the level of instructional control. For example, attention to directions, completion of assignments, and cessation of inappropriate behavior can all be cued simply by Ms. Kirk's presence (Minner & Prater, 1989). In addition, Ms. Kirk must be aware of what is actually going on in the classroom at all times. She arranges the classroom furniture and equipment so that she can make a visual sweep of the room in order to detect students who may need assistance and to check student interaction (Stainback, et al., 1987).

Sometimes teachers arrange bookcases and room dividers to create quiet areas in the classroom. However, this makes teacher monitoring of the classroom difficult, if not impossible. Some students may take advantage of blind spots to engage in behaviors that are not consistent with teacher expectations. The strategic placement of mirrors sometimes helps to avoid this problem (Minner & Prater, 1989).

Separation of space.   The clear demarcation of three kinds of space is important to the overall climate of the classroom. Ms. Kirk reserves one area of her classroom for group instruction, another area for individual seatwork, and a third for independent activities chosen by the children. In addition, she sets aside space for peer tutoring and team activities. In many classrooms, the desks are arranged in groups of fours or fives to enhance teamwork and are left in that arrangement for large-group instruction. Work areas should be separate from traffic areas, and quiet areas should be separate from noisy areas. Specific rules and procedures should also apply to each of the areas in order to provide structure and to improve the teacher's instructional control (Minner & Prater, 1989; O'Connor, 1988).

Traffic patterns.   Ms. Kirk also carefully considers how students will move about in her classroom. Points that will receive a lot of traffic (e.g., the pencil sharpener, waste basket, water fountain, and Ms. Kirk's desk) are placed so as to accommodate the traffic flow. Heavily traveled routes are free of obstacles. When traffic areas are not congested, the probability of disruptive behaviors is reduced (Stainback et al., 1987).

Extraneous stimuli.   Ms. Kirk considers the distractibility of her students when arranging the classroom and attempts to reduce extraneous stimuli. Students who are easily distracted work as far away as possible from high traffic areas, doors opening into hallways, and windows (Minner & Prater, 1989). Ms. Kirk never seats students who have difficulty concentrating near the area designated for independent activities. Sometimes she uses a study carrel as one solution to remove Travis and other easily distractible students from the extraneous stimuli that may keep them off task.

Seating arrangements. The arrangement of seats and the assignment of students to those seats contribute to student attention and participation. Mr. Mathis is aware that the students who sit in the front and center of a classroom frequently participate more and achieve higher grades. Since all students cannot sit front and center, he carefully chooses which students will be assigned to those seats. Mr. Mathis also moves around the room while teaching, checking to see that all students are attending as they should (O'Connor, 1988). Of course, seats must be arranged to allow easy teacher access to every area of the classroom and to every student's desk.

The special education teacher may be tempted to distinguish his or her classroom from that of the regular teacher by creating a homelike setting. This might include rocking chairs, lamps, and pillows or chairs for reading. Ms. Lopez, for example, once hoped to change the environment in her classroom to a more relaxed, informal one in order to make her students feel more comfortable. Since one goal of special education is to prepare children with disabilities for success in regular classrooms, however, this idea, although initially appealing, did not offer long-term benefits to Ms. Lopez's students. According to Minner and Prater (1989), "generalization of newly acquired behavior may be difficult for children who first acquire those skills in one type of environment and are expected to demonstrate them in a very different setting" (p. 95).

The Classroom Climate

Within the classroom, the term *climate* refers to the prevailing attitudes of students and teachers toward the process of learning and to prevailing behavioral expectations for students. A wholesome classroom climate is necessary for the growth and development of successful students and teachers.

A classroom climate that is nonpunitive and accepting promotes efficient learning more than a hostile or threatening climate. Ms. Kirk and other competent teachers know this. They recognize the need to understand what motivates them and their students. Since the affective climate is such an important component of the learning environment, teachers must know, first of all, what makes a climate wholesome, and then use that knowledge to create the best possible climate in their classrooms (O'Connor, 1988).

Sabatino (1987) suggests several ways to achieve a positive classroom climate and enhance student behavior:

1. Inform students of what is expected of them. Frequently, teachers neglect to tell students what behaviors are appropriate and expected. Teachers should always communicate classroom rules to their students and help them practice the rules to prevent discipline problems.

2. Act in a manner consistent with a positive learning climate. Students respect a teacher who is firm and decisive, but at the same time kind and patient. The application of consistent discipline teaches students that certain behaviors are or are not acceptable. Inconsistency, on the other hand, leaves students confused as to what the consequences are for particular behaviors. Optimism, planned instruction, appropriate and realistic expectations,

consistency, and human understanding are essential to a positive learning climate.

3. Provide meaningful learning experiences. Meaningfulness is important to all students, but it is especially important to students in special education programs who may not understand the value of what they are to learn. Learning must relate to students' needs and concerns. When learning is drawn from family and community experiences, students are motivated to become active participants in the process.

4. Avoid threats. Although students' obedience in the classroom is essential, the need for discipline should not result from threats. Threatening a student with some form of punishment for inappropriate behavior generally ensures that the student will, indeed, engage in the behavior. Further, when we use such language as "If you do it one more time . . . ," we are teaching that to do 'it' once is all right, but to do 'it' again is punishable.

5. Demonstrate fairness. Setting limits and dealing with misbehavior when it occurs are demonstrations of fairness. Treating all students in exactly the same way is not demonstrating fairness. Teachers must be willing to match learner needs and characteristics to disciplinary actions. When disciplinary action must be taken, the teacher should analyze the particular offense, state the reason for the action, and describe expectations for future behavior.

6. Exhibit self-confidence and build it in students. Teachers must be models of self-confidence. When teachers recognize each student as an individual and consider each student important enough to know personally, they are enhancing students' self-esteem and self-confidence.

7. Recognize positive student attributes. Sincere and specific praise creates feelings of self-worth in students. When teachers take the time to recognize appropriate behaviors rather than dwell on failures, they promote a positive classroom climate.

8. Time the recognition of student behavior. Timing is important in administering both rewards and punishment. In both cases, the teacher should respond as soon as possible following the student's behavior. Teachers need to anticipate situations before they occur, and then act in a consistent manner. Failing to affirm acceptable behavior, overreacting to minor events, or failing to fit a disciplinary action to a transgression make teachers less effective in training students to distinguish appropriate from inappropriate behaviors.

In addition, a professional demeanor reduces the chance that major discipline problems will develop from minor classroom infractions (Stainback et al., 1987). Teachers demonstrate a professional demeanor by remaining calm in the face of student misbehavior, by drawing as little attention as possible to the misbehavior, by redirecting the student back on task or into appropriate behavior, by handling discipline problems in private whenever possible, and by handling classroom problems themselves rather than passing them on to other school personnel.

9. Use positive modeling. A primary goal of classroom management is to help students move from externally controlled behavior to self-control. Teachers influence the success of this goal by the attitudes and behaviors they display. Teachers must first demonstrate positive attitudes toward the rules and regulations that govern their own behaviors. They must practice what they preach by modeling, for example, courtesy in the face of rudeness and respect for ideas different from their own. These attitudes will, in turn, influence student's respect for classroom and/or school rules.

10. Structure the curriculum and classroom environment. When the curriculum is too easy or too difficult, when the physical arrangement of the classroom does not facilitate student self-control and learning, and when expectations for student achievement are unrealistic, discipline problems are likely to occur.

Teachers must foster the attitude that each student shares responsibility with the teacher for achievement of personal learning objectives. This attitude focuses student attention on learning and may reduce behavior problems. Such an attitude may be promoted by working with each student to select appropriate objectives that will encourage a goal orientation in the classroom (Stainback, et al., 1987).

Teachers cannot prevent all behavior problems. However, they can structure a learning climate that supports problem solving and reduces friction between the learner and the environment. Deluke and Knoblock (1987) advise teachers to show respect for each of their students, letting each one know that he or she is appreciated and valued as an individual. Teachers like Ms. Lopez respond to students' verbal and nonverbal communications by listening, by taking the time to draw them out when they seem upset, by making eye contact, and by acknowledging what is being said. In this way, she communicates the message that what the students are saying is important (see Box 5.1).

One indicator of teacher respect is the ability to interpret the meaning of a student's behavior. Students misbehave for a variety of reasons, some of which are not readily apparent. Teachers often must delve deep to uncover the reason for problem behavior (Deluke & Knoblock, 1987).

Rules and Procedures

In the effectively managed classroom, rules and procedures are designed to create an orderly environment. Knowledge of what is expected of them goes a long way toward reducing inappropriate behavior on the part of students. Although very similar in meaning, rules and procedures may be distinguished by applying rules to classroom conduct and procedures to ways in which noninstructional activities are carried out (e.g., asking for help, turning in papers, getting a drink, using the restroom, etc.).

The first days of the new school year are a critical time for setting the tone for the remainder of the year and for establishing classroom order. Therefore, the teacher must give thought to selecting appropriate rules prior to the day school begins. By identifying the rules and procedures of the department, the

Box 5.1   Ms. Lopez Listens to Joey

Joey rushes into the classroom, slamming the door, hurling his books on his desk, and glaring defiantly at Ms. Lopez. Ordinarily, Ms. Lopez might remind Joey of the rules for making a proper entrance into the classroom. But Joey's facial expression and body posture cue her that he is upset. She decides to try to get Joey to talk so that she can find out what the problem is. She squats down next to Joey's desk.

Ms. Lopez: *[softly and calmly] Looks like you're upset, Joey.*

Joey: *[Slumps in his seat and continues to glare.]*

Ms. Lopez *Want to talk about whatever happened?*

Joey: *She shouldn't told me that.*

Ms. Lopez *Somebody told you to do something on your way to class today.*

Joey: *I was coming here.*

Ms. Lopez: *You were on your way to class and somebody told you something.*

Joey: *Yeah, that teacher, she told me to move along. I had to get the paper.*

Ms. Lopez: *You were coming to my classroom and you were getting a paper. Tell me about the paper.*

Joey: *It fell off the bulletin board in the hall and kids in her class were walking on it. I was just trying to get it, and she told me to get going. She shouldn't told me that.*

Ms. Lopez: *You were trying to help by picking up the paper off the bulletin board so that it didn't get messed up and a teacher told you to get to class. What did you do next?*

Joey: *I told her I was going to pick up the paper, and she couldn't stop me. She ain't my teacher to tell me to get to my room.*

Ms. Lopez: *Then what happened?*

Joey: *She said if I didn't get moving, she would get the principal to come and get me.*

Ms. Lopez: *So then you came on here to my class. Maybe, next time something like that happens you can try to explain that the paper fell off the bulletin board and that you were trying to pick it up. Maybe that way a teacher wouldn't get mad or think you were not being polite. I am very pleased that you shared that with me, Joey. It's hard to talk about things like that when we're angry, and especially when we're trying to be helpful. Do you feel ready to begin class now?*

Joey: *Yeah.*

school, and the district, Ms. Kirk, for example, may verify the appropriateness of intended classroom rules and procedures. In order to promote ownership of classroom rules, she may involve the students in generating and selecting rules. Ms. Kirk should have several rules in mind, first, however, and she should guide the students as they voice their ideas to ensure that all necessary rules are included. Whether or not the rules are teacher- or student-generated, they should be prioritized with the most important rules being introduced at first. Initially, three to five essential rules that clearly state what students are expected to do are sufficient (see Box 5.2 on page 85). Additional rules may be introduced as they are needed (Gartland, 1990).

Ms. Kirk must also consider certain aspects of the classroom that, although not instructional in nature, may play a large part in determining the efficiency of learning and the appropriateness of behavior. The daily operating procedures that students must follow—the "nitty-gritty" of classroom management—must be determined in advance by the teacher and introduced and practiced in much the same way as classroom rules. As shown in Figure 5.1, Olson (1989) offers some suggestions for handling nitty-gritty questions facing teachers.

Although all classroom rules and procedures should be posted using age-appropriate language and/or pictures, merely posting rules does not ensure that students will understand them. Gartland (1990) offers the following suggestions for teaching students the rules, the procedures, and their consequences:

1. Introduce classroom rules and procedures to students following a clear, specific plan.

2. Explain the rationale for each classroom rule and procedure.

3. Specify consequences for adherence to rules and procedures and for infractions.

4. Model appropriate behavior in accordance with the rules and procedures established.

5. Provide adequate time for students to practice appropriate behaviors.

Rules and procedures generated by the teacher and students and determined appropriate for classroom implementation should be transmitted to parents or guardians via newsletter (see Chapter 4). Knowledge of these rules and procedures may help parents solve problems with their children in the home setting.

Time Management and Transitions

Increasing student time on task is the major goal of time management. The longer students are on task, the more they learn and the better they achieve. In addition, when students are focused on productive activities they are less likely to present discipline problems (Stainback et al., 1987).

Time in the classroom falls into four broad categories: (1) allocated instructional time, (2) actual instructional time, (3) engaged time, (4) and academic learning time (Gartland & Rosenberg, 1987). *Allocated instructional time* refers to the amount of time the school or the teacher sets aside to teach a particular subject or lesson. *Actual instructional time* is a subset of allocated instructional time. This is the amount of time during which the instruction is actually delivered. *Engaged time* is the amount of time the student is attending to the teacher's lesson or to the task. *Academic learning time,* the most meaningful of the categories of instructional time, is the amount of time the student is actively attending to instruction at a correct level of difficulty and with a high rate of success. During academic learning time, the student's assessed strengths and weaknesses are accurately matched to the assignments or to the instruction.

In some schools, the amount of time in a particular period is limited by bells or by changing classrooms. In these circumstances, teachers may not be able to increase allocated instructional time. They may, however, increase actual instructional time by using several methods that have proven successful for both elementary and secondary grades (Gartland & Rosenberg, 1987).

Figure 5.1   Possible Answers to Nitty-Gritty Questions

From "Managing Life in the Classroom: Dealing with the Nitty Gritty" by J. Olson, 1989, Academic Therapy, *24(5), pp. 545–53. Copyright © 1989 by PRO-ED, Inc. Reprinted with permission.*

How Do You Plan to Begin Your Day?

1. Assign an "order" task to begin the day, such as copying assignments or paragraphs from the board. While the students are completing the task, the teacher can move from one to another, greeting each and exchanging friendly comments in an effort to establish rapport.

2. Establish a set routine for entering the class.

3. Take the first 5 or 10 minutes to review the classroom rules.

4. Give the students time to write in a personal diary or log that the teacher and others may read only with permission.

5. Assign a fun ditto or a manipulative activity that can be done independently at students' desks.

6. Allow 5 minutes for students to talk to their friends.

7. Begin with a goal-setting activity. Each student should then write and share an individual goal for the day, whether it is academic or behavioral.

8. Have older students who are on a token system plan a daily budget from the token salary they receive each week. The students must pay fees for their desks, books, utilities, etc., each morning.

9. Write a fun or challenging question on the board reviewing something you have taught that, if completed correctly within about 5 or 10 minutes, is worth extra credit.

How Do You Plan to End the Day or Period?

1. Have students evaluate course work or activities.

2. Have students discuss their goals for the day or conduct a 10-minute problem solving session on any problems that may have occurred during the day.

3. Review the main ideas of what was taught during the period either by dividing secondary students into small discussion groups or by having individuals summarize in writing the information they have learned. The teacher might suggest particular concepts for discussion.

4. Write a language experience story of the day's activities with younger children, which they copy off the board and take home. This is a great way of keeping in touch with parents.

5. Have students copy homework assignments in their notebooks.

(continued)

Figure 5.1   *(Continued)*
---

6. Give students a fun question to be copied and answered the next day from the newspaper or other reference sources (e.g., ''Which car had the best gas mileage in 1982?'' ''Who was the top hitter in the World Series?''). Students are given extra credit for correct answers.

7. Read a story or play a favorite record brought in by a student to quiet the class before final announcements.

8. Play soft music and do relaxation exercises with the students.

9. Play ''Trivial Pursuit'' with the class.

10. Pass out ''Atta Boy'' certificates or buttons for the students who have met their daily goals.

11. Have the students either write or discuss one good thing they did that day.

How Do Students Ask for Help?

1. Discuss with the student some alternative behaviors such as asking a friend, doing other folder work, skipping that problem and going on to the next, and so forth, while waiting for assistance.

2. Design a help sign for younger students to place on their desks. This prevents the necessity of a student keeping a hand raised while trying to complete the work.

3. Let the student write his or her name on the board, which is erased once help is given.

4. Use a ticket format like at the meat counter of a deli. Students take a number and when they have been helped by the teacher or aide, the number is replaced on the peg and the teacher writes the next number on the board.

How Do Students Turn in Work?

1. Place an ''in'' basket for incoming work and an ''out'' basket for corrected work on the the teacher's desk.

2. Have individual work folders, which are turned in daily.

3. Tape large manila envelopes on the side of each student's desk for completed work.

4. Appoint a different student each day to collect the work.

5. Put work in a class folder at the end of the period. There is a different folder for each period.

6. Place color-coded boxes for each subject in one area of the room.

7. Hang plastic wall baskets by the class door for students to place work in as they leave.

(continued)

Figure 5.1   (*Continued*)

How Do You Handle Pencils?

1. Allow students to sharpen two pencils as soon as they enter the room.

2. Keep extra pencils in a jar that students can either buy with points or exchange for some type of collateral such as a student's tennis shoe. Of course, the shoe is returned at the end of the class. If accidents occur, the pencils are free.

3. Institute a class rule whereby crayons are used if a student forgets to sharpen or to bring a pencil.

How Do Students Get Permission to Go to the Bathroom and Get Drinks?

1. Post a sign-out sheet by the door where students mark the time for leaving and returning to class. A good rule is that only one student at a time may leave the room.

2. Use two keys or hall passes, one for the girls' and one for the the boys' bathroom. Students take keys or passes to and from bathroom.

3. Have a rule that bathroom and drinks are available only when students are working individually (not during group instruction) or for emergencies.

4. If you are specifying time limits for breaks, but breaks are taking too long, try giving the laggards a count of 10 at the water fountain.

How Do You Handle Different Task Completion Rates?

1. Have a free area where students who have completed work may go. The free area may contain packets of fun activities, games, or listening activities and bean bag chairs or carpet strips. You may want to add an accuracy component, checking the correctness of the work before allowing students to go to the free area.

2. Allow students to read magazines such as *National Geographic, Time, People, Seventeen, Hot Rod,* etc., at their desks.

3. Have students sign up for computer time.

4. Arrange an area in the room for quiet chit-chat. Talking with friends is a powerful reinforcer for adolescents. The topics need not be structured by the teacher, as this time belongs to the student. However, the teacher will need to monitor the noise level.

5. Allow students to do homework.

6. Place old ditto sheets from past lessons in an area. Let students do any of the sheets for extra credit.

(continued)

Figure 5.1   (*Continued*)

7. Create a current events challenge, in which students must use the daily newspaper to find answers to questions written on the board.

8. Write different activities (reading a story to the fish, or discovering which of several materials magnets attract, etc.) on 3 × 5 index cards. Students complete one or two of the cards.

• *Establish rewards for school attendance and punctuality.* Teachers should make students aware of expectations regarding school attendance. Some school districts have mandated that students who are absent more than a certain number of school days will not be promoted to the next grade. Teachers must not assume that students and parents are aware of this regulation. By establishing rewards for school attendance and punctuality and by planning lessons that are meaningful and relevant for students, teachers help to ensure that students will spend more time in class. In addition, teachers should begin and end classes on time, thus becoming a model of punctuality.

• *Minimize interruptions.* Teachers must minimize interruptions during the presentation of instruction. Cohen and Hart-Hester (1987) suggest several

---

Box 5.2   Ms. Kirk Establishes Classroom Rules

Ms. Kirk begins each school year with four or five essential classroom rules. She posts the rules and tells students why each rule is important. Each rule is clear, and the consequences for rule violations are clear as well. Ms. Kirk is always willing to listen to student concerns about her rules, however, as the school year progresses. She is willing to modify the rules as circumstances require. She does insist, though, that students practice the rules that they have agreed upon, and she enforces each rule consistently. Ms. Kirk usually posts the following rules before a new school year begins:

1. Complete assignments and activities during each class period. (Consequences: Incomplete assignments will be completed during recess or after school as homework to be signed by a parent. Free time to choose an activity or book when assignment is completed early.)

2. Ask permission to leave your seat. (Consequences: You will lose the privilege that you failed to request properly. When you request permission to leave your seat, you may do so if the reason is legitimate.)

3. Speak politely to teachers, staff, and fellow students. (Consequence: You will give a written apology to anyone you speak to in a rude manner.)

4. Ask permission to speak during group lessons or independent work time. (Consequence: Those who speak without permission will not be acknowledged and will lose a minute of recess time.)

ways to reduce interruptions during instructional time, including the following:

1. Arrange the room so that the teacher is not facing the door and so that eye contact cannot be made with passers-by who might be encouraged to stop.

2. Use body language to indicate to would-be intruders that you are busy.

3. State to the intruder that this is not a good time for you to talk, indicating a more appropriate time.

• *Encourage disruption-free transitions between activities.* Transition time typically refers to the movement of students from one activity or place to another. Verbal and nonverbal signals may be used to eliminate confusion and to facilitate movement during transition times. In addition, teachers must give students clear and specific directions regarding what they are to do next. "Clams" (see Figure 5.2) is an example of a game-type activity for younger

Teachers who listen to their students promote a positive classroom atmosphere that supports problem solving and shared responsibility.

Figure 5.2   "Clams"

From "A Game to Prevent Disciplinary Problems," by P.C. Wood, Teaching Exceptional Children, *19(4), 1987, pp. 52–53. Copyright © 1987 by The Council for Exceptional Children. Reprinted with permission.*

"Clams" is a preventive discipline technique that can be used to avoid confusion and facilitate movement through typically disruptive times in a classroom. The activity is suitable for preschool through early elementary age students with mild disabilities as well as young nondisabled children in group settings.

PURPOSE: This technique can be used to prevent noise and disruption during potentially disruptive activities of short duration such as changing from one activity to another, preparing to go to recess, preparing to go home, or moving from one room to another. To be successful, the activity should take no more than 5 minutes to complete and be used occasionally, rather than daily. The objective of the activity is for students to remain quiet and monitor each other's silence during specific "high-contagion" times selected by the teacher.

MATERIALS: No specific materials are required.

PLAYING THE GAME:
1.   Before a short, high-contagion activity is to begin, tell the students you have a game you want to play. Explain that the game is hard to do, but that you think they are ready to play it.
2.   Tell the students that clams are animals who make no noise. They do not communicate like dogs, cats, birds, or even other sea animals. Even their movements make no sound. They certainly don't talk.
3.   Tell the students that when you say, "CLAMS!" all of them are to become completely silent immediately and remain silent as long as they can. Whoever forgets and speaks first or makes a loud noise first loses the game, and the game must begin again. Practice a few times by counting and starting the game, "One, two, three, CLAMS!" Close your lips tightly and give hand or touch signals to any child not complying. When everyone is silent, tell the students to begin talking so you can practice again. Practice several times in quick succession until all the children understand the game.
4.   After the children understand the game, begin a high-contagion activity. As soon as noise begins, say, "one, two, three, CLAMS!" Again, give hand or touch signals to any child not complying. Other children will soon begin to cooperate and give similar signals.
5.   When a child speaks or makes a loud noise, say, "That game is over. We'll begin again. One, two, three, CLAMS!" Repeat this sequence until the high-contagion activity is completed.

MODIFYING/ADAPTING THE TECHNIQUE: The teacher may want to keep track of the amount of time in seconds that the class manages to remain quiet for each game. Whenever a particular amount of quiet time is reached (e.g., 3 or 4 minutes or the entire amount of time needed for the activity), the entire class receives a predetermined reward such as extra recess time or a star on a chart.

(continued)

Figure 5.2   (*Continued*)

When enough stars have been earned, a larger reward is given, for example, free
time, a dance, or a party.

EVALUATING SUCCESS: This activity is successful if the students remain
silent and help remind each other with signals such as gestures and touching. If the
activity has to be repeated frequently, however, other management techniques
should be tried.

AT WORK IN THE CLASSROOM: Students respond favorably to this technique because it is a game rather than a threat or a lecture. The game can be used
at any high-stress time, such as after a fire drill or on the bus for a field trip.

---

students to encourage quiet transitions. (Also, see Figure 5.3 for additional
transition activities.)

Teachers at the secondary level may use their chalkboards to minimize
disruptions between activities. By listing the activities on the board prior to
class time, teachers prepare students for what is to come, thus maximizing
instructional time. Frequently, teachers at the secondary level inadvertently
allow students to determine when instruction will end. Students will, for
example, begin packing up to go to the next class well before the bell.
Teachers can use this time at the end of class for reviewing the day's lesson
and previewing what is to come tomorrow.

• *Maintain an academic focus.* By maintaining an academic focus and
limiting the amount of time devoted to noninstructional activities, teachers
increase the amount of actual instructional time available within the time
allocated. Noninstructional activities (e.g., classroom discipline,
organizational tasks, announcements, social interactions, transitions) are
negatively correlated with academic achievement. Teachers must ensure that
under 15% of class time is spent on such activities (Gartland & Rosenberg,
1987). Figure 5.1 offers suggestions for routines to enhance instructional
time and decrease noninstructional time. Remember, increased academic
learning time results in higher academic achievement.

• *Schedule activities carefully.* Scheduling is another important aspect of
time management and preventive discipline. Maintaining a daily schedule
provides structure for students and eliminates the need for constant
questioning about "what's next." Informing students in advance about
changes in the daily schedule keeps confusion to a minimum when changes
do occur.

In the regular classroom, the entire class has one schedule. Individual
students, especially those receiving special services, will have additional
schedules. The individual schedules will be a subset of the group schedule.
For example, within the block of time allotted for language arts or

---

Figure 5.3   Suggested Transition Activities

From "Transition Activities: A Classroom Management Tool," by B. S. Myles and L. J. Hronek, 1990, LD Forum, 15(3), pp. 20–22. Copyright © 1990 by Bowling Green State University. Reprinted with permission.

Lining up activities:

    Have students alphabetize themselves.

    Have students group themselves by specific characteristics ("All students wearing the color red line up first.")

    Have students discuss ordinal concepts (who is first, second) and prepositions (who is before, after).

Seated activities

    Have students see how many words they can spell from a word written on the blackboard.

    Have students write a story problem from an equation.

    Have each student write a story starter that will be used in a future creative writing lesson.

Relocating activities:

    Play "I Spy" ("Tommy, I spy something in the hallway that starts with D.").

    Play counting games ("Silently count the number of people we pass in the hall and divide that number by 3." "Count the number of classrooms we pass and estimate the number of children in the classrooms.")

Multiuse activities:

    Have students name two facts previously learned in a social studies or science lesson ("Name two facts about whales.")

    Have each student tell one sentence of a story—each sentence, however, must contain a newly learned vocabulary word.

---

mathematics in Ms. Kirk's classroom, Travis may go to the resource room for individualized instruction from Ms. Lopez. The remainder of his schedule may follow that of the group. (See Box 5.3 for a sample schedule for Travis.)

    Gallagher (1979) offers several suggestions for scheduling classrooms and students. These suggestions may be particularly helpful early in the school year for both classroom teachers and special educators:

1. Provide each student with a daily schedule.

2. Alternate high-probability tasks with low-probability tasks.

3. Schedule work that can be finished by the end of the school day.

4. Plan for some leeway time.

Box 5.3 Travis's Schedule

Travis reports to Ms. Lopez's classroom for reading and mathematics instruction on a daily basis. Ms. Kirk and the other members of the fourth-grade team at Oakhill Elementary School exchange students for both reading and mathematics so that students may be grouped by similar skills and needs. When reading and math time begin, therefore, Travis changes classes just like his peers, reporting to Ms. Lopez instead of to a regular fourth-grade classroom teacher. For all other subjects, Travis remains in Ms. Kirk's class. The following daily schedule is typical for Travis:

Daily Schedule for Travis

8:30–9:00	Morning activity/ Seatwork/Boardwork
9:00–10:00	Reading/Language arts with Ms. Lopez
10:00–10:30	Music or art
10:30–10:45	Bathroom break/Snack
10:45–11:45	Mathematics with Ms. Lopez
11:45–12:45	Lunch/Bathroom break/Recess
12:45–1:00	Story/Writing time
1:00–2:00	Social Studies or science (Ms. Lopez team teaches with Ms. Kirk.)
2:00–2:30	Health, Physical education, or Computer lab
2:30–3:00	Homework assignments/Jobs/ Preparation for dismissal

---

5. Require students to complete one task before beginning another whenever possible.

6. Provide time reminders.

7. Don't assign additional work if tasks are completed ahead of schedule, but rather structure routines to provide students with acceptable choices upon work completion.

8. Plan ahead and anticipate students' needs.

9. Establish expectations in advance and do not introduce unexpected activities.

10. Include feedback and evaluative marks with a student's daily schedule.

11. Provide positive feedback. (pp. 244–250)

• *Use positive teacher behaviors.* Several teacher behaviors are also related to engaged time, and thus to academic learning time, because they increase student attention to task. For example, at least 50% of class time should be spent on interactive activities, including demonstrating content material, monitoring oral reading, providing opportunities for student responses, providing corrective feedback, and reinforcing correct behaviors (Gartland & Rosenberg, 1987). Moreover, teachers should display enthusiasm during academic presentations and should try to engage all students in group activities. Approximately 35% of instructional time should be spent in monitoring controlled and independent practice. This practice might include teacher-directed seatwork, activities at the chalkboard, independent seatwork, or sustained silent reading. Teachers can increase the on-task rates of students during practice by giving clear instructions, by giving corrective feedback, by reinforcing correct responses, by using novel and motivating assignments, and by using study carrels (Gartland & Rosenberg, 1987). (See Figure 5.4 for some practical techniques for making the most of instructional time.)

Using Computers to Maximize Instructional Time

Teachers of exceptional students have many demands on their time. Unfortunately, some of the most important aspects of teaching, including planning and presenting instruction, receive less attention than they deserve because of paperwork and other administrative demands on the teacher. The technology available to schools of the 1990s may be used to decrease the time teachers spend managing paperwork and increase the productivity of instructional tools for use in the classroom. Specifically, the microcomputer can be used to produce teaching aids and tests, record grades, maintain information and performance data on individual students, and generate correspondence. The key idea behind using the microcomputer is that the teacher is not simply saving time, but rather finding ways to enhance the education of students.

In a survey of members of the Council for Exceptional Children, Blackhurst (1989) found that *AppleWorks* is the software most widely used by special educators. According to Blackhurst, "teachers can use *AppleWorks* to develop lesson plans, maintain student records, calculate grades, instruct students, and correspond with parents. Administrators can use the software to develop and update individualized education programs (IEPs); meet due process legal requirements related to parent contacts; prepare budgets and maintain records required for local, state, and federal accountability reports" (p. 68).

The three programs included in *AppleWorks,* designed for use on Apple computers, are word-processing, database, and spreadsheet applications. *AppleWorks,* however, is not the only software available for use in the classroom. Other programs are available for IBM PCs and IBM compatibles.

Word-processing applications enable educators to edit, move text, copy, print in various formats, and mail-merge with information from databases. The use of templates is a valuable time-saving feature of word processing that enables teachers to create letters, newsletters, forms, lesson-plan formats, student worksheets and assignments, and IEP objectives. This type of application saves time for the teacher when one format may need to be used on several occasions (Blackhurst, 1989).

The benefits of word processing are not limited to teachers, however. Students in special education programs, especially those with poor spelling or handwriting, can use word processing to improve their writing. Editing capabilities and spelling and grammar checkers work together to improve the readability of written documents (Blackhurst, 1989).

Database management offers the educator the capabilities of organization, storage, and retrieval of large bodies of information. Up to 30 categories of information can be stored in the *AppleWorks* database. In the classroom,

Figure 5.4   Time Management from the Kitchen

From "Time Management from the Kitchen" by E. Hoffman, 1988, Academic Therapy, *23(3), pp. 275–77. Copyright © 1988 by PRO-ED, Inc. Reprinted with permission.*

I am working with a small group of students while the others in my LD resource room are doing independent work. I have carefully explained the assignments to the other children so that I can concentrate on my group. We begin our lesson. We are interrupted not once but several times as I try to teach. I see that I am losing the attention of my students in the group. My frustrations increase. My calm answers become brusque, my patient requests to wait become irritated orders. Help! We need a better way to manage our time!

I first became aware of a need to teach time management to LD students when I changed from teaching at the high school level to an elementary resource room. In high school, the class periods are defined by bells. Older students are often able to wait to ask questions until it is their turn. But it is quite a different story with younger students.

After trial and error, I discovered help right in my own kitchen. A kitchen timer became our classroom bell. Here's how it works:

I get the students settled with their independent assignments. We have a question and answer period for a few moments until everyone is satisfied.

The timer is set for fifteen minutes (or more or less, depending on the ages of the students and our needs).

While the timer is running, I work with my group. No one may interrupt us for those fifteen minutes. "Peer tutors," who have been selected from older students, will answer questions that cannot wait. I also provide foolproof seat work that a student may turn to if he cannot proceed on his assignment until he is able to consult with me.

When the timer rings, we take a break, and I answer questions and change activities when appropriate.

The benefits of this simple technique are many:

1. Students working with me get a continuity of instruction and attention that was not possible when we were frequently interrupted.

2. Students working independently learn that they can often solve their own problems if they think about them for a few minutes.

3. Students who cannot proceed with their work learn to find alternatives so they can use their time effectively instead of sitting and wasting time.

4. "Tutors" have an opportunity to assume some classroom responsibility for their fellow students. This often reinforces skills, and it certainly builds egos.

5. Students improve their concept of time.

Another kitchen item that has helped my young students with time management is the three-minute egg timer. I use this small hour glass to motivate the "dreamers"—those students who sit and gaze into space unless I am working directly with them. I indicate a small section of the assignment to be completed, put the egg timer on the desk, and whisper, "Beat the clock!" It is amazing to see
(continued)

Figure 5.4   *(Continued)*

---

how the children sit up, grab their pencils, and get to work as the sand slips through the glass. My young students are learning the concept of using every minute productively.

Finally, another kitchen staple, the paper plate, has been useful as a private clock for those students who cannot yet tell time. In our class, students come in and out on different schedules. The younger children would always ask me, "When do I leave?" Now we set their individual clocks made of a paper plate with cardboard hands to their departure time (or any other time they need to remember). When their clock matches the wall clock, they know it is time to go. I also write the time in words and numbers on the clock, and they quickly learn their own schedule.

---

teachers may choose to create a database for history or geography, for example, or they may use commercially prepared databases that can be accessed from *AppleWorks* (Blackhurst, 1989).

Not only can a wide variety of formats be generated for displaying information in a database, but a wide variety of reports can also be generated. The kind of report is dependent upon the search strategy employed. For example, the program can generate a table-style report, grouping students alphabetically or by teacher. The program can also produce a label-style report that may typically be used as address labels (Blackhurst, 1989).

The spreadsheet application enables the educator to store and manipulate numerical data. Data are arranged in rows and columns and formulas are entered to perform a variety of calculations, such as averages, percentages, and ranges of scores. "The strength of the spreadsheet is that it can be set up so that all of the totals change when new figures are entered" (Blackhurst, 1989, p. 70).

The use of the microcomputer in education offers some teachers an exciting challenge, although it may be a source of stress for those who have not mastered it. Whether the computer is used as an instructional tool with students or as a management tool to handle a large volume of paperwork, it has the potential to be a valuable time-management asset for every teacher.

✎ Maintaining a Positive Classroom Environment

Recall that Gartland (1990) defined the three aspects of discipline as preventive, supportive, and corrective. Thus far, we have focused attention on the preventive aspect, in which the teacher organizes the environment and prepares for students to learn and behave appropriately within the structure provided. However, the teacher cannot always prevent misbehavior. The other aspects of discipline, supportive and corrective, may need to be implemented for particular students in specific instances. The effective use of reinforcement and punishment are necessary skills for the maintenance of a wholesome classroom environment.

Reinforcement may be defined as any consequence of a behavior that increases the likelihood of that behavioral response occurring again. When Joey brings his homework to class and receives Ms. Kirk's praise, and when that praise encourages him to bring his homework to school every day, Ms. Kirk's praise is considered to be reinforcement. If Ms. Kirk's praise does not result in Joey's turning in homework each day, that praise is not considered to be reinforcement. Students will repeat a response pattern in order to gain a particular desired reinforcer.

Two kinds of reinforcement exist: positive reinforcement and negative reinforcement. *Positive reinforcement* involves the delivery of a reward following a behavior, increasing the likelihood of the behavior in the future. Negative reinforcement also increases the likelihood of a behavior. Negative reinforcement, however, involves the removal of an aversive (unpleasant) stimulus as a consequence of the behavior. For example, if Ms. Kirk tells her students, "Those who complete their daily math worksheet and receive a grade of A will not have homework," she is using negative reinforcement, assuming, of course, that having homework is "unpleasant" and that "A-getting" increases.

Punishment, which is frequently confused with negative reinforcement, is designed to *reduce* the likelihood that a particular behavioral response will recur. Punishment carries with it unpleasant connotations and may occur in the form of an aversive consequence, such as scolding, following an inappropriate behavior. Punishment may also involve the removal of a privilege or the loss of points. The important idea behind punishment, however, is that the behavior of interest *decreases* when the consequence is applied. For example, punishment might occur when Ms. Kirk states, "Kevin you have been talking rather than working on your math problems, so you will finish your math during your free time this afternoon."

Reinforcement

Cohen and Hearn (1988) describe two forms of positive reinforcers: primary and secondary. *Primary reinforcers* are those that have biological significance to an individual, including reinforcers such as food or drinks. Although the use of snacks in the classroom on a regular basis may not be feasible, teachers who use such primary reinforcers (as candy, popcorn, or soft drinks) as rewards for good behavior have found them to be very effective.

Secondary reinforcers, on the other hand, receive their strength through frequent association with primary reinforcers. Parents, for example, often pair a secondary social reinforcer (verbal praise) with a primary reinforcer (a treat) for their young children. By the time the child enters school, many types of secondary reinforcers are well established. Teachers also may pair the primary reinforcer with a secondary reinforcer to which the child responds. For example, Ms. Lopez may pair a candy bar at the end of class (a primary reinforcer) with a sticker or verbal praise (secondary reinforcers). A transfer from the primary to the secondary reinforcer occurs when students are reinforced by the sticker or the verbal praise without the presence of the candy bar.

Secondary reinforcers may include praise, grades, tokens, stars, stickers, and permission to engage in preferred activities. These frequently are more appropriate in the school setting than food or soft drinks. (See Figure 5.5 for an activity using secondary reinforcers.) More naturally occurring secondary reinforcers include nonverbal expressions (smiles, for example) and teacher proximity. Should there be a student for whom secondary reinforcement has no "value," the teacher must first establish an association between a primary reinforcer and a secondary reinforcer. Cohen and Hearn (1988) suggest two things for teachers to keep in mind: First, never present a primary reinforcer without pairing it with a secondary reinforcer and, second, once the association has been made, gradually remove the primary reinforcer.

A number of reinforcers that teachers might use with students are presented in Figure 5.6. Some may be appropriate for any age or grade level, whereas others are likely to lose potency for older students. For example, verbal praise, lunch with the teacher, or working at the teacher's desk may be reinforcing for younger students, while older students like Robert may not wish to be singled out for such attention. Thus, Mr. Abel, who teaches in the middle school and high school, must be careful to select age-appropriate reinforcers that are based on student preferences and that are practical and available in the school setting (Reynolds, Salend, & Beahan, 1989). In each instance, teachers must know their students and observe what is reinforcing for them.

One way to ensure that effective reinforcers will be selected is to observe students' activities to determine which reinforcers they choose on their own. In addition, teachers might allow students to sample the available reinforcers or have them select desired reinforcers through a reinforcement survey (see Figure 5.7). For students who will not respond in detail to an open-ended survey, teachers may use interviews or provide a menu of possible reinforcers on which the student circles choices or provides answers by specific categories. For example, the student might choose:

Favorite snacks: _____type of candy bar

_____type of soft drink

_____type of snack food

Reynolds et al (1989) identify four types of positive reinforcers commonly used in school settings: edible, tangible, activity, and social. Edible reinforcers are at the lowest level in the hierarchy of reinforcement because they are highly intrusive in nature. Tangible reinforcers, such as pins, stickers, comic books, and posters, have a constantly changing value. Teachers must be prepared to adjust these reinforcers in order to keep up with the latest fad. Activity reinforcers are highly motivating alternatives to both edible and tangible reinforcers. They allow students to engage in a task that often serves as a learning experience as well as a reinforcer. Carefully structured free time, probably the most highly desired activity reinforcer, can be used to play an instructional game, visit the library or gymnasium, or make an art project. Extra computer time, or time allotted to listen to music or to watch a video, are also motivating reinforcers, especially for many secondary-level students.

Figure 5.5 "Punch Out"

From "Punch Out": A Behavior Management Technique, by G. B. Maher, Teaching Exceptional Children, *21(2), 1989, p. 74. Copyright © 1989 by The Council for Exceptional Children. Reprinted with permission.*

"Punch Out" is a behavior management technique that is especially useful for students who exhibit off-task behavior, both passive and active.

PURPOSE: The purpose of "Punch Out" is to motivate students to increase time on task and decrease inappropriate behavior. It provides both visual and auditory reinforcement for desired behavior. A variable-reinforcement schedule, paired with both verbal and tangible reinforcers, is used to increase appropriate behavior. Behavioral goals should be individualized. Target behaviors can be simple (e.g., raising hand for assistance) or complex (e.g., completing assignments). Contingencies can be established by the teacher, student, or both.

MATERIALS: Punchcard: 3″ × 5″ card with 50 to 75 small holes drawn in a picture or graph configuration. Hole-puncher: Used to punch holes in the cards. Various small tangible reinforcers: Given as rewards after all holes are punched on a student's card. Small bulletin board: Used to display children's cards after all holes are punched.

USING THE TECHNIQUE:

1. Give each student a punchcard with his or her name on it. Have the students place their cards at the corner of their desks each day.

2. Explain how the students will earn punches on the cards by displaying their target behaviors. Show them the "punched out" bulletin board on which they will staple their cards after all the holes are punched. Emphasize the tangible surprises they will receive after all the holes are punched on their cards.

3. Circulate through the class punching students' cards on a variable schedule and pairing the punches with verbal praises each time, or for an extra bonus, allow students to punch out card.

4. For variety, use the technique as a class reinforcer by giving the class a party or treat once all students' cards have been punched out.

AT WORK IN THE CLASSROOM: "Punch Out" has been used successfully in both resource class and regular classrooms with 40 elementary students who have learning disabilities, mental retardation, and behavior disorders. The technique has reduced behavior problems and increased time on task. "Punch Out" has been accepted readily by teachers because of its ease of implementation and maintenance.

Figure 5.6   Classroom Reinforcers

From S. B. Cohen and D. Hearn, Reinforcement. In R. McNergney (Ed.), Guide to Classroom Teaching. *Copyright © 1988. Reprinted with permission of Allyn & Bacon and the author.*

Receiving smiles, winks, etc.

Using the gym, library, during unassigned time

Getting stamps, stickers

Making a phone call home

Eating lunch with teacher

Bringing comic books to read

Writing notes to a classmate

Being line leader

Getting a chance to solve codes, puzzles

Getting time to spend in student lounge

Working with a volunteer

Getting peer recognition

Getting good grades

Being hall monitor

Getting a photo in newspaper

Getting free time

Watching films

Selecting time for completing assignments

Videotaping

Grading papers

Assisting custodian, secretary, etc.

Getting a snack

Choosing a special work spot

Speaking over address system

Using a calculator

Working at teacher's desk

Getting a soda from the lounge

Using felt tip pens

Spending a day interning with a local business

Displaying progress

Getting no homework

Assisting in another room, grade

Getting permission to miss a test

Participating in a special project

Taking class roll

Using a tape recorder, microcomputer

Creating a bulletin board

Having a class dance in the room

Social reinforcers are the least intrusive of the secondary reinforcers available because they closely match the environment and do not require the teacher to make or do anything special. Teacher comments (especially those in writing), free time with the teacher, and positive body language and smiles are teacher behaviors that may reinforce student behavior. Academic reinforcers are, perhaps, the most appropriate form of reinforcement that can be offered to secondary-level students. Academic reinforcers are logical consequences for appropriate school behavior. Such reinforcers might include schoolwide

Figure 5.7   Reinforcement Profile

From S. B. Cohen and D. Hearn, Reinforcement In R. McNergney (Ed.), Guide to Classroom Teaching. *Copyright © 1988. Reprinted with permission of Allyn & Bacon and the author.*

1. The thing I like best about school is _____

   _____ .

2. I feel really good when someone tells me that I _____

   _____ .

3. The school subject I like best is _____ .
4. My favorite snack is _____ .
5. If I could do anything in school that I wanted, I would _____

   _____ .

6. If I could do anything at all that I wanted, I would _____

   _____ .

7. The thing that makes me enjoy school the most is _____

   _____ .

8. In my free time I like to _____

   _____ .

announcements of achievement or effort, recognition of excellent work by displaying it in a hallway or display case, or midsemester reports of progress (Reynolds et al., 1989).

Another effective reinforcer for many secondary-level students is the removal of a certain amount of work. This is considered a negative reinforcer in that an aversive stimulus is removed with the goal of increasing the desired behavioral response. Appropriate behavior may be reinforced, for example, by eliminating a homework assignment or by waiving an upcoming test (Reynolds et al., 1989).

Group reinforcers, which can be delivered to the class contingent upon the behavior of the entire group or the behavior of individuals, are highly motivating to many students. Groups may be rewarded with structured free time, the opportunity to rent a video, a party for the entire class, or a special game the class enjoys. Although many students have access to videos or games, such activities often offer broadening experiences for students who do not have such access. Educational trips and outings also can provide both reinforcement for class behavior, as well as new learning experiences (Reynolds et al., 1989).

If reinforcement is to be used effectively, the reinforcer must be contingent on demonstration of the appropriate behavior. Students who receive their rewards whether or not they have behaved appropriately learn that they do not have to perform in order to get what they want.

Sometimes the teacher finds it necessary to implement a contingency contract with a student. A *contingency contract* is a document specifying the terms of an agreement in which the pupil and teacher jointly determine a task to be performed and an expected reward for the student (see Figure 5.8). When the

---

Figure 5.8   Sample Contingency Contract

I _____ will _____

_____ by _____

_____ .

After successfully completing this, I may _____

_____ .

Student Signature: _____

Teacher Signature: _____

Date signed _____   Date Completed _____

---

agreement involves several tasks or additional people, the contract may be more detailed and may be written and signed by all parties involved.

Some students seemingly defy reinforcement. That is to say, the things that we typically rely on as reinforcers may not be reinforcing to all students. Furthermore, scolding—a consequence most teachers believe to be unpleasant and punishing—may actually be reinforcing for some students. In such cases, teachers must determine exactly what it is that is reinforcing the inappropriate behavior and seek to remove it.

Punishment

As defined by Cohen and Hearn (1988), punishment means "the introduction of an aversive consequence following an inappropriate behavior" (p. 62). However, any intervention that is presented following a particular behavior may only be considered punishment provided it has the effect of eliminating or reducing the probability that the behavior will be repeated. Extinction and response-cost procedures, and sometimes scolding following inappropriate behavior, are forms of punishment appropriate to the educational setting.

Extinction refers to the process of eliminating an inappropriate behavior by withdrawing whatever reinforces it. Many times the reinforcer is teacher attention. When that attention is withheld, the behavior is reduced. For example, whenever Joey calls out in class without waiting to be called on, Ms. Kirk reprimands him. Joey, however, might be calling out to get his teacher's attention. The reprimand, while Ms. Kirk intends it to be aversive, actually functions as a reinforcer to maintain and increase Joey's behavior. If Ms. Kirk ignores Joey's call-outs consistently over time, they will gradually decrease and eventually disappear. When such a plan is implemented, Ms. Kirk must prepare for an initial increase in Joey's "call-out" behavior because he is accustomed to receiving attention for this behavior. This "preextinction burst" is the point at which many teachers state that planned ignoring doesn't work or that it only makes matters worse. Eventually, however, if Ms. Kirk continues to withhold her attention, the call-outs will decrease.

Cohen and Hearn (1988) add a note of warning concerning the use of extinction procedures: "Be sure you have pinpointed what is reinforcing the behavior" (p. 64). If the teacher has applied extinction techniques consistently over time and the inappropriate behavior has not decreased, something unaccounted for could be reinforcing the behavior. For example, Joey's classmates might laugh and giggle when he calls out so that he continues to receive the attention he is seeking. Extinction should not be used unless the teacher can be sure that the student is not receiving reinforcement.

Response-cost procedures are another form of punishment involving the withholding of certain amounts of a positive reinforcer each time a student demonstrates a specified inappropriate behavior. For example, in a token system where students are earning points for good behavior or academic accomplishments, a specified number of points are deducted each time an inappropriate behavior occurs. Reducing the minutes of recess or free time are additional examples of the response-cost procedure following inappropriate behaviors.

Parents often use scolding as a common child-rearing practice. This form of punishment, however, does not motivate learning and can backfire on teachers by creating a negative classroom climate and by drawing attention to inappropriate student behavior. Applying an aversive stimulus should only be used as a last resort for undesirable behaviors. If a teacher finds it necessary to use this form of punishment, the most effective practice is to pair the punishment of an inappropriate behavior with the reinforcement of an alternative appropriate behavior. In this way, the student is learning what to do as well as what not to do (Cohen & Hearn, 1988). In addition, teachers are advised first to check school policy regarding punishment and to obtain parental permission regarding the punishment to be used and the behaviors that might result in that punishment. Teachers must also make every effort to document the effectiveness of the form of punishment in question and to switch to less aversive forms of punishment as soon as possible.

All teachers must have a clear understanding of how to structure the classroom environment to prevent behavior problems and how to manage behavior problems when they occur. When "things get out of hand" is a bad time to implement a classroom-management program. The effective teacher plans the environment very carefully and begins to teach and reinforce desirable behavior on the first day of school. The effective teacher also learns quickly what motivates appropriate and inappropriate behaviors in each student. Finally, the effective teacher recognizes that no instruction and, certainly, no learning, can take place in a classroom that does not have a positive management system in as soon as possible.

✎ Summary

The goal of classroom management is to increase the amount of time available for instruction. Teachers must minimize the amount of time spent on behavior management and noninstructional activities and maximize the amount of time spent in demonstration and practice of academic tasks. Preventive discipline may eliminate many of the management crises that occur in the classroom. While teachers cannot prevent all discipline problems, they can plan an environment in which students are engaged in academic tasks to the maximum extent. The skillful use of reinforcement and punishment also helps teachers to maintain a positive classroom climate.

✎ Application Exercises

1. Interview a classroom teacher and a special educator. Ask them how the rules for their classes are determined. Ask them how they train their students to follow rules and procedures.

2. Observe in a regular and special education classroom. Watch for uses of primary and secondary reinforcers, group reinforcers, extinction, and response cost. Which reinforcers work best? Do certain students respond better to one form of reinforcement than to another? Do students respond better to reinforcement than to punishment?

Assessing Student Progress

Chapter 6

Focus

As you read, think about the following questions:

Why do teachers use various types of assessment methods, including informal and formal assessment?

How do teachers assess student progress in a particular curriculum?

How is assessment data used to plan and modify instruction?

What can the teacher do when assessment reveals that a student is not progressing as expected?

What is meant by referral, screening, and eligibility?

✎ Assessment refers to the process of gathering information that will enable the educator to identify specific problems and make decisions about students (Salvia and Ysseldyke, 1988). Assessment, then, is more than merely "testing" students. Rather, it involves collecting data to form a holistic picture of a student so that the teacher can plan instruction and promote student progress. If accurate objectives for students are to be maintained, assessment must become a daily strategy within the classroom.

Teachers use several types of assessment on a daily basis. Many of these methods are common in both regular and special education classrooms. Most methods of assessment help the teacher gain information about academic progress. Others provide clarification about social-emotional needs or behavioral problems. In addition, some assessment methods give the teacher information about the classroom environment, curricular materials, or teaching strategies. In combination, these various forms of assessment give the teacher the needed documentation by which to make informed educational decisions to promote student achievement. The following conversation between Ms. Kirk and Ms. Lopez illustrates how these two teachers use assessment to make instructional decisions:

Ms. Kirk: *Good Morning.*

Ms. Lopez: *Hi, how are you!*

Ms. Kirk: *I'm glad I happened to see you this morning. I have a question I want to ask you about Travis.*

Ms. Lopez: *Sure. What is it?*

Ms. Kirk: *Travis is having difficulty with his social studies written work. He's having trouble answering the comprehension questions in the book. I'm wondering if he's getting the words mixed up or if he's having trouble spelling some of the words for the answers.*

Ms. Lopez: *Can you think of an example?*

Ms. Kirk: *Let's see. I know. Many of the answers in this chapter involve the names of cities and places, and most of these are multisyllable words like Washington or Massachusetts.*

Ms. Lopez: *Hmmm . . . He does have difficulty spelling even simple words. Have you tried giving him a list of terms to use? That seems to help him in his other subjects.*

Ms. Kirk: *I've done that in the past and we just got rushed in this chapter. I'll write the terms and talk to him about them today.*

Ms. Lopez: *Great. I'll analyze some of his spelling errors today. When you write the list of terms, give me a copy and I'll review them with Travis in his resource period today to see if spelling is the problem. We can talk about it again this afternoon if you want.*

Ms. Kirk: *Okay, see you after school.*

Teachers use many types of assessment to gather data and make informed instructional decisions. Instructional decisions must be based on data, not opinion, or teachers will waste valuable time and effort. In this chapter, we will examine several assessment methods. First, we will examine informal assessment in the classroom, including curriculum-based assessment, criterion-referenced testing, observational recording procedures, and checklists and rating scales. Then, we will discuss formal assessments used in the referral, screening, and eligibility process.

✎ Informal Assessment in the Classroom

Informal assessment procedures make use of any data the teacher collects to monitor progress of students and make instructional decisions. These data may be collected through teacher-made or commercially prepared curriculum-based assessments, through error analysis using permanent products or work samples and probes, through criterion-referenced testing, through observational recording, or through checklists and rating scales. Informal assessment methods often employ the specific curricular materials used when teaching students.

Curriculum-Based Assessment

When assessment involves the curricular materials that students are using, the procedure is called *curriculum-based assessment* or *curriculum-based measurement*. Curriculum-based assessments may be teacher-made or commercially prepared curricular materials. Examples of common curriculum-based assessments are weekly spelling tests that include words from a unit in a spelling book, comprehension questions following a story in a basal reader, addition facts taken from an exercise in the student's mathematics workbook, and tests accompanying the basal reading series designed to assess mastery of specific grade-level skills, such as a first-grader's recognition of the consonants and their sounds.

Teachers often design their own curriculum-based tests to assess progress. In many cases, the commercially prepared assessment instrument includes a large body of information, such as an entire chapter or a whole topical unit. Students who are not monitored on an ongoing basis may struggle with a unit or chapter before the teacher realizes that they are not progressing through the curriculum as expected. For this reason, teachers should measure progress frequently. Frequent and direct assessment, when used to evaluate student objectives, results in more frequent teacher modification of instruction and in more specific goals for students (Fuchs, 1986; Fuchs, Fuchs, & Stecker, 1989). Moreover, teachers who use curriculum-based assessment tend to set more ambitious goals for their students (Fuchs, Fuchs, & Hamlett, 1989). Curriculum-based assessment also provides measurement that is sensitive to changes in student performance throughout the school year (Shinn, 1988).

Curriculum-based assessment may be used in any subject taught in school. The teacher simply uses the actual content of the curriculum to measure concept or skill acquisition. To assess student progress for one week in a social studies curriculum, for example, Ms. Kirk might survey the information in the text, select representative questions, and ask her students to answer the selected questions. Bennett (1982) suggests the following guidelines for teachers developing their own informal curriculum-based assessments:

1. Specify the purpose for the assessment. Teachers must clearly state an objective specifying what skill or behavior is to be measured. Ms. Lopez, for example, may wish to assess whether Travis can spell words using the "ay" spelling pattern when she dictates such words to him.

2. Construct or select procedures that are relevant to the purpose for assessment. In order to assess Travis's performance when writing words with the "ay" spelling pattern, Ms. Lopez must compile a list of words with this pattern (e.g., hay, play), and she must ask Travis to write the selected words.

3. Select assessment tasks that are representative of the objective of interest. Ms. Lopez must give Travis words using the "ay" pattern to write if she is to assess his performance on the objective. Asking Travis to read or point to words having the "ay" pattern requires a different behavioral response. To assess whether Travis can spell words using the "ay" pattern, Ms. Lopez must dictate such words and then observe whether or not Travis spells them correctly.

4. Specify dimensions on which performance will be judged and criteria for determining what will be considered a correct response. Ms. Lopez considers a correct response in spelling to be all letters present and in the correct sequence. She must decide, however, whether or not Travis's performance should be judged on the basis of legibility as well. Because handwriting must be legibile for others to be able to read it, Ms. Lopez decides that Travis must also write his letters clearly if his performance will be judged correct.

5. Specify criteria for evaluating overall performance and the rationale for selecting these criteria. Ms. Lopez determines that Travis must spell words having the "ay" pattern with 100% accuracy. She sets this criterion because using common spelling patterns without error must become automatic with Travis if he is to progress in his writing skills.

6. Use as long an assessment as possible. Ms. Lopez must gather a representative sample of work in order to assess Travis's ability to spell words having the "ay" pattern. If she gives Travis only two or three words with this pattern, she will not know whether he can spell "ay" words or whether he has simply memorized two or three particular words. Ms. Lopez may also wish to present Travis with some "nonexamples" of "ay" words (e.g., *cake* and *lake*) to be sure that Travis knows when to use the "ay" pattern.

According to Choate, Enright, Miller, Poteet, & Rakes (1992), curriculum-based assessment offers an "authentic" picture of student performance. Moreover, they maintain that it can provide teachers with numerous advantages; for example, curriculum-based assessment

- helps the teacher determine what to teach;

- facilitates evaluation of student progress and program effectiveness;

- provides an efficient, valid, and reliable means of evaluation;

- increases student achievement by assessing what is taught;

- helps with decision making in referring students for special education evaluation; and,

- complies with the requirements of Public Law 94-142 that a student's present level of educational performance be specified, that goals and objectives be written to address individual student needs, and that objective procedures be used for evaluating student progress toward instructional objectives.

Using student work samples and probes.   In addition to using teacher-made or commercially prepared tests, using the actual work products of the student is yet another form of curriculum-based assessment. Assessment based on a student's daily work is called *direct measurement*. Student worksheets, workbook pages, book reports, answers to questions at the end of a social studies chapter, and problems assigned for practice from the mathematics text are used in direct measurement.

Work samples are permanent products representing a student's performance at a given point in time. Permanent products may also include library records of books checked out, attendance records, or sign-up sheets for time to work on projects (Fagley, 1984). Permanent products provide a lasting picture of a student's strengths, interests, or weaknesses.

Probe sheets offer an additional way for teachers to gather permanent information about a student's performance. Probes are detailed assessments of a specific skill. Probes are administered in a specified (usually brief) period of time to assess student skill in a particular area. Correct and incorrect student responses per minute (rate) and percentage of correct responses are two measures that teachers may obtain by using probes (see Figure 6.1).

To construct a probe, teachers first specify an instructional objective and then select items by which to measure achievement of the objective. In the example provided in Figure 6.1, the objective is skill aquisition in solving two-digit plus two-digit addition problems with no regrouping. Only addition problems of this type are included as probe items. Of interest is the number of digits written correctly each minute. In order to assess the degree to which the student has mastered this particular skill, the probe must include more items than the student can complete in the allotted time. Salvia and Hughes (1990) suggest that teachers reduce student anxiety when using probes by informing them that there are more problems on the probe than any student can complete in the given time period.

Following assessment through a probe, the teacher may prepare a chart or graph to display student progress (see Figure 6.2). The teacher may also con-

---

Figure 6.1   Example of an Arithmetic Probe

Date: _____   Skill: 2-digit + 2-digit, no regrouping _____

Teacher: _____   Student: _____

                                    Text: _____

(digits)

11	20	72	13	23	21	11	82	10	35
+48	+44	+15	+25	+26	+66	+16	+14	+29	+22

(20)

10	29	35	40	34	24	40	23	20	87
+38	+60	+53	+18	+23	+35	+59	+51	+12	+12

(40)

32	41	50	34	41	30	26	50	50	75
+62	+26	+22	+44	+12	+28	+63	+21	+15	+12

(60)

60	32	34	20	10	23	62	11	48	35
+37	+34	+14	+63	+16	+76	+27	+67	+31	+44

(80)

57	10	51	33	20	19	45	11	23	22
+41	+35	+16	+62	+63	+80	+21	+51	+72	+76

(100)

41	50	19	45	87	20	11	10	13	11
+26	+22	+80	+21	+12	+12	+67	+16	+25	+48

(120)

Digits/Minute Correct _____   Digits/Minute Incorrect _____

---

struct a record sheet, such as the one for Travis's performance on arithmetic work samples shown in Figure 6.3.

Teachers use curriculum-based assessments, including teacher-made or commercially prepared tests, student work samples, and probes to measure student progress. Once the teacher completes a curriculum-based assessment, however, he or she must analyze student errors in order to make instructional decisions.

Analyzing student errors. In error analysis, the teacher examines the student's responses to determine whether there is a pattern of errors, or mistakes, indicating that the student has not yet mastered the specified task. For

---

Figure 6.2   Digits per Minute Correct as Determined by Arithmetic Probe

---

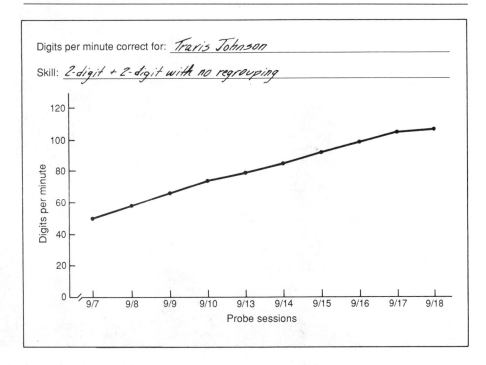

Digits per minute correct for: *Travis Johnson*

Skill: *2-digit + 2-digit with no regrouping*

example, Ms. Kirk might discern that a student is using a faulty algorithm in mathematics after observing the following errors on an arithmetic test:

705	217	342	438	814
−381	−123	−204	−269	−782
484	114	142	231	172

In this case, the student is subtracting the larger digit from the smaller digit without an understanding of place value and the need to regroup.

Through error analysis, the teacher can determine the reason for errors. For example, the student may not have understood the directions for the task, or the error may have been the result of carelessness. In other cases, errors are due to lack of understanding of the skill or concept. If the reason for the error is not clear, the teacher may ask the student to explain how he or she arrived at a particular answer (Howell, 1986). (See Box 6.1 for an example of an error analysis).

In Box 6.1 Ms. Lopez discovers that Travis has forgotten part of the rule for spelling words having the "ay" pattern. Therefore, she decides to provide additional practice activities for Travis using the "ay" pattern and to probe his mastery of that pattern before testing him again on the complete spelling list.

Dickinson (1980) recommends the following steps to help teachers with error analysis:

Teachers use informal assessments like curriculum-based measurement daily to help determine what to teach.

1. Pinpoint the problem. The problem must be defined in ways that are observable and measurable. For example, Ms. Kirk may find that Celie does not give complete information when asked, "What is your address?" Celie gives the correct apartment number, street name, city, and state, but she does not give the street number and zip code.

2. Determine if the task or behavior is in the student's repertoire. For example, Ms. Lopez may note that Joey knows how to get her attention appropriately in the resource room; however, he is not using the skill when necessary in his mainstreamed classroom with Ms. Kirk.

3. Determine what sets the occasion for the response. The teacher must determine exactly which stimuli set the occasion for an incorrect response. If Ms. Kirk were to observe, for example, that Joey was using the proper steps to get her attention during math but not during social studies, she might examine the stimuli to which Joey was generally exposed during math and social studies classes. She may note, for example, that several friends of Joey sit near him during social studies but not during math. Joey appears to enjoy attention from these friends.

4. Perform a task analysis. When a task is not in a student's repertoire, the teacher performs a task analysis to determine the lowest skill not mastered that is essential to the task.

Using task analysis.   Task analysis is used to break down a task into it's smallest steps or substeps, thus enabling teachers to determine exactly where a student's mastery of a particular skill begins and ends. According to Howell (1985), a student who is missing a substep of a task is missing one of the essential building blocks of the complete task.

Wolery, Bailey, and Sugai (1988) suggest that constructing a task analysis requires at least four steps.

1. Identify an instructional objective, (for example, the ability to say the letters of the alphabet in the correct order within a 30-second time limit).

2. Break down the desired skill into its component parts by watching someone else perform the skill, by performing it yourself, by logically

---

Figure 6.3   A Sample Record Sheet from Travis's Work Samples

Student: **TRAVIS JOHNSON**   Skill: **ADDITION WITH REGROUPING**

Objective: **GIVEN 2-DIGIT PLUS 2-DIGIT ADDITION PROBLEMS, TRAVIS WILL WRITE THE SUMS WITH 100% ACCURACY OVER 3 CONSECUTIVE DAYS**

Date	Number of problems	Number correct	Number wrong	Percentage correct	Comments
9/17	25- BEST EVER MATH SERIES, P.39	18	7	72	NO REGROUPING
9/18	25- BEST EVER MATH SERIES, P.40	21	4	84	NO REGROUPING CARELESS ERRORS
9/19	25- B.E.M.S., P.23	25	0	100	NO REGROUPING
9/20	25- B.E.M.S., P.24	25	0	100	NO REGROUPING
9/23	30- B.E.M.S., REVIEW P.41	30	0	100	NO REGROUPING
9/25	20- B.E.M.S., P.49	10	10	50	REGROUPING FROM ONES TO TENS

Reprinted with the permission of Macmillan Publishing Company from Curriculum-Based Assessment: Testing What Is Taught *(p. 104) by J. Salvia and C. Hughes. Copyright © 1990 by Macmillan Publishing Company.*

Box 6.1   Ms. Lopez Conducts an Error Analysis

Teachers often use curriculum-based assessment and student work samples to analyze student errors and plan for instruction. Let's listen to a conversation in Ms. Lopez's room during a spelling lesson with Travis.

Ms. Lopez: *Travis, let's look at the work you completed yesterday in spelling.*

Travis: *Okay.*

Ms. Lopez: *It looks like you had some trouble with the new vowel pattern we've been working on this week. What is your new vowel pattern?*

Travis: *Uh . . . the "ay"?*

Ms. Lopez: *That's right. Tell me the rule for the "ay" pattern.*

Travis: *Um . . . a long /a/ sound is spelled* ai wye.

Ms. Lopez: *Travis, a long /a/ sound at the end of a one-syllable word is spelled* ai wye.

Travis: *Oh . . . yeah!*

Ms. Lopez: *Tell me some words on the list that have the "ay" pattern.*

Travis: *Um . . .* hay *and* play.

Ms. Lopez: *Good. Those are some of the words with the "ay" pattern. Let's look through your spelling list again. The "ay" words are the only words that gave you trouble. I think you've figured out the "ee" words pretty well. We'll do a practice activity tomorrow on just the "ay" words, and I'll test you on just those words before we do the whole spelling list again. Okay, now let's take another look at those tricky "ay" words. . . .*

---

analyzing the skill, or by using a normal developmental sequence provided in a basal reading series. (For example, the student might first be required to say the letters A–F in correct sequence, then A–P, then A–Z).

3. Sequence the steps for teaching purposes, using either the temporal order for tasks or increasing levels of difficulty.

4. Specify any necessary prerequisite behaviors. For example, prerequisite skills for long division include the ability to write the numerals; recall the subtraction, multiplication, and division facts; and line up numbers on a page.

Error and task analysis are integral components of effective instruction. A teacher may, for example, analyze a student's errors on a work sample involving long division. Upon examining the work sample, the teacher may determine that the student knows the subtraction, multiplication, and division facts and that he or she is performing the operations in the correct sequence. However, the student is lining up numbers incorrectly following the multiplication step. The teacher now knows that the entry-level behavior for instruction with this student is the step of placing the multiplied number in the correct position prior to the subtraction step.

Task analyses may be conducted for any curricular area. Performing a task analysis prior to teaching a skill and analyzing student errors during instruction will provide the teacher with information necessary for sound educational decision making.

Criterion-Referenced Assessment

In addition to deciding which work samples to analyze for errors or which items to include on a teacher-made test, the teacher must decide the level of acceptable performance. In other words, how will the teacher determine that a student has mastered an objective? A test that has a preset level for mastery is called a criterion-referenced test. A criterion-referenced test compares a student's performance to a preset criterion rather than to the performance of other students.

The criterion is often an objective that states that a student can perform a particular task to a specified level. (See Chapter 7 for a discussion of writing educational objectives.) For example, an objective for Joey might state: Given a probe sheet of two-digit minus two-digit numbers without regrouping, Joey will write the correct answers at a rate of 50 digits per minute with three or fewer errors. In order to meet the specified criterion, Joey must correctly write answers to the subtraction problems on the probe at the given rate and accuracy level.

Criterion-referenced assessments are informal measurements that are either teacher-made or commercially available. One commercially prepared criterion-referenced test often used by teachers is the Brigance (Brigance, 1977, 1978, 1981). The Brigance, available through Curriculum Associates, assesses numer-

Some students still struggle in the classroom despite the teacher's best efforts to modify instruction. For these students, the multidisciplinary team collects both formal and informal assessment data to determine the child's eligibility for special education.

ous skills and subskills from the early childhood level through the secondary grades. The objectives wtih criterion levels for mastery provided by the Brigance are helpful to teachers when evaluating student performance toward educational goals on individualized education programs (IEPs).

Observational Recording Procedures

Another common method used for informal assessment of both academic and behavioral performance is direct observation. For example, the teacher may ask a student to solve a mathematical calculation on the chalkboard or on paper and listen as the student explains the steps. The teacher may also listen to a student read from a basal reader or observe a student as he or she presents an oral book report. Observational data may include, for example, the number of times Susan asks for help during a 30-minute period, the length of time Joey remains seated during social studies, or the percentage of time that Travis is on task during mathematics lessons. In order to gain an accurate picture of academic and behavioral performance through direct observation, the teacher may use anecdotal records, event recording, duration recording, or time-sampling procedures.

Anecdotal recording. An anecdotal record is a written description of a student's behavior in a particular setting or instructional time period (Alberto & Troutman, 1990). When completing an anecdotal record, the teacher may wish to use a format such as that shown in Figure 6.4. Using this form, the teacher writes the time of the observation; the antecedents, or events that occurred before the child's behavior; the observed behavior of the child; and any consequences following the child's behavior. The teacher must be careful to record only what the child and others actually say or do rather than interpret motivations or feelings.

Figure 6.4   A Sample Anecdotal Recording Form

Reprinted with permission of Merrill, an imprint of Macmillan Publishing Company, from Applied Behavior Analysis for Teachers, *Third Edition, by Paul A. Alberto and Anne C. Troutman. Copyright © 1990 by Macmillan Publishing Company.*

Time	Antecedent	Behavior	Consequence
9:30	Ms. Kirk says Group 1 may line up.	Joey walks to the line.	Ms. Kirk says Nice job for Group 1. Now Group 3 line up.
	Celie runs to line.	Joey says You ran. You can't run to line up	Celie talks to her friend
9:35	Kevin drops a ball and runs to get it.	Joey kicks ball away from Kevin.	Ms. Kirk says Go get the ball Joey.

Event recording.   Event recording, sometimes called frequency counting, is a simple method involving direct observation of student behavior. In event recording, the teacher simply tallies the number of times a particular behavior occurs over a specific period of time. This method is useful for behaviors that are discrete; that is, those behaviors having a distinct beginning and ending.

In order to observe changes in behavior over time, the teacher may display the data on a chart or graph. If the amount of time during an observational session stays constant, the teacher can use the actural number of behaviors counted. If however, the observational time varies from session to session, the teacher must convert frequency to rate (i.e., the number of times the behavior occurred divided by the amount of time observed gives the teacher the number of behaviors per unit of time) before graphing or charting the data.

As an example of event recording, Mr. Mathis might be concerned that Leon talks out inappropriately in his afternoon classes. He asks Mr. Abel to collect data on Leon's "talk outs" over a period of three days. The event recording might look like this:

Student name: *Leon*		Week of: *October 10-14*
Day	**Time**	**Number of talk outs**
Tuesday	12:30–1:30	⅃⅃⅂⅂ ⅃⅃⅂⅂
Wednesday	1:30–2:30	⅃⅃⅂⅂ ⅃⅃⅂⅂ //
Thursday	2:30–3:30	⅃⅃⅂⅂ ⅃⅃⅂⅂ ⅃⅃⅂⅂

The data gathered may suggest to Mr. Abel that Leon becomes more talkative in the late afternoon. Or perhaps he becomes more talkative as the week progresses. More data could be gathered to determine the validity of each hypothesis. This information would be particularly helpful to Mr. Abel when planning a behavior-management strategy for Mr. Mathis and Leon's other teachers.

Duration recording.   Duration recording is used to determine the length of time that a behavior lasts. For example, Ms. Lopez might record the amount of time Joey remains in his seat during reading or the length of time Celie sucks her thumb during observation periods. If Ms. Lopez records the number of seconds or minutes for each occurrence of the observed behavior separately, she will also know the number of times the behavior occurred. Again, if the length of the observation periods remains constant, Ms. Lopez may simply record the total amount of time for the behavior (e.g., 35 minutes in seat for Joey). If the observation times vary, however, Ms. Lopez must convert her data to a percentage of time before graphing (e.g., Celie spent 27% of the time observed sucking her thumb). The percentage would be the number of minutes engaged in thumb sucking divided by the total number of minutes in the observation period times 100.

Time sampling.   Time-sampling procedures enable the teacher to estimate the frequency and duration of behaviors without having to time or count every occurrence. To use momentary time sampling, the teacher divides a period of time into equal intervals. For example, Ms. Kirk divides the language arts period of one hour into twenty 3-minute intervals. She sets a small kitchen timer or the "beeper" on her watch to sound after 3 minutes, and at the sound, she looks to see if Travis is or is not on task at that exact moment. (On task for Ms. Kirk means that Travis is looking at his language arts book, writing on his paper, or looking at her when she is speaking.) If Travis is on task at that moment, Ms. Kirk places a + mark next to the observed interval on her observation sheet. If Travis is not on task, she places a − mark on her form (see Figure 6.5). At the end of the observation period, Ms. Kirk computes the percentage of time that Travis was on task by dividing the number of observed occurrences (the plus intervals) by the total number of intervals observed and multiplying by 100. (In this case, the total was only 17 intervals because Travis was excused to use the restroom for a few minutes.)

Figure 6.5   Time Sampling Data for Travis' On-Task Behavior

Student: TRAVIS JOHNSON   Date: 10/21
Time: 9:30 − 10:30AM (LANG. ARTS) Interval length: 3 MINUTES
Behavior observed: ON TASK − WRITING, READING, LA BOOK,
                    LOOKING AT TEACHER, SPEAKING WHEN
                    RECOGNIZED BY TEACHER

Interval number	+	−
1	+	
2	+	
3	+	
4	—	
5	—	
6	—	
7		−
8		−
9	+	
10	+	
11	+	
12	+	
13	+	
14	+	
15		−
16		−
17	+	
18	+	
19		−
20		−

Number of intervals observed: 17
Number of intervals on task: 11
Percent of intervals on task: 65%

Checklists and Rating Scales

Additional measures of behavior and academic performance include checklists and teacher rating scales. Checklists are sequential lists of skills that the teacher completes for a particular student. The checklist for reading, for example, may be taken from the scope and sequence chart included in the teacher's guide accompanying the basal reading series. Other examples of checklists include a sequential list of fine-motor skills necessary prior to beginning instruction in manuscript writing or a sequence of mathematics skills necessary for a specific vocational education program such as "auto mechanics." A portion of a mathematics checklist, listing the skills for multiplication and division, is presented in Table 6.1.

Rating scales are instruments by which the teacher judges a student's performance or behavior. The rating is often completed using a Likert scale measure, such as a rating of 1–5 on a social skills list, with a 1 indicating that the student has mastered the skill in the teacher's estimation, and a 5 indicating that the student has not mastered the skill. Thus, students receiving high scores on

Table 6.1   A Sample Checklist of Arithmetic Skills

Skill area	Above average 0	Average 1	Below average 2
Multiplication			
21. Tables 1–5			
22. Tables 6–10			
23. One-place multiplication			
24. Two-place multiplication			
25. Three-or-more-place multiplication			
26. Use of zero as a place-holder			
27. Multiplying by 10, 100, 1,000			
28. Decimals			
Division			
29. Tables 1–5			
30. Tables 6–10			
31. Short division			
32. Long division/subtractive method			
33. Long division/regular notation			
34. Use of zero as a place-holder			
35. Dividing by 10, 100, 1,000			
36. Decimals			
37. Conversion of fractions to decimals			

this instrument would be in need of social skills training. Those with lower scores would need relatively less training.

Commercially prepared rating scales are available to measure specific behavioral or social-emotional skills. For example, the Social Skills Rating System (Gresham & Elliott, 1990) available from American Guidance Service contains rating scales for parents and teachers of children aged 3 through 18. The Walker Social Skills Curriculum available from Pro-Ed (See Chapter 14) also includes a simple teacher rating scale (Walker, McConnell, Holmes, Todis, Walker, & Golden, 1983). Other instruments are in the developmental stages and show promising ability to discriminate between students who do and do not demonstrate acceptable academic performance or who are lacking social competencies. These include the Academic Performance Scale (DuPaul, Rapport, & Perriello, 1991) and the Teacher–Child Rating Scale (Hightower, Work, Cowen, Lotyczewski, Spinell, Guare, & Rohrbeck, 1986). Sample questions from the Academic Performance Rating Scale are shown in Table 6.2, pp. 120–21.

A Summary of Informal Assessment

Many forms of informal assessment provide valuable information on which to base instructional decisions. These include curriculum-based assessment, criterion-referenced testing, observational recording, and checklists and rating scales. Although some authorities caution teachers to use informal assessment techniques carefully (for example, Bennett, 1982), others argue that these procedures offer viable alternatives to formal, standardized testing (for example, Deno, 1985; Marston & Magnusson, 1985; Shinn, Tindal, & Stein, 1988).

✎ Referral, Screening, and Eligibility

From time to time, the classroom teacher may have students who continue to exhibit academic or behavioral problems despite the teacher's best efforts. By using curriculum-based assessment, criterion-referenced assessment, observation, and rating scales, the teacher determines that the student is not making progress at an acceptable rate. Informally, the teacher may ask another professional for advice. Regular classroom teachers, special education teachers, guidance counselors, principals, or school psychologists may be able to suggest intervention strategies that can be implemented in the classroom. In some cases, the teacher may be able to solve the problem without a referral for an evaluation to determine eligibility for special education.

Prereferral or Child Study

Recall from Chapter 3 that professionals in some school systems work together in structured problem-solving teams. Often, these professionals are able to help one another formulate instructional or behavioral interventions that enable students to make progress in the regular classroom. These interventions are implemented before a child is ever referred by the regular classroom teacher for formal evaluation to determine if he or she is eligible for special education services. According to Graden, Casey, and Bonstrom (1985), in schools using such prereferral intervention strategies the number of students who are referred, tested, and subsequently placed in special education programs decreases. Thus, these interventions may prevent needless assessment and placement in special education by solving students' learning or behavioral problems within their regular classrooms.

Prereferral intervention strategies suggested by a teacher assistance team or student support team may include a change in the curriculum for a particular student for whom the pace may be too rapid. An objective observer might also visit the classroom to determine whether such environmental factors as glare on the chalkboard or distracting seating arrangements may be creating difficulty for a student who is not making progress. In addition, changes in the teacher's instructional strategies may make the difference for a student with learning problems. Each activity conducted by the team gives team members additional information about the student and his or her responses to chosen interventions.

Referral and Screening

The teacher who has documented the failure of a substantial number of intervention efforts made on behalf of a struggling student may soon conclude that additional help is needed. The teacher, then, makes a referral for assessment by the school or school system's child-study or screening team. Although the exact procedures may vary for each state and/or school district, this referral usually includes any supporting documentation gathered by the teacher through such informal assessments as student work samples, time-sampling data, or skills checklists. Documentation should also include a description of the modifications attempted with the student, as well as data regarding the student's response to each intervention.

A referral by the classroom teacher usually begins the process of screening to determine whether or not a child should be evaluated for possible placement in special education. Because special education resources are limited, the procedures used to determine eligibility for special education programs are rigorous. The teacher's referral and supporting documentation is carefully reviewed by the screening team, which may include a regular educator, a special educator, the school principal, guidance counselors, the school psychologist, or a speech-language therapist. The task of this team is to determine whether additional interventions might be recommended to support the student in the regular classroom or whether the student requires formal evaluation.

Formal Psychoeducational Assessment

Upon examining the student's records and the teacher's referral, the screening team may submit a request for evaluation by the school or school system's multidisciplinary team. Again, the exact procedures and membership on the team may vary by state or school division; however, a multidisciplinary team is required by Public Law 94-142 for comprehensive evaluation of a student for special education services. The team may include a school administrator, a school psychologist, an educational diagnostician, a special education teacher, a school social worker or "visiting teacher," an occupational or physical thera-

Table 6.2   Academic Performance Rating Scale

ACADEMIC PERFORMANCE RATING SCALE

Student _____

Grade _____   Date _____

Age _____   Teacher _____

For each of the below items, please estimate the above student's performance over the **PAST WEEK.** For each item, please circle **one** choice only.

1. Estimate the percentage of written **math** work *completed* (regardless of accuracy) relative to classmates.	0–49% 1	50–69% 2	70–79% 3	80–89% 4	90–100% 5
2. Estimate the percentage of written **language arts** work *completed* (regardless of accuracy) relative to classmates.	0–49% 1	50–69% 2	70–79% 3	80–89% 4	90–100% 5
3. Estimate the *accuracy* of completed written **math** work (i.e., percent correct of work done).	0–64% 1	65–69% 2	70–79% 3	80–89% 4	90–100% 5

	1	2	3	4	5
4. Estimate the *accuracy* of completed written **language arts** work (i.e., percent correct of work done).	0–64%	65–69%	70–79%	80–89%	90–100%
5. How consistent has the quality of this child's academic work been over the past week?	Consistently Poor	More Poor than Successful	Variable	More Successful than Poor	Consistently Successful
6. How frequently does the student accurately follow teacher instructions and/or class discussion during *large-group* (e.g., whole class) instruction?	Never	Rarely	Sometimes	Often	Very often

From "Teacher Ratings of Academic Skills: The Development of the Academic Performance Rating Scale" by G. J. DuPaul, M. D. Rapport, and L. M. Perriello, 1991, School Psychology Review, 20(2), p. 299. Copyright 1991 by National Association of School Psychologists. Reprinted by permisison of the publisher.

pist, a school nurse, or a speech-language therapist. Team members determine what type of assessment is appropriate, and once parental permission for testing has been secured, the comprehensive evaluation is conducted.

The types of tests used by the multidisciplinary team may differ from those used by the classroom teacher. Many of the tests used by the team are called *norm-referenced tests*. Such tests have been administered to a large sample population to determine academic or intellectual performance of the typical student at a certain grade level. The score of the individual being tested is compared to the mean or average score of the sample group. Norm-referenced achievement testing, for example, enables the team to determine if a fourth-grade student who is having difficulty reading is significantly behind his or her peers. If norm-referenced tests indicate that the student is significantly behind peers, further diagnostic tests may be given to determine the specific reading skills that are presenting difficulty for the student. Examples of norm-referenced tests are given in Table 6.3.

Although norm-referenced tests may indicate whether a student's performance is discrepant from that of his or her peers, these tests have limitations (Marston & Magnusson, 1988). Salvia and Hughes (1990) report that the small number of items included in norm-referenced tests of achievement often do not match what the student is taught in the specific curriculum. Moreover, the limited number of items do not allow for the detection of small improvements over time (Good & Salvia, 1988). Norm-referenced tests of intelligence or ability are also criticized for cultural bias (Chinn & Hughes, 1987; Reschly, 1987) and for bias against the attentional problems and deficient strategic behaviors often exhibited by students with mild disabilities (Telzrow, 1988). In addition, Salvia and Ysseldyke (1988) state that students with mild disabilities often are not included in significant numbers in the population samples used in creating many norm-referenced tests.

Despite their limitations, norm-referenced tests are frequently used to determine whether a student differs significantly from his or her peers. In addition to tests of achievement, the student who has been referred for academic difficulties may be administered a measure of intellectual or cognitive ability by the school psychologist. A member of the multidisciplinary team may also conduct a classroom observation and interviews with the child's teachers and parents. Behavior rating scales, social-skills checklists or rating scales, and direct observation of behavior in various settings may be completed for students presenting behavioral or social-emotional difficulties, and a medical evaluation may help to determine whether a student has health problems that interfere with learning or behavior. The purpose for gathering such extensive information is, of course, to make the best possible decision regarding whether or not a child requires special education services.

Eligibility

When members of the multidisciplinary team have completed their assessment, a meeting is scheduled for the parents and team members. At this meeting, the team members and parents discuss test results and other information gathered from the comprehensive evaluation. It is at this point that parents and team

---

Table 6.3   Examples of Norm-Referenced Tests

Tests of Intelligence and Cognitive Ability

Wechsler Intelligence Scale for Children, Third Edition (Wechsler, 1991). This test is a measure of general intellectual ability. The test provides IQ scores and Indexes. Psychological Corporation.
Woodcock-Johnson Tests of Cognitive Ability—Revised (Woodcock & Johnson, 1989b). This is an individual measure of general intellectual ability. DLM Teaching Resources.

Tests of Achievement

Kaufman Test of Educational Achievement, Comprehensive and Brief Forms (Kaufman & Kaufman, 1985). These forms measure general academic achievement in grades 1–12. The brief form is a screening instrument. American Guidance Service.
Woodcock-Johnson Tests of Achievement—Revised (Woodcock & Johnson, 1989a). This is an individual measure of general academic achievement. DLM Teaching Resources.

Diagnostic Tests

Key Math—Revised (Connolly, 1988). This is a diagnostic math-assessment instrument that provides normative information about specific skills necessary for math achievement in grades K–6. American Guidance Service.
Test of Adolescent Language—2 (Hammill, Brown, Larsen, & Wiederhold, 1987). This instrument assesses spoken and written language skills for children in grades 6–12. Pro-ED.
Test of Language Development 2: Primary (Newcomer & Hammill, 1988). This instrument assesses understanding and use of spoken language in children aged 4–8. Pro-ED.
Test of Language Development 2: Intermediate (Hammill & Newcomer, 1988). This instrument assesses understanding and use of spoken language and grammar for children aged 8–12. Pro-ED.
Woodcock Reading Mastery Tests—Revised (Woodcock, 1987). This battery of tests assesses reading skills from initial letter identification to reading comprehension for individuals from kindergarten to adulthood. American Guidance Service.

Behavior Rating Scales

AAMR Adaptive Behavior Scale—School Edition (Nihira, Foster, Shellhaas, & Leland, 1981). This scale assesses social and daily living skills of children aged 3–16. American Association on Mental Retardation.
Behavior Rating Profile (Brown & Hammill, 1983). This instrument includes teacher, parent, and student rating scales for behavior of students in grades 1–12 at home, in school, and with peers. Pro-Ed.
Vineland Adaptive Behavior Scales (Sparrow, Balla, & Cichetti, 1984). These scales assess communication, daily living, motor, and socialization skills for individuals from birth through adulthood. American Guidance Service.

---

members must decide if the student is eligible for special education services according to the specific criteria for eligibility in use by the particular state and school system. If it is determined that the student is not eligible for special education services, the team will, it is hoped, make additional recommendations for the teacher to alleviate the child's learning or behavioral difficulty. If, however, the student is determined eligible for special education, the parents, the child's regular and/or special education teacher, members of the multidisciplinary team, and the student, when appropriate, will meet to negotiate an IEP detailing the individual educational program to be provided the child. (See Chapter 7 for a discussion of the IEP. See also Appendix A for a comprehensive evaluation for Travis and for other sample IEPs.)

According to Public Law 94-142, parents have a legal right to be informed, in a language and manner they can understand, of the types of tests to be given their child and the purpose for each test. Parents must give their consent, in writing, before the tests may be administered, and they have the right to be informed fully of the results of each of the tests. Parents must understand that their input is necessary and valued. Research indicates that parents tend to be passive during the eligibility and IEP process (Barnett, Zins, & Wise, 1984; Vaughn, Bos, Harrell, & Lasky, 1988), and that some low-income parents may not be fully informed or understand the process of eligibility concerning their children (Brantlinger, 1987). The teacher is encouraged to review the ideas suggested in Chapter 4 for increasing communication with parents.

✎ Summary

Teachers use many forms of informal assessment on a daily basis. Curriculum-based measurement, criterion-referenced tests, observations, checklists, and rating scales all may be used to help teachers evaluate student progress. By carefully analyzing the data obtained by these means, teachers can make better instructional decisions.

Teachers occasionally have students who do not make progress at the expected level or rate. These students may require changes in the curriculum or classroom environment. The teacher may consult a teacher assistance team or student support team for intervention strategies to help such children succeed in the regular classroom. Careful implementation and documentation of these intervention strategies, however, may not be enough support for some students. For these youngsters, the teacher may make a formal referral to a multidisciplinary team to screen and perhaps evaluate the child to determine his or her eligibility for special education services. Norm-referenced tests are formal, standardized measures used by the multidisciplinary team to determine whether a child's abilities are sufficiently discrepant from those of his or her peers that special education services are warranted.

✎ Application Exercises

1. Review a teacher's guide to a reading or mathematics series at a chosen grade level. Does the guide include a scope and sequence chart? Does the guide contain information that could be used to design a

criterion-referenced test? Locate and describe the types of tests included with the curricular materials.

2. Examine a teacher's guide for a reading, language arts, mathematics, science, or social studies series. Choose a skill for a given grade level. Perform a task analysis for your chosen skill.

3. Examine the psychoeducational evaluation for Travis shown in Appendix A. What additional information will the teacher need for instructional planning? If you found out that Travis would be entering your classroom next week, what informal assessments might you give him?

4. Visit a school or school system and ask to see information about parents' rights in special education. Was the information readily available? Describe the information. Was it easy to read and understand?

5. Kevin makes the following mistakes on his arithmetic paper:

$$\begin{array}{cccc} 22 & 73 & 24 & 45 \\ \underline{\times 7} & \underline{\times 4} & \underline{\times 4} & \underline{\times 2} \\ 214 & 712 & 216 & 410 \end{array}$$

Explain Kevin's error. List the preskills and perform a task analysis for this multiplication skill. Where will you begin instruction with Kevin in order to correct his error?

6. Interview a special education teacher and a regular classroom teacher at a chosen grade level. What forms of assessment do these teachers routinely use? How do these teachers use the information they gather through assessment? Include both informal and formal assessment in your discussion.

Planning for Successful Instruction

Chapter 7

Focus

As you read, think about the following questions:

How do teachers plan for both group and individual activities?

What are the elements of well-written educational objectives?

How do student stages of learning influence the teacher's planning?

What information is included on a student's individualized education program (IEP)?

✎ A smoothly running classroom, where students are actively engaged in appropriate academic tasks to achieve preset objectives, is the goal of the effective teacher. However, students do not successfully reach their academic potential by accident! A carefully planned, finely tuned, active classroom in which students achieve success is the result of considerable time and effort on the part of the teacher. Let's observe Joey as he works in Ms. Kirk's fourth-grade classroom and then goes to Ms. Lopez's resource room for his reading instruction.

Joey returns to his seat with the encyclopedia he has selected from the bookshelf in Ms. Kirk's room. He thumbs through the pages and can't quite remember what he was to do. He knows that Ms. Kirk color-codes her subjects: the green folder is for social studies, blue is for health, and red is for science. He takes the red folder out and turns to the weekly assignment page. Today is Wednesday and on his assignment page are the words: WEDNESDAY: Group I. Look up the geologic time scale. Write down the life forms of the Paleozoic era. Have a list of the life forms ready to report to the members of your group tomorrow.

Joey looks up the geologic time scale and begins to write down the life forms. He completes his assignment and puts the paper inside the pocket of his red folder. Tomorrow, he will meet with his group and they will exchange information about the eras of the geologic time scale. Joey knows that the groups will begin giving their reports to the class on Monday. He plans to help the group decide how to present the material when they meet on Friday. He wants to suggest drawing some pictures of the different life forms. Because he is interested in geology, Joey has some books and pictures at home. He will offer to bring in some pictures on Monday if his group thinks it's a good idea.

Ms. Kirk walks by Joey and smiles as she reads his answers. She moves around the room to survey students in the other groups. Other students are writing down information for their science reports. Group II students are using a special-materials science kit on the back table. Joey's group used the kit on Tuesday. Group III students are answering questions from their science textbook. Group I completed that task on Monday. By Friday, all three groups will be ready to plan their presentations.

Ms. Kirk informs the students of the time, and Joey begins putting his folders away. He returns the encyclopedia to the shelf. Then, he picks up a small piece of paper on the floor and begins to exit the room saying, "Bye, Ms. Kirk." Ms. Kirk responds, "Bye, Joey. Thanks for cleaning up. See you later."

Joey walks down the hall to Ms. Lopez's room. He enters saying, "Hi, Ms. Lopez." Ms. Lopez smiles and replies, "Hi Joey. I like that shirt. Is it new?" Joey answers, "Yeah, I got it for my birthday. Are we starting the new story today?" Ms. Lopez says, "Yes, we are! Look on your assignment sheet for the page number."

Joey takes his folder from the mailbox by the door. Inside, he sees the assignment for the day: "Winter Surprise, page 67." Joey takes the card out of the pocket in his folder. Ms. Lopez has written the new vocabulary words for the story on one side of the card, as well as a short outline of the story. Joey looks at the words, listens to them as Ms. Lopez pronounces them on a cassette tape she has placed in his folder, and tries to pronounce them silently. He skims the outline and then turns the card over to read his study strategy:

1. Read your new words. (Remember to review the words on the cassette tape if you have trouble.)
2. Read the story silently.
3. Reread the first sentence of each paragraph.
4. Write down the main events of the story.
5. Read the story aloud with your partner.
6. Answer the story questions. Check your answers.
7. Group discussion.

Joey places his folder on his desk and walks to the bookcase. He finds his reading book and returns to his seat. He quietly pronounces each of his new words. Then, he turns to his story and reads silently.

Ms. Lopez scans the room and notices that Joey is reading. She sits down at the group table with five students. Three other students are reading stories silently. Ms. Lopez directs the spelling instruction for the five students who are on the same spelling unit. As the spelling instruction continues, she notices Joey quietly walking to the box of answer keys to check his comprehension questions. He proudly marches to the wall chart and colors in a box by his name with a blue marker. Blue means that he has answered the questions with 100% accuracy. Joey then moves to the reading-partner table with Travis. They take turns reading the new story aloud.

Ms. Kirk organizes her classroom by using color codes, small groups, and weekly assignment sheets. Ms. Lopez employs small groups, partners, individual seatwork, individual folders, advanced organizers, study strategies, academic self-monitoring, and individual daily assignment sheets. Both teachers know the exact level of each student in their classes and assign work that will help the students achieve preset objectives.

Both teachers also use a variety of instructional methods and curricular materials to meet the needs of individual students. Each student in Ms. Lopez's class has an individual assignment sheet that consists of assignments designed to meet objectives written on his or her individualized education program (IEP). Whenever possible, Ms. Lopez groups students with similar needs for direct instruction. Ms. Kirk's students are working to meet the mastery levels set forth in the state curriculum guidelines for science in the fourth grade.

How do teachers plan appropriate activities to engage their students in learning? In this chapter, we will examine how teachers go about the tasks of planning and writing educational objectives. We will also examine how student stages of learning influence the teacher's planning. Finally, we will discuss the information to be included on the student's IEP, an essential component of the planning process for youngsters in special education programs.

✎ How Teachers Plan

Planning instruction for a classroom of students can be a complex and time-consuming task. Planning can also be an interesting and exciting challenge that will result in successful teaching and maximum learning. Good planning enables the teacher to use curricular materials and teaching methods effectively to help students reach educational goals.

Several factors influence teachers as they plan. According to Brown (1988), for example, plans made by middle school teachers are influenced by textbook content, applicability of curricular materials used in the school district, students' interests and abilities, availability of materials, knowledge of what worked in previous years, and time allocated to the class or subject. The middle school teachers in Brown's study felt that they were often governed by school policies, such as curriculum guides and school schedules.

Fuchs, Fuchs, and Bishop (1992) maintain that general and special educators may view the planning process somewhat differently. They suggest, for example, that general educators are more likely than special educators to focus on instructional activities as they plan. Special educators, on the other hand, focus more on specific procedures, such as direct instruction or metacognitive strategies. In addition, both general and special educators who use curriculum-based assessment may be more likely to use data to monitor student performance and adjust instruction than to yield to curricular pressures.

Similarly, Schumm and Vaughn (1992) report that mainstreamed teachers of students with mild disabilities view budget constraints, accountability, lack of equipment and materials, substandard physical environment of the classroom or school, large class size, and limited instructional time as barriers to planning. Although these teachers expressed willingness to adapt assignments or tests during instruction (a process called *interactive planning*), they were less likely to preplan these adaptations or to set new objectives for learning based on student performance (*postplanning*). Nevertheless, preplanning, postplanning, and interactive planning are essential responsibilities of teachers at all grade levels.

Backward Planning

Teachers approach planning in different ways. Long-range goals are a common starting place for teachers to begin planning for instruction (D.S. Brown, 1988; Slavin, 1991a). The process of beginning with long-range plans and moving to monthly, weekly, and daily plans is called the *backward planning process* (Slavin, 1991a). This process enables the teacher to keep the final outcome or long-term goal in mind as the students move through the daily curriculum. The teacher begins by examining curriculum scope and sequence charts, state curriculum guidelines, or current levels of performance and annual IEP goals for students who receive special education services. Having determined the goal for instruction, the teacher then breaks down the curriculum into smaller units for learning. Once this general blueprint has been designed, the teacher may begin planning for daily instruction.

Ms. Kirk, for example, reviews the curriculum at the beginning of the school year and determines that there are twelve topical chapters to cover in the science curriculum. She decides to cover each chapter in a 3-week period. This format allows her to use the textbook, assign group projects and experiments, assign introductory library research reports, and have weekly and unit tests.

Ms. Kirk varies the projects by topics and uses library visits to teach library skills within the context of her science topics. She also incorporates the unit topics into independent and class reading activities and into classroom mathematics exercises. Throughout the year, Ms. Kirk includes reading and discussion of each chapter in the science textbook, vocabulary exercises, comprehension questions, homework assignments, group projects, and peer review for tests. In addition, three times during the school year, Ms. Kirk arranges to take the class on field trips to the local science museum, to the aquarium, and to a geological dig being conducted by a local university.

Ms. Kirk follows essentially the same format for each chapter in the science textbook, but she creatively varies teaching methods and group-project ideas. She manages to keep her instruction on target because she has carefully planned the year by units, weeks, and days. She has organized her classroom so that students know what to expect and can independently move from one assignment to the next. This allows her the freedom to work with the whole class, with small groups, or with individual students as needed.

Ms. Lopez takes the approach of basing planning on the IEPs developed for each of her students. On each IEP, the student's current level of performance is specified for every area in which the student is having difficulty. Based on the child's current level of performance, Ms. Lopez and the other members of the student's IEP team plan annual goals. These annual goals are simply the "best estimate" of what a student with mild disabilities might accomplish by the end of the school year, given the special education services provided. For example, if assessment data indicate that Travis does not know the multiplication facts, then a reasonable goal for Travis for the current school year might be: Travis will write the product for multiplication facts through the nines. Notice that this goal states an observable student behavior ("write" the product) as an outcome of instruction. To enable Travis to accomplish this goal, Ms. Lopez breaks down the long-term goal into specific short-term objectives which she then uses to plan and monitor her daily instruction.

Writing Educational Objectives

Successful teachers prepare and plan for each day. Daily instruction is most effective when educational objectives are written for each class lesson or for an individual student when he or she is receiving special education services. Objectives help the teacher to articulate the purpose for instruction, the ways in which instruction will take place, and the criteria by which to judge when students have successfully mastered the material.

One of the most frequently used models for writing educational objectives, shown in Table 7.1, is Bloom's taxonomy (Bloom, Englehart, Furst, Hill, & Krathwohl, 1956). This system attempts to categorize objectives across cognitive, affective, and psychomotor domains of learning. According to Slavin (1991a), Blooms' taxonomy is not meant to imply a sequence from simple to more complex behavior, but rather is meant to remind teachers to use a variety of objectives from each of the three domains and on differing levels. The behavioral matrix shown in Table 7.2 provides examples of objectives at different levels for the cognitive domain.

Table 7.1   Bloom's Taxonomy: Sample Objectives for Each Level Across Three Domains

Level	Domain		
	Cognitive	*Affective*	*Psychomotor*
1. Knowledge—Recalling facts	Identify the state capitols of the states in the region.	Choose the most appealing architecture for a capitol building.	Construct a model of a capitol building.
2. Comprehension—Emphasizing meaning	Answer chapter questions about the history of each capitol city.	Describe an interesting tourist area he or she would like to visit.	Draw a city map of a specific capitol city.
3. Application—Using rules and generalizing	Write a set of rules for the class similar to those of the city.	Describe the advantages of the city rule that he or she feels is the most important.	Construct a mock town meeting to debate and vote on the city rules.
4. Analysis—Breaking information into parts	Identify the parts of city government.	Describe the qualities of an effective city leader.	Draw a chart to illustrate positions in the city government.
5. Synthesis—Putting elements together into a whole	Compile a list of state and city rules affecting the city school.	Create a brochure to inform new residents of favorite local attractions.	Make a model of the city to depict land forms and tourist areas.
6. Evaluation—Judging against a criterion	Compare and contrast the rules in the city with those of another city in the state of approximately the same size.	Select the most important rule for a particular city in the state.	Write an editorial for a local paper to justify the importance of the rule chosen.

Teachers of students in special education programs often write behavioral objectives. That is, the short-term objective on the student's IEP is written to specify a measurable and observable student behavior (e.g., "write," "point to," "state") that will move the student toward an annual goal. The objective also clearly delineates the conditions under which the student is expected to perform (e.g., the rate of presentation, the quantity or level of the material) and the criterion by which mastery of the objective will be judged (e.g., a percentage correct, a time duration). For example, to help Travis accomplish his year-end goal of being able to write the products for the multiplication facts through the

Table 7.2   Sample Objectives from a Behavioral Matrix for the Cognitive Domain

Level of Objective	Example I	Example II
	Main Idea of a Story	*Colonization of Africa*
1. Knowledge	Define "main idea."	Make a time line to illustrate how Africa was split into colonies.
2. Comprehension	Identify the main idea of a story.	Interpret a map of Africa showing its colonization by European nations.
3. Application	Identify the main idea of a newspaper article.	Locate articles that illustrate the influence of colonization in Africa today.
4. Analysis	Give ways to find the main idea in stories.	Contrast the goals and methods used by different European nations in colonizing Africa.
5. Synthesis	Write a new story based on the main idea of a story you've read.	Write an essay on the European colonization of Africa from the perspective of a Bantu chief.
6. Evaluation	Judge the author's effectiveness in presenting the main idea of a story.	Debate the positive versus negative impact of colonization on African countries today.

From Robert E. Salvin, Educational Psychology, *Third Edition. Copyright © 1991. Reprinted with the permission of Allyn & Bacon.*

nines, Ms. Lopez might write the following short-term objective: Given the multiplication facts from the ones through the fives presented in random order on a probe sheet, Travis will write the products with 100% accuracy within 2 minutes. The phrase "Given . . . on a probe sheet," specifies the conditions under which Travis will perform. The measurable student behavior is "write," and the criterion for mastery is "with 100% accuracy within two minutes." Ms. Lopez uses this short-term objective to guide her lesson planning in mathematics for Travis.

Wolery et al. (1988) offer several excellent suggestions for the teacher when writing behavioral objectives for students, including the following:

1. Keep the objective as brief as possible, omitting unnecessary words such as "will be able to." (Thus, "Travis will write . . ." rather than "Travis will be able to write . . .").

2. Be sure to include the exact conditions under which the student will perform the targeted student behavior, and the criteria for determining student mastery.

3. Phrase the objective in positive terms. State what the student will do rather than what he or she will not do.

4. State the desired learning outcomes in observable and measurable terms. Refrain from using such terms as *understands, knows,* or *comprehends;* use instead such terms as *reads orally, prints,* or *sorts.*

5. Choose objectives for students that are functional; that is, they should have immediate usefulness or lead students to more advanced skills. They should also be realistic—neither too hard nor too easy for the student.

6. Write the objectives to reflect not only the acquisition of knowledge or skills but also to demonstrate the ability to apply the skill to solve new problems or to use it in the natural environment.

Effective teachers carefully consider the objectives for each daily lesson plan and vary the conditions, student behaviors, domains, and levels of learning to promote student achievement. As lessons are planned, the teacher also considers the current mastery level of the students. In some school systems, students will not advance to more difficult skills or new topics unless the teacher has determined that sufficient mastery has occurred. For example, if most of the students in Ms. Kirk's class fail a unit test in math or achieve a mastery level below that specified in the preset objective, it is important that Ms. Kirk revise her plans to reteach the troublesome skill before progressing to the next instructional unit. For children in special education programs, mastery of objectives is essential before students progress to new skills or concepts. Special education teachers must document the progress of their students toward the goals and objectives specified on the IEP. Therefore, Ms. Lopez's planning is based on student performance data she gathers through ongoing assessment procedures, such as those described in Chapter 6.

Objectives are only one part of a daily lesson plan, but they are probably the most important element of the teacher's planning process. Daily lessons and activities flow from the chosen educational objectives, and the objectives are chosen based on student need and performance, in addition to curricular requirements for the specific grade level. A comprehensive lesson plan includes an objective, a lesson opening, a demonstration or presentation of new material, guided practice with the new skill or concept, independent practice, a lesson closing, and an evaluation to determine whether or not students have met the given objective. Each of these components of a lesson will be discussed in detail in Chapter 8. For now, however, the reader is reminded that without a carefully written educational objective, even the time spent pursuing the most exciting classroom activities may be time wasted.

Instructional Options and Grouping

Teachers may choose from a variety of instructional options when designing lesson plans for their students. The teacher may choose, for example, to modify the curriculum (See Chapter 13), to use specific teaching methods, to structure the classroom in a special way, or to give students organizational guides. As shown in Figure 7.1, teaching methods effective for students in special education programs include direct instruction with extensive guided practice (Lloyd, 1988; Rosenshine, 1986); modeling (Englert, 1984); and role playing (Rathjen, 1984). Classroom structure refers to how students are arranged for their instruc-

**Figure 7.1   Instructional Methods and Implications
for Learners with Mild Disabilities**

Method	Description	Implication for Learners
Direct instruction	Teacher actively involved with students. Demonstrates information and uses guided practice to check understanding.	Demands student attention. Uses learning time efficiently. May be used for rehearsal of facts and may promote automatic behavior. Provides opportunities to respond and receive feedback on accuracy.
Modeling	Teacher or peer demonstrates correct method or strategy to be used.	Improves learning when strategies or behaviors are clearly labeled and rehearsed or when peers receive rewards for their use.
Role playing	Teacher assigns meaningful and real-life roles to students to promote identification with others or problem solving.	Provides social-skills training, particularly when roles are clearly identified and relevant to student needs and when students are reinforced for problem solving.

tion. Students may, for example, receive instruction in large or small groups, through one-on-one instruction with the teacher or a paraprofessional, through peer tutoring, or in cooperative learning arrangements. Organizational guides help students understand the daily schedule, lessons, or activities. These may include advanced topical outlining of lessons on the chalkboard, projected on a screen, on sheets photocopied for individual use, on bulletin boards, or in work folders and self-monitoring guides.

In considering instructional options, teachers decide which will best help students achieve preset objectives. Ms. Kirk, for example, may choose to use small-group instruction for the reading groups in her classroom and large-group instruction for the presentation of new information in her health lessons. Classwide peer tutoring (Maheady, Sacca, & Harper, 1988) may be an appropriate instructional choice for Ms. Kirk's fourth-graders who are practicing newly learned social studies content. On the other hand, direct instruction may be Ms. Kirk's preferred method for introducing new social studies skills and concepts to her students. Instructional decisions are always made with objectives and student needs in mind.

A teacher may select a particular option for a specific reason, such as to use time most efficiently or to allow for incidental learning to occur. (Incidental learning is nontargeted learning as a result of interaction during a lesson.) For example, large-group instruction may be an efficient use of teacher time, but small-group instruction increases the acquisition of information through observational and incidental learning for students with mild learning problems (Keel & Gast, 1992; Stinson, Gast, Wolery, & Collins, 1991). To help a student catch up with peers, however, intensive one-on-one instruction is more effective than group instruction (Baker, Young & Martin, 1990). A teacher might use large-group instruction with students who are able to acquire information at approximately the same rate, one-on-one instruction with a student who is far behind the others, and small-group instruction with students who are likely to acquire additional information through observational or incidental learning. A 3-day rough outline of the science activities to be completed by groups in Ms. Kirk's class is presented in Figure 7.2.

Planning for effective instruction becomes easier as teachers gain experience. Slavin and Madden (1989) offer the following general planning tips, which beginning teachers may find particularly useful:

- Use the backward planning process. Look at the whole unit you will cover and break it down into manageable parts. Look at the student's

Figure 7.2   Ms. Kirk's Three-Day Outline for Science

Group I	*Group II*	*Group III*	*Individual*
2-24-93			
Review terms (teacher-directed)	Group Project (individual assignments)	Research with science kit at back table	Provide advanced organizers to Celie, Kevin, Joey, and Travis.
2-25-93			
Group project (individual assignments)	Research with science kit at back table	Review terms (teacher-directed)	Check contract for Joey.
2-26-93			
Research with science kit at back table.	Reviews terms (teacher-directed)	Group Project (individual assignments)	Check contract for Joey.
2-27-93			

Whole-Group Instruction: Explain presentations for next week. Check homework and collect homework notebooks.
Group Work: Work on presentations by groups for Monday.

current level of performance, annual goals, and short-term objectives. Break these down into small learning steps.

• Always monitor the progress of each student. Know whether students have mastered objectives and plan instruction accordingly.

• Plan more than you can cover in a period. It is much easier to move the activities or concepts to the next day than to be caught with 30 minutes of unprepared time!

• Have extra content-related activities ready. Always provide enrichment activities or additional games for drill and practice for students who finish work early. Never use this additional work as punishment for inappropriate behavior, however.

• Have a substitute folder ready with several days worth of lessons. The substitute folder might include the names of students listed on a seating chart, specific comments about individual student needs, information about classroom rules and routines, and detailed daily lesson plans. Substitute folders will, of course, require frequent updating.

• Arrange instructional groups for various subjects and use the groups in your planning process. Once students learn the classroom routines, alternate

Students may receive instruction in large or small groups depending on the lesson objectives. Here the teacher uses group instruction for students who are performing at approximately the same level and rate.

teacher-directed lessons with independent work, peer tutoring, or cooperative learning. Alternating the classroom structure will allow you to give direct instruction to one small group while other children are engaged in appropriate learning activities with one another or under the supervision of a paraprofessional.

• Alternate group membership. Place students in small, flexible groupings based on their performance and interests.

✎ Stages of Learning

In addition to grouping and curricular considerations, teachers keep learning stages in mind when planning lessons for their students. As students progress from lack of knowledge or limited knowledge of a skill or concept to knowing how to use the skill appropriately in differing contexts, they pass through four stages in their learning. These stages include acquisition, proficiency, maintenance, and generalization.

Teachers cannot assume that students will pass through these stages on their own! To help students acquire and become proficient with new skills requires careful planning. To ensure that students maintain their newly acquired skills over time and that they use these skills appropriately when necessary entails even more systematic and detailed planning. Objectives and instructional methods chosen by teachers must reflect student performance at each stage of learning and must change as students progress from one stage to the next.

The Acquisition Stage

The acquisition stage is the initial stage of learning when the student is thought to have only limited knowledge or no knowledge of a skill or concept. This stage is considered to be the entry level of learning. Students may, in fact, vary somewhat at this beginning stage of learning; some may have a little knowledge of the skill and others may have no knowledge at all. Students at this stage, however, are unable to perform the skill without teacher assistance.

In order to help students acquire a new skill or concept as rapidly as possible, teachers use direct instruction. That is, they tell students what is to be learned and why the skill or concept is important, clearly demonstrate the new skill or concept, and provide guided practice so that the students receive immediate feedback as to how well they are doing. At the acquisition stage, learning is highly teacher-directed and interactive, with the teacher posing questions and offering all students many opportunities to respond correctly.

Earlier in this chapter we mentioned Travis's long-term goal of being able to write the products for the multiplication facts through the nines. At this point, Travis may know some, but not all, of the multiplication facts. He is at the acquisition stage of learning. To help Travis acquire the multiplication facts through the nines, Ms. Lopez will determine which facts Travis does and does not know, and she will plan direct instructional lessons focused on the short-term objectives for multiplication written on Travis's IEP. Ms. Lopez will also use manipulatives to help Travis acquire the concept that multiplication is a fast way to add equal-sized groups (e.g., that $3 \times 4 = 12$ means three groups of four each).

The Proficiency Stage

Once students have acquired a new skill or concept, they then must become automatic or fluent in its use. Students in the proficiency stage of learning require drill and practice until they have demonstrated mastery of the new material. At the proficiency stage, instruction is still highly interactive, although students may now work with a peer tutor or paraprofessional to receive corrective feedback. Students at the proficiency stage of learning now "know" the new material, but they may make numerous errors or respond hesitantly rather than confidently.

For example, when Travis "understands" the concept of multiplication and has had practice using manipulatives to illustrate the multiplication facts through the fives, he is entering the proficiency stage of learning. Now, Travis must learn, for example, to respond automatically that $3 \times 4 = 12$. Recall the short-term objective Ms. Lopez wrote for Travis: Given the multiplication facts from the ones through the fives presented in random order on a probe sheet, Travis will write the products with 100% accuracy within 2 minutes. This objective is written for the proficiency stage of learning to ensure that Travis recalls the given multiplication facts accurately and rapidly. Travis will have daily supervised drill and practice activities and periodic probes to determine when he has mastered this objective.

The Maintenance Stage

As students become proficient with a new skill or concept, teachers must help them retain the material over time with little or no teacher assistance. At the maintenance stage, students receive periodic review or practice in the skill so that they will maintain accuracy and speed. Practice activities at the maintenance stage are more independent than those at the acquisition and proficiency stages of learning. Students at this stage may, for example, complete homework assignments and independent seatwork activities that are not immediately checked for accuracy by the teacher or the paraprofessional. Students also may play instructional games or use computer programs that have built-in self-checking features.

To ensure that Travis retains the multiplication facts through the fives even though he is now entering the proficiency stage with the "six" and "seven" facts, Ms. Lopez plans periodic review activities, games, and probes using the "one through five" facts. She also adds a maintenance criterion to Travis's objective: Given the multiplication facts through the fives presented in random order on a probe sheet, Travis will write the products with 100% accuracy within two minutes *on four consecutive probes conducted at 1-week intervals.* By adding the maintenance criterion, Ms. Lopez plans systematically to provide and check for Travis's retention of the targeted multiplication facts.

The Generalization Stage

During the generalization stage, students begin to use skills or concepts appropriately in new situations. For example, Travis may now apply the multiplication facts to solving word problems in mathematics or science in his regular classroom, or he may use these facts when assisting his grandmother to compute totals for purchases of identical items at the supermarket.

Generalization of skills is problematic for many learners with mild disabilities. Teachers cannot assume that generalization will take place naturally; hence, they must plan systematically for it to occur (Stokes & Baer, 1977). Unfortunately, IEP objectives written by teachers often do not address generalization of skills (Billingsley, 1984).

Wolery et al., (1988) suggest that teachers include a generalization objective for each acquisition objective written. These authors argue that for an objective to be considered mastered, the behavior must be performed fluently with someone other than the person who taught it to the child, in different settings, with different directions and/or materials, and in naturally occurring situations in which it is appropriate and necessary. To accomplish generalization, then, teachers must begin during the acquisition stage to systematically vary people, settings, materials, and directions in teaching a new skill or concept. In addition, teachers may ask students, or tell them, where a new skill or concept may be useful at school, at home, or in the community. Teachers may also enlist the help of parents, other teachers, and peers to prompt or reward appropriate demonstration of a skill in the natural setting.

Stages of Learning and Planning

In planning instruction, teachers set objectives appropriate for the level of performance and stage of learning of their students. They also plan instructional activities to reflect the degree of teacher assistance required by students at each learning stage.

Planning will be most accurate if the teacher knows exactly how well students are performing in the curriculum. If there are two students with learning problems who need instruction in specific areas, for example, the teacher may plan time for one-on-one instruction with these youngsters. At the same time, other students in the classroom may be engaged in independent tasks at the maintenance stage of learning, or they may be working with a paraprofessional or peer tutor on tasks designed to promote proficiency. Teachers who know student performance levels and who adjust instructional arrangements and activities accordingly are able to plan for a group diverse in abilities and interests (Bennett & Desforges, 1988).

Inaccurate planning may result if student progress is not monitored closely. According to Bennett and Desforges (1988), teachers may underestimate the progress of high achievers and overestimate the progress of low achievers when performance has not been monitored. Moreover, inaccurate assessment of student progress results in lack of adequate instructional time for students who are struggling or wasted instructional time for students who have already mastered skills or content.

Cohen and deBettencourt (1991) suggest pretesting students to determine academic needs and skill levels in order to prevent wasted instructional time and to increase academic learning time. (Recall that academic learning time is the time in which students are actively engaged in appropriate tasks with a high rate of success.) These authors state that a high level of academic learning time may actually lower the probability of at-risk students dropping out of school. In addition to knowing the skill level of students, Kameenui and Simmons (1990) suggest that teachers identify skills that may present problems for students and preteach those skills to at-risk learners before introducing lessons that require use of the skills. These preteaching lessons may be brief, but they should ensure that students have mastered prerequisite skills or tasks.

Rappaport (1991) advocates the holistic assessment of students with reading disabilities in order to provide accurate instruction. Holistic assessment takes into account student interests, skill levels, strengths, and weaknesses. Airasian (1991) argues that teachers must consider pupil characteristics along with instructional factors in planning for instruction (see Table 7.3).

Accurate assessment of student skill levels is attained through direct daily measurement and curriculum-based assessment. Student performance data, obtained through the measurement procedures described in Chapter 6, are used to write educational objectives, plan instructional activities, and monitor student progress. For students receiving special education services, these objectives are included on the IEP.

Individualized Education Programs

When it has been determined that a student is eligible for special education services, the multidisciplinary team must develop an individualized education program, or IEP, for that student before special education services can begin.

Table 7.3   **Factors to Consider When Planning for Instruction**

Pupil characteristics:
- Ability
- Work habits/socialization
- Special learning needs
- Prerequisite skills

Instructional Resources:
- State curriculum mandates
- Time
- Textbook/instructional packages
- Other resources (space, aides, equipment, etc.)

From Classroom Assessment, *by P. W. Airasian, 1991. Copyright © 1991 by McGraw-Hill. Reprinted by permission of McGraw-Hill.*

Team members include the student's parents or guardians, the special education teacher, the regular classroom teacher, a school administrator or designee, and whenever appropriate, the student himself or herself. The IEP details the exact special education services to be provided to the student; therefore, it may be no older than one calendar year. Every year, or more frequently if required, the team meets to renegotiate the IEP.

Public Law 94-142 requires several components to be included on the IEP. These include

- a description of the special education and related services to be provided to the student;

- the dates of initiation and estimated length of duration for the special education and related services provided;

- the current level of student performance;

- annual goals based on the current level of student performance;

- short-term objectives designed to enable the student to meet the annual goals; and

- evaluation methods and time schedules for determining whether the goals and objectives have been met.

An IEP for Travis is shown in Figure 7.3 and an example of one annual goal with objectives for Joey is presented in Figure 7.4. Sample IEPs for Travis, Joey, Susan, and Robert are included in Appendix A.

The concept of backward planning is often used in developing the IEP. That is, the multidisciplinary team uses the information regarding the student's current level of performance to write annual goals first. The annual goals are then broken down into short-term objectives. Later, the teacher may break down these short-term objectives further for daily lesson planning and instruction.

Short-term objectives are stated in behavioral terms and are monitored frequently. Recall that well-phrased objectives specify conditions, observable student behaviors, and criteria for measuring success. In other words, a short-term objective on the IEP would not be phrased "Travis will know his multiplication facts" or "Travis will increase his reading comprehension." Rather, the objective might read, "Given any 200-word passage selected at random by the teacher from the third-grade basal reader, Travis will read the passage aloud at a rate of 150 words per minute with fewer than three oral reading errors." Stated in this manner, the objective conveys to the teacher the precise behavior expected of Travis, (i.e., read a passage aloud); the conditions under which he will be expected to perform (i.e., a timed reading of a 200-word passage randomly selected from the third-grade reader); and the level of performance required for mastery (i.e., an oral reading rate of 150 words per minute with no more than two errors). The well-written instructional objective guides teacher planning and enables the teacher to determine student progress toward the annual goal.

Figure 7.3   Part of an IEP for Travis

INDIVIDUALIZED EDUCATION PROGRAM
CONFIDENTIAL

Name: TRAVIS JOHNSON   Current Grade/Year: 4th / 1992-93
Teacher: MS. KIRK   Eligibility: SPECIFIC LEARNING
                                           DISABILITIES

Services Begin: 9/8/92   Services End: 9/7/93

Special education services	Person responsible	Time
Resource room for reading and mathematics instruction	Ms. Lopez	2 hours per day
Regular classroom for all other instruction with consultation services to Ms. Kirk, 4th grade teacher.	Ms. Kirk and Ms. Lopez	4 1/2 hours per day

Related services	Person responsible	Time
None		

Signatures: Date:

Susan Lopez _____ LD teacher _____   9/7/92
Ms. Kirk _____   4th grade teacher _____   9-7-92
Mr. Vuon _____   Principal _____   9-7-92
Mrs. L. Johnson _____ Mother _____   9-7-92

NOT CONFIDENTIAL

Annual Goal: Travis will write the sum for 2-digit plus 2-digit addition problems with regrouping.

Short-Term Objective	Strategies/ Materials	Teacher	Date Met
Given a probe with fifty 2-digit plus 2-digit addition problems with no regrouping, Travis will write the sums with 100% accuracy within 3 minutes.	Teacher-made probe sheets. Best Ever Math Series. Manipulatives. Flash cards.	Ms. Lopez	9/22
Given base-10 blocks and any 2-digit plus 2-digit addition problem requiring regrouping from the ones to the tens, Travis will exchange 10	Base-10 blocks. Best Ever Math Series	Ms. Lopez	10/3

(continued)

Figure 7.3   *(Continued)*

---

ones blocks for 1 tens block correctly within 30 seconds.			
Given a probe sheet with fifty 2-digit plus 2-digit addition problems with regrouping only from the ones to the tens, Travis will write the sums with 100% accuracy within 3 minutes.	Teacher-made probe sheets. Best Ever Math Series	Ms. Lopez	10/9
Given a probe sheet with any 2-digit plus 2-digit addition problem, Travis will write the sums with at least 90% accuracy within 3 minutes.	Teacher-made probe sheets. Best Ever Math Series. Base-10 blocks	Ms. Lopez	

In addition, the teacher must write objectives that will promote generalization of skills or concepts to new environments. Billingsley, Burgess, Lynch, and Matlock (1991) provide guidelines for writing objectives with generalization in mind (see Table 7.4).

Frequent measurement of student performance helps the teacher to make informed instructional decisions. The teacher sets a criterion level for mastery under a specified set of conditions for a targeted student behavior, and then changes the conditions, behavior, or required level of performance when data indicate that the initial objective has been met. Giek (1992) recommends considering the student's learning rate and past retention rate as guidelines for setting the criterion for mastery.

In addition, in order to save teacher time and promote student independence and ownership of learning, students may log their own progress on a chart or graph. Such self-monitoring increases student motivation (Giek, 1992). Ms. Lopez, for example, uses a self-monitoring wall chart for reading. Her students color in the appropriate box for the story they read, selecting the color that is coded for the degree of accuracy they have attained upon self-checking their story-comprehension questions. By looking at the wall chart, Ms. Lopez and the student both know the last story read, as well as how accurately the comprehension questions were answered.

Writing behavioral objectives and measuring student progress toward these objectives directly and frequently is at the heart of the IEP. The most important outcome of well-written objectives is accurate measurement of how well students are learning. This information, in turn, guides the teacher in planning daily instruction and providing appropriate special education services.

Figure 7.4   A Sample Annual Goal with Objectives From Joey's IEP

Name: <u>Joey Greenhill</u>   Academic Year: <u>1992–93</u>

Teacher: <u>Ms. Lopez</u>   Date: <u>September 9, 1992</u>

Annual Goal: Joey will complete the third-grade reader by the end of the academic year.

Objective	*Evaluation*	*Date of Completion*
Given 100 new vocabulary words from the first reader at the third-grade level shown randomly in written phrases, Joey will verbally decode the words with at least 90% accuracy by January.	Individually administered list of phrases from the Best Ever Third-Grade Reader Number 1. (Untimed)	1/15/93
Given five comprehension questions following each story in the first reader at the third-grade level, Joey will verbally answer the comprehension questions with at least 80% accuracy by January.	Comprehension questions following each story in the first reader at the third-grade level in the Best Ever Reading Series. (Untimed unit tests given orally to Joey)	

✎ Summary

Accurate planning is necessary for maximum educational achievement. Special and regular education teachers may use a variety of methods to plan and organize for instruction. Teaching methods, grouping arrangements, and organizational guides for students all fit together in a smoothly running classroom.

Teachers must write educational objectives to guide the planning and provision of appropriate instructional activities for their students. Well-written behavioral objectives include conditions under which a student will perform, observable student behaviors, and criteria for determining success. Objectives also must reflect the levels and stages of learning. If students are to progress from the acquisition of new material to the generalization of skills in different situations, teachers must plan for this learning to occur.

Students receiving special education services must have up-to-date IEPs developed by a multidisciplinary team. The IEP consists of annual goals and

Table 7.4   A Checklist for Instructional
Objectives with Generalized Outcomes

Components of Generalization Objectives:
1. Is the learner specified?
2. Is the behavior specified (and functional)?
3. Are the performance conditions specified?
4. Are the criteria specified?
5. Are those responsible for reporting success named?
6. Is a target date set?
7. Is this a realistic objective?
Dimensions of Generalization:
1. Do the conditions indicate the need for the behavior among people in general?
2. Do the conditions indicate the need for the behavior with respect to various objects and materials?
3. Do the conditions indicate the need for the behavior across settings/time?
4. Do the conditions indicate the need for the behavior on a ''spontaneous'' basis on an ''as needed'' basis, or on an ''as appropriate'' basis?

Adapted from ''Toward Generalized Outcomes: Considerations and Guidelines for Writing Instructional Objectives'' by F. F. Billingsley, D. Burgess, V. Lynch, and B. L. Matlock, Education and Training in Mental Retardation, *26, 1991, p. 357. Copyright © 1991 by the Council for Exceptional Children, Division on Mental Retardation. Adapted with permission.*

short-term objectives written in behavioral terms. Frequent and direct measurement of student progress enables the teacher to determine when the student has mastered an objective. New objectives may then be written so that valuable academic time is not wasted.

✎ Application Exercises

1. Interview a special education teacher in a local school system. What strategies does this teacher use when developing daily lesson plans? What factors influence his or her planning decisions?

2. Interview a regular classroom teacher in a local school system. Gather the same information as in Question 1. Are there similarities in the planning strategies used by regular and special educators? Are there differences? Compare and contrast the strategies used by these teachers and the factors that influence their planning.

3. An annual goal for Robert in geography this year is as follows: Robert will label the states of the United States on a blank map. Write a short-term objective for this goal. Be sure to include conditions, behavior, and a criterion for mastery.

4. Using Bloom's taxonomy, write an objective in the cognitive, the affective, and the psychomotor domain for the annual goal given for Robert in Exercise 3. If you can, write a goal at each level for the cognitive domain!

5. Assume Robert is at the acquisition stage of learning for the short-term objective you wrote in Exercise 3. What activities might you plan at this stage of learning? What activities will you plan to help Robert become proficient with the skill? How will you ensure that Robert maintains the skill? How will you plan for generalization to occur?

6. Arrange to examine an IEP for a student receiving special education services in a local school system. Remember to keep the information on the IEP confidential as required by PL 94-142. Can you locate each component on the IEP?

Part Three

Providing Instruction

Effective Teacher Behaviors

Chapter 8

Focus

As you read, think about the following questions:

Why should teachers of children with special needs consider the allocation of time, the management of transitions, and the provision of academic learning time important instructional variables?

What specific behaviors indicate that a teacher is teaching "effectively"?

How do teaching behaviors differ from one phase of a lesson to another and from one stage of learning to another?

✎ Teachers sometimes attribute the failure of students to lack of ability or poor home environment. Such statements as "His parents aren't very supportive" or "She's really a slow learner" reflect a belief that the final responsibility for academic achievement rests with the child and his or her family rather than with the school and the teacher. Effective teachers, however, assume full responsibility for the performance of all children in their classrooms, and they focus on the variables over which they have control. Let's listen to a conversation in the faculty lunchroom at Apple County Middle School.

> Mr. Mathis: *What's this "Success" project supposed to be about? I got a flyer in my box this morning for the meeting tomorrow afternoon.*

> Ms. Booker: *I think it's to help us figure out more ways to reach our difficult students. I heard that some of the special education children would be involved, along with other kids the guidance counselors think might drop out of school.*

> Mr. Abel: *I think you're right. I heard in the office yesterday that we were going to brainstorm ways to motivate and teach our at-risk kids to help keep them in school. I think it's supposed to be a schoolwide effort to improve the performance of kids who are having trouble.*

> Mr. Mathis: *The project sounds good. Some of my kids are hard to teach—Leon, for example. I'm worried we could lose him, and I'm open for any suggestions I can get to help him and the other kids stay in school and like learning.*

Teachers can and do make a tremendous difference in how much and how well students learn. Effective teachers, therefore, focus on their own skills and behaviors rather than on variables over which they have no control.

In this chapter, we will focus on variables controlled largely by teachers. First, we will review the teacher's use of time. Next, we will examine teaching behaviors that affect the academic achievement of students with mild disabilities. Finally, we will explore elements of the direct instructional teaching model.

✎ Research on the Use of Time

During the 1970s, research efforts focused on those variables linked to the academic achievement of students, particularly in reading and mathematics, over which teachers could exert control. Berliner (1984), for example, stressed the importance of the teacher's use of time. Teachers must first allocate time for instruction, both across and within given content areas, if their students are to achieve academically.

Simply allocating time for instruction, however, is not enough to effect positive student outcomes. Students must also be *on task* and *engaged* in an instructional activity if learning is to occur. Although teachers in different classrooms may schedule similar amounts of time for instruction in an academic area, the actual time children spend involved in learning tasks varies greatly from classroom to classroom. Haynes and Jenkins (1986), for example, report that students in resource rooms spend only 44% of their allocated time engaged in instructional activities. Yet, engaged time is more closely related to student academic achievement than allocated time.

Clearly, how teachers organize and use instructional time influences student performance. This means that teachers must plan ways to convene instructional groups quickly. Materials must be prepared in advance and placed in accessible locations, and directions must be given so that they are easily understood. Clear rules, routines, and signals must be established to ensure smooth movement from one activity to another. Unless teachers plan organized transitions from one activity or place to the next over the course of the school day, the time used for transitions will considerably decrease the amount of time available for instruction.

What students actually do during instruction, however, is the most critical factor influencing their achievement. Students must be actively engaged in an appropriate task with a high rate of success. Berliner (1984) calls this important variable *academic learning time* (see Chapter 5). Thus, it is not enough for students with low achievement to be simply on task. The task must be an appropriate one, chosen because it relates directly to the content for which they will later be held accountable. Moreover, the students must be active participants, experiencing a high level of success with that task. Rosenshine (1983), for example, emphasizes the importance of a very high success rate with a task before assuming student mastery. It is extremely important, then, that teachers carefully plan how to maximize academic learning time for their students (see Box 8.1).

✎ Research on Teacher Effectiveness

According to Rosenshine (1983), six specific teacher behaviors are exhibited by effective teachers:

1. reviewing and reteaching previous work;
2. clearly presenting new concepts and skills;
3. providing supervised student practice in order to check understanding;
4. giving immediate positive and corrective feedback during practice sessions and reteaching if necessary;
5. providing structured independent practice opportunities to promote mastery; and
6. using periodic reviews to ensure maintenance of concepts and skills learned.

Effective teachers assume an active role in directing the learning of all students. They orient students to lesson goals and objectives, present key skills and concepts clearly and concisely, and use questions to check student understanding and focus attention on important elements of the lesson (Brophy & Good, 1986; Stallings, 1985). Effective teachers also pace their instruction

---

Box 8.1   Maximizing Academic Learning Time

During the 1970s and 1980s, the educational research literature reflected an increased knowledge of how teachers affect student academic achievement. According to research syntheses produced by the Northwest Regional Educational Laboratory (1990), effective teachers plan for optimal use of student time. The following recommendations are based on the practices of effective teachers:

1. Use a preplanned curriculum in which learning goals and objectives are sequenced to facilitate student learning. Maintain a brisk pace during instruction, introducing new learning objectives as rapidly as possible (Englert, 1984; Good, Grouws, & Backerman, 1978)

2. Form instructional groups within the classroom to be sure all students thoroughly learn the material. These groups should be formed according to student achievement levels for specific academic skills, and group membership should be reviewed and adjusted frequently as skill levels change.

3. Keep noninstructional time to a minimum, using classroom-management strategies that minimize disruptive behaviors. Effective teachers continue to be aware of all students in the classroom while working with individuals or small groups, and they communicate that awareness to other students. Effective teachers also establish classroom rules and routines and prepare activities and materials before students arrive.

4. Set challenging but attainable standards for all learners. All students should be held accountable for appropriate behavior and achievement and given help immediately and intensively when they experience difficulty.

5. Provide additional learning time and activities on priority objectives for at-risk students. Effective teachers continue to communicate the expectation that all students will be held accountable for meeting classroom performance standards. Comparisons are made, however, only to the student's own past performance rather than to that of other children.

Adapted from "Effective Teachers," Effective Schooling Practices: A Research Synthesis *(1990 Update). Copyright © 1990 by Northwest Regional Educational Laboratory. Adapted with permission.*

---

appropriately, introducing new objectives and learning activities as rapidly as possible while still ensuring thorough mastery of content by students (Good, Grouws, & Backerman, 1978). Appropriate pacing keeps students alert and interested and reduces student error.

These indicators of effective instruction are particularly applicable when teaching academic skills to students with mild disabilities. Stevens and Rosenshine (1981), for example, maintain that, for students with academic deficits, effective instruction takes place in teacher-directed groups that are academically focused. In these groups, students receive more teacher demonstration and feedback and spend more time engaged in learning tasks than when they work alone. Moreover, effective instruction is also individualized for members within each group. This does not mean, however, that individual students are given additional workbook or worksheet practice pages to complete on their own during time allocated to special education. Students are instead given many opportunities to respond correctly to questions posed by their teachers during interactive teaching sessions. Extensive content coverage, task engagement, feedback, and success are critical to the academic achievement of children with learning difficulties (Englert, 1983, 1984; Sindelar, Smith, Harriman, Hale, & Wilson, 1986).

✎ Direct Instructional Strategies

Direct instruction is an effective teaching model that emphasizes fast-paced, well-sequenced, highly focused lessons (Gersten & Keating, 1987; White, 1988). These lessons are delivered to small groups of students who are given many opportunities to respond and receive feedback about the accuracy of their responses (Lloyd, 1988). Teachers provide repetition of key lesson elements and enthusiastically engage all students equally in active practice. For students who are already behind their same-age peers, students with mild disabilities, or students facing possible school failure, the quality, intensity, and clarity of instruction are of vital importance. Therefore, direct instruction appears particularly well-suited to meet their needs (Englert, 1984). (See Box 8.2 for an illustration of the direct instructional model.)

Teachers using direct instruction plan lessons that are congruent with a necessary student outcome. That is, if students must later demonstrate on a test or by other means that they can add decimal numbers to the hundreths place, correctly placing the decimal points in the answers, then the teacher writes an appropriate instructional objective and focuses all teaching and practice on that objective. Typically, such lessons follow a predictable pattern. The teacher opens the lesson, clearly demonstrates the skill or concept to be learned, guides the student through practice using the new skill, and closes the lesson. The teacher also provides ample opportunity for every student to become proficient with the new skill and to use the skill independently (Hunter, 1982).

Opening the Lesson

At the beginning of the lesson, teachers must gain the students' attention and orient them to the purpose for the lesson. They must tell (orally or in writing) students what will be learned, why the information is important, and how new learning relates to what they already know (Englert, 1983, 1984). During this phase of the lesson, teachers must quickly set the pace for the lesson to come and motivate students to learn the material. To open a lesson, teachers might choose to do any combination of the following:

1. Gain student attention. Begin the lesson on time and with enthusiasm. Give a clear signal that the lesson is about to start (e.g., "Look," "Let's begin," "Eyes on me").

2. Review or summarize previous learning. Provide a few quick practice trials using important preskills previously learned. Relate the new lesson to past learning or to future needs.

Box 8.2   Mr. Mathis Uses Direct Instruction

Mr. Mathis, at Apple County Middle School, is about to begin a lesson with his sixth-grade general math class. Susan is a student with mild mental retardation mainstreamed into the class of approximately 19 children. Leon, also in the class, is a young man "at risk" for school failure. Mr. Mathis maintains that all of the students in this class have academic and behavioral difficulties and are children with special needs. Therefore, his lessons are highly interactive and follow the direct instructional model.

Mr. Mathis plans to teach a lesson on adding decimal numerals. His lesson plan states the following objective: "Given 10 addition problems with no regrouping, using decimal numerals to the hundreths place, the students will write the correct sum with at least 90% accuracy and with a correctly placed decimal point." Mr. Mathis has decided to present the lesson in the form of a rule for adding decimals. On the board, he has written the objective and the steps to follow: (1) Line up the decimal points, (2) bring the decimal point down, and (3) add the numbers. In addition, Mr. Mathis has items of interest to the children, with accompanying price tags, hidden in a box on his desk. After the children are seated, he begins his lesson. (Note key elements of the direct instructional method enclosed in parentheses.)

Mr. Mathis: *We've been working hard writing decimal numerals like money. Let's review. Help me write the price for this notebook from the school store.* [He pulls the notebook from the box so that the children cannot see the price tag and states the price.] *Let's see. This notebook costs three dollars and forty-five cents. Write that cost on your paper, everybody. [Waits about 5 seconds.] Now, tell me how to write that number . . . Anna? (Lesson opening and review of preskills)*

Anna: *You write the three. Then, a decimal point. And then you write the four and the five.*

Mr. Mathis: [Writing] *Super! Is this correct?* [Pointing to the number on the board] *Yep. That's right. Three dollars and forty-five cents.*

Remember the word and *stands for that decimal point in the number. Let's try another one.* [He pulls a school banner from the box, repeating the process to review this skill with the children.] *Now, suppose I wanted to buy both this school notebook and this school banner. How would I know how much money that would cost? John?*

John: *You'd have to add the two things together.*

Mr. Mathis: *Good. I'd have to add together the price of the notebook and the banner. Today, we are going to learn how to add decimal numerals together. (Statement of purpose) Watch me. On the board are three steps I must follow to add decimal numerals together. (Demonstration)* [Pointing and reading aloud] *I must line up the decimal points, bring a decimal point down into my answer, and add as I always do. This notebook costs $3.45, and this banner costs $1.12.* [Points to prices written on the board.] *The first thing I must do is write the numbers so that I line up the decimal points.* [Writes numbers on the board and points to the decimal points one over the other.] *Now, I must bring a decimal point down into my answer* [placing a decimal point in the answer], *and make sure it's lined up with the other decimal points. Now, all I have to do is add as I always do.* [Writing] *Five plus two is seven. Four plus one is five. Three plus one is four. The cost of the notebook and the banner together is $4.57. Let's do one another. (Guided practice)* [He pulls a school hat from the box and puts it on his head so that the children laugh as the price tag, clearly visible, dangles down.] *How much does this cost, Susan?*

Susan: *Two dollars and fifty-five cents.*

Mr. Mathis: *Come up and write that price on the board, Juan. Good. $2.55. Stay here, Juan, and let's get the others to help us find out how much it would cost to get ready for the game*

(continued)

Box 8.2   *(Continued)*

Friday night if I wanted to buy a school hat to wear and a school banner to carry. [Pointing to the first step on the board] *What's the first thing Juan must do, Leon? (Focused questions)*

Leon: *He's gotta write the numbers so the decimal points line up.*

Mr. Mathis: *Yep. Okay Juan, you've written the price of the hat, $2.55, and the price of the banner is $1.12.* [Pointing to the price written on the board earlier in the lesson] *Leon says the first step is to line up the decimal points. Watch and be sure he's correct, everyone.* [Juan writes $1.12 correctly under the $2.55.] *Is he correct, Leon?*

Leon: *Yeah.*

Mr. Mathis: *Sure is.* (Feedback and involving others) *Now, what's the next step, Pete?*

Pete: *Bring a decimal point down to the answer.*

Mr. Mathis: *Exactly. Bring a decimal point down to the answer.* [Juan does this as Mr. Mathis talks.] *Good job, Juan. Now, what's the last step, Shanda?*

Shanda: *Add the numbers.*

Mr. Mathis: *Yes, add the numbers as we always do. Now, while Juan is working the problem on the board, check to be sure his addition is correct, everyone.* [Juan writes $3.67 as the answer.] Is he correct, Susan?

Susan: [Shyly] *Yes.*

Mr. Mathis: *That's correct. Good job! Thank you, Juan. Now, let's work the next one together. You do it at your seat, and I'll do the problem up here at the board. Let's see.* [He pulls a small calculator from the box tagged with the price $6.24.] *Suppose I want to buy this calculator and a notebook. How much does the calculator cost, Marvin?*

Marvin: *Six dollars and twenty four cents.*

Mr. Mathis: *Yes. And the notebook, Leon?*

Leon: *Uh . . .* [Mr. Mathis holds up the notebook with the price tag so that Leon can see it.] *. . . yeah. It cost three dollars and forty five cents.*

Mr. Mathis: *Good. Now, what's the first thing we must do, Emily?*

Emily: *Write the numbers and line up the decimal points.*

Mr. Mathis: *Super! Do that on your own paper, everyone.* [As the children write, Mr. Mathis puts the problem on the board and then moves to quickly check student work.] *Excellent! Now, what must we do next, Sam?*

Sam: *Bring the decimal point down into the answer.*

Mr. Mathis: *Yes, bring a decimal point down into the answer. Do that on your paper, and I'll put one in my problem up here. Okay, check and be sure your problem looks just like mine.* [He quickly scans the room to be sure all decimal points are lined up correctly.] *Now, what is the last step, Juan?*

Juan: *Add.*

Mr. Mathis: *Okay. Add on your papers, everyone. Be sure to check my answer to see if its right.* [Writing the sum $9.69 on the board after the students begin to work] *What's the correct answer, Mike?*

Mike: *You're right. It's nine dollars and sixty-nine cents.*

Mr. Mathis: *Good job. It's easy to add decimal numerals like money together. All we have to remember is to write the numbers so that the decimal points all line up. Then, we bring a decimal point down into our answer and add as we always do. (Closing Review of important concepts) Now it's your turn to practice.* [He pulls several more items from the box, each with a clearly visible price tag, and places them along the chalk tray with the notebook, banner, hat, and calculator.] *On this*

(continued)

Box 8.2   *(Continued)*

---

worksheet are ten prices to find. You will need to write the cost for the two items in each problem so that the decimal points line up. Then, you will bring a decimal point down into the answer and add just as we always do. (Independent practice) When you get your practice sheet, we'll do the sample problem at the top together. [He passes out the worksheets.] *What are the items to buy in the sample problem, Susan?*

Susan: *The hat and the calculator.*

Mr. Mathis: *Yes, so what will we write first, Marvin?*

Marvin: *The $2.55 for the hat and the $6.24 for the calculator.*

Mr. Mathis: *Yep. And how will I write these numbers, Marvin?* [He points to the steps still on the board as a reminder.]

Marvin: *Oh. Write them so the decimal points line up.*

Mr. Mathis: *Good. Do that on your paper, everyone.* [He writes this on the board, as well.] *Now, what do we do, Josh?*

Josh: *Put the decimal point down in the answer and add the numbers up.*

Mr. Mathis: *Okay. You gave us the two last steps to do. We put the decimal point down in the answer* [writing a decimal point in his problem on the board] *and we add as usual. Do that, everyone.* [He walks around checking papers to be sure all decimals are properly lined up.] *What did you get, Sarah?*

Sarah: *Eight dollars and seventy-nine cents.*

Mr. Mathis: *Is she right, Pete?* [Pete nods yes.] *Good.* [He writes the correct answer on the board for his sample problem.] *Now, we have 15 minutes to finish the 10 problems on the page . . .*

---

3. If appropriate, remind students of rules to follow during the lesson.

4. Succinctly state the purpose for the lesson. Some teachers like to write the lesson objective on the chalkboard in an abbreviated form as well. This, of course, must be done before students enter the classroom. Main points to be emphasized also can be written on the board in advance and referred to during the lesson. This outline or overview (whether written or oral) is called an *advance organizer*.

5. State why the skill or concept should be learned. For example, relate it to the students' daily lives or to something they already know. Help them to see the usefulness or relevance of the skill and help them to set a performance goal, such as number correct on a mathematics practice sheet or quiz.

Once students have been oriented to the lesson and know the purpose and importance of the information to follow, the teacher can introduce the new skill or concept to be learned. This next important phase of the lesson is often referred to as a teacher "demonstration."

Demonstrating the New Skill or Concept

For low-achieving students, a short demonstration that is *explicit, repetitive,* and *focused* on the lesson objective is vital (Ysseldyke, Christenson, & Thurlow, 1987). This means that teachers must devise concise, well-organized, step-by-step explanations, using language the students will understand, explaining all new vocabulary terms, and repeating essential lesson elements. Teachers must task-analyze—breaking the new skill or concept into carefully sequenced, manageable steps. Examples must be carefully chosen for the demonstration, and teachers must constantly focus student attention on the key features of these items.

For example, if Ms. Lopez were to present a lesson on the CVCe rule, she might begin with the words *made, dime, hope, Pete,* and *cube* on the chalkboard. She would clearly state the rule "When words end in the letter *e*, we say this (pointing to the initial vowel) letter name," and she would then move students to many practice opportunities reading the words under her supervision and guidance (Carnine et al., 1990). Later, Ms. Lopez might include words such as *cap, tub,* and *hid* in her word list to check student understanding and to be sure that students could identify the relevant feature of the task (i.e., the CVCe pattern).

Once the teacher has clearly demonstrated the new skill or concept, he or she must immediately move students to numerous controlled practice trials with close teacher supervision. This interactive teaching phase of the lesson is often called *prompted practice* or *guided practice.*

Giving Guided Practice

Although a clear demonstration is critical for the academic success of students with mild disabilities, of even greater importance is the opportunity to practice the new skill or concept under direct teacher supervision (Ysseldyke et al., 1987). During guided practice sessions, teachers ask many questions, providing all students equally with numerous opportunities to respond successfully and to receive immediate feedback regarding the accuracy of their answers (Hunter, 1982). Thus, asking questions and giving feedback are related and critical skills for special education teachers to master.

Asking questions.   Questions allow the teacher to check whether or not students understand the information presented. Effective questions also result in accurate, substantive responses by pupils. That is, good questions should "lead" students to the correct answer, focus student attention on important features of the learning task, and require active participation by all students. Some authorities maintain that students must respond correctly to questions posed by teachers at least 80% of the time in order for learning to occur (Wittrock, 1986). This means that questions should be planned in advance so that both the meaning of the question and the type of response called for are clear to the student.

At the acquisition stage of learning, particularly for instruction in basic skills, the questions posed by teachers should be narrowly focused and rapidly paced. These questions have only one correct answer. At the initial stage of learning, questions that require only lower levels of thinking enable students to respond successfully until they become firm or automatic with the new information (Englert, 1984; Mastropieri & Scruggs, 1987). Later, as students apply their newly acquired skills in different situations, the questions posed by teachers will become more open-ended, challenging students to use higher-level thought processes and to make slower, more carefully considered responses.

Regardless of the level of questioning, however, teachers must ensure active participation by all students throughout the lesson. To accomplish this, teachers should ask a question first, then call on particular students to answer. In addition, teachers might ask questions needing only a one- or two-word answer and then signal all students in the group to respond together in what is known as *choral responding*. For example, the teacher might say "Everyone" or use a preestablished hand signal to ensure that all students answer simultaneously. Alternatively, the teacher might ask a question, direct all students to think about the answer for a moment, then ask for all students to respond.

Whether the teacher chooses individual or choral responding, students must know the type of response they are to make, and they must have adequate time to think and answer. Teachers should allow at least three seconds of "wait time" for lower-level questions and additional time for higher-level questions before signaling students to respond (Northwest Regional Educational Library, 1990). Moreover, if a student gives an incorrect or incomplete response, the teacher must stay with the child, asking additional questions and giving feedback until an accurate answer has been given.

Giving feedback.   Students must know whether their answers to questions are correct or incorrect. In addition, teachers must help students correct inaccurate answers as quickly as possible. Giving feedback, then, is another critical skill for special education teachers to master (see Box 8.3).

When students respond correctly to questions asked, the teacher must immediately acknowledge the accuracy of the answer. Failure to do so may produce uncertainty and confusion for children in special education programs. If students are hesitant or not yet firm with the answers they give, the teacher should provide an immediate and explicit statement indicating to everyone that the answer was correct. Often, this can be accomplished by simply restating the answer given by the child (e.g., "Yes, the word is 'hope'."). In this way, all students have one more opportunity to hear the correct response. If students are answering questions quickly and accurately, the teacher may choose to acknowledge correctness with a nod, a yes, a thumb's-up sign, or some other overt signal indicating acceptance of the answer given. Teachers must take care, however, not to interrupt the pace of a lesson with an overabundance of artificial, nonspecific praise. If praise is used, it should be delivered quickly, sincerely, and specifically, so that students know what was correct about the answer given.

When students give an inaccurate answer, the teacher should immediately and specifically indicate any portion of the response that was correct. Then, the teacher should rephrase the question, redirecting the child's attention to important features of the task and leading the child to the correct answer. If students

Box 8.3   Examples of Questions and Feedback During Guided Practice

Question	Example	Feedback	Example
Fact/Recall	What's the word?	Restate correct answers	Yes! The word is *rope*.
Focus student attention	Does the ending begin with a vowel?	Acknowledge correct answers overtly	Smile and give a thumbs-up sign.
Lead to right answer/Ensure high accuracy	Are the decimal points lined up?	Give specific praise quickly	Good, your decimal points are lined up.
Check student understanding	What is the next step?	Reinforce by confirming correct part of answer and rephrase the question	Yes, add is the third step. But what do we do *before* we add?
Ask question, then give a clear signal to respond	Is the word a proper noun? (pause) Susan? or Everybody?	Prompt	Joe is the name of a person.

are still unable to answer the question, prompts may assist them to respond correctly (see Box 8.4). Teachers should not, however, continue to probe students when they obviously do not know the answer to a question asked of them. Stating the correct answer without embarrassing the student and moving on without interrupting the pace of the lesson is usually wise in this instance. The teacher should, of course, give the student the same question again later in the lesson in order to check for understanding. Teachers must provide numerous opportunities for all students to respond with high levels of success (Greenwood, Delquadri, & Hall, 1984).

Kline, Schumaker, and Deshler (1991) offer an excellent sequence for giving individual feedback to students with mild disabilities. These authors maintain that effective feedback routines can be easily mastered by teachers and that these routines should include the following elements:

1. at least three positive statements about the work product made by the student or by the teacher;

2. a description given by the teacher of one error made by the student and specific examples of the error;

3. modeling by the teacher and supervised practice by the student of ways to correct the error; and

4. summary statements about what was learned in the feedback conference to be rephrased by the student later as written goals.

Through the interactive teaching process used during guided practice—asking questions and giving feedback—teachers are able to monitor student

---

Box 8.4   Giving Feedback Using Prompts

Prompts help students to achieve a high rate of successful responding during guided practice sessions. To be most effective, prompts should be planned *before* a lesson begins. In this way, teachers can give students only that level of assistance necessary to reach accuracy levels of 80% to 90% or better during the initial stages of learning. For most students with mild disabilities, prompts will fall loosely on a hierarchy from the least amount of assistance to the greatest amount of assistance. (See Wolery et al., 1988, for an excellent description of the system of least prompts). For example, when a student makes an error, the teacher might begin prompting at the "top" of the hierarchy, cueing the student to respond. If the cue fails to produce a correct answer, the teacher might then move down the hierarchy, systematically giving increasing levels of assistance.

	Type of Prompt	Example
Cue:	Ask again, student may not have attended to the question.	Read the word.
Visual:	Highlight correct response in some way.	Feet (Teacher underlines the double-vowel pattern)
Verbal:	Partially supply or describe the answer.	The *smallest* coin. Line up the _____.
Model:	Show or tell the correct answer.	The word is *rope*. What's the word?
Manual:	Give physical assistance.	Place hand over the child's to write his name.

---

performance and adjust instruction immediately. If students are unable to respond, teachers rephrase questions, provide prompts, or reteach the skill or concept using different examples and smaller teaching steps. When students are responding to the teacher's questions confidently and with at least 80% to 90% accuracy, they are ready to practice the new material independently.

Providing Independent Practice

Once students have achieved a high level of correct responding during guided practice, the teacher must provide them with opportunities to practice new skills and concepts independently. Independent practice allows the student to become proficient (faster and more accurate) with new information. The teacher also may plan independent practice activities to help students maintain or apply previously learned information. Moreover, student performance during independent practice helps the teacher evaluate accomplishment of lesson objectives and adjust additional instruction accordingly.

Often, independent practice takes the form of a seatwork task. To be effective at the initial stages of learning, however, it is essential that seatwork be directly related to the lesson objective and require a response similar to that demonstrated and practiced under teacher guidance. For example, if the demonstration and guided practice involved children stating the time to the hour as the teacher moved the hands on a large clock, the independent practice activity must follow a similar oral format. If students in special education programs are suddenly asked during independent practice to draw the hands on a clock to illustrate a given hour, their performance will likely deteriorate. "Stating" time to the hour and "drawing" the hands on a clock are two different behavioral responses, and students with special educational needs do not readily generalize unless they are explicitly taught to do so (Stokes & Baer, 1977). Unfortunately, the teacher might be left with the mistaken impression that "these students never pay attention or retain what they learn," when, in fact, the teacher has set up the conditions for student failure.

In addition, teachers sometimes wrongly use independent practice activities to fill class time and to keep students busy. Seatwork should *never* be used merely to fill time in any classroom. Independent seatwork should be used only when it will enable students to become proficient with new information, or when it will help them to maintain and/or apply previously learned skills. If the seatwork task is not related to lesson objectives, teachers should choose another activity.

As students complete independent practice activities, the teacher must still actively monitor their performance. Teachers should "walk" students through the first few problems or examples and then circulate among the students to check their understanding and accuracy, to provide clarification or assistance, and to reteach when necessary. Often, however, the teacher of special education or other at-risk children must give direct instruction to another small group of students after the first group has begun to work independently. This means that teachers must communicate the expectation that all seatwork will be accurately completed during a specified time period. In addition, teachers must establish rules regarding appropriate ways to get help or acceptable activities to choose upon completion of seatwork if independent practice is to flow smoothly.

Independent practice does not have to be conducted solely as individual paper-and-pencil tasks, however. A paraprofessional, parent volunteer, or peer tutor can be enlisted to continue teacher-directed practice, providing additional opportunities for children in special education programs to answer questions and receive immediate feedback. Similarly, students may participate in cooperative learning arrangements, with both group incentives and individual accountability, to help one another master new skills and concepts. Computerized drill-and-practice programs may also be useful as independent activities to provide immediate feedback *if* they are directly related to the lesson objective and to the guided practice given by the teacher.

Closing the Lesson

As teachers come to the end of a direct instructional sequence, they either follow guided practice with independent practice or move students into a new lesson. Regardless of the next instructional activity, teachers must signal to students that the lesson has ended.

To bring closure to a lesson, the teacher may choose to review or summarize the main points learned. For example, students could read a list of new vocabulary words in a final "firm-up" trial. The teacher may also remind students about the importance or usefulness of the new information, reestablishing the relevance of what has been learned. Students could also be asked to summarize the new information and explain its relevance. Finally, the teacher may give specific directions regarding what students are to do next (See Box 8.5). These directions, of course, could refer to either the independent practice or to a totally new instructional activity. When giving directions, though, teachers must always remember to be specific (e.g., "Now, please put your reading cards on the shelf, get out your math book, and open it to page 23") and to check students' understanding by observing what they do or by asking them to restate the directions given.

Evaluating Instruction

Following each lesson, teachers must systematically evaluate whether or not students have accomplished the instructional objective(s). This ongoing process of reflecting about student performance is known as *formative evaluation*. Formative evaluation allows for immediate corrective action on the part of teachers. (By contrast, *summative evaluation* is done through achievement tests given once a year.) Gathering information regarding student performance on a daily, or even moment-to-moment, basis permits teachers to adjust instruction immediately to suit the needs of students.

Box 8.5   Directions For Independent Practice

In special education classrooms, directions must be clear, concise, and specific. The following suggestions may help teachers provide proper directions for independent practice activities:

1. Gain everyone's attention *before* giving directions.

2. As you give the directions, watch each student. Look for signs of confusion or inattention as you speak.

3. Ask students to repeat or rephrase the instructions when you finish. You may wish to ask students who are likely to have difficulty to repeat the directions after you.

4. Ask specific, step-by-step questions of the students to be sure that they understand what they are to do.

5. Work through one or two items with the group, following the directions given, before allowing students to begin independent work.

6. Place a clear reminder of the directions and/or a sample work item on the board for all students to see.

7. Circulate around the room as students work independently.

8. If you cannot circulate, be sure to remind students of the rules for obtaining help (e.g., check with an assigned peer) and for acceptable behavior upon work completion.

Suppose, for example, students were achieving accuracy leveis of 80% to 90% during practice sessions. In this case, the teacher would probably maintain or increase the pace of instruction. However, if students were making frequent errors, the teacher would critically examine all instructional variables, with the following questions in mind:

1. Is the lesson objective appropriate? Is the objective stated appropriately for the stage of learning (i.e., acquisition, proficiency, maintenance, or generalization)? Is the criterion level set too high or too low?

2. Are students properly motivated to learn the lesson? Do they see the relevance and usefulness of the content? Are student goals realistic?

3. Do students have the necessary preskills for this lesson? Is the pace of instruction on target?

4. Is the demonstration clear? Is the demonstration task properly sequenced? Do the examples clarify the information? Are important parts of the task clear to students and are they repeated numerous times?

5. Are questions clear and designed to lead students to correct responses? Do all students have sufficient opportunity to respond? Do they have adequate ''wait time'' to think and answer?

6. Are students given immediate and specific feedback for each answer? Do students know when answers are correct? Are questions and prompts designed to focus student attention on the correct answer?

7. Does the guided practice match the lesson objective and the demonstration? Do students need additional guided practice?

8. Does the independent practice activity match the instructional objective? Does the independent practice activity require the same behavioral response as the demonstration and guided practice? Do students understand the directions and know what they are to do? Do students need additional independent practice opportunities before evaluation of their performance?

9. Does the evaluation procedure, whether the independent practice activity or an oral or written test, match the instructional objective and require the same behavioral response as was required during guided practice?

✎ Summary

Teachers are responsible for the academic performance of children in special education programs. Teachers who increase the achievement levels of their students allocate sufficient time to instruction and then provide lessons designed to maximize academic learning time for all pupils. Effective teachers, then, focus on their own teaching behaviors, examining how they plan lessons and deliver instruction.

Direct instruction is one particularly effective method for teaching children with mild disabilities. It allows for instruction that is highly structured, repetitive, and interactive. Teachers focus lessons on appropriate instructional objectives and orient students to the lesson purpose. Teachers give clear demonstrations, ask many questions to elicit correct answers from all students equally, and offer students immediate corrective feedback. Following the demonstration and guided practice, teachers afford students numerous opportunities to practice new skills and concepts independently. Teachers also close lessons clearly by reviewing key lesson elements, summarizing the purpose and usefulness of the lesson, or issuing clear directions regarding what students are to do next. Throughout the lesson, student performance is monitored closely by the teacher, and instruction is adjusted immediately to increase the success rate for all students. Structure, repetition, and high rates of successful responding are necessary elements for effective instruction in special education classrooms.

✎ Application Exercises

1. In Box 8.2, Mr. Mathis is delivering a lesson on adding decimal numbers. Does he state the lesson objective or purpose? How does he make the material relevant for the students and motivate them to learn? Does Mr. Mathis give students a clear demonstration of the new skill? What questions does he use consistently to focus student attention on the important features of the task? Are all students responding actively and successfully? Are they receiving immediate feedback as to the accuracy of their answers?

2. On page 159, Ms. Lopez is conducting a lesson on the CVCe rule. Use the format that follows to write a lesson plan for Ms. Lopez. (Be specific and write exactly what you will say and do.)

   • *Objective:* (Be sure to include a condition, a measurable student behavior, and the criterion for determining success.)

   • *Opening:* (What will you say or do to establish interest in the topic and relate the forthcoming new information to what is already known by the students? Will you review preskills or state the lesson purpose? What rules will you establish to structure the lesson?)

   • *Demonstration:* (How will you present the new skill or concept? What examples will you use? How will you focus student attention on the important features of the task?)

   • *Guided Practice:* (What examples will you use? What questions will you ask to structure this practice, check student understanding, focus student attention, and keep all students actively engaged in the learning task? What prompts might you plan to ensure successful student responding?)

   • *Closing:* (What will you say or do to close the lesson? Will you restate the relevance or review and/or summarize the material? Will you give specific directions for what students are to do next?)

• *Independent Practice:* (What task will students complete independently? Are you sure that this activity directly matches the lesson objective and corresponds to both the demonstration and the guided practice?)

• *Evaluation:* (How will you evaluate whether students did or did not accomplish the objective? Are you sure that your evaluation procedure matches the objective, the demonstration, and the practice activities?)

Student-Mediated Learning

Chapter 9

Focus

As you read, think about the following questions:

What is meant by "individualized instruction"?

How can teachers use cooperative learning groups to individualize instruction?

How can peer tutoring work to the advantage of both tutors and tutees?

Can students with disabilities be taught to work independently using cognitive behavior modification and learning strategies?

✎ Because each student with disabilities must have an IEP to receive services, and because that IEP must specify specially designed instruction unique to the needs of the student, many teachers have construed PL 94-142 to mean that students with disabilities must have one-on-one instruction from a special educator at all times. Although some students with disabilities may require instruction in a one-on-one teacher–student mode, most do not need it all the time. Many of the needs of students with mild disabilities may be met through small, cooperative learning groups, peer tutoring, and learning strategies.

For example, in Mr. McNally's geography class, the students have different ability levels. In order to accommodate these varying levels, Mr. McNally knows that he must provide a variety of reading materials and activities for his students. He plans to use cooperative learning groups, recognizing that they can help him to accomplish several goals. Activities that involve all students in the learning process not only improve achievement but also facilitate the social integration of students with disabilities.

Ms. Kirk has students with both disabilities and exceptional abilities in her classroom. She has considered several methods by which to give each student the instruction he or she needs to achieve academically. Grouping by ability seems to be the most commonly used technique, but Ms. Kirk recognizes that this may not be the best method. By investigating the current educational journals and talking with teachers in other schools, she has become aware of several peer-tutoring strategies that are being used successfully to meet the academic needs of many diverse students. When she implements peer tutoring in her classroom, Ms. Kirk realizes many benefits, not the least of which is improved academic performance.

Mr. Abel has 20 students who visit his classroom daily. These students are all assigned to general education classrooms where they receive the majority of their instruction. In the resource room, Mr. Abel knows that he must maximize time by training his students in strategies that will enhance their performance in the regular classroom rather than simply tutoring them in content areas. He has chosen to teach learning strategies and use cognitive behavior modification techniques to improve his students' academic and behavioral performance in the mainstream.

In each of the preceding examples, the teacher is striving to meet the unique needs of students by using the most appropriate methods. With careful teacher planning and supervision, these methods will enable the students to assume greater responsibility for their own learning, as well as that of others. Such student-mediated methods as cooperative learning, peer tutoring, and strategy training may increase academic learning time for students with mild disabilities by providing more opportunities for active engagement with appropriate tasks when the teacher is involved in direct instruction with others.

✎ Cooperative Learning

Placing students with mild disabilities in the regular classroom influences their lives deeply. It allows for the development of constructive relationships between them and their peers without disabilities. The risk of making things worse, as well as the potential for making things better, is a possibility that cannot be overlooked, however (Johnson & Johnson, 1986). Friendships and positive relationships may result for both students with and without disabilities when mainstreaming is successful. But if mainstreaming is unsuccessful, students with disabilities may experience rejection, stereotyping, or ill treatment from their peers. According to Johnson and Johnson, simply placing students with mild disabilities in the general education classroom does not ensure that mainstreaming will go well. Successful integration of students with mild disabilities into the general education classroom depends on how well the teacher structures relationships among students.

Teachers may structure academic lessons in any of three basic ways: (1) in a competitive struggle to determine who's "best"; (2) along individual lines, without peer interaction; and (3) in a cooperative manner, in which students help each other master the assigned material (Johnson & Johnson, 1986). Options 1 and 2 tend to isolate students from one another. Each one is out for himself or herself. By contrast, the third option allows teachers to structure lessons around shared goals toward which students work together—encouraging, discussing, and helping one another to understand the material. Thus, Johnson and Johnson suggest that teachers use cooperative learning whenever they want students "to learn more, like school better, like each other better, have higher self-esteem, and learn more effective social skills" (p. 554). Cooperative learning may be used both in general education classrooms that include mainstreamed students with mild disabilities and in special education classrooms that include students with varying levels of achievement.

The basic elements that must be present for cooperative learning to take place are positive interdependence, individual accountability, collaborative skills, and group processing (Johnson & Johnson, 1986). Cooperative learning is also characterized by heterogeneity and teacher intervention when appropriate (Center for Special Education Technology, 1990). (See Figure 9.1 for a listing of cooperative learning elements.) *Positive interdependence* refers to the perception that each individual is linked with the other individuals in the group, and that the success of one is dependent upon the success of all (see Figure 9.2). By *individual accountability* is meant the assessment of each group member's performance to determine who needs additional help in mastering the material or completing the assignment. In this process, group points may be assigned for improvement in individual scores. *Collaborative skills* include leadership, decision making, trust building, communication, and conflict management. Because groups cannot function without collaborative skills, they must be taught in the same way that academic skills are taught. *Group processing* refers to discussions on how the group is functioning; for example, whether or not members are achieving their goals and whether or not the actions of members are helpful. Such discussions provide the feedback necessary for students to determine the success of their participation (Johnson & Johnson, 1986).

Although cooperative learning may take many different forms, all are characterized by students working in small groups to help one another master academic material (Slavin, 1991b). Student team learning (STL), developed at Johns Hopkins University, is a collection of cooperative methods in which

Figure 9.1   Elements of Cooperative Learning

This material was developed by the Center for Special Education Technology (September 1990) under contract No. 300-87-0115 with the Office of Special Education Programs, U.S. Department of Education.

Cooperative learning is more than just putting students together in groups. It is a teaching strategy characterized by:

- Positive goal interdependence of group members. This may consist of having a common goal, sharing materials, or assigning members different parts of the task.

- Individual accountability. Each group member is asked to be responsible for his or her own learning, as well as responsible for helping others learn.

- Heterogeneous groups. The composition of the class should be reflected in each of the groups. The teacher assigns students who differ in ability, culture, gender, and race to work together. These differences enable students to make unique contributions toward the group goal.

- Teacher observation and intervention when appropriate. While students are working, the role of the teacher ideally should be to monitor the groups. When problems in understanding the content or in interactions occur, the teacher may help focus the group on the problem. Rather than solving the problem, the teacher should try to help the group discuss possible situations.

- Instruction in collaborative skills. Emphasis is on building skills which help students to work together. Role playing and examples of the skill are used to depict the expected behavior. "How to actively listen," or "how to disagree in an agreeable way" are two skills that may be modeled.

- Group processing/debriefing at the conclusion of the lesson. There needs to be discussion of the content, as well as how the group functioned while working together. The observations of the teacher, as well as student input, would be used to create a plan for the next time the group meets.

These features distinguish the cooperative group from the traditional student groups. Cooperative groups foster positive interactions that result in student academic achievement and in development of collaborative skills.

Mainstreamed students should be welcome in these cooperative groups because they provide additional group heterogeneity. Each member should be valued, as his or her diversity of skills and background are useful for some aspect of the work. Thus a member with disabilities as well as a nondisabled member ought to be viewed as an asset to the group. Working together can provide an opportunity for stereotypes to fall away and for students with disabilities to become friends with classmates. These relationships might not develop if the class works competitively or individually.

attainment of team goals depends on all team members learning the objectives. "The students' tasks are not to *do* something as a team but to *learn* something as a team" (Slavin, 1991b, p. 73). Team rewards, individual accountability, and equal opportunities for success are concepts that are central to STL methods. As described by Slavin,

> using STL techniques, teams earn certificates or other team rewards if they achieve above a designated criterion. The teams are not in competition to earn scarce rewards; all (or none) of the teams may achieve the criterion in a given week. Individual accountability means that the team's success depends on the individual learning of all team members. This focuses the activity of the team members on explaining concepts to one another and making sure that everyone on the team is ready for a quiz or other assessment that they

Figure 9.2   Positive Interdependence

From "Mainstreaming and Cooperative Learning Strategies," D.W. Johnson, and R.T. Johnson, Exceptional Children, *52(6), 1986, p. 555. Copyright © 1986 by The Council for Exceptional Children. Reprinted with permission.*

The perception that one is linked with others in a way that one cannot succeed unless the others do (and vice versa) and, therefore, that their work benefits one and one's work benefits them is referred to as positive interdependence. It is a sense of fate and mutual causation. The ways in which a teacher may structure positive interdependence include the following:

1. Positive goal interdependence exists when students perceive that the goal of the group is to ensure the learning of all group members. This may be done by giving each student an individual test and taking a group average for each member's grade or requiring one product from the group.

2. Positive reward interdependence exists when all group members receive a reward based on their overall achievement. Giving a single grade for the group's efforts, adding bonus points to each member's individual score when every member achieves up to criteria, or giving nonacademic rewards such as free-time or food when all group members reach criteria are examples.

3. Positive resource interdependence exists when resources are distributed so that coordination among members is required if the goal is to be achieved. Jigsawing materials so that each member has part of a set of materials or information or limiting the resources given to the group (e.g., only one pencil, book, dictionary) is an example.

4. Positive role interdependence exists when members are given specific complementary roles to play in the group.

5. Positive task interdependence exists when a division of labor is structured so that the actions of one member have to be completed if the next group member is to complete his or her responsibilities.

will take without teammate help. Equal opportunity for success means that students contribute to their teams by improving over their own past performances. This ensures that high, average, and low achievers are equally challenged to do their best and that the contributions of all team members will be valued. (p. 73)

Slavin (1991b) identifies four STL methods: student teams achievement divisions (STADs) and teams-games-tournaments (TGTs), both of which are adaptable to many subjects and grade levels; team-assisted individualization (TAI) for mathematics in grades 3–6; and cooperative integrated reading and composition (CIRC) for reading and writing instruction in grades 3–5. Another cooperative learning technique that has received attention in the literature is called Numbered Heads Together (Kagan, 1990).

Student Teams Achievement Divisions

In the STAD approach, a heterogeneous group of students is divided into four-member teams. After Ms. Stone presents a lesson, for example, her students work within their teams to ensure that all have mastered the material. Then, her students take individual quizzes independently. Students' quiz grades are compared to their own past grades and each student is awarded points based on the amount of improvement over earlier performances. The points of all team members are then combined to determine the team score. Teams reaching a predetermined criterion receive certificates or some other reinforcer.

STAD has been used for many subject areas at many grade levels. Slavin (1991b), however, suggests that it works best with fact-oriented material, such as math computations, language usage, geography and map skills, and science facts.

Teams-Games-Tournaments

The TGT approach also is structured around teams working together, but weekly tournaments take the place of the quizzes of STAD. In the tournaments, students compete with members of the other teams to provide points for their team. In Mr. McNally's class, the tournaments take place at tournament tables, each with three to four students of comparable abilities. The winner of each table contributes the same number of points to his or her team, regardless of which table played. This method ensures equal opportunity for success for low achievers who compete against low achievers and high achievers who compete against high achievers. High-performing teams earn the rewards (Slavin, 1991b).

Team-Assisted Individualization

TAI also uses learning teams with members of mixed ability. The high-performing teams, as in TGT and STAD, receive certificates. However, this approach combines cooperative learning with individualized instruction and is designed to teach mathematics to students in grades 3 through 6. Students are placed in an individualized mathematics sequence based on their scores on a placement test. Team members work on different units, help each other with problems, then check each other's work. The unit tests are taken independently, and team rewards are determined by points assigned for passing scores and perfect papers. Using this method, the amount of materials management that teachers must do is reduced. Teachers are able to spend time giving instruction to small groups of students who are working on the same objectives (Slavin, 1991b).

TAI uses the same motivational factors as STAD and TGT, with students encouraging and helping one another so that the team can succeed. The individualization of TAI is what distinguishes it from STAD and TGT. Because most concepts in mathematics are built on prerequisite concepts, students must master the prerequisites before later skills can be mastered. In TAI, since students are working at their own levels, they have the opportunity to master the prerequisites before moving on to higher-level concepts. TAI depends on a specific set of instructional materials that covers skills and concepts from addition to algebra. The materials include lesson guides with suggested methods for introducing mathematics with manipulatives, demonstrations, and examples (Slavin, 1987).

Cooperative Integrated Reading and Composition

CIRC is a program for teaching reading and writing in upper elementary school. The teacher uses a basal or literature-based reading series and traditional reading groups (see Chapter 10). For example, while Ms. Kirk is meeting with the "Blue Jays," pairs of students from the "Cardinals" and the "Orioles" are working together on other activities, such as reading to one another, making predictions, practicing spelling and vocabulary, or completing comprehension activities. The sequence is generally teacher instruction; team practice; team preassessments, during which team members determine who's ready for the quiz; and quizzes. Teams receive certificates based on the average performance of team members on all of the activities (Slavin, 1991b).

Numbered Heads Together

According to Kagan (1990), Numbered Heads Together is a cooperative learning structure that can be used with almost any subject matter at almost any grade level. It has been described as a "teacher questioning strategy designed to actively engage all students during adult-led instruction and discussion" (Maheady, Mallette, Harper, & Sacca, 1991, p. 25). In most teacher-questioning situations, the students are forced to compete for teacher attention and praise. As one student is called on to respond, the others lose their turn; moreover, should a student give an incorrect response, there may be additional loss of teacher attention and praise (Kagan, 1990). Numbered Heads Together provides a way to increase the participation of students with lower achievement, at the same time maintaining the participation of those with higher achievement. As described by Maheady et al. (1991), Numbered Heads Together works in the following way:

First students are placed into small (four-member) heterogeneous learning teams consisting of one high achieving, two average achieving, and one low achieving pupil(s). Students number themselves 1 to 4 and sit together during teacher-directed lessons. After the teacher directs a question to the entire class, pupils are instructed to "put their heads together, come up with their best answer, and make sure that everyone on the team knows the answer." The teacher then asks, "How many Number ____ (1, 2, 3, or 4) know the answer?" After one randomly selected student responds, the teacher can ask, "How many other Number ____ agree with that answer?" or, "Can any Number ____ expand upon the answer?" Teachers then recognize and/or reward all students who provide or agree with correct answers, as well as those who offer meaningful expansions. Since students are given time to discuss possible answers prior to responding, it is more likely that everyone, including low achievers, will know the correct responses. Moreover, since teams cannot predict which group member will be called upon to respond, they are more likely to ensure that everyone knows the answer.

Forming Cooperative Teams

Kagan (1990) identifies four major types of team structure for cooperative learning groups: (1) heterogeneous teams, (2) random groups, (3) interest groups, and (4) homogeneous/heterogeneous language-ability groups. Each type has its advantages and disadvantages. For example, if heterogeneous grouping is the only formation, then high achievers never have the opportunity for the academic stimulation of interacting with each other and low achievers are likely to miss leadership opportunities, since they are never on the same team. According to Kagan, the exclusive use of homogeneous grouping eliminates the opportunity for peer tutoring and support.

Heterogeneous groups may be formed by placing one high achiever, two average achievers, and one low achiever on each team. The teacher assigns the teams, ensuring heterogeneity of ability levels, gender, and ethnic groups. Nonheterogeneous teams may be formed by allowing students to group themselves according to their own friendships or interests, or by random selection in which students draw a number for team assignments. Each of these team-formation methods, however, may pose problems. Self-selection runs the risk of promoting cliques of students, with some being the "in" groups and others being the "out" groups. Random selection may result in "loser" groups, with those students having the lowest achievement being assigned to the same team. For these reasons, teacher-selected heterogeneous groups are generally preferred. Figure 9.3 presents Kagan's (1990) approach for forming heterogeneous teams.

To facilitate the formation of cooperative learning groups, teachers may choose to use a classroom sociogram (Peck 1989). (See Figure 9.4 for the sociometric grid.) Students with high group status are identified by the sociogram. These students have demonstrated the ability to influence their peers. The teacher then can strategically place students with high ratings in cooperative learning groups so as to maximize positive peer pressure.

Figure 9.3 How to Form Heterogeneous Teams: Teacher Assignment Using the Ranked-List Approach

From Cooperative Learning: Resources for Teachers, *by Spencer Kagan, Ph.D. Copyright* © *1990. Reprinted by permission of Resources for Teachers, San Juan Capistrano, CA 92675.*

Step 1: Rank Order Students. Produce a numbered list of students, from highest to lowest achiever. The list does not have to be perfect. To produce the list, use one of the following (in order of preference): pretest, recent past test, past grades, or best guess.

Step 2: Select First Team. Choose top, bottom, and two middle achievers. Assign them to team one, unless (a) they are all of one sex; (b) they do not mirror the ethnic composition of the class; (c) they are worst enemies or best friends; (d) they are unfavored choices on the Sociometric Grid [see Figure 9.4], in which case, you move up or down one student from the middle to readjust.

Step 3: Select Remaining Teams. To produce Team 2, repeat Step 2 with the reduced list. Then use the even more reduced list to assign to teams 3, 4, and so on. If you end up with one or two students left over, distribute them to other teams so that you have one or two five-member teams (pick teams with a frequently absent student); with three left over, have a team of three.

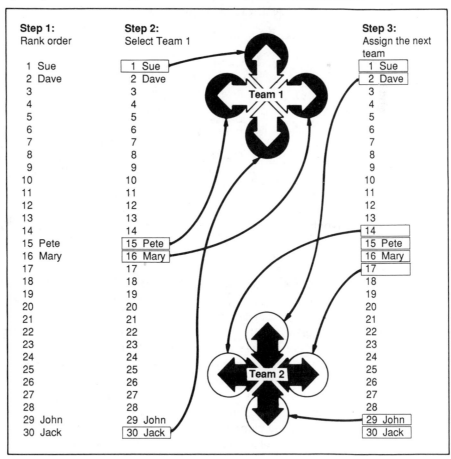

Figure 9.4   The Sociometric Grid

From Cooperative Learning: Resources for Teachers, *by Spencer Kagan, Ph.D. Copyright ©*
1990. Reprinted by permission of Resources for Teachers, San Juan Capistrano, CA 92675.

This approach was developed by Susan Masters and Lucille Tambara (Maple Hill
Elementary School, Diamond Bar, CA). It allows consideration of the relations
among students. To use the Sociometric Grid, first present students with a list of
their classmates and have them place a plus by the names of the three persons they
would most like on their team and a minus or check mark by the names of the
three persons they would least like to be on their team. For instructions consider:

> "We are forming new teams and to form the best teams possible I would like to
> know your preferences. Here is a list of your classmates. Please put a plus by the
> names of the three classmates you would most like to have on a team for the next
> six weeks, and a check mark by three people you would prefer not to be on a team
> with this time. You may want to make new friends, so you might place a check
> mark by the names of your best friends. I cannot promise you will be on a team
> with someone you have given a plus, or that you will not be on a team with
> someone you have given a check, but I will consider your preferences when I
> make the new team assignments."

Next, make a grid which contains all of that information, like so:

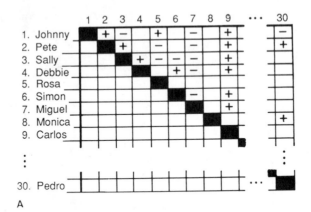

A

In the sociometric grid above, the choices of each student toward each other
are indicated by a +, −, or blank. The black squares are filled in to indicate that
students cannot nominate themselves. Thus, Johnny indicated he would like to
have as teammates students 2 (Pete), 5 (Rosa), and 9 (Carlos), and that he would
prefer not to have as teammates students 3 (Sally), 7 (Miguel), and 30 (Pedro).
Note, the chart is filled out with the choices for only the first four students. Carlos
is very popular; Miguel is very unpopular.

For teacher's use: Write in the three pluses and three minuses following the
name of each student, indicating their preferences. While assigning teams you may
wish to avoid pairing students if a minus occurs. Although some students may not
be a favorite of anyone, and may have quite a number of students who do not want

(continued)

Figure 9.4   (Continued)

to be on their team, it is almost always possible to find at least three others for whom the unpopular student is not a least favored alternative. You may want also to avoid certain pluses as they represent "best friends" who can pair, minimizing interaction along many lines within teams.

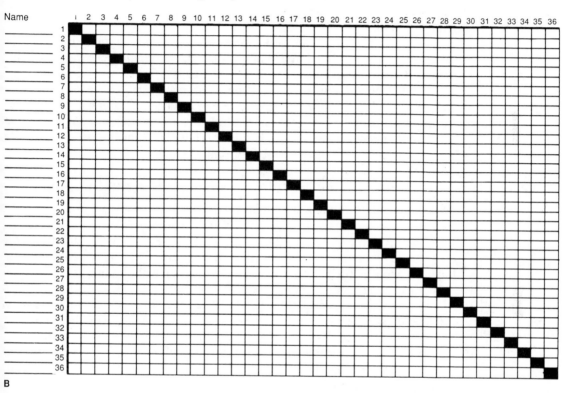

B

When the teacher chooses to use random teams, a simple method for assigning team members is to have students draw numbers from a hat. The Puzzled People method uses a picture torn into four parts, four sentences in a content-related statement, or four lines of a proverb or poem (Kagan, 1990). The steps for Puzzled People using torn pictures are as follows:

1. Have students tear pictures into four parts.

2. Have them mill around the room and trade pieces—each with one other person. (They keep their hand raised until they have made a trade, so those who have not yet traded can see who to trade with.)

3. Then, let them solve the puzzle by grouping with the others who hold pieces of the same picture.

Random teams offer variety and the opportunity to transfer skills to a new group. As stated previously, however, this method might lead to the four lowest achievers in the class being in the same group. Generally, random groups cannot stay together for as long a period of time as heterogeneous teams can (Kagan, 1990).

Occasionally teachers find it useful to allow students to form their own teams. For certain projects, allowing students with similar interests to explore a topic in depth results in learning opportunities not otherwise possible. Sometimes permitting best friends to work together brings new energy into learning (Kagan, 1990).

A fourth basis of team formation is homogeneous grouping by language abilities or needs. At certain times in the instructional cycle (for example, when teachers have students with limited English proficiency), teams formed by homogeneous English language ability are necessary. However, as Kagan (1990) points out, "while homogeneous by language, an attempt is still made to make the team heterogeneous on other dimensions such as content ability, sex, and, if possible, ethnic background. Thus the team is really a homogeneous language/heterogeneous ability team" (p. 69).

Integrating Students with Disabilities into Cooperative Learning Groups

When students with mild disabilities are in general education classes like Ms. Stone's, teachers may need to make special efforts so that the cooperative learning process can be as effective as possible. For example, Johnson and Johnson (1986) point out that (1) students with disabilities may be fearful and anxious about participating in groups, (2) students without disabilities may be afraid that their grades will be affected by having students with disabilities in their groups, and (3) students with disabilities may be passive and withdrawn in the group. Figure 9.5 offers some suggestions for dealing with these issues.

Although cooperative learning arrangements provide students with extra support and encouragement, they are not the only means by which students can help one another. Peer tutoring offers teachers yet another technique to increase instructional time in the classroom.

✎ Peer Tutoring

Within every classroom the potential exists for additional instructional assistance for teachers pressed for time and resources. Students who have reached higher levels of achievement can be trained to tutor classmates who are not achieving as well. Peer tutoring provides teachers with a way of ensuring that every student will receive additional instruction and/or practice that may be needed in acquiring particular skills. Peer tutoring may take the form of same-age tutors, cross-age tutors, regular class students tutoring students with mild disabilities, students with mild disabilities tutoring other students with disabilities, and students with mild disabilities tutoring students without disabilities.

Peer tutoring offers a number of advantages to both tutors and tutees. Peer tutoring promotes interaction between two students by allowing them to work with and help each other. Moreover, some children learn better from other students than from an adult, perhaps because the communication is more

---

Figure 9.5   Overcoming Concerns About Cooperative Learning Groups

---

From "Mainstreaming and Cooperative Learning Strategies," D.W. Johnson, and R.T. Johnson, Exceptional Children, 52(6), 1986, pp. 555–60. Copyright © 1986 by The Council for Exceptional Children. Reprinted with permission.

Anxious Students with Disabilities

Many students with disabilities may be fearful about participating in a cooperative learning group with nondisabled peers. Their anxiety may be alleviated through the following actions:

1. Explain the procedures the learning group will follow.

2. Give the students with disabilities a structured role so that they understand their responsibilities. Even if a student cannot read, he or she can listen carefully and summarize what everyone in the group is saying, provide leadership, help to keep the group's work organized, and so forth. There is always some way to facilitate group work, no matter what disability a student may have.

3. Enlist the aid of a special education teacher to coach the students with disabilities in the behaviors and collaborative skills needed within the cooperative group. Pretraining in collaborative skills and periodic sessions to monitor how well the skills are being implemented will increase the confidence of the students with disabilities.

4. Enlist the aid of a special education teacher to pretrain the students with disabilities in the academic skills needed to complete the group's work. Try to give the student with disabilities a source of expertise the group will need.

Anxious Nondisabled Students

Many nondisabled students may be concerned that the student with disabilities will lower the overall performance of their group. The three major ways of alleviating their concerns are as follows:

1. Train nondisabled students in helping, tutoring, teaching, and sharing skills. The special education teacher may wish to explain to the group how best to teach the group member with disabilities. Many teaching skills, such as the use of praise and prompting, are easily taught to students.

2. Make the academic requirements for the students with disabilities reasonable. Ways in which lessons can be adapted so the students at different achievement levels can participate in the same cooperative group are to
   (a) use different criteria for success for each group member;
   (b) vary the amount each group member is expected to master;
   (c) give group members different assignments, lists, work, or problems and then use the average percentage worked correctly as the groups score; and
   (d) use improvement scores for the students with disabilities. If it is unclear how to implement these procedures, consult with the special education teacher to decide what is appropriate for the specific student.

(continued)

Figure 9.5   *(Continued)*

---

3. Give bonus points to the groups that have students with disabilities. This will create a situation in which nondisabled students want to work with their disabled classmates to receive the bonus points.

Passively Uninvolved Students with Disabilities
When students with disabilities are turning away from the group, not participating, not paying attention to the group's work, saying little or nothing, showing no enthusiasm, or not bringing their work or materials, the teacher may wish to try the following:

1. Jigsaw materials so that each group member has information the others need. If the passive uninvolved student does not voluntarily contribute his or her information, the other group members will actively involve the student.

2. Divide up roles and assign the passive uninvolved student one that is essential to the group's success.

3. Reward the group on the basis of average performance. This will encourage other group members to derive strategies for increasing the problem member's involvement.

---

straightforward, or perhaps because the tutors remember what the problems were when they were learning the material, and thus can explain it better. Both tutors and tutees tend to sharpen their academic skills as a result of reviewing the material. Students who act as tutors also gain confidence (Eiserman, 1988).

Same-Age Tutorial Programs

Same-age or same-grade tutorial programs may be implemented from pre-school to college. The use of students to tutor their classmates is probably the most prevalent form of peer tutoring because teachers do not have to be involved in a specific program with other teachers in order to initiate the process. In the classroom, teachers can use peers to drill each other, check each other's work, and reinforce teacher instruction.

Same-age peer tutoring between students with and without disabilities helps those with mild disabilities to improve academically and stimulates others to be creative in their approaches to learning. The opportunity peer tutoring affords all students to interact and to learn about one another is, however, the most important aspect of the program. "Students are able to interact on a regular basis and to grow in their knowledge that all people are more alike—and special—than they are different" (Henrico County Public Schools, 1989, p. iv).

In one middle school in Virginia, talented and gifted students designed a peer-tutoring program for students with learning disabilities, mild mental retardation, and behavioral disorders, as well as for those taking English as a Second Language (ESL) (Henrico County Public Schools, 1989). To participate in the tutoring program, students in the talented and gifted program must conduct research on educational, social, physical, and psychological needs of special education students and take an examination. Once accepted into the peer-tutoring program and trained in methods for tutoring, student tutors work under the supervision of an experienced tutor. Sometimes a group of tutors will work with an entire special education class, but most tutoring is done on a one-on-one basis. Tutoring sessions usually take place once or twice per week, but some tutors schedule more sessions. All tutors work under the supervision of a faculty member.

The tutoring manual, *Tutoring: Lending a Helping Hand,* was written by a group of students in the Talented and Gifted program under the guidance of their teacher (Henrico County Public Schools, 1989). The students have included such topics as "Lesson Plans," "Confidentiality," and "Rewards" in their manual, as well as observation forms, the tutoring calendar, lesson-plan forms, a tutoring record, and the tutor's pledge. The manual gives background information on each of the types of disabilities and tips and techniques for tutoring students with disabilities. (See Figure 9.6 for the tips these students recommend, as well as for an address to obtain a copy of the manual.)

Cross-Age Peer Tutoring

Recognizing the benefits that accrue for the tutors in a peer-tutoring program, the use of students with mild disabilities as tutors for younger children with lower-level skills offers promise for reinforcing skills that students in special education programs have learned. Schrader and Valus (1990) describe a tutoring program that uses high school students with severe learning disabilities in a cross-age tutoring project. These students provide reading instruction to primary-grade students who are having difficulty with reading. The tutors are trained in such teacher behaviors as "giving clear directions, giving positive and corrective feedback, and avoiding over prompting. [They] are also trained in the use of established techniques for teaching reading" (pp. 590–591). The tutors spend one class period per day for a nine-week period in this project. The daily and weekly activities of the tutors are described in Figure 9.7.

Peer-tutoring activities, when carefully structured and supervised by teachers, can be an effective technique by which to increase the academic learning time of students in both regular and special education classrooms. Sometimes, however, students must engage in independent learning activities. In these instances, teachers need to help students take greater responsibility for their own learning.

✎ Cognitive Behavior Modification Strategies

Education involves more than just providing the students with a body of knowledge or a set of skills. Teachers are also concerned with training students to know how to learn and to assume responsibility for themselves. Cognitive behavior modification (CBM) offers the potential for teaching

Figure 9.6   Tips and Techniques for
Tutoring Students with Mild Disabilities

From Tutoring: Lending a Helping Hand, *1989. Henrico County Public Schools, Programs for the
Gifted at Tuckahoe Middle School, Richmond, VA 23221.*

1. Make a calendar showing when you are to tutor and keep it handy. Never skip a tutoring session.

2. Schedule frequent talks with the teacher to gain information about the individual needs of each student and to discuss problems and progress.

3. Know beforehand what you are going to be tutoring so that you can plan ahead. Ask to borrow copies of textbooks and workbooks.

4. Always keep a record of whom you tutored, when you tutored, and what subjects you taught. You need these records to help monitor your students' progress.

5. Be a good role model. Always use good manners and be considerate.

6. Be patient. Remember that these students need a lot of time to learn something new.

7. Keep the student on task. Ask questions to get him or her to pay attention.

8. Never do the students' work for them. When they get stuck, ask questions to lead them to find the answer for themselves.

9. When working on reading, read aloud with the student. Ask the student to read the first paragraph. Then, you read the next one. Continue alternating until the assignment is finished. Remember to ask questions at the end of each paragraph to be sure that the student understands what has been read before starting a new paragraph.

10. When the student stumbles over a hard word in a reading assignment, use a folded piece of paper to cover up all but the first part of the word. Have the student sound out the first part. Then, move the paper to the right, just enough to show the second part of the word. Continue gradually moving the paper to the right until the student has sounded out the whole word. Have the student repeat the word until he or she is comfortable with it. Come back to the same word a few more times as you continue reading to be sure that the student really knows it.

11. Make flash cards to teach new vocabulary words. Use the set of cards several times to be sure that the student knows the word. Also use flash cards to review basic mathematics skills.

12. When working on written assignments, do not allow the student to settle for phrases and incomplete sentences. Encourage him or her to write a complete sentence by asking questions (who, what, when, where, how, why).

13. When working on math problems involving more than one column of

(continued)

Figure 9.6   *(Continued)*

numbers, have the student use a folded sheet of paper to cover one column while working out the other one.

14. Use pictures and objects to illustrate concepts. They make learning interesting and fun and help students understand abstract concepts. For example, use concrete objects to illustrate fractions or concepts from geometry. Use maps in history to show where specific events took place.

15. Be positive and give lots of praise. Try to avoid using words like *wrong* or *incorrect*. If the student gives a wrong answer, try something like, "Let's try that again" and be ready to ask questions to lead the student in the right direction.

16. Review, Review, and Review even more. Students often learn best when something is repeated many times.

17. Be a good friend. Listen to the student and ask questions about his or her interests. Be friendly whenever you see the student at school.

18. At the beginning of each session, ask the student to tell you what the assignment for the day is. Ask why it is important to know the material covered.

19. If you have access to a computer, find or write some educational games to use as rewards. Help the students learn to use word processing programs.

20. If the student says something negative to you during the tutoring session, don't get upset. Remain calm and ask, "Do you really mean what you said or are you just frustrated?" Most of the time the student will admit that he or she was frustrated. Take time to talk about feelings and then get students back on task by asking questions.

21. Use your knowledge about the student's personal interests in making up practice problems and exercises. For example, when studying grammar and composition, create sentences about favorite topics.

22. Make pictures and diagrams to illustrate lessons that require reading and comprehension. Playing games like Win, Lose, or Draw; Pictionary; Trivial Pursuit; or Jeopardy can be helpful.

23. Help students develop a system of highlighting in their notes. For example, in history notes, all dates could be highlighted in one color and the names of people in another color.

24. After passages have been read or concepts have been taught, ask the student to explain orally what he or she has learned. Do not ask such questions as, "Do you understand?" or accept the answer, "Yes, I do." Be sure to have the student demonstrate that understanding has occurred.

25. Be careful never to talk about tutoring when other students are around.

Figure 9.7   Daily Activities for Tutors with Learning Disabilities

From "Disabled Learners as Able Teachers: A Cross-Age Tutoring Project," by B. Schrader and A. Valus, 1990, Academic Therapy, *25(5), pp. 589–97. Copyright © 1990, by PRO-ED, Inc. Reprinted with permission.*

The tutors' daily activities are as follows:

Monday and Tuesday. Each week, the tutors are instructed in a new technique to be used with the tutees. The teacher models the technique and directs the tutors to prepare and practice the technique in role-play situations.

Wednesday. The tutors conduct and tape-record their tutoring sessions.

Thursday. The tutors listen to their tapes and evaluate the session. Tutors also work on memory books and word banks for their tutees.

Friday. This is a "break day." This time is reserved for various thinking activities on the senior high student's interest level.

Reading Activities

Week 1. The first week's reading activity is choosing and reading a story to the tutee. This activity has two objectives: first, to practice reading fluency and expression and, second, to offer the tutor a controlled, structured, nonthreatening format for meeting the tutee and beginning a relationship. Preparation for this activity includes:

1. Reminding tutors of what it was like when someone read to them.

2. A discussion of small children.

3. A modeling activity.

4. Guided selection of a story.

5. Practice reading the story.

6. Role-playing the reading of the story.

Week 2. The second week deviates from the schedule of activities previously detailed because the tutors conduct two sessions with their tutees. This week's activity is a Language Experience Activity. On Tuesday, a story is told by the child tutee and tape-recorded by the student tutor. A concrete stimulus, such as a stuffed toy or picture, may be used to focus the tutee's attention and help structure the story. On Wednesday, the student tutor listens to the tape and writes the story exactly as told by the tutee. Thursday, the tutor meets again with the tutee. At this time the story is read and reread by the tutee several times until the reading becomes fluent and automatic. The objective of this activity is to show the tutee the association of thoughts with words and the stringing together of ideas into sentences and groups of sentences. The student tutors gain experience in writing from dictation, in editing a written product, and in preparing an accurate, complete, neat final draft.

(continued)

Figure 9.7   (Continued)

Weeks 3 and 4. Weeks 3 and 4 involve two Directed Reading/Thinking Activities (DRTA) (Stauffer, 1975). The student tutor uses three basic questions repeatedly to keep the tutee stimulated, motivated, and purposeful in his or her reading. The first question sets a purpose for reading by asking the child, "What do you think will happen?" The second question allows the child to process his or her answer by asking, "Why do you think so?" The child then reads a portion of the story or article. The final question sequence requires the child tutee to support or justify his or her ideas by asking, "Were you right? Can you prove it?"

The activity gives the senior high student practice in identifying main events or ideas, in simple questioning techniques of a divergent and open-ended nature, in developing alternative predictions, and in locating specific information, both explicit and implied, to justify predictions. It gives the elementary child practice in making and justifying predictions, in divergent thinking, and in establishing a purpose for reading, through their [*sic*] own predictions.

The third week, the activity is prepared as a class activity. All student tutors prepare the DRTA using the same story, with teacher help and guidance. The fourth week's DRTA is prepared individually, with each student tutor using material of his or her choice.

Weeks 5 and 6. Weeks 5 and 6 involve two activities with Reciprocal Questioning (ReQuest) (Manzo, 1969). In ReQuest, the student tutor and child tutee silently read the same passage. The student then closes the book, and the child asks the tutor any questions he or she may have about the passage. The tutor may have to do a great deal of prompting and cuing at the beginning of this activity to stimulate questions from the child. When the child has no more questions, the student tutor asks any questions that have not already been asked. The tutor requires careful preparation for this activity. First, an understanding of the questioning levels (literal, interpretive, and applied) is necessary. Second, the tutor needs to be able to develop questions about a passage; and finally, the tutor needs to be able to apply techniques to cue the tutee if the tutee has difficulty with the activity.

The fifth week's activity is prepared as a class activity, using the same material and building the questions as a class. The sixth week, each student tutor prepares an individual ReQuest activity for his or her child tutee, with teacher help.

Week 7. Week 7's activity involves oral reading using the Echo Reading technique (Gillet & Temple, 1982). In Echo Reading, the student tutor reads a sentence of phrase, using good fluency and expression, and the child tutee reads the same sentence, trying to use the same expression and inflections. This provides an opportunity for the student tutor to practice fluency and expression in his or her own reading. It makes rereading and oral practice of a selection purposeful. The child tutee gains from practicing oral reading in a strongly supportive context on material that he or she normally would not be able to read without repeated practice. Preparation for this activity does not need to be as intense as preparation for previous activities. This activity is used at this time because it fosters a feeling of

(continued)

Figure 9.7   *(Continued)*

---

mastery in the student tutors, and it gives them a chance to assume more initial control in preparing an activity.

Week 8. Throughout the project, the student tutors build word banks for their tutees. In Week 8, the tutors use these banks to work with the tutees on both closed and open sorts. Words can be sorted into such categories as words that name things, words that show action, words with the same beginning sound, and words that describe something. Severely LD students often find it difficult to recognize criteria needed to classify and categorize. This activity, in a very nonthreatening format, provides practice and review in recognizing aspects of words that they can use in analyzing groups of words. The benefits are the same for the tutee, who may, depending on his or her thinking ability, reverse roles with the student tutor and help the tutor recognize various similarities and contrasts in groups of words.

The second activity using the word banks involves adapting card games, such as Go Fish, to incorporate classifying and categorizing words. The benefits to both the tutor and tutee lie in the repetition of the various sorts, the exploration of new relationships, and the game format, which stimulates motivation and encourages quick thinking and responses.

Week 9. In preparation for the last day of the project, each tutor makes a memory book to be given to the tutee. The memory book includes a cover illustrated by the tutee that incorporates a photo of the tutor and tutee and a story dictated by the tutee to the tutor. Each tutor also selects a story and prepares a lesson using a technique of his or her choice to help the tutee with comprehension.

Another possible activity for Week 9 is a field trip giving the tutees the opportunity to visit the tutors' class at the high school. This can include refreshments, a tour of the high school, and meeting the high school principal.

A good cross-age tutoring project requires careful preparation. It is necessary to establish contact with elementary personnel regarding selection of tutees, scheduling the tutoring session, and locating a room for the project. The necessary materials, such as children's books and tape recorders, need to be organized and ready to take to the elementary school the day of the tutoring. Transportation needs to be arranged. Finally, the tutors need to be guided in their preparation for tutoring. The rewards of such a project, however, greatly exceed the effort and time required for its preparation.

---

students to take charge of their own learning and to control their own behaviors (Meichenbaum, 1980).

Teachers cannot be expected to keep a classroom full of students actively involved in the education process all the time. However, students with learning or behavior problems frequently become passive learners. They depend on teachers to direct their learning, control their behavior, and reward their performance. Teachers cannot be expected to monitor every student's actions and reinforce every response. Students must be taught to take responsibility for their own performance. For teacher and student well-being, students must learn to act independently so that reliance on teacher direction is reduced. Students, however, may not know how to take responsibility for their own learning and behavior. Cognitive behavior modification may be used to teach students learning strategies and to improve their academic performance and behavior in the classroom (Williams & Rooney, 1986). (See Figure 9.8 for general procedures in cognitive behavior modification.)

Cognitive behavior modification procedures may be adapted to fit numerous classroom tasks that students must perform. In addition, CBM curricula are available, including Rooney's Independent Strategies for Efficient Study (Rooney, 1990) and the Strategies Intervention Model developed by researchers at the University of Kansas Institute for Research on Learning Disabilities (Deshler & Schumaker, 1988).

Independent Strategies for Efficient Study

Using cognitive behavior modification as a foundation, Rooney (1990) has devised a number of independent strategies for efficient study. Because most students are never taught how to learn, many students with and without mild disabilities struggle with the learning process. They need direct instruction in how to organize for learning. Rooney's field-tested strategies are "designed to activate the individual in the learning process through simple strategies that will make organizing, learning, and reviewing information easier'' (p. 5).

Organizational strategies help students who cannot seem to manage their time or their school supplies. The time-management strategy presented in Figure 9.9 is based on a week; however, it may be adapted for a smaller unit of time (e.g., a two-hour period for Robert to complete his homework on Tuesday evening) or for a longer unit (e.g., Robert's entire semester). It may also be adapted for a particular activity, such as preparing for a party or studying for an exam. First, the basic strategy is taught. Later, students learn adaptations that may be used in various situations.

Students with learning problems frequently have difficulty knowing what to study and how to study. In the mainstreamed classroom, especially in the content areas such as science and social studies, students like Robert are expected to read the text, participate in class discussions, and take tests in the same manner as students without disabilities. If students with mild disabilities are to survive in the mainstream, they must be taught how to study efficiently. Rooney (1990) has developed and researched a strategy for textbook reading that enables students to read actively and prepare for quizzes and tests using index cards. This Systematic Study System, when used in conjunction with other organizational note-taking and test-taking strategies (see also Chapter 13), results in significantly improved grades.

Teachers with mainstreamed students in their classrooms often complain that these students are not prepared for classes; that is, they frequently forget to bring in pencils, paper, homework, books, or assignments. Teachers can improve the probability that students will come to class prepared by helping

Figure 9.8   General Procedures for Cognitive Behavior Modification

From A Handbook of Cognitive Modification Procedures for Teachers, *by R.M. Williams and K.J. Rooney. Copyright © 1986 by the University of Virginia Learning Disabilities Research Institute. Reprinted with permission.*

There are some CBM techniques that are not content-specific; they can be used for a variety of academic or social behaviors. Five such general procedures are self-recording, self-graphing, self-reinforcement, self-instruction, and self-instruction through attack-strategy training. Following are brief descriptions of each of these five procedures.

Self-Recording. Self-recording is a very effective, very simple means to change behavior. The student simply keeps track of his or her behaviors in order to become more aware of behaviors that are either present or absent. Self-recording can be used to increase or decrease particular behaviors.

The student simply makes a record of each time the behavior occurs. Merely counting the behaviors makes the student automatically more aware of the behavior. Any type of recording sheet can be used depending on the behavior to be recorded.

Self-Graphing. Self-graphing is an extremely versatile CBM technique. In conjunction with self-recording, it may be used to increase appropriate behaviors, to decrease inappropriate behaviors, or to improve the accuracy or frequency of academic responses.

After checking to be sure the student really knows what the behavior is, he or she may be instructed first to record a targeted behavior or skill and then to transfer this recorded information to a simple graph. Information plotted on a graph provides a visual clue for the student regarding his or her progress, which may serve as a form of self-reinforcement. Older students may wish to establish a goal and graph progress toward that goal. The following are examples of specific uses of self-graphing that might be used by Joey:

1. recording and/or graphing the number of correct (or incorrect) arithmetic problems completed;

2. recording and/or graphing the number of sentences written in a composition (or the number of action verbs, adjectives, adverbs, etc., used);

3. recording and/or graphing the amount of time spent studying each day;

4. recording and/or graphing the number of "talk outs" occurring during class time; and

5. recording and/or graphing the number of "polite" words used ("please," "thank you," etc.).

Self-Reinforcement. Self-reinforcement is a technique geared to promote student independence of external reinforcers. For example, if Joey must have a candy bar at the end of each good day (an external reinforcer), his performance is dependent on the availability of a reward. Self-reinforcement trains the student to tell himself

(continued)

Figure 9.8   *(Continued)*

---

or herself if he or she was doing a good job. For example, Joey might say to himself, "Good. I have completed all 10 steps and I have done a good job." Self-reinforcement can be used in a great variety of ways according to the needs of the situation.

Self-Instructional Training. Training children to talk to themselves is an effective means of teaching many academic and social skills. Donald Meichenbaum, the "father" of self-instruction, recommends that the following steps be used when administering self-instructional training:

1. The teacher performs a task while talking aloud (cognitive modeling). The demonstration should include
   (a) problem definition ("What is it I have to do?")
   (b) focusing attention and response guidance ("Go slowly . . . draw the line down.")
   (c) self-reinforcement ("Good, I'm doing fine.")
   (d) coping skills ("If I make a mistake, I can fix it by going slowly.")

2. The child performs the task under the direction of the teacher (overt, external guidance).

3. The child performs the task while instructing himself or herself aloud (overt self-guidance).

4. The child whispers the instructions while performing the task (faded, overt self-guidance).

5. The child performs the task while guiding his or her actions via private speech (covert self-instruction).

The teacher should be aware that it may not be necessary for some children to follow exactly all of the preceding steps. In addition, permit the child to use his or her own verbalizations as long as the meaning remains unchanged. Ten guidelines to follow for the development of a self-instructional training program are (Meichenbaum, 1981):

1. Analyze the target behavior including all requirements for successful performance.

2. Listen for ineffective strategies children currently use.

3. Select training tasks that approximate the target behavior.

4. Involve the child in devising the self-instruction.

5. Make sure the child has the necessary component skills for using self-instruction.

6. Tell the child how the self-instructions will be useful for performance.

7. Point out specific tasks and settings where the instructions may be used.

(continued)

Figure 9.8   *(Continued)*

8. Use multiple trainers, tasks, and settings to promote generalization.

9. Include in the training program specific coping skills for the management of failure.

10. Continue training until a specific criterion level is reached; then provide follow-up maintenance sessions.

Self-Instruction Through Attack-Strategy Training. Teaching children to use academic attack strategies is not new. Strategy training has been used effectively to teach children of all ages a wide range of academic skills. A strategy-training approach to instruction includes the following steps:

1. Define a group of related problems that a student needs to be able to solve (e.g., addition with regrouping).

2. Devise a strategy for attacking and solving the problems.

3. Specify the skills required in each step of the strategy.

4. Assess student performance on each of the component skills and teach separately those preskills not yet mastered by the student.

5. Model the strategy for the student while "talking aloud" (see the previous section on self-instructional training).

6. Guide the student through the strategy, verbalizing each step.

7. Provide practice and give corrective feedback.

8. Reinforce (praise) the student for correct use of the strategy.

---

them to organize their materials into a notebook (Rooney, 1990). The notebook should be large enough to be missed if it is forgotten. A large three-ring binder can be organized with spiral notebooks for each class or with dividers and looseleaf paper. Rooney suggests including the following items in student notebooks:

1. a plastic pouch to hold pencils, pens, and erasers;

2. pocket inserts to hold all homework to be handed in as well as to store handouts or returned tests;

3. graphs of grades for each class placed at the beginning of each subject section; and

4. self-monitoring homework charts to track homework assignments and their completion.

In addition, students may include a pocket calculator if allowed by the classroom teacher, a monthly calendar with large squares for each day on

---

Figure 9.9   Time Management

From Independent Strategies for Efficient Study, *by K.J. Rooney. Copyright © 1990 by J.R. Enterprises. Reprinted by permission of J.R. Enterprises, Richmond, VA 23230.*

A simple wheel (oval) can be used to organize tasks or activities in a visual format. Any amount of time or any activity can be organized using this system. Wheels have been used to organize weeks, semesters, hours, parties, and projects. The process is very simple.

1. Put whatever is being organized inside the wheel and attach the tasks or activities as spokes around the wheel.

2. Number all the attached items around the wheel.

3. Next, figure out how much time is available to complete the numbered items. Then, break the amount of available time down into manageable units. For example, if 1 week was given for the above tasks to be completed, the units of time would probably be 7 days. A box is drawn to represent each unit of time.

4. Distribute the numbers of the tasks over units of time and set a timer so that the end of each unit serves as a point to monitor progress. Consider deadlines so that the items that need to be completed by a specific time are scheduled accordingly.

5. When the unit of time (one day in this case) is over, cross out the completed items and move uncompleted items into the next unit of time. The visual presentation of the units of time and the self-monitoring of progress allows for speeding up, adjusting time limits, or slowing down as necessary. The strategy is also designed to sharpen time estimation skills to improve time management.

1. Math: Page 42, examples 1–8
2. Science: Study for test
3. Literature: Read pages 18–29
4. History: Read and answer
   questions on page 87
5. Five-minute break

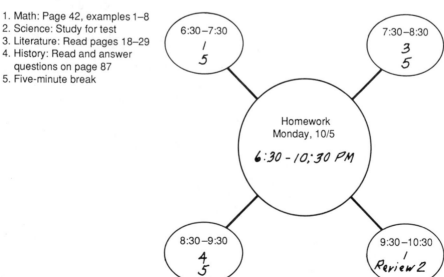

Box 9.1   Robert Uses the Systematic Study Strategy

Robert is practicing a study strategy Mr. Abel taught him. As Robert reads each section in his geography textbook, he takes special notice of the names of people and places, as well as important numbers, dates, and new terms. He writes each name, term, and date on a separate index card. He also prepares a card containing a question, using each subheading of the chapter. Thus, when Robert has completed the chapter, he has a set of cards to help him review the chapter information for the geography test. (See also Chapter 13 for a complete explanation of this study strategy.) Below are four cards prepared by Robert for the first paragraph he read:

latitude	longitude
degrees	equator

---

which to write activities and assignment due-dates, and plastic-covered pages outlining steps for particular study strategies the student may be learning. The teacher may also suggest that the student use plastic pencil pouches for index cards prepared for the Systematic Study System. With notebook organization, students should have all the materials necessary for participation in their classes.

In addition to the Time Management and Systematic Study System strategies, Rooney (1990) gives directions for "Wheels for Writing" (see Figure 9.10) and suggests the use of "wheels" for math, speech writing, literature, and "feelings." She also uses index cards for vocabulary, foreign languages, and spelling. In each case, the student prepares flash cards for drill and for future reference. The student also is encouraged to use "pictorials," or visual representations of words or concepts, to aid in learning. For example, the student who is learning vocabulary words may write the new word on the front of a card. On the back, he or she would draw a picture to illustrate the concept and write a short definition or synonym for the word. According to Rooney,

> the drawing of the picture forces an understanding of the concept or an association that will aid memory retrieval. The most important point about the pictorial is that you should make the picture based on your personal

experience. If the picture is supplied by someone else, it is only another piece of information to be memorized. The association must be natural so it will be easier to retrieve. (p. 64)

Finally, students must be taught how to proofread their work for errors. Here again, Rooney (1990) uses index cards. She suggests that, together with the teacher, the student identify the kinds of errors he or she usually makes. Then, the student prepares a set of questions to use when proofreading written work. With each question placed on a separate card, the student reads through the written assignment to see if there are errors that relate to that card. The student should proofread for each question separately. For general proofreading, the student should read aloud with a finger or pencil eraser placed on each

---

Figure 9.10   "Wheels for Writing"

From Independent Strategies for Efficient Study, *by K.J. Rooney. Copyright © 1990 by J.R. Enterprises. Reprinted by permission of J.R. Enterprises, Richmond, VA 23230.*

Wheels are basic organizational units used for tracking details and main ideas as well as for breaking larger tasks into smaller tasks. Writing is a sophisticated process involving memory, creativity, spelling, punctuation, organization, sequencing, capitalization, and word usage rules. In order to simplify the process, the wheels are used to organize the separate sections so the work can be divided into manageable units according to the individual's attention span or schedule. The strategy involves the use of wheels but the number of wheels depends on the assignment. The basic strategy is presented below but is adjusted for use with essay questions, paragraphs, compositions, and term papers:

1. Place the title at the top of a sheet of lined paper.

2. Draw 5 wheels (ovals) on the first sheet. Mark the first oval with the word START and the last oval with the word END or THEREFORE. Place a word, a phrase, or a sentence in the first wheel to identify the idea/ideas that will be used to start (Introduction).

3. Inside each of the three middle wheels, write one main idea to be developed.

4. In the last wheel, marked END or THEREFORE, write a word, phrase, or sentence to identify the conclusion.

5. Reproduce each oval on a separate sheet of paper. Around each wheel, attach all possible details, ideas, or thoughts that are related to the idea in a spoke-like fashion around the wheel.

6. When all the ideas are around the wheels, go back and number the ideas in the order that they will be used.

The strategy results in a set of six pages. The first page has the five-circle overview, and the other pages have the individual wheels. The wheels can be used to develop an outline or write a rough draft.

word as it is read. This helps the student see whether extra words have been inserted or if words are missing. To check for spelling errors, Rooney recommends reading each word separately, beginning at the end of the paper and working backwards. Often, in proofreading from the beginning, the meaning of the text tricks readers into missing misspellings because they see what they think should be written rather than what is actually written.

The Strategies Intervention Model

The ultimate purpose of cognitive behavior modification and strategy training is independence. With the "self" emphasis of CBM, the student is learning not to depend solely on the teacher or anyone else for control, instruction, or reinforcement. The student is also enhancing self-confidence and self-esteem by knowing that he or she has the ability to gain self-control. In order to promote this independence, researchers at the University of Kansas devised the Learning Strategies Curriculum (Deshler & Schumaker, 1988; Ellis, Deshler, Lenz, Schumaker, & Clark, 1991). This curriculum teaches students strategies for acquiring, storing, and expressing information learned in content classrooms. (See Figure 9.11 for examples of strategies from this curriculum.)

For strategy training to be effective, however, the teacher should keep in mind several guidelines. The required task, the strategies currently in use by the student, the setting in which the task must be performed, the student's level of motivation, and the materials which the student must use are all important considerations in choosing the learning strategies to teach a particular student. When using the Strategies Intervention Model (Deshler & Schumaker, 1988), teachers of students with mild disabilities should follow the essential steps described in Figure 9.12.

One representative learning strategy described by Alley and Deshler (1979) is SCORER, a test-taking strategy that will improve student performance on objective tests. The SCORER strategy is taught using the procedures described in Figure 9.12. The letters in the acronym, SCORER, stand for the following steps in the strategy:

S = Schedule your time. Allot more time for the harder questions and those with a greater point value.

C = Clue words. Look for tip-off words in true/false items. For example, *all, always, none,* and *never* frequently indicate false answers. *Usually* and *sometimes* frequently indicate true answers.

O = Omit the difficult questions on the first pass. Mark the questions you skip with a light check mark in the margin.

R = Read your answers. Look for clues in other test items to help you answer questions you are uncertain about. Eliminate alternatives you are certain are incorrect, then make your best guess. When you have answered the easy questions, go back to the checked questions. If you are still uncertain about the answer, add another light check mark in the margin.

Figure 9.11   Sample Strategies from the Learning Strategies Curriculum

---

Note: Information about the Learning Strategies Curriculum and each of these strategies may be purchased by writing to Coordinator, Institute for Research in Learning Disabilities, 3061 Dole Human Development Center, University of Kansas, Lawrence, Kansas 66045–2342.

The Learning Strategies Curriculum offers several strategies in three different strands: acquiring, storing, and expressing information.

Acquiring Information	*Storing Information*	*Expressing Information and Demonstrating Competence*
Interpreting visuals	First-letter mnemonic	Assignment completion
Multipass	Listening and notetaking	Error monitoring
Paraphrasing	Paired associates	Paragraph writing
Self-questioning		Sentence writing
Visual imagery		Test taking
Word identification		Theme writing

E = Estimate your answers. On test items that require calculations, roughly estimate the answer to help prevent careless errors.

R = Review your work. Read through all the questions as time permits. Don't be eager to change answers. Change only those you have a good reason for changing. Start with the questions with two check marks, then those with one check mark, then the unmarked questions. If there is no penalty for guessing, be sure to take your best guess and do not leave any questions blank.

Although not a part of the Learning Strategies Curriculum, the FORCE strategy (Wehrung-Schaffner & Sapona, 1990), is a similar step-by-step procedure designed to assist students in preparing for tests. This strategy also follows the guidelines for teaching learning strategies suggested by Deshler and Schumaker and their colleagues at the University of Kansas Institute for Research on Learning Disabilities (Deshler, Alley, Warner, & Schumaker, 1981). (See Chapter 13 for additional learning strategies.)

A Summary of Strategies

Although cognitive behavior modification procedures and learning strategies hold promise for improving the academic and behavioral skills of students with mild disabilities, the generalization of skills learned in the special classroom to the regular classroom setting remains problematic (Rooney & Hallahan, 1985). If teachers are to maximize the probability that their students will use learning strategies appropriately, they must teach only those strategies that relate to their student's needs and carefully follow the procedures described in Figure 9.12.

Figure 9.12   The Steps of FORCE

From "May the FORCE Be with You: A Test Preparation Strategy for Learning Disabled Adolescents, by L. Wehrung and R. H. Sapona, 1990, Academic Therapy, 25(3), pp. 293–96. Copyright © 1990 by PRO-ED, Inc. Reprinted with permission.

F = Find Out   Your teacher announces a test. If you don't receive all of the information that you need, ask questions, for example, "What will the test cover?" "What types of questions will be used?"

O = Organize   Collect all necessary materials for taking the test, such as notes, old tests, or books.

R = Review   Do the general review necessary to study for this test; for example, skim chapters, charts, maps, summaries, questions, or vocabulary; highlight notes; review old tests and assignments.

C = Concentrate Make a study sheet (cue sheet) by putting important information in question/answer form.

E = Early Exam   Practice the test by pretesting. For example, take turns asking questions with a partner (study buddy); have your parents or other adults help you drill from your study sheet; take your own test from your study sheet. Now review those weak spots until you are certain of what you know. There may be a few items you want to review right before the test.

When teaching learning strategies, include the following important steps:

1. *Measure preskills, current study habits, and current attitudes* toward test taking. A preskill and attitude questionnaire (developed by the teacher) is presented in a true/false format. Examples include the following: "I can take notes easily from the board"; "I keep most of my old tests, notes, and so forth"; "I do not feel frustrated when I take tests"; "I don't mind asking a teacher for help"; and "I have an obligation to ask questions when I need help." Results from this questionnaire and other student data, as well as teacher observation, help to establish whether a student is ready for instruction in the FORCE strategy. Preskills include knowledge of parts of a book, organizational skills, note taking, outlining, and knowledge of various test formats (e.g., objective, essay, matching). Approximately 75% mastery of preskills is needed prior to implementation of the strategy.

2. *Describe the new strategy* and how the previously learned preskills relate to its effectiveness. *Present a rationale for using the strategy.* Why should a student bother to use it? A teacher might pose the following question to the class: "If I could show you a way to study for a test that would improve your grades in most cases, would you be interested?"

(continued)

Figure 9.12 *(Continued)*

---

3. *Offer specific and isolated instruction of the strategy.* If the strategy is supposed to be important to the students, then it must be important to you, their teacher, to provide specific class time for instruction and implementation.

4. *Model each component of the strategy* using role play whenever possible. The teacher might say, for example, "F stands for FIND OUT. If the teacher announces a test, but doesn't fill you in on sufficient details about it, ask the appropriate questions at an appropriate time and in an appropriate manner. The key word here seems to be 'appropriate.' Let's role play some appropriate and inappropriate questions."

5. *Rehearse verbally* with students often. There are always times of the day when one might say, "Which part of FORCE is that?" or "Which component of FORCE could you use to improve your grade?" Sometimes, one of the questions on a quiz will be "What does the F stand for in FORCE?"

6. *Practice on controlled materials.* Begin implementation with high-interest materials that are at a comfortable reading level for the students. The primary concern at this point is for the students to learn the strategy.

7. *Practice on actual classroom materials.* It is important to use the strategy in a relevant situation as soon as possible. A pretest checklist can be given to students to assist them in monitoring their use of the strategy. Examples of items on the checklist are (1) "What will the test cover? Notes, maps, old tests, chapter questions, handouts, homework assignments, text, worksheets." (2) "What pages will be covered in the text, if any?"

8. *Reinforce the use of the strategy* after the test with a post-test evaluation sheet (developed by the teacher). This questionnaire will help determine the extent to which the student used the strategy. Sample questions include, "Did you prepare a study sheet in a question/answer format from materials that were covered on the test?" "Did you test yourself either alone or with another person by asking questions from a study sheet?" Also teach students to provide reinforcement for one another and themselves. A conversation with Robert who did not do as well on a test as he had a few weeks before went something like this: "I usually study with Joe, but I didn't this week. Next week I'll work with him. It seems to help—studying with him right before the test." At this point Mr. Abel may ask, "That's great you realize that, Robert. What part of FORCE is that?"

9. *Provide frequent opportunities to use the strategy.* It might be helpful to test frequently, at least once a week, in order to give the students plenty of chances to put the strategy into action.

(continued)

Figure 9.12 *(Continued)*

---

10. Chart the test scores and *post-test* evaluation sheets. Evaluate the results and discuss with the student the relationships between the two graphs (test scores and information gained from post-test evaluation sheets). It is important to point out any patterns that establish a correlation between test scores and strategy use.

11. *Explicitly suggest the use of FORCE in other classes.* If the teacher offers assistance to the students in self-monitoring and self-evaluation, students learn to depend on themselves to organize and study materials for tests. Frequent reminders help. This is an area in which parents can become powerful allies. They can remind students to use the strategy when studying other subjects and find ways in which the strategy can be used in the home setting.

✎ Summary

Both classroom teachers and special educators encounter students with widely varying ability levels and needs. Such diversity may challenge the teacher when providing individualized instruction for students with mild disabilities. Through cooperative learning groups and peer-tutoring arrangements, students with disabilities and other students with low achievement can receive additional instruction and reinforcement of skills. Students with and without mild disabilities will also benefit from instruction in cognitive behavior modification procedures that may enhance their ability to study and guide them in monitoring and controlling their own behaviors. Independent strategies for study and learning strategies also enable students with mild disabilities to help themselves to learn.

✎ Application Exercises

1. Observe cooperative learning groups in a general education classroom. Ask the teacher how the team members were selected and what the responsibilities of each team member are.

2. Interview a student with a learning disability in a secondary school to determine the types of tasks required of him or her in general education classes. Inquire as to what kind of activities best facilitate the student's

learning process (e.g., cooperative learning groups; peer tutoring, either as a tutor or a tutee; learning strategies).

3. Observe in a classroom using peer tutoring. Ask the teacher how peer tutors are selected, trained, and monitored. Ask some of the tutor/tutee pairs to express the things they like the most about peer tutoring.

Reading Instruction

Chapter 10

Focus

As you read, think about the following questions:

What is meant by a ''whole-language'' approach to reading and the language arts?

How do authorities differ in their ideas about the nature of reading and reading instruction?

What role does direct instruction of phonics skills play within a whole-language curriculum?

Which approaches to initial reading instruction are supported by research for use with children with mild disabilities?

What are some effective methods for helping children with mild disabilities comprehend materials they read?

✎ Children and youth with mild disabilities have numerous deficits in the language arts. Reading is, without a doubt, the area in which most of these youngsters experience difficulty; however, spelling, handwriting, and written expression are three related language arts that also present significant hurdles (Fessler, Rosenberg, & Rosenberg, 1991; Scruggs & Mastropieri, 1986). Listening and speaking are additional skills considered to be language arts; however, in this chapter we will focus primarily on reading instruction—an area crucial to all school success. Although specific methods for teaching spelling, handwriting, and written expression are not discussed until Chapter 11, we will explore the interrelated nature of reading and the language arts within this chapter. Keep this relationship in mind as you read both Chapters 10 and 11.

As children move up the grade levels, they are expected to use reading and writing skills more and more to obtain and demonstrate knowledge. Youngsters lacking these basic skills, therefore, face a serious disadvantage across the entire curriculum when compared with their normally achieving peers. Consider, for example, the case of Robert in his earth science class with Ms. Stone:

Ms. Stone: [Having completed her introduction of igneous, metamorphic, and sedimentary rocks, she is passing out a study guide and assigning homework.] *Tonight, please read Section 5.2 in your text, pages 314–320, and answer the five questions on your study guide. You have 10 minutes left in the class period to go ahead and start your homework with your lab team.* [She writes the page numbers on the board as students begin working.]

Robert: [Opening his textbook to the proper page, he reads silently.] *Scientists have id, i-den, identified three ba, basi, basic pro, pro, processes by which rocks are formed. These pro, processes are used, useful class, classi, classifying. . . . These processes are used by geo, geo, geologists when class, classifying rocks for study. I-ge-neous, Ig-e-neous, Ign-ne-ous rocks are formed when . . .* [He looks up as he becomes aware that the other three students on his lab team have located the answer to the first question on the study guide: *How do geologists classify rocks? He writes on his paper: "Geolugists clasify rocks by igneus, metmorfic, and saidamentery."*]

Students like Robert, who must struggle to read the textbook or to write coherent answers to questions posed by teachers, fall farther and farther behind their classmates every day (Coutinho, 1986). How can teachers help youngsters with mild disabilities learn to read and write more effectively? This question will serve as the central theme for both Chapters 10 and 11. Let us turn first, however, to a discussion of the reading process, a summary of the difficulties encountered by students with mild disabilities when learning to read, and an examination of the interrelated nature of reading and the language arts. Then, we will present effective methods for teaching children with mild disabilities to read.

✎ The Nature of Reading and Reading Problems

Researchers use many models to explain how children learn to read. For example, authorities may consider reading to be a "top-down," a "bottom-up," or an "interactive" process. In addition, some researchers emphasize developmental or information-processing models when explaining the nature of reading. All models, however, emphasize two major elements: decoding or recognizing words and comprehending the meaning of written text.

Goodman (1970) and Smith (1971) were among the first to describe reading as a top-down process. According to these authorities, the reader brings to the reading task past experiences and background knowledge about language and about the world. Rather than relying on individual words or parts of words to obtain meaning, the reader predicts meaning as reading occurs, advancing hypotheses about what is read based on prior knowledge and reading to confirm these predictions. Thus, the reader is an active participant in constructing his or her own meaning from the text. Proponents of a bottom-up model, on the other hand, view reading as a process of decoding individual letters and words and of putting words and sentences together to achieve meaning (Liberman & Shankweiler, 1985). Rather than bringing meaning to the text, the skillful reader extracts the meaning by fluently decoding or recognizing words.

Today, however, many authorities consider reading an interactive process (Spiro & Meyers, 1984; Stanovich, 1980). This view holds that the reading task is composed of alternating or simultaneous use of *both* top-down and bottom-up processes. The mature reader brings to the printed page background knowledge and experience, using these to predict and construct meaning from the text. When unknown words are encountered, though, the reader may switch to a bottom-up strategy. Thus, background knowledge and decoding skill interact as the reader engages with the text.

Similarly, Chall (1983) proposes a developmental model of reading in which children progress through a sequence of stages. In stage I, children learn the alphabet and the sounds of letters. During stage II, youngsters practice the basic decoding and word-recognition skills learned in stage I in order to achieve fluency and speed and to gain meaning from the text. By stage III (grades 4–8), children must learn from reading so that in high school, stage IV, they can read substantial amounts of text with differing points of view. Although this model emphasizes mastery of component reading skills, particularly in stages I and II, Chall believes that the child's prior experience and knowledge influence how rapidly the youngster will progress. Moreover, when faced with difficult text or unknown words, children will revert to stage I or II skills.

LaBerge and Samuels (1974) also hold that children progress through a hierarchy of reading skills, from decoding to comprehension. In their information-processing model, however, attention is a critical element. Children must become automatic and fluent with lower-level reading skills, recognizing letters and remembering letter–sound correspondences, in order to free a limited attentional capacity for comprehension skills. Therefore, the goal of initial reading instruction according to this model is fluent decoding.

Each of these models helps to explain the difficulty children with mild disabilities may have when learning to read. For example, Stanovich (1986a) maintains that much of the variance in reading ability among children and youth may be due to differing levels of decoding ability. Because poor readers are deficient in decoding skills, they may be too dependent on top-down processes, guessing at words based on the first letters and on the context. On the other hand, Samuels (1987) holds that poor readers rely on bottom-up processes more than do mature readers. That is, poor readers often use the single letter as the unit of recognition, placing heavy demands on short-term memory and hindering comprehension. Most authorities now agree, though, that poor readers have deficits in phonological processes—the skills necessary for segmenting, blending, and manipulating phonemes (units of sound)—rather than deficits in visual processes, such as letter reversals (Foorman & Liberman, 1989; Lenchner, Gerber, & Routh, 1990; Mann, Cowin, & Schoenheimer, 1989).

Although poor readers may have problems with reading comprehension that cannot be explained solely by deficient decoding ability, there is evidence to suggest that the primary difficulty for most poor readers originates with inadequate decoding skills (Spear & Sternberg, 1986). Deficits in decoding ability limit the child's future interaction with text, thus limiting the knowledge and experience the child may gain from reading (Stanovich, 1986b). Unfortunately, children in the bottom reading groups may not receive the intense instruction in decoding skills, coupled with exposure to extended text, necessary to accelerate their progress and allow them to access school knowledge (McGill-Franzen & Allington, 1991).

Because children with mild disabilities often encounter difficulty with decoding and word recognition, special educators must emphasize these essential skills during initial reading instruction. Teachers must remember, however, that students with mild disabilities also need instruction and practice with connected text if they are to learn to comprehend what they read. Finally, rather than endless drill and practice of isolated skills on workbook pages, youngsters with mild disabilities must have opportunities to integrate reading and writing activities.

✎ Whole Language and Reading Instruction

Recently, literature-based approaches to teaching reading have become increasingly popular. Criticism of skills-oriented reading materials and instruction in such national reports as *Becoming a Nation of Readers* (Anderson, Hiebert, Scott, & Wilkinson, 1985) at least partly account for the popularity of a "whole-language" approach to reading and the language arts. Advocates of a whole-language approach believe that children must learn to read and to write in a natural context, and that reading and writing skills are inherently connected (Goodman, 1986). Rather than breaking reading and writing into separate component skills, whole-language proponents maintain that all skill instruction must be integrated with the literature being read. Therefore, as described by Butler (1987), teachers using a whole-language approach typically

1. read quality literature to children;

2. read and reread rhymes, songs, poems, and stories, particularly those with predictable or repetitive lines (e.g., "I'll huff, and I'll puff, and . . .");

3. set aside time each day for sustained silent reading for everyone, including the teacher;

4. provide guided reading for small groups of children using books selected to suit the interests and abilities of group members;

5. provide individualized reading opportunities;

6. organize language-experience activities so that children may write about what they do;

7. afford children numerous opportunities to write about topics of interest, focusing initially on the content rather than on the form;

8. model "expert" writing for children;

9. provide opportunities for children to share or publish finished writing; and

10. demonstrate reading and writing with content-area text.

Although whole-language advocates realize that some time must be spent on decoding skills, they maintain that this instruction must always be integrated with quality literature. They criticize the skill-building drill-and-practice activities of traditional classrooms as boring exercises, bearing little resemblance to authentic reading and writing experiences. They suggest instead that teachers use repetitive lines within stories and poems to help children figure out the code on their own (Cullinan, 1987). Moreover, whole-language proponents argue that the books often used with poor readers are so contrived in vocabulary and style that most children find them unappealing. According to whole-language advocates, poor readers do not understand why they are completing drill-and-practice activities; moreover, they are frustrated with the dull stories they are expected to read (Routman, 1988).

Whole-language proponents properly remind us that all children need exposure to quality literature and that reading and writing are related activities. Nevertheless, the reader must remember that children with mild disabilities do not learn well from indirect instruction. Although whole language may increase a student's motivation to read, the teacher must provide systematic instruction in decoding and comprehension skills if youngsters with mild disabilities are to learn *how* to read (Chall, 1989; Gersten & Dimino, 1990; Stahl & Miller, 1989). We will return to this discussion later in the chapter; however, for now, let's examine the major approaches used during initial, or developmental, reading instruction.

✎ Developmental Reading

Developmental reading refers to a sequence of daily activities designed to teach children to read for the first time. Many children with mild disabilities fail in their developmental reading programs. Others may participate in these programs, to some extent, in their mainstreamed classrooms. For these reasons, special education teachers must understand the developmental reading programs used in their schools.

Typically, a series of books (the basal readers) form the core of a developmental reading program. These books gradually increase in difficulty from preprimers, primers, and the first reader through about the eighth-grade level. In addition, the basal reading series provides the teacher with lesson plans, supplementary activities, and skill-building workbooks and worksheets to guide instruction.

Within the teachers' manuals are suggestions for specific instructional procedures. Most basal reading series use either a directed reading activity or a directed reading-thinking activity as a guide for reading lessons. In the *directed reading activity,* the teacher begins by motivating students to learn the material. Next, the teacher presents new vocabulary or concepts and actively guides students while they read the story by asking specific questions to establish a purpose for reading. Finally, the teacher develops related skills using drill, workbook pages, and independent assignments, and evaluates the effectiveness of the lesson. By contrast, in the directed *reading-thinking activity,* the teacher serves to facilitate, rather than guide, lessons. With teacher assistance, children come up with their own purposes for reading and formulate their own questions. The teacher then challenges them to think about the validity of the answers they propose or the conclusions they draw (e.g., "What evidence is there in the story to support your statement?").

Although basal reading series are comprehensive instructional programs, they usually emphasize one of two major approaches to initial reading instruction: a code-emphasis approach (i.e., a bottom-up philosophy of the reading process) or a meaning-emphasis approach (i.e., a top-down theory). All basals include activities designed to increase both decoding and comprehension skills; however, the relative emphasis each receives within the series defines the approach used.

Code-emphasis basals begin with letters and letter sounds. Children learn consistent letter–sound associations and other essential phonics skills to help them unlock the code and become independent readers. Comprehension skills are included within these series, but the primary focus, initially, is on decoding.

Although all code-emphasis basals obviously begin with decoding skills, they differ in how these skills are presented. Direct-synthetic phonics programs present letter–sound (i.e., grapheme–phoneme) correspondences and sound blending explicitly. For example, children learn the sounds of *m, a,* and *n* individually, and then learn to move from one sound to another to blend the word *man.* Indirect, or analytic, phonics programs, on the other hand, present letter sounds only within the context of whole words. Children learn the sound of *d* as in *daddy* or, in the special case of linguistic approaches, the sounds within word families (e.g., *can, ran, man, tan, pan*).

Meaning-emphasis basals, however, begin with words children often use. Because these frequently occurring words are familiar to most children, they are presumably easier for children to recognize. Youngsters learn to read words by sight, as whole units having meaning, and to use context clues to identify unknown words. Throughout reading instruction, the focus is on comprehension and the meaning of words within connected text. The whole-language movement represents a recent resurgence of interest in the meaning-emphasis approach.

Research on Developmental Reading Approaches

Over the years, debate has raged regarding the "best" approach for initial reading instruction. In a classic review of both experimental and correlational research on reading instruction, *Learning to Read: The Great Debate,* Chall (1967) draws the following conclusions:

1. A code-emphasis approach produces better reading achievement by the third grade than a meaning emphasis approach.

2. Children of average and below-average intelligence and children of low socioeconomic backgrounds learn to read better with a code-emphasis approach.

3. Both code-emphasis and meaning-emphasis approaches produce reading failures, but failures are more serious within the meaning-emphasis approach.

Later, in an updated version of this classic, Chall (1983) states that, although phonics instruction has become widely accepted and taught early in the grades, authorities are now debating the "best" method for phonics instruction. She adds, however, that experimental and correlational evidence favors a direct-synthetic phonics approach, particularly for children with mild disabilities.

Recently, in response to a congressional request for a reevaluation of phonics instruction and a renewed interest in meaning-emphasis approaches, Adams (1990) reviewed a substantial body of research on the teaching of reading. Although very little research in her review involved special education populations, Adams stated:

1. Programs using systematic phonics instruction in addition to connected reading are superior to those that use either alone.

2. A child's knowledge of the letters of the alphabet and his or her ability to discriminate phonemes are the two best predictors of first-grade reading achievement.

3. Teaching explicit (direct-synthetic) phonics is more effective than teaching indirect phonics.

4. The most important outcome of phonics instruction is not the ability to sound out words, but rather the ability to recognize letters, letter patterns, and words automatically.

Ideally, with intensive decoding instruction early in the grades, only a very few children would fail to learn to read. Unfortunately, though, most children with mild disabilities are referred to special education programs *because* of reading problems. Initial reading instruction for these children must be explicit, direct, and focused on essential phonics skills. As children become automatic and fluent with decoding and word recognition, their teachers may emphasize direct instruction of comprehension skills and comprehension strategies. Although initial reading instruction should be structured and highly focused, teachers can still read quality literature to children with mild disabilities and provide them with opportunities to talk and write about what they read. Let's now turn to a discussion of remedial reading instruction for youngsters with reading disabilities.

✎ Remedial Reading Approaches

For many children with mild disabilities, the typical reading lesson in the regular classroom is inadequate (Simmons, Fuchs, & Fuchs, 1991). Words are not repeated frequently enough in the basal readers for children with learning disabilities, emotional disturbance, or mild mental retardation to master them (Chall, 1983). In addition, many familiar first words introduced in meaning-emphasis or whole-language preprimers and primers (*you* or *the,* for example) are difficult to decode, containing irregularities or letters representing other than their most common sounds (Kameenui & Simmons, 1990).

Repetition and explicit teaching are hallmarks of special education classrooms. Successful remedial reading instruction, therefore, adheres to these principles of effective teaching and includes an early emphasis on phonics skills and sight word recognition. In addition, teachers maintain that, for some children, a specialized multisensory approach or the language-experience approach (LEA) may be useful. Finally, as children in special education classrooms become fluent with decoding and word recognition, their teachers must provide direct instruction in comprehension skills and strategies.

Phonics Instruction and Phonics Programs

Children with mild disabilities must be directly taught the phonics skills necessary to "unlock" the code. Initially, students learn the most common letter–sound associations for the consonants and the short vowels. Carnine et al. (1990) suggest that teachers begin with "more useful" letter sounds (i.e., the short vowels and the consonants *b, c, d, f, g, h, k, l, m, n, p, r, s,* and *t,* although not necessarily in that order) and that they separate, auditorily or visually, similar letters by at least three dissimilar ones. As students become automatic with five or six grapheme–phoneme relationships, sound blending may be introduced using regular consonant-vowel (CV) or consonant-vowel-consonant (CVC) words (e.g., *at, map*). The sequence described in Table 10.1 is recommended for teaching blending with regular one-syllable words with short vowels.

When students have mastered basic letter–sound correspondences and are successfully sound blending, they must learn useful letter combinations and phonics rules. Letter combinations include:

1. the vowel and consonant digraphs: two vowels or two consonants that together make one sound, such as *oa* in *boat* or *sh* in *ship;*

2. the diphthongs: two vowels, each modifying one another and both contributing to the sound produced, such as *oy* in *boy;*

3. the "*r*-controlled" vowels: a vowel followed by the letter *r*, such as *ar* in *smart;* and

4. the "*l*-controlled" vowels, such as *ol* in *cold.*

Teaching these letter combinations permits the child to attack words generally considered to be "irregular" as if they were "regular." That is, once students have mastered the basic letter combinations, they can be prompted to "look in the middle of the word" for spelling patterns whenever mispronunciation occurs (Schworm, 1988). In addition, useful phonics rules that may be taught include the CVCe pattern (e.g., *made, hope*); *c* followed by *e* or *i* makes the *s* sound (e.g., *cent*); and *c* followed by *o* or *a* makes the *k* sound (e.g., *cotton*) (Carnine et al. 1990).

Table 10.1   A Teaching Sequence for Blending Regular One-Syllable Words with Short Vowels

---

Carnine, Silbert, and Kameenui (1990) recommend the following sequence when teaching blending:

1. VC and CVC words beginning with continuous sounds (i.e., sounds that may be prolonged and stretched, such as /m/, or all vowels, as in *me* or *man*);

2. CVCC words beginning with continuous sounds (e.g., *fill, mist*);

3. CVC words that begin with stop sounds (i.e., sounds that can't be prolonged, such as /p/ in *pat*);

4. CVCC words that begin with stop sounds (e.g., *band, past*);

5. CCVC words beginning with two continuous consonant sounds (i.e., the two-letter consonant blends, such as in *slam* or *flat*);

6. CCVC words beginning with one continuous and one stop sound (e.g., *stop, skip*); and

7. CCVCC words (e.g., *blast, crust*) and CCCVCC words (e.g., *struck, splint*).

More advanced decoding skills involve the structural, or morphemic, analysis of words. That is, children learn to break words into meaningful parts. These may include compound words, such as *baseball,* or a base word plus frequently occurring prefixes, such as *un-;* suffixes, such as *-ness;* or inflectional endings, such as *ing, ed,* or *s.* Again, teaching useful rules may assist youngsters with mild disabilities to recognize or spell unknown words. Examples of useful rules include the following:

1. The doubling rule: When suffixes beginning with a vowel are added to a CVC word, the final consonant in the word is doubled (e.g., *fat* becomes *fatter,* but *sing* stays the same in *singing* and *sad* stays the same in *sadness*).

2. The *y* rule: When a consonant comes before a *y* in a base word, the *y* changes to *i* before an ending is added (e.g., *happy* changes to *happiness* or *happiest,* but *play* remains the same, as in *played*).

Special education teachers often supplement the basal reading series with direct instruction of phonics skills. In order to provide explicit and comprehensive instruction with enough repetition to ensure proficient decoding, teachers may wish to choose one of several code-based programs available commercially as the core for reading lessons. Many of these programs are total reading curricula that could also be considered developmental; however, they are most often used for remedial reading, and therefore will be included here in our discussion. Teachers may also wish to consult several older phonics programs, including *The Writing Road to Reading* (Spalding & Spalding, 1962); *Phonetic Keys to Reading* (Harris, Creekmore, & Greenman, 1967); and *The Phonovisual Method* (Schoolfield & Timberlake, 1974).

The Reading Mastery Series: DISTAR reading and corrective reading. "Reading Mastery: DISTAR" (Direct Instructional System for Teaching Arithmetic and Reading) is a highly structured and rapidly paced reading program at two levels (Engelmann & Bruner, 1984), designed for children through grade 3. The program uses a direct-synthetic phonics approach and provides teachers with scripted 30-minute lessons, detailed hand signals to guide student responding, and specific error-correction procedures (see Box 10.1). Because the authors believe letter sounds to be the most useful association to learn (Engelman & Bruner, 1984), students are initially taught to recognize the sounds of letters rather than the letter names. In addition to letter–sound correspondence, sound blending, and letter combinations, DISTAR gives the student practice in both literal and inferential comprehension skills.

The "Corrective Reading Program" (Engelmann, Becker, Hanner, & Johnson, 1980) follows an instructional sequence similar to that of DISTAR; however, the format is more appropriate for older children. Designed for remedial or nonreading students in grade 4 or above, Corrective Reading provides 340 lessons in two strands: decoding and comprehension. Again, lessons are scripted for teachers to follow, but real-life applications and a group-reward system provide motivation for older children with reading problems.

Both DISTAR and Corrective Reading have an extensive research base. Although most studies report favorable results for low-achieving children (Carnine & Silbert, 1979; Stallings, 1974) and for students with learning disabilities, mild mental retardation, or emotional disturbance (Polloway, Epstein, Polloway, Patton, & Ball, 1986), some suggest only mixed effectiveness (for example, Kuder, 1990, 1991). In addition, some teachers object to the scripted nature of the materials, maintaining that these programs inhibit "teaching creatively." One must remember, however, that the progress of children, not the whims of the teacher, should dictate program selection.

The Gillingham–Stillman method.   Although originally said to be a multisensory procedure using the Visual-Auditory-Kinesthetic-Tactile (VAKT) approach, the Gillingham–Stillman method (Gillingham & Stillman, 1973) consists of direct-synthetic phonics instruction. This program emphasizes how letters and words look, how they sound, and how the speech organs or the hands feel when producing the letter or the word. In addition, the history of

---

Box 10.1   Direct-Synthetic Phonics Instruction

When using a direct-synthetic phonics approach, letter–sound correspondence and sound blending are taught explicitly. The following example from *DISTAR Reading* is illustrative of this approach. The teacher is given the following instructions:

Say, "Everybody look at the book," and offer praise to children who look.
Say, "mmm. This is mmm." While pointing to the *m*.
Say, "Say mmm." Pause and say, "Good."

(The teacher continues this procedure pointing to *m* and to a picture of an ice-cream cone as a distractor. Notice that the *m* is introduced by its sound rather than by its name.)

Later, sound blending is introduced through a "sound-sliding" game. Children are taught to hold sounds and to slide slowly from one sound to another, using an arrow from left to right under the letters as a directional clue. Next, youngsters "say it fast" to produce a word, as in the following example:

1. "Let's follow the arrow and say the sounds." Point to *a:* "aaa. Keep it going. Louder."

2. Have the children hold *a* until you point to *m*. Do not pause. Point to *m* and say, "mmm."

3. Return to the beginning of the arrow. "Let's do it again." Move rapidly from *a* to *m*, saying "aaammm." Pause, then say, "Again." Repeat three times. Then say, "Say it fast!" Pause and say, "Yes, am."

4. "Let's follow the arrow and see what word this is: aaammm. Say it fast!" Pause and say, "Yes, am. Am. I am happy."

Adapted from DISTAR Reading I: Sounds and Reading Sounds, Book A, *by S. Engelman and E.C. Bruner. Copyright © 1974 by SRA, Macmillan/Mc-Graw Hill. Adapted by permission of Science Research Associates, Chicago, IL 60606-1780.*

the English language is included as a fundamental part of the program so as to enable the child to understand inconsistencies in pronunciation and spelling and to attack unknown words more effectively. Originally designed for pupils at the high school level, the method is successful with older and younger individuals as well (Guyer & Sabatino, 1989).

Within the teacher's manual are explicit guidelines for the instructor to follow. For example, the program requires a minimum of 2 years of lessons for approximately 45 minutes to 1 hour each day. Moreover, teachers and parents are requested not to permit the child access to any materials that do not conform to the method until new habits and skills are acquired. Parents and teachers, may, of course, read content textbooks or other literature aloud to the child so that he or she may keep up with classwork.

Instruction begins with the introduction of letters on letter cards, starting with the consonants *b, f, h, j, k, m, p, t* and the short vowel sounds. White cards are used for the consonants; salmon-colored cards are used for the vowels. Later, buff-colored cards introduce additional phonemes for reading and spelling. Each letter is shown initially with a key word, which is always repeated before the child states the letter name or sound. Letter names and sounds are introduced using the following procedures:

1. Show the letter card, say the letter name, and have the child repeat it.

2. Show the letter card, say the letter sound, and have the child repeat it.

3. Have the child feel your throat and his or her own throat for vibrations or have the child feel the breath flow from your mouth and his or her own mouth.

4. Write the letter in cursive, pointing out the strokes and any identifying visual clues for the letters, and have the child trace the letter while saying first the letter name and then the letter sound until he or she can write the letter correctly from memory.

5. You say the letter name and the child says the sound.

6. You say the letter sound and the child says the name.

7. You say the letter sound and the child writes the letter from memory.

8. Use the first six letters introduced for practice in sound blending.

9. Progress to simultaneous oral spelling (SOS), during which the child repeats a word dictated by you, names the letters in the word, writes the word while again naming each letter, and reads the word he or she has written.

10. Teach additional phongrams (e.g., digraphs *ch* or *sh*) and word-attack/spelling rules (e.g., For a one-syllable word ending in *f, l,* or *s* following only one vowel, double the *f, l,* or *s,* as in *puff, tell,* or *kiss*).

Children keep new words in word boxes and progress to reading controlled stories containing mostly CVC words and a few irregular sight words. Teachers give students any sight words necessary for story reading, and students silently prepare to read each sentence, asking for assistance only if necessary. When students finally read orally, they are expected to read fluently and with expression. Later, teachers dictate the same stories for pupils to write. Timed readings and graphs are also used to enhance motivation and record progress.

The Gillingham-Stillman method is a highly structured and repetitive approach to teaching synthetic phonics skills. Critics suggest, however, that students with mild disabilities may become confused when asked to learn both the letter name and the letter sound. In addition, the contrived stories may be boring, particularly to older students. Finally, school districts may be unable to allocate the extended time necessary for the program when faced with standards for learning objectives at each grade level and content requirements for graduation credits. (For information on this approach, write to Orton Dyslexia Society, Inc., 724 York Rd., Towson, Maryland 21204.)

The Herman method for reversing reading failure. Like DISTAR, the Herman reading program (Romar Publications) developed by Renee Herman is a highly structured direct-synthetic phonics approach requiring a minimum of 2 years of daily lessons. Similar also to the Gillingham-Stillman method, the Herman program was developed to be multisensory in nature. The materials are designed for children in grades 3–12 who are below the 25th percentile in reading achievement. Detailed lesson plans and objectives are included in the teacher's manual and skills are presented using a multimedia format: 20 instructional filmstrips in two sets of 10, and more recently, computer software. In filmstrip Set A, children progress from basic consonant and short vowel sounds associated with key words to digraphs, beginning blends, sight words, and phrase reading. In Set B, more difficult letter combinations, prefixes, suffixes, and syllable-division rules are introduced. In addition, handwriting and spelling are integral parts of the total package. Although little research evidence exists in the literature to support the program itself, the heavy emphasis on structured phonics makes the Herman reading program attractive to many special education teachers. (For information on this program, write to Romar Publications, 4700 Tyrone Ave., Sherman Oaks, California 91423.)

Writing to Read. "Writing to Read" is a computer software package produced by International Business Machines (IBM) for beginning readers in kindergarten and grade 1. The program contains a blend of whole-language and phonics instruction using computerized voice capabilities. In drill-and-practice tutorials, children learn a special phonemic alphabet in which all letter–sound correspondences are made regular. They listen to taped stories containing the words and sounds they have learned and then write stories of their own using invented spellings.

"Writing to Read" is an expensive program, however, that is drawing criticism. Like other modified alphabet approaches used in the past (e.g., the *Initial Teaching Alphabet* introduced by Downing in 1965), "Writing to Read" offers no empirical evidence to support the use of its phonemically regular spelling system with regular or special education students (Freyd & Lytle, 1990). The primary strength of the program appears to be that of helping young children make the connection between speaking, reading, and writing. (For information on "Writing to Read" write IBM, One Culver Rd., Dayton, New Jersey 08810.)

The Merrill linguistic reading program.   This widely used indirect analytic phonics program is available from Science Research Associates, 860 Taylor Station Rd., P.O. Box 543, Blacklick, OH 43004. Rather than direct teaching of letter–sound correspondence and sound blending, children learn sounds through consistent word families following the CVC pattern (see Box 10.2). Later, additional spelling patterns and irregular sight words are introduced. Although the program follows a whole-word orientation, consistent letter–sound combinations are stressed. Because words are grouped in families, the stories are often contrived and stilted, making comprehension difficult for students with mild disabilities. Thus, the primary strength of the program, the controlled vocabulary, is also its greatest weakness.

Phonic remedial reading lessons.   "Phonic Remedial Reading Lessons" (Kirk, Kirk, & Minskoff, 1985) consists of 77 analytic phonics lessons providing repeated practice in sound blending through whole words. In each lesson, children first sound out the phonetic elements and then blend them into the given words. The lessons are designed for children reading below the third-grade level who require structure and repetition. "Phonic Remedial Reading Lessons" includes excellent word lists for constructing drill-and-practice activities. (These lessons are available through Academic Therapy Publications, 20 Commercial Blvd., Novato, California 94949.)

Computer software programs for phonics practice.   In order to make phonics practice more enjoyable for children with mild disabilities, teachers are increasingly turning to computer software programs. Two of these programs for use with Apple II computers, "Construct-a-Word" and "Hint and Hunt," both available from DLM Teaching Resources, P.O. Box 4000, Allen, Texas 75002, are effective in increasing decoding fluency in children with reading problems (Beck & Roth, 1984a, 1984b; Torgesen, 1986). In "Construct-a-Word," children create words by manipulating consonants, consonant blends, and other phonograms. A computerized voice (a "Supertalker," also from DLM Teaching Resources) pronounces each word for the student. "Hint" provides initial instruction with vowel sounds using animated graphics and the Supertalker. "Hunt" gives students additional practice with decoding skills through a fast-paced game format.

A summary of decoding-skills instruction.   Without a doubt, fluent decoding skills are necessary if children with mild disabilities are to become independent readers. Single-consonant and short vowel sounds, sound blending with CVC words, the most frequent sounds of common letter combinations, and high-utility rules are the basic ingredients for structured practice with phonics skills. These are also the elements of many direct-synthetic phonics programs. Although each of the programs we have described has both its proponents and critics, the choice of a particular program is probably less important than a

---

Box 10.2   Indirect Analytic Phonics Through a Linguistic Approach

In an indirect, or analytic, phonics approach, children learn the letter–sound associations through an examination of sounds within whole words. Some indirect analytic phonics programs present new words in word families, so that children can spot consistent letter–sound patterns. The following example from the *Merrill Linguistic Reading Program* (1986) is representative of this approach. Teachers introduce new words using the following procedure:

1. Write the word on the chalkboard.

2. Pronounce the word.

3. Spell it, pointing to each letter.

4. Pronounce the word again.

5. Pronounce the word in the context of a sentence.

6. Have pupils offer sentences using the word.

7. Have pupils read the word and spell it as you point to each letter. (Be sure pupils look at the word.)

Then, when introducing new words of the same pattern, teachers present the word in minimum contrast with familiar words:

1. Write the familiar word on the chalkboard.

2. Write the new word directly beneath it. For example, *cat*
        can

3. Have pupils read the familiar word.

4. Pronounce the new word and spell it.

5. Ask pupils how the two words differ.

6. Use steps 5, 6, and 7 described in the preceding procedure.

7. After the minimum contrast with a familiar word has been established, present subsequent words in the new pattern together. For example, *can*
          man

8. Ask pupils how the words differ.

The following is an example of a story from the *Merrill Linguistic Reading Program*. As you read the story, note the consistent word pattern:

> *A Man in a Van*
> Look at the van, Jan.
> A man is in the van.
> Jan ran to the van.
> Dan ran to the van.
> The man ran the van.
> Dan is not in the van.
> Jan is not in the van.

Adapted from I Can, Teacher's Edition, Level A: Merrill Linguistic Reading Program *(pp. 6, 46) by M. K. Rudolf and R. G. Wilson. Copyright © 1986 by SRA, Macmillan/ Mc-Graw Hill. Adapted by permission of Science Research Associates, Chicago, IL 60606-1780.*

---

basic commitment to *systematic* and *intensive* instruction in the essential decoding skills.

Many words in the English language, however, are not phonetically regular. These words must be taught and practiced as sight words—words to be recognized immediately as whole units. In addition, if students are to become fluent readers, they must progress from letter-by-letter decoding strategies to rapid and automatic recognition of whole words and phrases. Let's now turn to a discussion of sight word instruction and sight word programs used in special education classrooms.

Sight Word Instruction and Sight Word Programs

Students who understand the phonemic code and the morphemic rules of our language are able to attack most unknown words. In addition, as children become more skillful readers, they are often able to use the context of the sentence along with phonic and structural analysis to determine word possibilities.

Some children with mild disabilities are unable, however, to master the many phonics skills necessary to become fluent decoders. These students need to develop a functional sight word vocabulary consisting of necessary survival words (e.g., *women, exit, danger*) or vocational words—words necessary for completing job applications and other forms. Teachers of adolescents often must curtail decoding practice in order to focus on words essential for independent living or content-course completion. Teachers at the elementary or middle school may choose to supplement phonics instruction with sight words from the basal reader or from a list of high-frequency words arranged by grade levels, such as the Dolch words (Johnson, 1971). These words must be taught in phrases from text, however, if students with mild disabilities are to recognize them in context. (See Table 10.2 for the Dolch list.)

Edmark. The "Edmark Reading Program" is appropriate for children with mental retardation, learning disabilities, or emotional disturbance, as well as for low-achieving students who are having difficulty with traditional reading materials. Edmark is a highly repetitive reading system originally designed for institutionalized individuals with mental retardation. In Level One of the program, 150 sight words, capital letters, punctuation, and the endings *s, ing,* and *ed* are introduced. A software version of Level One, using a voice synthesizer, is also available for use with Apple computers. Level Two introduces 200 additional sight words and includes stories about adolescents in true-to-life situations. At completion of the program, students are reading at approximately the third-grade level. (For literature on this program, write to Edmark Corporation, P.O. Box 3903, Bellevue, Washington 98009–3903.)

Input organization.   Simms and Falcon (1987) suggest that teachers rearrange lists of sight words into more meaningful groupings than grade-level categories. For example, through direct instructional procedures, teachers may introduce children with mild disabilities to "action" words (*put, pull, open*); "when" words (*before, after, soon*); "no" words (*don't, never, no, not*); or "color" or "number" words. Drill-and-practice activities are then planned to ensure mastery of each category before moving on to a new one. Again, teachers must remember to present words in meaningful phrases rather than as isolated list items during demonstration and practice activities.

Another method by which "input" might be organized is by words that are known (i.e., immediately recognized) and words that are unknown. In order to enhance motivation during drill-and-practice activities, teachers can mix in a few "known" words with those the student has not yet mastered. Use of this technique also provides a review of words learned previously, and thus helps to ensure that they are maintained.

Table 10.2 The Dolch Basic Sight Words

Preprimer	Primer	First	Second	Third
1. the	45. when	89. many	133. know	177. don't
2. of	46. who	90. before	134. while	178. does
3. and	47. will	91. must	135. last	179. got
4. to	48. more	92. through	136. might	180. united
5. a	49. no	93. back	137. us	181. left
6. in	50. if	94. years	138. great	182. number
7. that	51. out	95. where	139. old	183. course
8. is	52. so	96. much	140. year	184. war
9. was	53. said	97. your	141. off	185. until
10. he	54. what	98. may	142. come	186. always
11. for	55. up	99. well	143. since	187. away
12. it	56. its	100. down	144. against	188. something
13. with	57. about	101. should	145. go	189. fact
14. as	58. into	102. because	146. came	190. through
15. his	59. than	103. each	147. right	191. water
16. on	60. them	104. just	148. used	192. less
17. be	61. can	105. those	149. take	193. public
18. at	62. only	106. people	150. three	194. put
19. by	63. other	107. Mr.	152. states	195. thing
20. I	64. new	108. how	152. himself	196. almost
21. this	65. some	109. too	153. few	197. hand
22. had	66. could	110. little	154. house	198. enough
23. not	67. time	111. state	155. use	199. far
24. are	68. these	112. good	156. during	200. took
25. but	69. two	113. very	157. without	201. head
26. from	70. may	114. make	158. again	202. yet
27. or	71. then	115. would	159. place	203. government
28. have	72. do	116. still	160. American	204. system
29. an	73. first	117. own	161. around	205. better
30. they	74. any	118. see	162. however	206. set
31. which	75. my	119. men	163. home	207. told
32. one	76. now	120. work	164. small	208. nothing
33. you	77. such	121. long	165. found	209. night
34. were	78. like	122. get	166. Mrs.	210. end
35. her	79. our	123. here	167. thought	211. why
36. all	80. over	124. between	168. went	212. called
37. she	81. man	125. both	169. say	213. didn't
38. there	82. me	126. life	170. part	214. eyes
39. would	83. even	127. being	171. once	215. find
40. their	84. most	128. under	172. general	216. going
41. we	85. made	129. never	173. high	217. look
42. him	86. after	130. day	174. upon	218. asked
43. been	87. also	131. same	175. school	219. later
44. has	88. did	132. another	176. every	220. knew

From "The Dolch List Reexamined," by Dale D. Johnson, 1971, The Reading Teacher, 24, pp. 455–456. Copyright © 1971 by the International Reading Association. Reprinted with the permission of Dale D. Johnson and the International Reading Association.

Time delay.   When providing drill and practice with sight words, teachers may use time-delay procedures (Touchette, 1971) to enhance student responding. Time delay is a data-based procedure designed to minimize student error and maximize reinforcement for correct answers by providing consistent prompts when children are unable to respond independently (Stevens & Schuster, 1988). However, rather than providing an immediate prompt, the teacher might delay prompting for a few seconds in order to allow the child an opportunity to respond. The delay may be constant or progressive (Kleinert & Gast, 1982).

Using a zero-second time delay, for example, the teacher might present the sight word *put* along with three other words on a flash card, cue the student to point to put, and immediately prompt by pointing to the word *put.* Later, the teacher might begin to fade the prompt by increasing the time delay to 5 seconds. That is, after presenting the words on a flash card and cuing the student to point to *put,* the teacher would wait for 5 seconds before prompting (Touchette & Howard, 1984). The student could also be told to wait if he or she was unsure of the correct response and a prompt delivered only if it became necessary. The student could *begin* to read the word at any time before the end of the 5-second interval without prompting, receiving reinforcement for successful reading or teacher assistance to correct errors.

The time-delay procedure is useful for teaching sight words to individual students with mild disabilities (Browder, Hines, McCarthy, & Fees, 1984) or to children in small groups (Keel & Gast, 1992). When using a time delay with groups of children, however, the teacher should first obtain and reinforce the attention of all members of the group (i.e., ''Everyone look'') and then call for choral or individual responding to the cue, ''Read the word'' (Gast, Wolery, Morris, Doyle, & Meyer, 1990; Wolery, Ault, Gast, Doyle, & Mills, 1990). Again, in the initial trials, the teacher may use a zero-second time delay. When students respond individually or collectively at a criterion of 100% under a zero-second time delay, the teacher may increase the delay. Under each time-delay condition, the teacher must take care to collect data. Knowing the percentage of unprompted correct responses, prompted correct responses, unprompted errors (errors made before delivery of the prompt), and prompted errors (errors made within a specified number of seconds following delivery of the prompt) enables the teacher to adjust instruction accordingly to improve learning and decrease errors.

Imagery and paired association.   High-imagery words (Hargis, 1982) are typically nouns or verbs that bring to mind an immediate picture (e.g., *horse* for children in a rural community or *bus* for those in an urban environment). To use these visual associations for instructional purposes, the teacher places the sight word on one flash card and a picture to illustrate it on another card (Bos & Vaughn, 1991). Instruction begins by presenting both cards simultaneously, pronouncing the word, and asking students to read the word. Gradually, the picture cards may be removed, using them for prompts only if necessary. In addition, students may point to a word, given two or three choices for a picture, in a word-recognition rather than a recall task. Or they may choose the correct word to ''fill in the blank'' when the teacher reads a sentence.

An alternative association for some children with mild disabilities is the word-configuration clue. Again, the teacher places the sight word on a flash card, but this time draws a box around the word to illustrate the overall shape of the word. Gradually, the box would be faded as the child successfully read the word.

Word-identification strategy. The word-identification strategy (Lenz, Schumaker, Deshler, & Beals, 1984) is useful for decreasing the oral reading errors and, to a lesser extent, increasing the reading comprehension of older students needing assistance in content courses, such as science or social studies. The procedure harnesses what these students may know about phonics, structural analysis, and context clues to give them a systematic strategy for attacking unknown words. The seven steps of the strategy can be remembered by using the mnemonic illustrated in Table 10.3.

Table 10.3   The DISSECT Strategy

According to Lenz, Schumaker, Deshler, and Beals (1984), students with mild disabilities can learn strategies to identify words. DISSECT gives students a seven-step process:

D = Discover the context by skipping the unknown word and reading to the end of the sentence to see if the word can be determined by the meaning of the sentence.

I = Isolate the prefix and box it off.

S = Separate the suffix and box it off.

S = Say the stem and then say it along with any prefixes or suffixes.

E = Examine the stem, if it cannot be named easily, by following one of three rules:
   1. If the stem or a part of the stem begins with a vowel, separate the first two letters. If the stem or a part of the stem begins with a consonant, separate the first three letters from the stem.
   2. If rule 1 does not work, isolate the first letter of the stem and then try to apply rule 1.
   3. When two different vowels are together in the stem, pronounce both vowel sounds. If that does not "sound right," try again, saying each vowel sound in turn until the word is identified.

C = Check with someone else if the word is still unknown.

T = Try the dictionary if no help is available.

Using the procedures for teaching learning strategies developed by researchers at the University of Kansas (Deshler, Alley, Warner, & Schumaker, 1981; Ellis, Deshler, Lenz, Schumaker, & Clark, 1991), students with learning disabilities can successfully learn the word-identification method to determine unknown words in content-area classes. The teacher must remember, however, that improved word identification (i.e., fewer oral reading errors) does not necessarily lead to improved reading comprehension (Lenz & Hughes, 1990). (See Chapter 9 for additional information on learning strategies.)

Computer software programs for sight word practice. Several software packages provide optional activities for student practice with sight words. For example, in "Word Radar," part of the Academic Skill Builders in Language Arts series (available through Developmental Learning Materials of Allen, Texas) for use with Apple or IBM computers, students pretend to be air-traffic-control operators who scan for words of increasing length. In "Cloze-Plus," available for use with Apple computers from Milliken Publishing Company of St. Louis, Missouri, the traditional cloze technique is used (i.e., one word is omitted from a sentence and students use context clues to determine the unknown word). Students select one of five possible words to fill in the blank after reading a factual paragraph, and they may request additional assistance with context clues if necessary. "Cloze-Plus" is appropriate for older students, although it was originally intended for use with students in grades 3–8. In addition, teachers may wish to obtain one of many software programs for producing crossword or word-search puzzles tailored to specific sight word needs of individual students. For example, "Crossword Magic," available from Mindscape, Inc., 3444 Dundee Rd., Northbrook, Illinois 60062 is available for use with both Apple and IBM Pcs).

A summary of sight word instruction and programs. Students with mild disabilities must practice irregular or commonly used words as "sight words." Automatic recognition of these words as whole units is necessary if children are to progress beyond laborious letter-by-letter decoding to fluent, independent reading with comprehension.

Many materials and techniques are available to help students master essential sight words. The teacher may also wish to use more "specialized" methods for teaching reading skills through a whole-word approach. Let's first examine these "special" techniques before turning our attention to reading comprehension.

Specialized Remedial Reading Approaches

A few remedial reading methods follow the meaning-emphasis philosophy, connecting whole words and sentences directly with their meaning in context. Although phonics skills may be woven into reading programs using these methods, decoding is not a core element of instruction. Therefore, teachers might choose one of these special methods for students who are not motivated to practice reading or for those unable to master decoding skills even after extensive instruction. These specialized methods include the multisensory approach, the language-experience approach, and Reading Recovery. Data-based instruction is yet another specialized approach useful for teaching decoding or sight word skills.

Fernald's multisensory approach.   Grace Fernald worked initially with adolescents with behavioral problems who were having difficulty reading. Her multisensory VAKT (Visual-Auditory-Kinesthetic-Tactile) approach (Fernald, 1943) represented a "new way" for these students, low in motivation, to learn to read and spell. The teacher using the VAKT method allows the child to select words he or she wants to learn. The teacher then prints or writes one of these words in crayon on a card, models the strategy for the child, and asks the child to practice the word by

1. saying the word, tracing the word with a finger while saying each part of the word, and then saying the whole word again;

2. writing the word without looking at the card and then comparing this effort with the original on the card; and

3. continuing to trace the word until he or she can write it correctly from memory at least three consecutive times.

Fernald (1943) stresses the importance of always writing the word as a total unit. That is, if the child makes an error while writing a word, he or she must begin the word all over again rather than erasing and starting from the middle of the word. In addition, Fernald recommends that children begin writing stories on topics they choose after they have learned to read and write several words. Any additional words the child requires for the story are supplied by the teacher and practiced by the child using the steps described. As children complete their stories, they file all new words in a word bank or word box and then read their stories to the teacher and/or the group from a typewritten copy provided by the teacher.

Essentially, this approach emphasizes the meaning of words in a context determined by the student. In addition, the method fosters student reliance on repetition and the visual configuration of words as useful strategies for practicing and mastering unknown words. Fernald maintains that students will soon progress from the tracing stage to looking at a printed word, saying it, and writing it from memory. Later, the student will no longer need to write words in order to remember them. Although teachers believe that multisensory approaches such as Fernald's help students with mild disabilities learn to read new words, supportive research evidence is lacking. Teachers who want to try multisensory methods should use them only to supplement direct instruction with repetitive, systematic practice activities and not as a primary instructional method.

The language-experience approach.   The language-experience approach (LEA) stems from the philosophy that what a child experiences he or she can talk about, and that what a child can talk about he or she can write about and then read (Stauffer, 1970). The LEA, therefore, integrates oral language, reading, and writing through activities meaningful for an individual child or for a small group. To implement the LEA, the teacher selects a topic or provides an activity of interest for the children. The teacher then discusses the activity with the children, helping them to organize their thoughts and plan what they want to say.

Following the discussion, the students dictate a story to the teacher, who records it exactly as told by the children (see Box 10.3). For an individual pupil, the teacher may wish to sit next to the youngster so that he or she can see the page as dictation is taken. For small groups of students, the teacher may use large chart paper or the chalkboard, having each child contribute to the story. After dictation, the teacher rereads the story to the children, asking them whether they want to make any changes or additions. Next, the children read the story, individually or chorally, as the teacher points to each word. Finally, the teacher provides each child with a typed copy of the story, and the children practice reading the story to one another. New words are put on word cards, practiced, and filed in word banks by individual students.

The LEA is a highly motivating approach for reluctant readers and a useful introduction to the meaningfulness of reading and writing for beginning readers. Alone, however, the LEA is insufficient as an initial reading method for most children with mild disabilities. For these youngsters, beginning reading instruction must emphasize phonics and structural analysis skills.

Reading Recovery.   Reading Recovery is an early intervention program for "high-risk" first-graders, originally developed by researchers in New Zealand (Boehnlein, 1987). The method offers one-on-one tutorial assistance for 30 minutes each day to children having difficulty during their first year of learning to read. The program is intended to supplement the ongoing reading and writing instruction in the regular classroom with literacy strategies used naturally by good readers. At the heart of Reading Recovery is interaction with a caring, supportive teacher, trained to use the following sequence of activities during each lesson (Pinnell, 1990).

1. Familiar rereading. The child reads and rereads favorite books he or she has read previously. These books may be selected by the child or by the teacher and are read for enjoyment and fluency.

Box 10.3   A Language-Experience Story

The following story was written by Joey with assistance from Ms. Lopez:

In art class we made these kites. We had to take some sticks and put them together across. Then we cut some paper and drew whatever we wanted. I made mine look like a shark. It was cool with these big teeth. We had to wrap the paper around the sticks and staple it on. And we put a tail on the kite out of string and tied these knots around some paper. The best part was when we got to take the kites outside and fly them. Mine was awesome. It was the best. Nobody could get their kites to fly very good.

2. Rereading new books and obtaining a running record analysis. The child reads the new book from the previous day's lesson. The teacher may assist the child when he or she is "stuck"; however, the primary goal here is for the child to read as independently as possible while the teacher records the types of word-identification, comprehension, and other strategies the child is using.

3. Writing a message. The child composes a message or story over one or more days. The story is written with teacher assistance so that the child can predict, when possible, letters to represent the sounds. The child reads the message or story aloud and reassembles the story from sentence strips made and cut apart by the teacher.

4. Reading a new book. The teacher or child selects a new book to explore, looking at pictures, making predictions, and identifying one or two key words after examining the initial letter. Finally, the child reads the new book with teacher assistance.

Books selected for reading are at the correct level if the child can recognize the words with 90% to 95% accuracy. In addition, many familiar books are "patterned" stories or poems that contain predictable, repetitious lines. Children often delight in repeating these known words alone or with the teacher, and patterned books are well suited to the prediction of letter–sound associations.

Reading Recovery is receiving acclaim and research support, although little evidence exists to suggest its effectiveness with children already in special education programs (Pinnell, 1990; Slavin et al., 1989). Critics argue, too, that the method demands more highly trained personnel than many school districts can presently afford.

Data-based instruction.   Data-based teaching of reading skills is rooted in applied behavior analysis and direct instruction. This approach focuses on establishing precise instructional objectives and then directly measuring student progress toward those objectives. This data analysis enables teachers to make informed decisions about pupil performance, materials, and instructional procedures.

Using curricular materials at the appropriate level, the teacher might time and record a student's oral reading rate, compute the percentage of words read correctly or incorrectly from a passage or from a sight word list, or administer a probe to determine whether the student can decode CVC or CVCe words correctly. Reading errors made by students are directly recorded and analyzed by the teacher to determine instructional needs. For example, Ms. Lopez might present Travis with a list of regular CVC and CVCe words including *hat, can, bake,* and *hope.* As Travis reads the words on the list, Ms. Lopez would follow along with an identical list, placing a plus sign next to the words that Travis reads correctly (say *hat* and *can*) and a minus sign and approximate pronunciation next to the words that he reads incorrectly (say, *bake* read as *back* and *hope* read as *hop*). Ms. Lopez would then use this information to plan additional instruction for Travis using the CVCe pattern.

A summary of specialized remedial reading approaches.   Specialized remedial reading approaches such as Fernald's VAKT method are believed by teachers to motivate reluctant learners to read. In addition, the language-experience approach and Reading Recovery may help at-risk youngsters associate meaning with the printed word and provide enjoyable, successful experiences with books. However, these approaches do not provide the intensive, systematic, and direct phonics instruction required by students with mild disabilities. Very few teachers have the expertise to integrate the necessary instruction in decoding skills when one of these techniques is used as a primary approach to initial reading instruction. Special education teachers may wish, therefore, to focus intervention on decoding skills first, supplementing lessons with whole-word approaches, such as the LEA or a multisensory approach. Data-based instruction also ensures student progress with essential decoding and sight word skills. A focus on decoding does not mean, however, that teachers should neglect comprehension. We will now turn to a discussion of this important goal of remedial reading instruction.

✎ Teaching Comprehension Skills

The ultimate goal of reading instruction is for students to obtain meaning from what they read. As they advance up the grades, students are expected to read for pleasure and to read for content. These expectations require the student to understand different types of text, to read for different purposes, and to bring to the printed page background knowledge or experience from which meaning may be constructed (Carnine et al., 1990). Good readers, then, read fluently and with expression; moreover, they comprehend what they read.

The comprehension skills found in most basal reading series include those listed in Table 10.4. Typically, teachers in regular classrooms teach comprehension skills indirectly through a directed reading activity or a directed reading-thinking activity. That is, the teacher sets the purpose for reading, or elicits a purpose from student predictions, and then follows reading with questions designed to monitor comprehension or evaluate conclusions. Most questions asked by teachers during reading lessons are at the literal comprehension level (Guszak, 1972); furthermore, teachers provide very little systematic demonstration or explanation of *how* to comprehend what is read (Jenkins, Stein, & Osborn, 1981).

For students with mild disabilities, comprehension skills may be difficult to master, even at the level of recognition or recall of facts and main ideas explicitly stated in the text, particularly if instruction is not systematic (Carnine et al., 1990). For example, youngsters with mild disabilities may lack fluent decoding and word-recognition skills, hampering their reading comprehension. Moreover, many children with mild disabilities may not have the vocabulary or background knowledge, built from experiences both in the real world and with text, to enable them to understand the language of instruction or to comprehend what they read (Samuels, 1981). Other students lack knowledge of differing text structures and of comprehension strategies (Dyck &

Table 10.4

Comprehension Levels and Skills

Literal: Understand word meanings in context. Recognize or recall details, main ideas, sequences of events, cause-and-effect statements, and comparisons when directly stated in the text.

Inferential: Infer details, main ideas, sequences of events, cause and effect, and comparisons when not directly stated in the text. Predict outcomes. Use figurative language.

Evaluative: Judge fact versus opinion and reality versus fantasy. Judge adequacy, validity, or worth of arguments, conclusions, or sources.

Appreciative: Respond emotionally to plot and theme. Identify with characters or plot. React to author's use of language or imagery.

Sundbye, 1988; Laughton & Morris, 1989; Seidenberg, 1989). Fluency, vocabulary, and direct instruction of comprehension skills and strategies, then, are important features of initial or remedial reading instruction for youngsters with mild disabilities.

Fluency Building

LaBerge and Samuels (1974) suggest that students have only a limited attentional capacity to allocate to the simultaneous tasks of decoding and comprehension. Those students who, because of deficient word-attack skills, must allocate an excessive amount of attention to the task of decoding have very little remaining attentional capacity to remember and comprehend what was read. Although fluency alone is insufficient for reading comprehension, it is an important initial goal of reading instruction for students with mild disabilities. Teachers can help students build fluency through such activities as repeated reading and previewing of text.

Repeated reading.   Repeated reading is an effective technique designed to facilitate active student practice with reading materials (O'Shea, Sindelar, & O'Shea, 1985; Samuels, 1979). The technique is based on the theory of limited attentional capacity offered by LaBerge and Samuels (1974). Rather than expecting students with mild disabilities to read stories and passages fluently with only one reading and to progress through the basal reading series at the "normal" rate, repeated reading provides the student with additional opportunities to read each passage or story until a criterion level has been attained. The basic idea is that students with mild disabilities must master reading material before moving to a new reading selection, and that mastery is rarely achieved following a single reading experience.

Repeated reading is a relatively simple procedure. Students read and re-read passages to a specified criterion for reading rate (e.g., 85 words per minute) and/or for reading accuracy (e.g., fewer than five word-recognition errors). Students begin with timed readings of passages containing from 50 to 200 words at a specified reading level. Gradually, longer and more difficult passages are introduced, and the student records his or her progress on a chart or graph (Samuels, 1979). As fluency improves, comprehension is cued by prompting students to think about and remember what is read (O'Shea et al., 1985). Rather than finding the procedure boring or repetitive, teachers report that children enjoy trying to beat their own records in successive reading trials.

Variations on the technique of repeated reading include tape recording, choral and paired readings, and repeated reading of language-experience stories. Tape recording the repeated reading session affords the student an opportunity to hear himself or herself reading. Tape recording also gives the teacher the freedom to work with other children by producing a permanent product for later review (Henk, Helfeldt, & Platt, 1986).

Bos (1982) suggests that students listen to the teacher read a passage or story at the appropriate instructional level and then read the story aloud along with the teacher. The student would then read the passage or story independently and record his or her word-recognition and reading rate on a chart. Bos and Vaughn (1991) recommend that this practice of choral or paired reading begin with predictable, patterned books and that the method be combined with discussion of the reading selection to set purposes and to make predictions. Additional variations offered by these authors include making cards for practicing words students have consistent difficulty recognizing and using repeated readings with tape-recorded stories or books.

Still another variation of repeated reading was studied by Peterson, Scott, and Sroka, 1990. Children read language-experience stories for 1-minute timed trials. At the end of the minute, the teacher pointed to each word the child had missed, clearly pronounced the word, and requested that the child repeat the word. The teacher then used the word in its context, with the child repeating the phrase, and then the child read the remainder of the passage untimed. Both reading rate and error rate, graphed on a standard behavior chart, improved through this technique.

Previewing.   Another simple, but effective, method for improving fluency is previewing. That is, the child is given the opportunity to read silently (silent previewing) or listen to a passage or story before attempting oral reading (listening previewing). In studies comparing silent and listening previewing (Rose, 1984; Rose & Sherry, 1984), listening previewing resulted in improved reading rates for children with learning disabilities, as well as for those with behavior disorders.

Another form of previewing involves a structured overview of passage topics and subtopics, including prompts for self-questioning (Billingsley & Wildman, 1988). Using this procedure, the teacher arranges cards to illustrate the relationships among the major topics, subtopics, and details for each passage read. In addition, the teacher prompts students to generate as many who, what, when, where, and how questions as possible before actual reading begins. Billingsley and Wildman suggest that this prereading activity can increase student involvement with the text during actual reading, and thus improve comprehension.

A summary of fluency-building activities. Students can improve their oral reading rate and decrease word-recognition errors through such fluency-building activities as repeated readings and previewing. These activities alone, however, are not enough for some children with mild disabilities to comprehend what they read. Other deficits, such as poor vocabulary, also may hinder reading comprehension.

Vocabulary Building

Students with mild disabilities often lack the necessary vocabulary to fully comprehend text (Carnine et al., 1990). In addition, vocabulary, word-recognition, and decoding difficulty may, in turn, prohibit these youngsters from reading material that would help them build additional vocabulary (Stanovich, 1986c). Moreover, children with mild disabilities may have particular difficulty with words having several meanings (e.g., *run*), which are often used in basal readers (Paul & O'Rourke, 1988) or with specific tasks they are asked to perform during vocabulary instruction and assessment (Simmons & Kameenui, 1990). Although the exact relationship between vocabulary development and reading comprehension is unknown, teachers must help students to develop a ''deep'' understanding of vocabulary through both direct instruction and multiple uses of words in context (Shake, Allington, Gaskins, & Marr, 1989).

Preteaching vocabulary in phrases using hypothesis testing. When preteaching vocabulary, teachers must remember to teach words in meaningful phrases from the text rather than in isolation. For example, the teacher can make sentence or phrase strips using words from the reading passage and then underline the new vocabulary word or omit the new word, or all but the first letter of the new word. Using the context and/or the letter clue, students are asked to hypothesize the word choice or meaning (e.g., ''What could this word be?'' or ''What could this word mean?'') and then read on to test their hypothesis (Sindelar, 1982). Dixon (1987) suggests that teachers should ''think aloud'' to demonstrate this hypothesis-testing approach using unknown words encountered in text, and then guide students as they practice the procedure.

Keywords. Mastropieri and Scruggs (1987) describe a strategy in which teachers help students to associate a visual image of the meaning with a word to be remembered. The visual image can be constructed to represent the word itself or a sound-alike or synonym for the word. For example, if the student must remember that the word *persuade* means ''to convince,'' he or she might construct a visual image of one woman convincing another to buy a *purse* (a word similar in sound). Of course, if the student is unfamiliar with the word, the teacher must use direct instructional procedures to teach that *persuade* means ''to convince'' before using the mnemonic (Mastropieri & Scruggs, 1987).

Rooney (1988) describes a similar technique. The student writes the new vocabulary word on one side of a card and a brief version of the most common definition on the back. Under the definition, the student draws a picture to illustrate the meaning and associate the definition with the word. For example, if the student must learn that *belligerent* means ''argumentative,'' he or she might draw a picture of two bells fighting under the word *argumentative* on the back of the card. Children may use the cards for drill-and-practice activities and file mastered words in a word box. Although the keyword strategies described previously may help students associate words with their meanings, there is no evidence to support the transfer of this strategy to comprehending passages when the words are used in context (Carnine et al., 1990).

Word webbing.   Paul and O'Rourke (1988) suggest that teachers can help students activate prior knowledge of topics and vocabulary by word webbing. Teachers can take phrases containing new vocabulary from the text (e.g., ''along the river bank'') and ask students, ''What does the word *bank* mean?'' or ''What else is called a *bank?*'' (e.g., a pile of snow, an inclined curve on a road, a place where money is stored) using pictures as clues if necessary. Interrelationships among these definitions can then be illustrated visually by using lines branching out to each from the word *bank*. In a similar activity, teachers can web synonyms or sentences around the central word (Paul & O'Rourke, 1988). (See Figure 10.1 for an illustration of webbing with synonyms.)

A summary of vocabulary-building activities.   Students with mild disabilities need many opportunities to read and use words in context. Preteaching vocabulary words in phrases, hypothesis testing, keywords, and word webbing may help many children expand their vocabulary. Nevertheless, most youngsters with mild disabilities also require direct instruction in comprehension skills, such as finding the main idea.

Direct Instruction of "Main Idea"

Although not the only necessary comprehension skill, one early and important task children are expected to master is that of finding the main idea. Frequently, basal reading materials begin this instruction by asking children to choose the ''best'' title for a story or the main idea of a passage when presented with a series of four or five choices. This level of difficulty, however, is often above that of many students with mild disabilities, who may not understand the concept of ''main idea'' or how the main idea relates to other elements of the text.

Graves (1987) outlines a sequence for direct instruction in finding the main idea. According to this sequence, students first generate a main idea when presented with a series of pictures that clearly illustrates an activity or tells a story. For example, a picture of Susan swinging a bat, a picture of Susan running the bases, and a picture of Susan catching a ball with a glove can be used to generate the idea that Susan plays baseball. Next, students must generate the main idea for three or four sentences that contain similar elements

Figure 10.1   A Synonym Web for *Joke*

Ms. Kirk and the students in her fourth-grade class produced the following web to illustrate synonyms for a word overused in her students' writing—*Joke*.

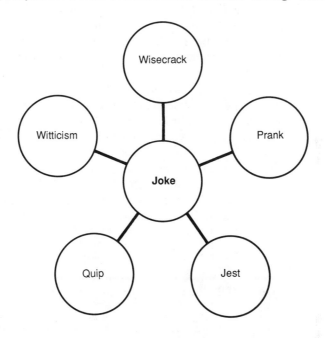

(e.g., dogs need oxygen to live, cats need oxygen to live, horses need oxygen to live). The main idea here is that "animals need oxygen to live." The student is then ready to progress to short passages, picking out the main idea from among three or four choices presented.

Teachers should begin instruction at the literal level, helping children find the main idea and details when they are explicitly stated in the text. To do this, teachers might point out to children the most common positions for the main-idea sentence (i.e., the first sentence, the last sentence, then a sentence in the middle) within paragraphs. Using exact wording from the paragraph, the teacher can illustrate the relationship between the main-idea sentence and the supporting detail sentences by likening the paragraph to a table. The main idea is represented by the broad tabletop and the details are represented by the table legs that offer support. In addition, the teacher can make sentence strips in which one color is used for the main idea and a different color for the supporting details. The teacher and children can then manipulate the strips to demonstrate the various positions for the main idea and detail sentences within paragraphs. Gradually, the paragraphs can be lengthened and the wording can be changed, making the choices for the main idea less and less like the actual wording in the text.

Similarly, Hanau (1974) used the illustration of Statement-PIE to represent the relationship of main ideas and details in paragraphs (see Figure 10.2). The "statement" is the main idea and the "PIE" is all the proof, information, and examples offered by the author in support of the main idea. Again, the teacher might begin instruction with short paragraphs containing the statement in the first sentence and the PIE in subsequent sentences. Later, the order of sentences can be rearranged so that students can practice identifying the statement and the PIE.

A summary of main-idea instruction.   Children with mild disabilities may need explicit and sequenced direct instruction of comprehension skills, such as finding the main idea. In addition, students in special education programs may need extensive practice if they are to master these skills even at the literal level. Finally, direct teaching of comprehension strategies, in combination with direct instruction, may help youngsters with mild disabilities to comprehend and remember what they read more effectively than either procedure used alone (Graves, 1986). Some authorities caution, however, that reducing instruction in comprehension skills to discrete steps may focus on student

Figure 10.2   Statement-PIE

From "Using Statement-PIE to Teach Reading and Writing Skills," by C. S. Englert and A. Lichter, Teaching Exceptional Children, 14, 1982, p. 165. Copyright © 1982 by The Council for Exceptional Children. Reprinted with permission.

Teachers can use a concrete visual example, such as Statement-PIE (Hanau, 1974), to illustrate the relationship between main-idea statements and detail statements at the literal level. By means of the graphic aid pictured below, teachers can demonstrate that the main-idea statement tells what a passage is all about and that the PIE statements are all the proof, information, and examples that support the statement.

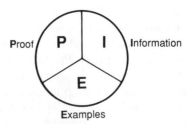

Statement—This is a super pair of shoes!

PIE—They don't cost a whole lot.

PIE—They have neon shoelaces and designs on them.

PIE—They are really comfortable.

deficits rather than on the whole child and his or her background experiences and reasons for reading—factors considered critical for comprehension (McGill-Franzen et al., 1991; Poplin, 1988).

Comprehension Strategies

Students with mild disabilities may possess adequate skill in decoding, recognizing words, and determining the main idea; however, they may still fail to comprehend what they read. Good readers engage in summarization or retelling, answering questions, and other strategic behaviors to improve comprehension or to address comprehension difficulties. Poor readers, on the other hand, do not spontaneously use these strategies to improve or monitor their comprehension. These youngsters need explicit instruction in comprehension strategies including self-questioning, paraphrasing or story retelling, using text structures, and surveying and reviewing.

Self-questioning.   In a 1982 study, Wong and Jones demonstrated that some students with mild disabilities do not engage in self-questioning while reading. Even when students are able to identify main ideas, they may not ask questions to help themselves find and remember the main idea when reading a passage. The self-questioning strategy developed by Wong and Jones lists five

High-imagery sight words, like nouns and verbs, may be paired with a visual prompt to increase student success during initial instruction.

important steps for students to follow to improve their reading comprehension:

1. Ask "Why am I studying this passage?"

2. Find the main idea or ideas and underline it/them.

3. Think of a good question about the main idea(s).

4. Read to learn the answer to the question.

5. Remember to look back to see how each question and answer gives you more information.

Similarly, researchers at the University of Kansas used a self-questioning strategy in combination with visual imagery to help students with learning disabilities comprehend written material (Clark, Deshler, Schumaker, Alley, & Warner, 1984). Students were taught the RIDER strategy for visual imagery and the RAM self-questioning strategy. During RIDER, students: Read the first sentence, Image a picture in the mind, Describe the image, Evaluate the image for completeness, and Repeat the steps with each subsequent sentence. When students can generate common "WH" questions (who, what, when, where, why) and recognize cue symbols for each type of question (e.g., a clock face for "when" questions), they can use the RAM strategy by: Reading a passage and asking "WH" questions, Answering the questions while reading, and Marking the answers with the appropriate symbols. According to these researchers, the use of both strategies resulted in greater comprehension for students in the study.

Paraphrasing and story retelling. There a number of strategies to help students summarize paragraphs or retell stories in their own words. For example, Jean Schumaker and her colleagues at the University of Kansas taught students with learning disabilities to use a paraphrasing strategy for remembering the main idea and details in written materials (Schumaker, Denton, & Deshler, 1984). Using the acronym RAP, students: Read a paragraph, Ask themselves what the main ideas and details were, and Put the main ideas and details into their own words. In addition, students are instructed to look in the first sentence and to look for words that are repeated in order to find the main ideas.

In a procedure known as reciprocal teaching, Palincsar and Brown (1984) taught students summarizing, questioning, clarifying, and predicting strategies during interactive teaching sessions. Using reciprocal teaching procedures, students slowly assume, with teacher assistance, the role of "co-instructor" during reading lessons. After modeling the four strategies, the teacher prompts and gives feedback until students are able to lead discussions about stories themselves. That is, students take turns retelling stories, asking questions, clarifying information, and making predictions (see Box 10.4).

During reciprocal teaching, teachers begin reading selections by having students make predictions based on story titles, headings, or other appropriate features. In this way, students are encouraged to activate background knowledge and information and to set a purpose for reading. Teachers then foster practice of good questioning strategies by requiring students to ask "teacherlike" questions rather than fill-in-the-blanks. In addition, if students are unable to ask a question, the teacher might provide an appropriate question word as a prompt. Summarizing strategies for students include finding the main idea and supporting details and stating this information in their own words without looking at the text. Students are told to look for a topic sentence or to give a name to a list of items as ways to identify main ideas. Finally, students point out information that is unclear or unknown as they clarify new vocabulary, unfamiliar expressions, or ambiguous information. The essential element of reciprocal teaching is an interactive dialogue between students and teacher.

Using text structures and story grammars. When retelling stories, children typically rely on certain structures they have come to understand (e.g., a character in a particular setting encounters some type of conflict, which is finally resolved). These essential elements, called *story grammar,* are organizational devices for narratives across many cultures. Understanding story grammar, then, may enhance the reader's comprehension of narrative passages (Stein & Trabasso, 1982).

In a study by Griffey, Zigmond, and Leinhardt (1988), story-grammar training and self-questioning strategies were combined to improve the reading

---

Box 10.4   Ms. Kirk Uses Reciprocal Teaching Strategies

The following conversation takes place between Ms. Kirk and the fourth-graders in one of her reading groups:

Celie: *My question I want to answer is what the man buy with all his money?*

Kevin: *Probably a big car and a new house.*

Sarabeth: *Maybe a boat.*

Holden: *I think presents for everybody.*

Ms. Kirk: *Interesting answers. My question, though, is since the man can only buy one thing with all that money, how can he buy all these things that he wants?*

Sarabeth: *I'm not sure, but I wish I had all that money!*

Celie: *My summary is someone this man didn't even know give him a bunch of money, but told the man he could buy only one thing with it. The man has to decide how to spend it.*

Ms. Kirk: *Good summary, Celie. It says in the story that because the man doesn't know who gave him all the money or why, he "ponders" who the mystery man might be. What do you suppose "ponders" means here?*

Holden: *Wonders.*

Sarabeth: *He thinks about it.*

Ms. Kirk: *Yes. Well, who do you predict gave him all that money?*

Kevin: *Maybe his uncle.*

Mark: *No, it was probably someone who didn't want to get caught because it was stolen money.*

Celie: *Someone to teach the man a lesson.*

Ms. Kirk: *Great answers! Let's read on to see if our predictions are accurate. Who would like to be the next teacher? Holden?*

comprehension of elementary-level poor readers. First, teachers provided lessons on the story elements using the acronym CAPS (Character, Aim, Problem, Solution). Next, the teacher initiated training with self-questioning related to each of these story elements. For example, during reading, the teacher interjected the following questions at appropriate points in the story:

1. Who are the characters?

2. What is the aim of the story?

3. What problem occurs?

4. How is the problem solved?

The teacher then summarized by retelling the story, providing answers to each of the questions, and writing these on the chalkboard. Later, students were reminded to use the CAPS questions when reading stories on their own.

Idol (1987) used the concept of story grammar along with story mapping to improve the reading comprehension of third- and fourth-graders with reading disabilities. During instruction, the teacher modeled how to locate the story components and write them on a story map. Students first copied information generated by the group onto their own story maps. Later, however, the children completed individual story maps while reading independently. According to Idol, ten key questions were used to generate information for story mapping and comprehension:

1. Where did the story take place?

2. When did the story take place?

3. Who were the main characters in the story?

4. Were there any other important characters in the story? Who?

5. What was the problem in the story?

6. How did _____ try to solve the problem?

7. Was it hard to solve the problem? Explain.

8. Was the problem solved? Explain.

9. What did you learn from reading this story? Explain.

10. Can you think of a different ending?

Using more sophisticated language and story-map formats, (e.g., protagonist, conflict, theme), students with mild disabilities can also comprehend high school literature (Gurney, Gersten, Dimino, & Carnine, 1990) and expository text structures (Englert & Mariage, 1991). For example, graphic aids can be constructed to represent a sequence of events or cause-and-effect statements. Visual aids can also represent attributes along which items can be compared (Carnine et al., 1990). With teacher assistance, students can complete these "story maps" and then use the map structure to facilitate comprehension of similar material in the future (see Figure 10.3).

Figure 10.3   Two Examples of Graphic Aids to Improve Student Comprehension of Differing Text Structures

(A) From "Group Story Mapping: A Comprehensive Strategy," by L. Idol, 1987, Journal of Learning Disabilities, *20, p. 199. Copyright © 1987 by the Donald D. Hammill Foundation. Reprinted with permission. (B) From "Developing Successful Writers through Cognitive Strategy Instruction," by C. S. Englert and T. E. Raphael, 1990. In J. Brody (Ed.),* Advances in Research on Teaching. *Copyright © 1990 JAI Press, Inc. Reprinted with permission.*

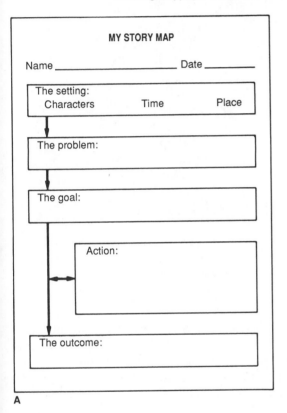

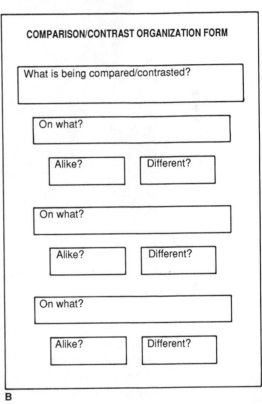

A   B

Surveying and reviewing.   One "study skill" often emphasized for reading content area textbooks is SQ3R (Survey, Question, Read, Recite, Review), originally developed by Francis Robinson in 1961. Good readers preview reading materials before actual reading occurs, noting chapter headings and subheadings, introductory and summary paragraphs, focusing and final questions, pictures, graphs, and new words. In this way, they get a general idea of the content, the organizational structure of the material, and a set of questions and/or purposes for reading. While reading and immediately following reading, students are encouraged to recite new information and to review or summarize what has been learned. Children with mild disabilities, however, may not have the skills or background knowledge to survey, question, read, recite, and review without explicit instruction from the teacher.

Elements of a whole language approach, such as having children dramatize or retell favorite stories, may supplement direct instruction in reading skills for students with mild disabilities by providing them meaningful experiences with connected text.

Archer and Gleason (1989) adapted the SQ3R procedure to include a teacher-directed "warm-up" and an "active-reading" strategy for children in grades 3–6. During "warm-up," the teacher guides students through a survey of the material to be read. Later, students are given a written reminder of the five warm-up steps and follow them independently:

Step 1: Read the title of the chapter and the introduction. (Ask, "What is the title? What will this chapter be about?")

Step 2: Read the headings and subheadings. (Ask, "What will this section be about?")

Step 3: Read the chapter summary. (Ask, "What are some important ideas from this chapter?")

Step 4: Read the questions at the end of the chapter. (Teachers should stress that the questions are very important because they indicate what students are expected to learn as they read the chapter.)

Step 5: Say to yourself, "This chapter will talk about . . . ."

Following warm-up, students learn a strategy to become actively involved during actual reading. Called *active reading,* the strategy emphasizes recitation of topics and details after each paragraph has been completed. Archer and Gleason (1989) used the acronym RCRC to guide active reading:

R = *Read*
    Read a paragraph.
    Think about the topic.
    Think about the important details.

C = *Cover*
    Cover the material with your hand.

R = *Recite*
    Tell yourself what you have read.
    Say the topic.
    Say the important details.
    Say it in your own words.

C = *Check*
    Lift your hand and check.
    If you forget something important, begin again.

In a more complex and sophisticated strategy designed for adolescents with mild disabilities, students are taught to make three systematic passes through content-area reading materials (Schumaker, Deshler, Alley, Warner, & Denton, 1982). The strategy, called *multipass,* consists of three sub-strategies to help students comprehend textbook reading selections: a survey pass, a size-up pass, and a sort-out pass. Each pass is taught separately using textbook materials that students can read with speed and accuracy.

1. Survey Pass: To get the main ideas and a feeling for the structure of the chapter, students (a) read the chapter title and the introductory paragraph, (b) review the chapter's relationship to other chapters by looking at the table of contents, (c) read the subtitles of the chapter and think about how the chapter is organized, (d) look at the pictures and read their captions (e) read the summary paragraph, and (f) paraphrase everything learned during the pass.

2. Size-Up Pass: To get specific information and details without reading the entire chapter, students (a) read the questions at the end of the chapter to see what is important to learn, (b) put a check mark beside each question that can be answered from the survey pass, (c) go through the chapter page by page looking for clues like boldfaced or italicized type and subheadings, (d) turn each clue into a question and skim through the surrounding text to answer the question, (e) put the answer to the question into their own words, and (f) paraphrase all facts and ideas they can remember from the chapter.

3. Sort-Out Pass: To self-test comprehension of the chapter, students again read and answer the questions at the end of the chapter. If they can answer a question based on the size-up pass, they place a check mark next to the question. If not, they think of a section where the answer might be located and skim for the answer. If the answer is not there, they try another section, repeating this procedure until the answer is found.

A summary of comprehension strategies.   Teachers must provide youngsters with mild disabilities explicit instruction and practice using comprehension strategies. Successful strategies are those that activate student background knowledge and information, focus student attention on the organizational structure of the material, help students set purposes for reading, and involve students actively throughout the reading process.

Computer Software for Building Comprehension Skills

Several computer software programs are now available to provide enjoyable activities for drill and practice of comprehension skills. For example, "Comprehension Power" is a program designed to improve the comprehension skills of students in grades 4–12. The program is available from Milliken Publishing Company of St. Louis, Missouri, for use with Apple computers. Vocabulary in context, previewing, and comprehension questions at all levels from literal to evaluative are part of the package. In addition, students may read and reread the selection page by page or line by line at a preset reading rate to build fluency.

A new form of computer software, called *hypertext,* is currently receiving much attention as an aid in comprehension instruction (see Figure 10.4). In the hypertext format, students may seek additional text, computer speech, or graphics as comprehension aids, much like "pulling down" a help menu or screen during word processing (Higgins & Boone, 1990). Although not yet commonly found in schools, several authoring programs are available for Apple and IBM computers to enable educators to produce curriculum-based hypertext.

A Summary of Comprehension Instruction

As students master phonics and word-recognition skills, teachers must emphasize that the goal of reading instruction is not decoding, but rather comprehension. Comprehension involves both the knowledge a student brings to a reading selection and his or her understanding of the varied types of text and purposes for reading. Comprehension instruction for children with mild disabilities must be systematic and must help students engage actively with materials before, during, and after the reading task. Fluency- and vocabulary-building activities and direct teaching of comprehension skills and strategies are components of comprehension instruction for students with mild disabilities.

✎ Integrating Reading Instruction and the Language Arts

At the beginning of this chapter, we discussed the whole-language approach to reading instruction. Recall that proponents of whole language advocate the use of quality children's literature as a vehicle through which children can learn to read and to write. By reading, rereading, and writing about favorite stories, poems, and topics, children discover the phonetic code and connect

Figure 10.4   An Example of Hypertext

From "Hypertext: A New Vehicle for Computer Use in Reading Instruction," by K. Higgins and R. Boone, 1990, Intervention in School and Clinic, 26, p. 30. Copyright © 1990 by PRO-ED, Inc. Reprinted by permission.

When hypertext is used to improve reading comprehension, the student answers a question from a second-layer window on the computer screen before continuing to the next page of text. If the student chooses a correct answer, a third-layer window reinforces the correct choice and shows the student where in the text the answer is located. If the student gives an incorrect choice, hypertext prompts students through steps to find where the answer is located.

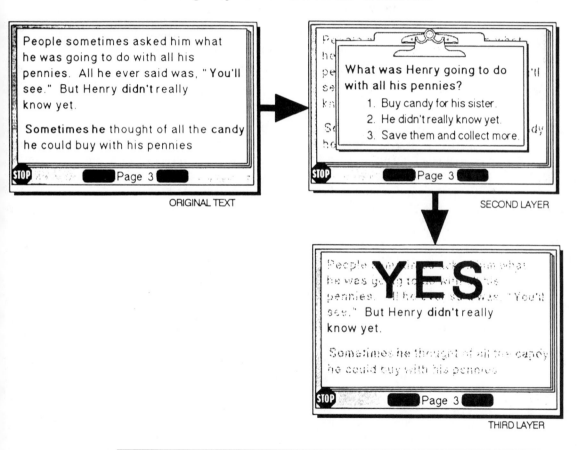

reading with meaning. Reading and writing are interrelated skills that are not easily separated in real life; therefore, the integration of reading and writing activities intuitively makes sense to teachers.

We cautioned, however, that for children with mild disabilities, indirect teaching methods are rarely effective. These youngsters need explicit instruction and practice in decoding skills and comprehension strategies if they are to learn to read. Nevertheless, certain elements of a whole-language approach can play a vital role in reading and language arts instruction for children with mild disabilities. For example, teachers can

1. read quality children's literature to youngsters with mild disabilities;

2. choose reading selections based on student interest or useful content-area topics under study;

3. have students read repetitive lines of poems or stories individually or chorally;

4. follow up reading selections with activities such as a dramatization, retelling, or illustration of the story or poem;

5. engage children in writing activities, such as changing the ending of a story or writing a letter to the main character after reading a selection; and

6. model skillful reading and writing strategies by "thinking aloud" during both reading and writing activities.

Whole-language approaches, at present, lack sufficient research support for use as a primary method of instruction for youngsters with mild disabilities. Whole language can, however, supplement direct instruction in essential reading and language arts skills for these children, providing them with motivating and meaningful experiences with connected text.

✎ Summary

Authorities debate whether reading is a top-down, a bottom-up, or an interactive process. Today, however, most professionals do agree that mature readers draw on both their background knowledge and experience and their knowledge of phonics and word-recognition skills to derive meaning from the printed page. Poor readers, on the other hand, have deficient decoding skills and more limited background information. They must depend on either a top-down or a bottom-up strategy to gain meaning from written materials.

Children in special education programs often have significant reading problems, hindering their performance in other academic areas as well. Research supports the use of systematic direct-synthetic phonics instruction for most students with mild disabilities. In addition, these youngsters require explicit instruction in and extensive practice with sight word recognition and comprehension skills and strategies. For those students who still fail to master decoding and comprehension skills after intensive and quality instruction, building a functional sight word vocabulary or using a specialized remedial reading technique, such as Fernald's VAKT method, might become the approach of choice.

An integrated approach to reading and the language arts, the whole-language curriculum, is receiving attention in both regular and special education classrooms. A whole-language approach will provide children with mild disabilities experience with well-written connected text and with meaningful reading and writing activities. If these youngsters are to learn to read, however, whole-language programs must supplement, rather than replace, explicit instruction in decoding and comprehension skills.

✎ Application Exercises

1. Examine two different basal reading series used in local school districts. Would you classify these as primarily meaning-emphasis or code-emphasis approaches? Justify your answer by explaining how phonics instruction is treated within each series. Examine a whole-language basal reading program. How does this series differ from the other two you examined?

2. Examine two phonics-based reading programs. Compare and contrast the sequence of phonics skills and the recommended instructional techniques.

3. Robert has difficulty comprehending the language and organizational structure of his textbooks. Plan a program to help him build more fluent decoding and word-recognition skills. In addition, select a strategy to help Robert comprehend his science and social studies textbooks. If you were Mr. Abel, how would you justify the program and strategy selected?

4. Travis's school district uses a whole-language approach to the reading program, indirectly teaching phonics skills through literature and writing activities. If you were Ms. Lopez, what suggestions would you make to the IEP team regarding phonics instruction for Travis? Design an instructional plan to help Travis master decoding skills.

5. Assume the role of Mr. Abel at an IEP meeting. Defend the choice of a reading program to build a functional sight word vocabulary for Susan, rather than continued instruction in decoding skills. Describe how time-delay procedures and input-organization techniques might be used when teaching functional sight words to Susan.

6. Select a representative passage of 100–300 words from a basal reading series used in a local school system. Ask a child at the series grade level to read the passage orally for you. Record words the child reads incorrectly or repeats and any words the child substitutes for a word in the passage. Time the child during reading. Compute the number of words read per minute. Do you see any pattern in words missed by the child (e.g., words substituted that do or do not make sense in the story)?

7. Design a probe to assess the following objective for Joey: Given a probe of CCVC words beginning with two continuous consonant sounds that are randomly presented in list form, Joey will verbally decode the words with 100% accuracy at a rate of at least 60 words per minute. Ms. Lopez notes that Joey consistently omits the second consonant sound in the consonant blend. How might you correct Joey's error?

Language Arts Instruction

Chapter 11

Focus

As you read, think about the following questions:

How can teachers provide students with practice using oral language skills?

What are some effective methods for teaching spelling and handwriting skills to children with mild disabilities?

How can reading, oral language, and written language instruction be integrated for learners with mild disabilities?

✎ Several interrelated skills are collectively known as the "language arts." In addition to reading skills, discussed in Chapter 10, oral language, spelling, handwriting, and written expression are all considered to be language arts. Unfortunately, most students in special programs experience difficulty in one or more of these areas. Let's listen to a conversation between Ms. Kirk and Ms. Lopez regarding some of Ms. Kirk's fourth-graders.

> Ms. Kirk: *I'm trying to provide more opportunities for my students to talk with one another and to write and share what they write. I've paired up Travis, Joey, and two other students having difficulty—Celie and Kevin—with partners, and they're also on cooperative teams. Still, I'm concerned about their progress.*

> Ms. Lopez: *Can you tell me some of the things that you're concerned about?*

> Ms. Kirk: *Well, Joey, of course, has trouble interacting with the other children on his team. He always seems to say the wrong thing and ends up antagonizing his teammates. Travis is polite and helpful to his team, but his handwriting and spelling skills are very weak. He, himself, can't even read what he's written when he's done. I tried a partner as a "secretary," but Travis wants to do his own work. Kevin can write only simple sentences that are very concrete, and Celie is one of my ESL [English as a Second Language] students. She understands more English than she can speak or write.*

> Ms. Lopez: *I agree that it's important to have students interact with one another—to write and share and talk about what they're doing. Perhaps, I can help by setting up some role-playing situations in my classroom for Joey. I could help him practice appropriate social language skills for working in a group, like accepting and giving compliments and criticism. As for Travis, maybe he could come to my class to use the word processor to write and then go back to your class to share and revise. What do you think?*

As in most classrooms, the children in Ms. Kirk's fourth grade have diverse language abilities and needs. Yet, enabling all students to communicate effectively, to understand and use both written and oral language, is a major goal of education. Providing all students with appropriate language arts instruction, therefore, merits careful consideration and planning.

In this chapter, we will briefly examine the difficulties children with mild disabilities may experience with oral language, and we will discuss how teachers can help their students develop better listening and speaking skills. Next, we will present effective methods for teaching two written language skills—spelling and handwriting—to youngsters with mild disabilities. Finally, we will return to our discussion of the interrelated nature of reading and the other language arts as we discuss written expression.

✎ Oral Language

Oral language involves the child's ability to understand and use spoken language. Children with mild disabilities may have difficulty with receptive language (i.e., understanding oral communications) or with expressive language (i.e., communicating ideas or thoughts to others through spoken language) that inhibits their progress in school. For example, youngsters having difficulty comprehending spoken language may have problems following a sequence of directions or understanding multiple-meaning words, figurative language, and complex sentence structures (Wiig & Semel, 1984). Students experiencing production difficulty—those having expressive language problems—may use incorrect grammar and only simple sentence structures, or they may find it difficult to retrieve the proper word for communicating a concept. In addition, many children with mild disabilities exhibit pragmatic language deficits. That is, like Joey, they have difficulty understanding and using language in social contexts. These youngsters may fail to adapt their communicative style to suit the needs of the listener, and they may be unable to maintain conversations or repair communication breakdowns (Bryan, Donahue, & Pearl, 1981; McDonough, 1989). (See Table 11.1 for an overview of language terminology.)

Although children exhibiting severe language difficulties may be referred to a speech and language specialist for intensive language development and training, teachers can take advantage of the many opportunities in their own

---

Table 11.1   Components of Oral Language Instruction

The teacher must consider many components of oral language when providing instruction to children with mild disabilities. The following are critical elements of any program for oral language development:

- *Semantics:* With reference to vocabulary for labeling objects and concepts; relationships between ideas expressed.

- *Phonology:* With reference to the smallest unit of sound produced by speakers in our language (e.g., /ch/); rules governing the order of sounds to produce words and the intonations used to give meaning.

- *Morphology:* With reference to the smallest unit of language having meaning. *Free morphemes* have meaning and can be used alone (e.g., the word *big*). *Bound morphemes* are attached to the root word and change its meaning (e.g., *est* added to *big* to make *biggest*).

- *Syntax:* The word order in sentences and the rules used to govern the order of words in the language.

- *Pragmatics:* The use of language for social functions and communicative purposes.

---

classrooms for youngsters with mild disabilities to practice oral language skills. Rather than breaking down oral communication into isolated receptive and expressive language skills for drill and practice, the teacher can use the natural environment to enhance oral language development. Children can talk about the numerous activities that take place in the classroom. Classroom events provide opportunities for instruction and practice of language in context throughout the school day. The following suggestions can easily be incorporated within ongoing programs in most classrooms:

1. Model good listening skills:
   (a) Allow children to finish what they have to say rather than interrupting or finishing statements for them.
   (b) Give a child your attention when he or she is speaking.
   (c) Focus on what a child has to say rather than on whether the child is using proper grammar and sentence structure.

2. Model good speaking skills:
   (a) Use proper grammar yourself.
   (b) Use "self-talk" to think aloud and to model "expert" use of particular language structures. For example, when modeling verb tenses or syntax for Celie, Ms. Kirk models, "The storm *blew* the ship off course" to validate, and also to correct, Celie's statement that "the ship blowed off course).
   (c) Expand on what children say, modeling for them longer and more complex sentence structures to express the same ideas. For example, when Kevin says, "I like to make kites. Mine didn't go up," Ms. Kirk might reply, "You enjoy making kites, but yours didn't go up."
   (d) Elaborate on what children say, providing for them, or eliciting from them, additional details or ideas regarding the topic at hand. For example, in science, when Kevin answers that the habitat for a giraffe is a grassland, Ms. Kirk might say, "Yes, the habitat for a giraffe is a grassland. That's also the habitat for some types of elephants and for zebra. A grassland is a habitat for grazing animals."
   (e) Describe for children what they are doing to link language use with their actions and environment. Say, for example, "When you mixed the red and yellow paints together, you made orange."

3. Consistently reinforce children for good listening and for good speaking with peers and teachers.

4. Use concrete activities and experiences for language development:
   (a) Provide pictures to illustrate new vocabulary or sentence structures.
   (b) Ask children to act out new sentence forms and structures.
   (c) Use simple language forms and vocabulary when teaching new concepts, trying unknown words and structures to familiar ones.
   (d) Allow children to give and follow directions to help each other make something, play a game, and so forth.
   (e) Have children role play making telephone calls, interviewing for a job, greeting someone, ordering from a menu, and so forth, to practice pragmatic language skills in realistic social contexts.

5. Use subject areas for language instruction and practice throughout the day:
    (a) Have students retell stories to one another or summarize the main idea or sequence of events after listening to a speaker or reader.
    (b) Have students generate questions before reading or listening to a lesson.
    (c) Follow reading and writing activities with discussion to clarify and expand on ideas.

Oral language skills, both receptive and expressive, play a vital role in a student's progress through school; therefore, teachers must help their students understand and use spoken language effectively. When teachers capitalize on the language-rich nature of classrooms to provide meaningful activities for language development and practice, most students with mild disabilities experience oral language as a functional tool for communicating with peers and teachers within a natural context. For those youngsters requiring more intensive intervention, the teacher must work collaboratively with a speech and language specialist or consult one of the language development programs listed in Table 11.2.

In providing opportunities to enhance oral language development, teachers must remember that oral language cannot be separated from written language. After all, the language arts are a series of interrelated skills. Let's turn now to a discussion of written language instruction for children with mild disabilities.

✎ Written Language

Written language is a complex area within the language arts. To communicate through writing, students must apply both oral language skills and reading skills. In addition, students must be able to think about and organize a topic, spell words, and legibly produce letters in manuscript or cursive form. Although in this section we will examine spelling and handwriting as separate written language skills, the reader must remember that spelling and handwriting, as well as oral language and reading, are interrelated skills used simultaneously to achieve the final goal of written language instruction—written expression.

Spelling

Spelling is a difficult skill for many students to master. Rather than recognizing letter patterns and combinations and their corresponding sounds, as when decoding words while reading, the student must recall and encode the correct sequence of letters when spelling. The task is made more difficult when we consider that even though there are only 26 letters in the alphabet, there are approximately 256 different spelling patterns to represent the more than 40 sounds in the English language. Inconsistent letter–sound correspondence and

Table 11.2   Language Programs for Students with Mild Disabilities

Program	Uses and Publishers
Communicative Competence: A Functional-Pragmatic Language Program (C. Simon, 1980).	A program for teaching the use of language in social contexts and the rules for conversation. Communication Skill Builders, Tucson, AZ.
Conversations: Language Intervention for Adolescents (B. Hoskins, 1987).	A pragmatic language program for students in middle or high school. Developmental Learning Materials, Allen, TX.
Developing Understanding of Self and Others (DUSO) (D. Dinkmeyer, 1972).	A language enrichment program for grades K–4 adaptable for special education children. American Guidance Service, Circle Pines, MN.
Direct Instruction for Teaching and Remediation (DISTAR) (S. Engelmann & J. Osborn, 1976).	A systematic language program at three levels. Uses scripted direct instruction appropriate for preschool to grade 4. Science Research Associates, Chicago, IL.
Fokes Sentence Builder and Expander (J. Fokes, 1984).	A program for systematic instruction in syntax to improve sentence construction and understanding. Developmental Learning Materials, Allen, TX.
Let's Talk: Developing Prosocial Communication Skills (E. Wiig, 1982).	A program for developing pragmatic language skills in children and young adults. Also appropriate for children with a language difference. Merrill Press, Columbus, OH.
Peabody Language Development Kits (Rev.) (Dunn, Smith, Dunn, Horton, & Smith, 1981).	Hands-on games and activities for language stimulation and development in preschool through grade 3. American Guidance Service, Circle Pines, MN.
Pragmatic Language Trivia (M. A. Marquis, 1985, 1988).	Games for promoting effective communication in older children and adolescents. Communication Skill Builders, Tucson, AZ.

words borrowed from other languages create difficulty for students in both regular and special education classrooms.

Although students who are not in special education programs may still have difficulty with spelling, most children with mild disabilities inevitably experience problems in this area, particularly if they are poor readers. Authorities suggest that students having trouble learning to read also have trouble learning to spell (Carpenter & Miller, 1982). Poor readers often exhibit deficits in phonological skills, such as detecting and remembering sounds in words (Mann & Liberman, 1984). Phonological skills must be mastered in order to spell words, as well as to say them out loud. Moreover, difficulty learning to read and to spell may affect phonological awareness (Ehri, 1989). Thus, reading and spelling are interrelated skills having a reciprocal effect on one another and on the development of phonological ability.

Ekwall (1989) suggests that children may make similar errors in both reading and spelling. For example, "phonetic readers" may also be "phonetic spellers." In addition, most students are consistent in the types of spelling errors they make (DeMaster, Crossland, & Hasselbring, 1986), with the majority of errors resulting in phonetically acceptable incorrect spellings (Tovey, 1978). Children with mild disabilities, then, may be using limited information and strategies in a "best attempt" to spell unknown words (Gerber, 1984). Teachers, therefore, must engage in systematic analysis of errors made by students and tailor spelling instruction accordingly (Fuchs, Allinder, Hamlett, & Fuchs, 1990; Fuchs, Fuchs, Hamlett, & Allinder, 1991).

Spelling requires the student to apply knowledge of phonics and structural analysis, to visualize a word, and to write properly formed letters in the correct sequence. Because there is only one correct way to spell any given word, some authorities suggest that repetition and meaningful practice in spelling frequently used whole words (i.e., learning by rote) is more useful than teaching spelling rules and phonics generalizations (Polloway, Patton, Payne, & Payne, 1989). Others argue, on the other hand, that teaching highly generalizable phonics rules or morphemic rules may enable students to spell a greater number of words than rote memorization alone (Dixon, 1991). Most professionals agree, however, that the approach used in the typical basal spelling series (e.g., assigning on Monday a "weekly list" of spelling words that are based on a particular pattern for practice throughout the week and a test on Friday) is inadequate for children with mild disabilities. (See Table 11.3 for a summary of recommendations for spelling instruction based on the research literature.)

Youngsters in special education programs require explicit instruction and extensive practice if they are to retain spelling words and use them correctly in written work. Although not yet substantiated by research, we suspect that the following suggestions offered by Dixon (1991) promise more powerful spelling instruction for most children with mild disabilities than the instruction typically provided:

1. Focus instruction for younger spellers on true phonemic generalizations (e.g., a *k* sound at the end of a word is spelled *ck*) rather than on

---

Table 11.3   Recommendations for Spelling Instruction

Templeton (1986) offers the following recommendations in planning spelling instruction for children with mild disabilities:

1. Present spelling words in list form rather than in sentences or paragraphs.

2. Give students a pretest. Allow students to practice only those words missed on the pretest.

3. Have students self-correct spelling tests. This is an extremely effective procedure for children at all grade levels.

4. Use the test-study-test method, which is superior to the study-test method for most learners.

5. Rather than present words in syllable form and teach syllable-division rules, teach and have students practice whole words.

6. Give students frequent oportunities to use spelling words in context through purposeful writing activities.

7. Give students specific strategies for studying their spelling words. Writing words in the air, repeatedly copying a word, and oral spelling are not effective ways to practice spelling words. Some children do, however, use oral spelling as a support strategy to prompt or cue correct spelling when writing a word.

8. Focus most spelling practice on the word as a whole unit. Teaching highly generalizable phonemic and morphemic rules, however, can supplement rote memory.

---

phonemic patterns (e.g., the long *e* sound in the middle of a word may be spelled in several different ways).

2. As students become proficient phonemic spellers, begin to emphasize generalizable morphemic rules to prevent overgeneralization of phonemic spelling.

3. Provide rote memory practice for words that do not conform to any rules.

Teachers can link phonics and structural analysis practice in reading with spelling instruction while still providing numerous opportunities for rote memory drill. For example, after reading the word *bake* in a story, the teacher might pause and challenge students to spell the word *baking,* requiring pupils to apply a newly acquired spelling skill. In addition, teachers must create ways for students with mild disabilities to use spelling words in context if these children are to transfer the spelling skills they learn. Beyond these two major suggestions, we hope that the practices we are about to recommend will be helpful to teachers in their spelling instruction. In addition, teachers may wish to obtain one of the programs for spelling instruction listed in Table 11.4.

Short word lists and self-correction.   Poor spellers are more likely to succeed with relatively short word lists. Authorities suggest that between five and ten words per list is a sufficient number for poor spellers (Bryant, Drabin, & Gettinger, 1981). Moreover, "flow" word lists may be more effective for youngsters with spelling difficulty than "fixed" word lists (Mercer & Mercer, 1989). On a flow word list, new words are added to replace words mastered,

Table 11.4   Spelling Programs for Students with Mild Disabilities

Programs	*Uses and Publishers*
Common Words	High-frequency words often misspelled for use with grades 9–12. Merrill Press, Columbus, OH.
Corrective Spelling Through Morphographs	A program for students in grades 4 and up. Intensive instruction in morphemic rules. Science Research Associates, Chicago, IL.
Gateways to Correct Spelling	A functional list of 720 words commonly misspelled for use with grades 7–12. Steck-Vaughn Company, Austin, TX.
Instant Spelling Words for Writing	A spelling series across five different levels. Curriculum Associates, North Billerica, MA.
Speed Spelling and *Advanced Speed Spelling*	*Speed Spelling* teaches children in grades 1–3 phonetic regularities; *Advanced Speed Spelling* addresses irregularly spelled words for students in grades 7–12. C. C. Publications, Tigard, OR.
Spelling Workbook Series	Elementary and secondary workbooks on phonetic regularities, visual recall of whole words, and spelling rules. Educators Publishing Service, Cambridge, MA.
The Quick Word Handbook for Everyday Writers	Words frequently used in writing arranged alphabetically. Curriculum Associates, North Billerica, MA.

while those words not yet learned to a specified criterion level remain on the list. By contrast, all words remain on the more typical fixed word list, even if the child has mastered some of them. Moreover, an entire fixed word list is replaced with a new one, even if the child has not yet mastered words on the old list.

Another procedure that can be used effectively with the flow word list is the "test-study-test" method. Rather than assigning words to be studied all week and then tested on Friday (i.e., a "study-test" method), the teacher gives a pretest first. Those words spelled incorrectly on the pretest then become targets for practice. Both flow word lists and the "test-study-test" method allow children with mild disabilities to focus attention on words they need to practice.

Self-correction immediately after a spelling test or pretest also may focus student attention on troublesome words or parts of words (Graham & Miller, 1979). That is, the child should correct his or her own spelling paper, with teacher assistance and feedback. In addition, with words that do not follow regular phonetic rules, imitation plus modeling may be an effective error-correction procedure (Kauffman, Hallahan, Haas, Brame, & Boren, 1978). Using this technique, the teacher first writes the spelling word to include the same error made by the child. Then, the teacher immediately provides the correct spelling beside the incorrectly spelled word. For example, Mr. Abel might tell Susan, "Here's how you spelled *field,*" while he writes "feeld." Next, he says, "Now, here's how to spell *field,*" while he writes the word correctly.

Drill-and-practice activities for retention. Teachers can use numerous games, such as variations on traditional tic-tac-toe or board games in which students must correctly spell words to move a game piece or to place an X or O, and drill activities to ensure memorization of spelling words, particularly those not conforming to phonemic rules. Time-delay procedures such as those used with sight word drills (See Chapter 10) may also be used to provide nearly errorless practice. For example, using a zero-second time delay, the teacher can cue a student, "Spell _____" and then follow the cue with an immediate presentation of the word correctly written on a card (Stevens & Schuster, 1987). Later, the teacher may increase the time delay to 5 or more seconds before providing the prompt. Using time-delay procedures with a small group to practice writing and spelling words also improves sight word recognition (Winterling, 1990).

In order to increase motivation during spelling practice, the teacher can intersperse words the child knows among those he or she still needs to learn. Again, as with sight word drills, this procedure allows for repetition of previously mastered words to ensure that they are retained. As an additional incentive for spelling practice, students may earn rewards for correctly spelled words on spelling tests. For example, students can receive reinforcement either for individual improvement over past performance or as a member of a cooperative learning team. Moreover, self-graphing of spelling words mastered may be a motivating activity for older youngsters with mild disabilities.

Finally, a few computer programs also provide motivating drill and practice. In "Spelling Wiz," available from DLM Teaching Resources, Allen, Texas, for use with most types of computers found in classrooms, students in grades 1–6 compete at nine different speeds as a wizard uses his wand to put missing letters into words. When playing "Dieting Dinosaur," available from the Charles Clark Company of Brentwood, New York, children in grades 3–8 help a dinosaur stay on his diet by providing correct letters to complete spelling words in a computer-age rendition of the traditional hangman game.

Strategies for studying spelling words.   Children with mild disabilities also need direct instruction and practice in appropriate ways of studying their spelling words. Research does not support having children copy their spelling words repeatedly for practice. Research also does not support having children practice spelling words in the air or orally (Templeton, 1986). Many authorities advocate a "See it, Say it, Cover it, Write it, Check it, Repeat" cycle as an effective spelling-practice strategy (Graham & Miller, 1979). Rooney (1988), however, offers a slightly different strategy to help older students study unknown spelling or content-area words. In her field-tested strategy, the students are taught to follow seven steps:

1. Write the correct spelling of the word on a card.

2. Spell the word aloud.

3. Say the word and write the word, breaking it into parts.

4. Look for and mark visual clues, such as little words within the word.

5. With the card turned over, write the word from memory.

6. Again, mark all the visual clues.

7. Write the word with eyes closed.

Dangel (1987) used a sequential strategy to help students aged 9–14 improve spelling study. The Coach's Spelling Approach uses a trace-cover-write sequence in which spelling practice is analogous to coaching a football team. The strategy involves several steps across three "coaching" phases:

1. During scouting, the student must
   (a) know the opposition by reading each word correctly;
   (b) identify the tendencies of opponents by sorting spelling words written on cards into groups that are phonetically regular or irregular; and
   (c) identify the opponent's strengths and weaknesses by arranging cards into stacks of easy and hard words.

2. During practice, the student must
   (a) practice phonetically regular words by looking at the word and saying it, tracing the word while saying it and listening to the sounds, covering the word and writing it from memory while saying it, and checking for errors; and
   (b) practice phonetically irregular words by looking at the word and saying it, tracing the word and naming the letters, covering the

word and writing it from memory while saying the letters, and
checking for errors.

3. During the postgame period, the student must
   (a) compile statistics, keeping a record of spelling performance during
       practice and testing sessions; and
   (b) adjust practice based on the stats.

Functional words and whole-word practice.   Some students with mild disabilities may be unable to master phonemic and morphemic rules even with
intensive and quality instruction. For these children, it is useful to construct
an individualized and functional word list. For example, Marcus may need to
spell number words, the months of the year, and words pertaining to personal
information (e.g., place of birth, occupation, address) in order to write a check
or complete a job or credit application. Similarly, Robert may need these
words written on "wallet-sized" cards so that they will be available to him
when needed upon leaving school.

In addition, multisensory techniques may provide focused, repetitive
practice of whole words (see Chapter 10). Although these approaches lack
research evidence of their effectiveness, teachers report that multisensory
practice helps some students with mild disabilities spell new words. Using the
Fernald (1943) method, for example, the teacher

1. writes the word and pronounces it;

2. asks the child to repeat the word;

3. has the child trace the word while saying it and then copy the word while
   saying it;

4. asks the child to write the word from memory; and

5. files mastered words for later use in stories.

In the Gillingham-Stillman method (1973), the teacher uses a technique called
simultaneous oral spelling. Following dictation of a word by the teacher, the
child repeats the word and names the letters in the word. Next, the child
writes the word while naming each letter and reads the word he or she has
written. Whereas the Fernald (1943) method emphasizes the whole word as a
unit through visual, auditory, kinesthetic, and tactile stimulation, the child
must rely more on letter–sound correspondences when using the Gillingham-
Stillman (1973) approach.

The Johnson and Myklebust (1967) procedure is an alternative practice
method that moves the student from recognition to partial recall to total recall
of letter sequences within whole words. To practice the word *said*, for example, the teacher might present a sequence like the following while pronouncing
the word slowly and distinctly:

s a i d

s _ i d

s a _ d

s _ _ d

s a i _

_ _ _ _

Finally, students like Robert or Marcus may benefit from using technological aids such as spell-checkers included with word processing programs. Moreover, hand-held computers such as the Franklin Spellmaster, available through most school-supply catalogues or local electronics stores, enable students to obtain the correct spelling for many frequently used words by entering the word "as it sounds."

A summary of spelling instruction. Children with mild disabilities require direct instruction of useful spelling words and highly generalizable phonemic/morphemic rules. Providing words in short lists that "flow" and helping students self-correct spelling words are two other procedures effective with children in special education classrooms. Drill-and-practice activities and specific strategies for studying spelling words are also necessary components of spelling instruction for youngsters with mild disabilities.

Handwriting

The goal of handwriting instruction is for students to produce legible written communications fluently. To do so, they must maintain proper posture, pencil grip, and paper slant; produce letters of the correct size and shape; align letters evenly on the baseline; and properly space letters in words. Moreover, they must accomplish each of these tasks automatically and recall letter shapes immediately so that they may write with ease and speed. Although some students may claim that they do not need to write frequently, they must have legible handwriting to successfully perform such tasks as completing an order form for themselves or for a customer, filling out a job or credit application, or taking notes in class or messages over the phone. Unfortunately, many students balk when faced with laborious handwriting practice, and many others develop poor handwriting habits as they get older.

Handwriting instruction usually begins in either kindergarten or the first grade. Children first learn uppercase and lowercase manuscript letters composed of simple sticks and circles. Those letters composed solely of vertical and horizontal lines (e.g., E, F, H, L, T, etc.) are easier to produce and are usually taught before those made up of both straight and curved lines (e.g., b, f, p, etc.). Typically, the teacher demonstrates the correct letter formation, emphasizing correct starting points and directions for letter strokes (e.g., "Start at the top. Go down. Start at the top. Go around."). Children are then provided with guided practice, first tracing the whole letter and then tracing a faded model of the letter containing only dashed lines. Later, students copy letters from near point and then far point, and finally produce them independently.

Cursive writing instruction usually begins in the second or third grade following an instructional sequence similar to that used with manuscript. Cursive handwriting programs often group letters in families for instruction according to the types of strokes used (Hanover, 1983). For example, cursive letters may be looped (e.g., *e, l*), humped (e.g., *n, m*), or members of the "c" or "two o'clock" family (e.g., *c, a, d*). During cursive writing instruction, the teacher also must emphasize both letter formation and connective strokes. For example, some letters end swinging up, such as *a* and *c*; others end swinging out to form a "bridge," such as *b, o, v,* and *w.* (See Table 11.5 for a list of programs for handwriting instruction.)

Whether it is best to begin handwriting instruction with cursive writing or with manuscript writing, particularly for youngsters with mild disabilities, is debated among professionals. Those advocating manuscript maintain that it is similar to the print children are just learning to read and that the letters are easier to produce (for example, Barbe, Milone, & Wasylyk, 1983). Others

Table 11.5   Handwriting Programs

Programs	*Uses and Publishers*
Better Handwriting for You (Noble, 1966).	A basal handwriting series of eight workbooks for both manuscript and cursive. Noble and Noble Publishers, New York, NY.
D'Nealian Handwriting Program (Thurber & Jordan, 1981).	Workbooks, teachers' editions, and alphabet strips in a basal program for teaching manuscript and cursive. Scott-Foresman, Glenview, IL.
Improve Your Handwriting for Job Success: Peterson Handwriting System.	A workbook that emphasizes proper grip and posture and correct letter formation, with a focus on the functional uses of handwriting on the job. Macmillan, New York, NY.
The Palmer Method	A handwriting series for both manuscript and cursive. A.N. Palmer, Schaumburg, IL.
Writing Manual for Teaching the Left Handed (Plunkett, 1954).	A manual that includes excellent models and practice activities in cursive writing for left-handed students. Educators Publishing Service, Cambridge, MA.
Zaner-Bloser Handwriting: Basic Skills and Application (Barbe, Lucas, Hackney, Braun, & Wasylyk, 1984).	A basal workbook series for handwriting instruction and evaluation of handwriting performance in grades K–8; Manuscript and cursive alphabet. Zaner-Bloser, Columbus, OH.

point out that cursive writing has a natural flow and rhythm that tends to prevent reversals, and that beginning with cursive eliminates the confusing transition from manuscript to a different form of writing (for example, Strauss & Lehtinen, 1947). Most authorities would agree, though, that children with mild disabilities want to be like their peers; therefore, the teacher must help the child learn the form of handwriting used in the regular classroom. In addition, teachers must always remember that handwriting becomes a personal and idiosyncratic tool with time. If a student is producing legible work at an adequate speed, with writing that does not detract from communication, small irregularities in handwriting should not be of concern to teachers.

Today, in an attempt to ease the transition from manuscript to cursive handwriting, many school districts are adopting a "transitional" handwriting approach. For example, D'Nealian handwriting (Thurber & Jordan, 1981) looks like a simplified version of cursive (see Figure 11.1). To produce the cursive alphabet, simple connective strokes are added.

Youngsters with mild disabilities may have numerous difficulties with both manuscript and cursive handwriting. Some students have difficulty producing clearly formed letters. In fact, illegibilities in only four letters—*a, e, r,* and *t*—account for 50% of all improperly shaped cursive letters across the grade levels (Newland, 1932). Improper letter formation may be due to carelessness, misunderstanding of letter strokes, improper pencil grip, or improper paper position. If the last two factors are contributing to illegible handwriting, the teacher can tape the paper to the desk or provide the child with a special pencil grip. For example, rubber grips available from DLM Teaching Resources or masking tape around the pencil tend to produce the correct three-point grip. Teachers must also reinforce children for properly formed letters and provide clear directions and motivating activities for handwriting instruction and practice.

In addition, students with mild disabilities may have difficulty aligning letters on the paper and properly positioning them on the baseline. To address this problem, teachers may wish to use "Right Line" paper available through Pro-Ed (see Appendix B). This paper has raised lines so that the child can feel when he or she brings a stroke to the baseline. Alternatively, the teacher can draw color-coded horizontal lines on the child's paper.

Finally, fluency may be a difficulty experienced by many children in special programs. Some youngsters with mild disabilities may not have an appropriate handwriting speed. They may rush to form their letters, producing many illegibilities, or they may produce each letter slowly and laboriously. Again, teachers can reinforce legibly written, rather than perfectly formed, letters, and they can engage children in such activities as self-checking and graphing legible letters within a given period of time.

Sometimes parents and teachers become concerned about children who reverse letters or numbers when writing. Children younger than age 5 make frequent reversals, and those between the ages of 5 and 7 often will reverse letters or numbers when first learning to write. The letters *N, b, d, p, q, s,* and *y* are often reversed by young children (Lewis & Lewis, 1965). Although teachers should correct reversal errors, they should not become overly concerned that the child may have a learning disability.

Figure 11.1   D'Nealian Manuscript and Cursive Alphabets

From D'Nealian® Handwriting *by Donald Neal Thurber. Copyright © 1987 by Scott, Foresman and Company. Reprinted by permission.*

D'Nealian® Manuscript Alphabet

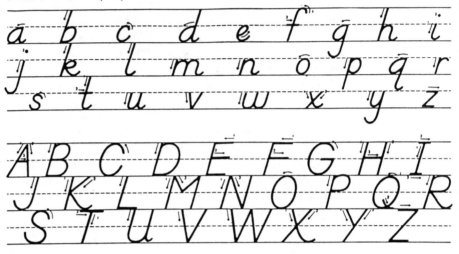

D'Nealian® Cursive Alphabet

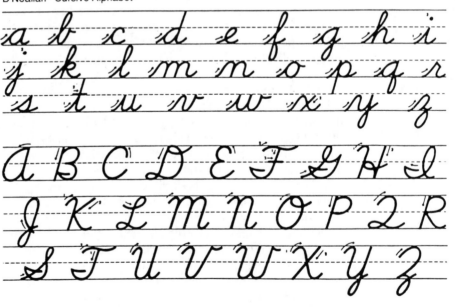

If children persist in making reversal errors at a frequent rate, teachers may wish to emphasize the correct starting point and strokes by using color-coded start–stop cues and directional arrows. For example, a green dot might be placed on the line as a starting point, and a red dot placed as a stopping point, during practice forming manuscript letters. In addition, the following suggestions may be helpful when assisting children to overcome reversal errors:

1. Have the child name the letter before writing it. Then, have the child verbalize the strokes used to form the letter as he or she is writing it.

2. Give the child mnemonic clues for remembering the letter. For example, have the child make a fist with each hand, extending the thumbs straight up. Then, ask the child to place his or her knuckles together. The child should see a *b* and a *d* and should be reminded that *b* comes before *d* in the alphabet. In this way the child will know which letter is to the left.

3. Post a manuscript alphabet at the child's desk and require the child to refer to the alphabet before writing the letter and then to self-check against the alphabet after writing the letter.

4. Separate instruction with frequently reversed letters. For example, rather than progressing through the alphabet with letters in order, separate practice with *b* and *d* by three or four other letters rather than just with *c*.

5. For children having severe difficulty with letter reversals, build a visual clue into the letter as a prompt and then slowly fade the clue. For example, superimpose an uppercase *B* over the lowercase *b,* then fade the upper, curved portion of the capital letter.

Hoffmeister (1981) offers the following excellent suggestions for providing instruction and practice in handwriting:

1. Use supervised practice while handwriting skills are being formed. In this way, students will receive immediate reinforcement or corrective feedback to minimize the chance that errors will be practiced and habituated. Limit practice sessions to about 15 minutes and focus on only one aspect of handwriting at a time (i.e., emphasize posture, grip, slant, size, or shape, but not all simultaneously).

2. Emphasize student self-checking of letters. Children can make individual checklists for troublesome letters, so that they can concentrate on those creating the most difficulty for them.

3. Provide close-range models of correct letter formation (e.g., an alphabet strip or chart taped to the student's desk). Be sure the student receives the appropriate right- or left-handed model.

4. Avoid repeated drill of correct letter formation. Special education students may rush to finish this work and practice poor habits.

5. Post good handwriting on the bulletin board and reinforce handwriting performance with points, stars, or privileges of value to the student. Build legibility criteria for handwriting into all assignments when appropriate.

6. Stress legibility rather than perfection.

7. Use creative writing assignments or content-area study as opportunities for handwriting practice. For example, children can write invitations, letters,

stories, poems, announcements, book reports, journals, or news articles to practice handwriting throughout the day.

A summary of handwriting instruction.   Children with mild disabilities need supervised practice with immediate reinforcement and correction during handwriting instruction. Generally, methods for teaching manuscript or cursive handwriting skills to youngsters in special education programs are similar to those used in regular classrooms. Special paper, pencil grips, or mnemonics also may be used to assist some students when learning to form letters. In addition, children require practice and reinforcement to produce well-formed letters at an appropriate speed. Legibility and fluency are two major interrelated components of handwriting instruction for children with special needs.

✎ Written Expression

We have defined the final goal of written language instruction to be written expression. Adequate written expression requires a solid foundation in oral language, reading, and written language skills, such as spelling and handwriting. As a matter of fact, because written expression is the most complex of all the language arts, special education teachers often overlook instruction in this area. They concentrate instead on handwriting and spelling as "prerequisite skills," or they focus instruction on the mechanical aspects of writing, such as punctuation, capitalization, or word usage. Although oral language, reading, spelling, and handwriting are associated with written expression, they are not sufficient to produce it (Isaacson, 1988). Each must be taught, and all must be combined when composing written communications.

To be sure, children with mild disabilities must master mechanical or functional aspects of writing if they are to complete written assignments successfully in content-area classrooms. Furthermore, knowledge of the mechanics of writing is necessary to produce a proper business or personal letter or to fill out an application for a job. An overemphasis on mechanical skills, however, frequently makes all writing activities distasteful for youngsters. The typical drill-and-practice exercises found in grammar textbooks (e.g., correcting punctuation, capitalization, or word-usage errors in sentences or identifying the parts of speech) bear little resemblance to the actual processes used by good writers (Hayes & Flower, 1986). Moreover, many children fail to transfer the skills practiced during these exercises to their own spontaneous writing.

Teachers are rightfully concerned about fluency (i.e., the number of words and sentences children write); syntax (i.e., using more complex sentence structures such as subordinate clauses and appositives), vocabulary (i.e., varying word choice and increasingly using more "mature" words), and the aforementioned mechanical conventions of writing. Youngsters with mild disabilities require direct instruction and practice in these areas (Isaacson, 1992). This practice, however, should complement rather than replace experience with real writing tasks (Graham & Harris, 1988). That is, if youngsters with mild disabilities are to learn *how* to write for varying purposes, they must receive instruction and practice *with writing as a process.*

Indeed, students in special education classrooms have numerous difficulties with written expression (see Figure 11.2). For example, most youngsters with mild disabilities exhibit problems with the mechanical aspects of written expression, producing written work containing a greater number of handwriting, punctuation, grammar, or spelling errors than that produced by peers (Thomas, Englert, & Gregg, 1987). In addition, some children may focus

Figure 11.2 A Writing Sample from a Student with a Learning Disability

From "A Student's Perspective on Good Teaching: Michael," by A.Y. Gallegos and M.L. Gallegos, 1990, Intervention in School and Clinic, 26, *pp. 14–15. Copyright © 1990 by PRO-ED, Inc. Reprinted with permission.*

This writing sample, a list of those things believed to contribute to "good teaching," was produced by a student with a learning disability. Difficulties with spelling, letter size, spacing, and alignment are apparent. Although not his work, this paper could just as easily have been produced by Robert!

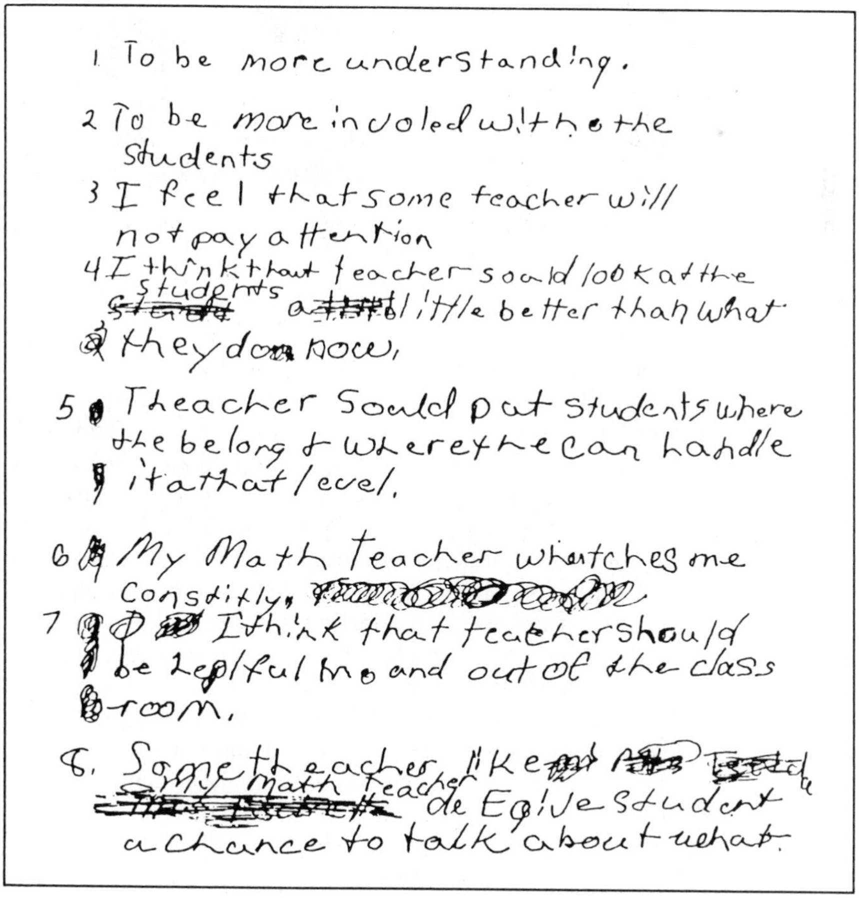

1. To be more understanding.
2 To be more invoyled with the students
3 I feel that some teacher will not pay attention
4 I think that teacher sould look at the students a little better than what they do now,
5 Theacher Sould put students where the belong & where the can handle it at that level.
6 My Math teacher whatches me consditly,
7 I think that teacher should be helpful in and out of the class room.
8. Some theacher like My Math teacher de Egive student a chance to talk about what.

Students with mild disabilities may experience difficulty with both manuscript and cursive handwriting.

so much attention on these "lower level" processes that they fail to generate sufficient ideas about the topic chosen. Their written reports, then, tend to be short in comparison with those of their peers (Englert, Raphael, Anderson, Anthony, Fear, & Gregg, 1988). Finally, many students lack understanding of varying text structures and of the communicative purpose of writing (Englert et al., 1988; Newcomer & Barenbaum, 1991). A writing program for students with mild disabilities, therefore, must include instruction regarding how to plan, organize, draft, and revise written work to meet the needs of various readers, as well as instruction in mechanical skills to improve fluency.

Most authorities today view written expression as a recursive process. That is, good writers think about the topic and audience before they write, planning and organizing ideas accordingly. As the expert writes, he or she keeps the audience and purpose in mind while producing the initial draft. Then, good writers make revisions, eliminating ideas that are not connected to the central thesis, clarifying ambiguous statements, or inserting connectives where needed to ensure cohesive text. Finally, the expert writer edits his or her end product, proofreading for mechanical errors or for inconsistencies, before sharing the text with the intended audience (Bos, 1988). Prewriting, drafting, revising, and editing, then, are the major components of the recursive writing process. Teachers must build instructional activities and strategies around these components to help their students produce good written work. (See Table 11.6 for a description of the writing processes and products of skilled and unskilled writers.)

Prewriting Activities

Students must consider the intended audience and plan and organize a topic during the prewriting stage. Some students find it difficult to generate topical ideas. For these youngsters, teachers must provide stimulation to write. Viewing films, reading stories, or discussing activities or areas of interest could provide needed stimulation; however, Bos and Vaughn (1991) caution that students must be helped to choose their *own* topics about which to write. For example, youngsters may keep a list of ideas in a folder, generated with peer or teacher assistance, to serve as future topics for writing. Additionally, teachers find it helpful to read quality literature to students or to have children share their writing with one another, modeling fresh ideas and differing writing styles. Some teachers encourage students to explore ideas in personal journals or give them opportunities to write poetry (see Figure 11.3). Focusing on idea generation rather than on mechanics and providing students with a real audience and a meaningful purpose for writing are critical elements of all prewriting activities. Children can be given such tasks as writing a letter to request information, writing a letter to be mailed to a family member, writing an article for the school newspaper, or writing a story to be placed in the school library.

Many children with mild disabilities also need help in generating vocabulary to use when writing about a selected topic. To address this need, the teacher and student can list words or phrases to describe an object before the student writes a descriptive paragraph. Similarly, teachers can elicit content-area vocabulary from students, posting this information on the chalkboard or bulletin board so that youngsters may refer to it when writing.

In addition, most youngsters in special education classrooms require assistance organizing topics according to varying text structures (Vallecorsa & Garriss, 1990). When writing simple paragraphs about a topic, special education teachers can provide children with the formats illustrated in Figure 11.4 or Statement-PIE discussed in Chapter 10 (Wallace & Bott, 1989). Welch and Jensen (1990) also offer a strategy for generating and organizing ideas in simple paragraph form. Their strategy, Write PLEASE, consists of the following steps prompted by the mnemonic PLEASE:

P = Pick a topic.

L = List ideas about the topic.

E = Evaluate your list of ideas.

A = Activate with a topic sentence to introduce the paragraph.

S = Supply supporting sentences.

E = End with a clincher sentence to summarize the paragraph and hold the ideas together.

Table 11.6   A Comparison of Skilled and Unskilled Writers

Process	Skilled	Unskilled
Prewriting	Jots notes and makes diagrams. Discusses and explores topics. Considers both purpose and intended audience.	Does not sketch out ideas or plans. Does not participate in prewriting discussion. Does not consider either purpose or intended audience.
Drafting	Writes in style appropriate for audience. Stops frequently to reread and think.	Writes in an informal style. Stops infrequently to reread and think; overemphasizes spelling and the mechanics of writing.
Revising and editing	Reviews and often changes content. Makes corrections for all errors. Keeps audience in mind while revising and editing.	Does not review or make content changes. Looks only for surface errors. Recopies only to make a neat version in ink.

Product Dimension	Skilled	Unskilled
Fluency	Writes many words in allotted time. Writes complete sentences.	Writes few words in allotted time. Writes incomplete sentences.
Syntax	Writes complex sentences using clauses or phrases.	Writes only simple S-V or S-V-O sentences.
Vocabulary	Uses "mature" words; avoids favorite words.	Repeats favorite words; uses high-frequency words.
Content	Uses appropriate style for topic and audience; sticks to topic. Develops topic logically and organizes material well.	Disregards audience; includes irrelevant information. Does not organize or structure material coherently.
Conventions	Makes few or no errors; writes neatly.	Makes many errors; writes illegibly.

For more sophisticated text structures, "mapping" may be a useful pre-writing activity. For example, a story map, such as that offered by Idol (1987), may improve the child's production of narratives or stories (See Chapter 10). In a study by Englert and Raphael (1990), the written products of children were improved by providing them with formats for organizing explanatory and other text structures (see Figure 11.5). The teacher first modeled each text structure while thinking aloud and then gave students ample practice in the use of each for actual writing.

Carnine and Kinder (1985) also taught elementary-age children to ask themselves a series of "story-grammar" questions to generate narrative text: "Who is the story about?" "What are they trying to do?" "What happens when they try to do it?" and "What happens in the end?" Similarly, Graham, Harris, and Sawyer (1987) suggest a mnemonic to help students remember essential questions they should ask themselves so as to include all the necessary elements when writing stories:

W-W-W; What = 2; How = 2

Who is the main character? Who else is in the story?

When does the story take place?

Figure 11.3   Using Personal Journals and Poetry in Writing Instruction

---

The following is a journal entry and poetry sample written by the author and her students during writing time in a ninth-grade English class composed of six boys with learning disabilities.

Journal Entry for March 1992

Spring is coming! I can sense its approach in the change of wind and the changes in people. There is something about spring that always speaks to my heart and renews my spirit.

I stood atop a building yesterday, caressed by sun and warm fresh breezes. Later, I could smell the soil, rich and moist after a gentle spring shower. I watched a rainbow appear in a darkened sky and felt the poetry of spring.

Wind

Scintillating touch!
Lifting strands from my shoulders
And strings from my heart.

Rainbow

Cascading color,
The blue sky smiles a rainbow
Caressing green Earth.

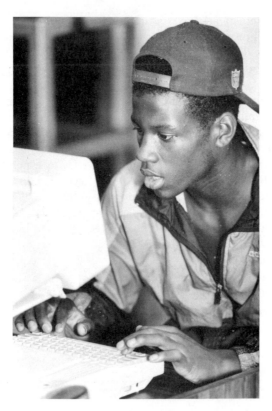

Students who use word processors may spend more time writing and revising. Consequently, they may produce a more readable written product.

Where does the story take place?

What does the main character do?

What happens when he/she tries to do it?

How does the story end?

How does the main character feel?

Additionally, these authorities offer a self-instructional strategy for expository writing: Think of the audience and the purpose for writing. Then, plan what to say using TREE (i.e., note topic sentence, note reasons, examine reasons, note ending). Finally, write and say more. Self-instructional strategies may help children with mild disabilities to generate ideas and then organize them coherently before actual writing takes place (Graham & Harris, 1989a, 1989b).

Drafting Activities

After children have the opportunity to generate ideas and plan what they want to say, they must write their stories or essays. During this stage of the writing process, the teacher must help students focus on their ideas rather than on the

Figure 11.4   Formats for Organizing Writing

From "Strategies for Teaching Students with Learning Disabilities," by A.L. Vallecorse, R.R. Ledford and B.B. Parnell, Teaching Exceptional Children, 23, 1991, p. 53. Copyright © 1991 by *The Council for Exceptional Children. Reprinted with permission.*

JOT LIST

(Main ideas)

1. _____

(Support) ⟶ _____
            _____

2. _____
            _____
            _____
            _____

3. _____
            _____
            _____
            _____
            _____

PARAGRAPH PLANNER

Topic sentence

Supporting details

Conclusion

The Hamburger paragraph

**COMPARISON/CONTRAST
JOT LIST**

Similarities   Differences

_____   _____
_____   _____
_____   _____
_____   _____
_____   _____
_____   _____
_____   _____

Conclusion:

RELATIONSHIP PLANNER

Topic:

Fact:

Relate:

Fact:

Relate:

Fact:

Relate:

Conclusion:

mechanical aspects of written expression. Teachers may tell students not to worry about punctuation, capitalization, grammar, or spelling while producing the first draft (Clarke, 1988). A. S. Brown (1988) cautions, however, that "invented" spellings may hinder later spelling accuracy with older students.

In addition, dialogue between students or between students and the teacher may enhance the clarity of written communications. For example, children may be paired with partners and given ample time to share their

Figure 11.5   Expert Writing Organization Format

*From "Developing Successful Writers Through Cognitive Strategy Instruction," by C.S. Englert
and T.E. Raphael, 1990. In J. Brody (ed.),* Advances in Research on Teaching. *Copyright © 1990
JAI Press, Inc. Reprinted with permission.*

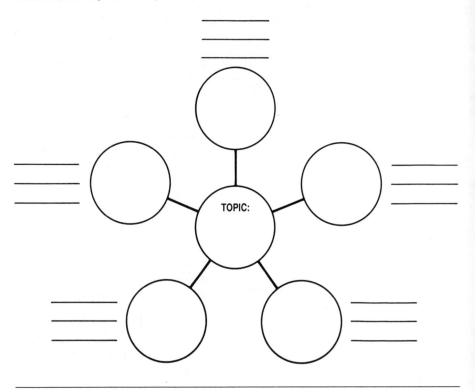

writing attempts with one another as they write. Of course, teachers will need
to supervise this activity carefully to be sure students ask appropriate questions and give appropriate feedback to their peers.

Some teachers like to use a different color paper for the "sloppy copy" so
that students can easily tell which version is the draft and which version is the
final product (Englert et al., 1988). Also, teachers should require students to
write the first draft on every other line so that revision will be easier.

Revising Activities

Revision is a difficult process even for experienced writers. During the revision stage, writers judge and improve the content and clarity of their initial
writing efforts. Although mechanical errors may be detected and corrected
during this stage, the primary focus when revising is on *what* is said.

Often, children are reluctant to revise their written work; therefore,
teachers must model and reward appropriate revision skills. While reading a
draft version of a written product aloud, the teacher might pause to ask for
clarification at certain points and help the student formulate a better way to

phrase what is being said (Wong, Wong, Darlington, & Jones, 1991). In addition, the teacher will need to "think aloud," modeling evaluative and directive thoughts (e.g., "People may not understand what I mean here"; "This doesn't sound quite right"; "I'd better move this sentence"; "I'd better support what I'm saying here") (Bereiter & Scardamalia, 1982).

As in drafting activities, teachers must provide numerous opportunities for children to interact when revising. Children can share their drafts with one another and use questions designed to accompany each specific text structure (e.g., "Did I explain what was happening? "Did I include a main character?" "Did I use key words to show the order?") to evaluate their own writing or that of peers. Englert et al. (1987) require children to rate themselves or others on "Did I . . ." type questions using a three -choice scale (i.e., "Yes," "Sort of," "No"). In addition, they encourage children to place question marks next to parts of their drafts that they think may be unclear.

Finally, word processors may make it easier for children with mild disabilities to revise their compositions. Vacc (1987) maintains that when children with mild disabilities use word processors they spend more time writing and revising, and consequently produce better writing samples, than when they complete written work by hand. Such word processing programs as "Bank-street Writer III" and the "Talking Text Writer," both available from Scholastic for Apple and IBM computers, are invaluable tools to aid youngsters in special education programs. With "Bank Street Writer," the teacher can provide "frozen text"—giving students on-screen prompts that do not affect the actual product written by the student. "Talking Text Writer" allows the student to hear what he or she has written as writing occurs. In addition, programs containing a spell-checker or a thesaurus help youngsters vary word choice and achieve more accurate spelling.

Teachers can also help students to use revision activities similar to those described previously as they use word processing programs. Graham and MacArthur (1988), for example, helped students with learning disabilities to use both a self-instructional revision strategy and a word processor to improve the length and quality of written work. Youngsters learned the following six-step strategy for revising essays produced on the word processor:

1. Read your essay.

2. Find the sentence that tells what you believe. Is it clear?

3. Add two reasons why you believe it.

4. SCAN each sentence:

   Does it make sense?

   Is it connected to your belief?

   Can you add more?

   Note errors.

5. Make changes on the computer.

6. Reread your essay and make final changes.

Editing Activities

The last stage of the writing process involves editing and rewriting the final copy, which will be shared with an audience. The emphasis during editing is on correcting mechanical errors of punctuation, capitalization, spelling, or grammar; however, students may also make any additional changes to improve the clarity and content of their compositions. When helping students edit written work, teachers should concentrate on only one or two key elements at a time, and not overwhelm students with papers covered with editing marks. By focusing direct instruction on a limited number of mechanical skills needed to complete a final written product, the teacher can provide the student, or a small group of students making similar errors, with mini-lessons designed to give meaningful practice with essential skills in context (Dowis & Schloss, 1992).

Englert et al. (1988) point out that students can serve as "editors" for themselves or others, placing question marks next to unclear sentences, stars next to passages that seem particularly well-written, and standard editing symbols near errors (see Figure 11.6). Students with mild disabilities will require explicit instruction and practice using specific procedures to detect errors in written work, however. One helpful strategy for error monitoring combines revision and editing activities and uses the mnemonic WRITER within a "policing" theme (Ellis & Lenz, 1987; Schumaker, Nolan, & Deshler, 1985):

W = Write on every other line.

R = Read the paper for meaning.

I = Interrogate yourself using the "COPS" questions:

   C = Have I capitalized the first word and all proper nouns?

   O = How is the overall appearance of the paper?

   P = = Have I used end punctuation and commas correctly?

   S = Are the words spelled correctly?

T = Take the paper to someone else to proofread again.

E = Execute a final copy.

R = Reread your paper a final time.

Promoting a Classroom Atmosphere Conducive to Writing

Many children with mild disabilities dislike writing. Therefore, at first teachers may need to disregard mechanical errors in an effort to make these children feel more comfortable with writing. Teachers must promote a classroom atmosphere in which everyone writes about topics of interest without fear of being penalized for mistakes. According to Englert (1992), writing is best taught as the children and the teacher engage in dialogue about real writing (see Box 11.1).

Figure 11.6   Commonly Used Editing Symbols

From "Motivate Reluctant Learning Disabled Writers," by J. Whit, P.V. Paul and C.J. Rey-nolds, Teaching Exceptional Children, 20, p. 38. Copyright © 1991 by The Council for Exceptional Children. Reprinted with permission.

Mark	Explanation	Example
⬯	Circle words that are spelled incorrectly.	My (freind) and I went to the zoo last Sunday.
/	Change a capital letter to a small letter.	Mary and Jim watched ⫽elevision for one hour.
≡	Change a small letter to a capital letter.	bob loves the way I play horn.
∧	Add letters, words, or sentences.	*brick* My friend lives in the ∧ house next door.
⊙	Add a period.	My dog, Frisky, and I are private detectives⊙
℘	Take out letters, words, or punctuation.	Last summer Bob (went and) flew an airplane⊙in Alaska.
⟨⸴⟩	Add a comma.	Bob visited Alaska⸴Ohio⸴and Florida.

Promoting an atmosphere conducive to writing may involve teachers sharing their own writing efforts with students. Furthermore, when teachers select quality books, poems, and stories to read in the classroom, students may discover new styles or topics for their own writing. Conferences about writing between teachers and students or among students should focus on prewriting, drafting, revising, and editing activities that are likely to result in clear written communications. Finally, Graves (1985) offers several suggestions to help teachers engage their students in writing:

1. Allow students to choose their own topics.

2. Provide time for children to write. Children must write daily, preferably for about 30 minutes.

3. Permit children to own a "topical turf," a topic about which they are the "expert" and on which they can expand over time as they write.

4. Collect all writing samples for each child and keep these in a portfolio or folder. Periodically "publish" the best works for each child or for the class in "hardcover" form.

5. Provide a predictable pattern for writing. Try to write at about the same time each day, and share your own writing with children. Move about

Box 11.1   Writing Time in Ms. Booker's Sixth-Grade Language Arts Class

Ms. Booker integrates reading and writing activities in her classroom. This year, her students have a daily writing period of about 20 minutes. During this time, they jot down ideas for writing in a personal folder and work on their creations.

Ms. Booker has organized the class in four cooperative groups of six members each. During writing time, the students in each group may talk quietly with one another, sharing their writing, making suggestions, and asking questions. In addition, each group elects a weekly "editor" to review manuscripts before recopying. Twice a month, Ms. Booker plans time for children from each group to share their "best work" with the rest of the class. Periodically, she types stories and poems selected by the students for "publication" in a classroom literary magazine, a copy of which is placed in the library. The magazine is also sent home to parents. During daily writing time, Ms. Booker is constantly on the move, chatting with students and supervising groups. Although she is pressed for time, she tries to hold a 5-minute "conference" with each child at least once every two weeks.

Let's listen to a conference between Ms. Booker and Leon. Ms. Booker is very pleased that Leon has read a book, which the librarian helped him select. Although the reading was somewhat difficult for Leon, he did enjoy the book, reacting to the plight of the main character, "Jimmy." Ms. Booker believes that Leon, an extremely reluctant writer, may be motivated to write about this book.

Ms. Booker: *Okay, so you're saying that if you had been Jimmy you wouldn't have let them treat you the same way.*

Leon: *No, man. I'd bust heads off!*

Ms. Booker: *Do you think Jimmy had a choice? I mean, what might have happened to him if he had tried to fight?*

Leon: *I don't know.*

Ms. Booker: *Would they have killed him?*

Leon: *Maybe, but you don't stand for that stuff!*

Ms. Booker: *Do you think Jimmy had courage?*

Leon: *No, he didn't fight them guys!*

Ms. Booker: *Okay, so you believe Jimmy should have stood up to those guys right away. But didn't he finally trick them?*

Leon: *Yeah, Jimmy, he gottem in the end.*

Ms. Booker: *So, he used his brains to get the men arrested. What would you have done if you had been Jimmy? Can you change the story to say what you would have done differently?*

Leon: *Maybe.*

Ms. Booker: *That might make a good thing to write about, if you want to put that on your list. . . .*

A day later, Ms. Booker checks back with Leon as she moves about the classroom. Leon has decided to change the story to reflect what he would have done had he been Jimmy. Ms. Booker reads Leon's version: "Jimmy wait until they guys go buy. He have a gun. A AK-47 and he go to use it to. Them guy they shoodn do Jimmy what they done. He come done from up there."

Ms. Booker: *Hmm . . . An AK-47. I wonder if your readers will know what that is?*

Leon: *It's an automatic.*

Ms. Booker: *That might be a good thing to tell your readers. Maybe you could explain how he got an AK-47! I think that would make a whole story by itself!*

(continued)

Box 11.1   *(Continued)*

Leon: *Yeah, man.*

Ms. Booker: *Now, here, I'm not real sure what is meant by this part, ". . . they shouldn't do Jimmy what they done."*

Leon: *You know, how they took his stuff from him and said they was gonna hurt him.*

Ms. Booker: *You may need to tell your reader what these men did, or else they won't understand Jimmy's motive.*

Leon: *Okay, I can fix that.*

Ms. Booker: *Great! I just have one more question. When you write, "He come down from up there," do you mean Jimmy or one of the men?*

Leon: [Crossing out "He" and writing "The man"] *Yeah.*

Ms. Booker: *Super! That should make your readers want to read that book for themselves! Okay, I'll check back with you later to see your progress.* [She moves on to another student. . . .]

---

during writing time, conferring with children and asking questions to help them improve their own writing. Provide direct instruction on the mechanical skills necessary for completing a piece of written work, but focus on the composing process rather than on specific skills.

6. Let children listen to and revise their own writing.

7. Have children share their writing with one another during every writing period. Encourage children to ask questions to help them improve their writing.

A Summary of Written Expression

Written expression is the most complex area of all the language arts. To write, children must combine knowledge of oral language, reading, spelling, and handwriting. In order to communicate through writing, children also must understand the differing purposes for writing, as well as various text structures. Teachers can help students learn to write by providing them with numerous opportunities to engage in purposeful writing. Prewriting, drafting, revising, and editing activities, focused on the content rather than on the structural aspects of writing, are important ways to improve a child's written expression.

✎ Summary

The language arts include both oral and written language. Listening, speaking, reading, and writing are considered interrelated language arts skills that cannot be artificially separated for instructional purposes.

Teachers can capitalize on the natural environment of the classroom to promote oral language development. Listening and speaking activities may be planned to ensure that students with mild disabilities understand that oral language is a functional tool for communicating with others.

In order to teach the written language skills of spelling and handwriting, however, teachers must provide children with direct instruction and practice. Teaching highly generalizable phonemic and morphemic rules, repetition for rote memory, a limited number of words on a flow list, self-correction, and specific strategies for study and practice are useful techniques by which to improve the spelling performance of children with mild disabilities. The goal of handwriting instruction is legible, fluent written communication. Students with mild disabilities must receive supervised practice during handwriting instruction.

Children must use all of the language arts skills in combination when expressing themselves in writing. In addition, written expression requires children to plan and organize ideas, to write for differing purposes, and to use varying text structures. Teachers must promote a classroom atmosphere conducive to writing in which children engage daily in interactive conferences and dialogues about their writing. The teacher can plan prewriting, drafting, revising, and editing activities designed to help children write about self-selected topics for a real audience.

✎ Application Exercises

1. Examine two of the oral language programs listed in Table 11.2. Compare and contrast the approach to oral language instruction taken by these programs.

2. Interview a speech/language specialist from a local school district. In what ways does this professional interact with other teachers in order to serve children with mild disabilities?

3. In the opening vignette for this chapter, Ms. Lopez says that she can help Ms. Kirk by planning activities to improve Joey's use of pragmatic language skills. Assume you are Ms. Lopez and design two role-playing activities appropriate for Joey. Justify your choices.

4. Obtain two writing samples from a child with a mild disability in a local school district. Taking care not to use any identifying information, analyze the writing samples for spelling errors. Compare the samples to a same-grade-level handwriting standard from one of the handwriting programs listed in Table 11.5. List any errors that you see.

5. Choose one of the text-structure formats presented in this chapter (e.g., explanatory organization, paragraph planner). Design a direct instructional lesson for Ms. Booker's sixth-grade language arts class

using this text structure. Recall that Susan and Leon are members of this class.

6. Choose a revision strategy presented in the chapter. Again, design a lesson to teach this strategy to the children in Ms. Booker's sixth-grade language arts class.

Mathematics Instruction

Chapter 12

Focus

As you read, think about the following questions:

What are some factors likely to impair the mathematics performance of students with mild disabilities?

If children with mild disabilities are to function successfully as adults, which mathematics skills are essential for them to master?

What are some effective methods for teaching basic math facts and operations to youngsters with mild disabilities?

What are some effective teaching methods and strategies for enabling students in special education programs to problem-solve?

✎ Many children with mild disabilities experience significant difficulty with mathematics (Epstein, Kinder, & Bursuck, 1989; McLeod & Armstrong, 1982). If these students are to function independently as adults, however, they must be able to apply mathematics skills. Despite the importance of mathematics skills in everyday life, not until recently has research focused on effective methods for teaching mathematics to youngsters in special education programs. Consider, for example, the following class session in Ms. Lopez's resource room:

> Ms. Lopez: [Placing on the table several "base-10" blocks] *"We've been dividing our blocks into equal groups, and you can do that very well. Today, we're going to divide and have remainders left. Watch me. I have one 10-stick and seven 1 units. I have seventeen units all together. I want to divide seventeen into equal groups of three."* [She writes 17 ÷ 3 = .] *"Let's see. Can I divide these blocks into equal groups now, Travis?"*
>
> Travis: *"No, cause you got one 10-stick and seven singles."*
>
> Ms. Lopez: *"Good answer! So, what must I do, Joey?"*
>
> Joey: *"Trade the 10 stick in for ten 1s."*
>
> Ms. Lopez: *"Excellent! If I trade the 10-stick in for ten 1s, I have seventeen 1s; I still have seventeen. Now, can I divide the seventeen 1s into equal groups of three? Let's see . . . "* [She puts three 1 blocks in a pile on the table and then continues making groups of three until she has five piles of three blocks each.] *"Now I have five stacks of three blocks each, and I have two 1s blocks left over. Since 2 is less than 3, I can't divide these blocks any further without making my five piles unequal. So, 17 divided by 3 equals 5 with a remainder of 2."* [She writes the answer as she says it.]

Using concrete manipulatives is one effective instructional method for developing an understanding of mathematical concepts in students with mild disabilities (Peterson, Mercer, & O'Shea, 1988). In this chapter, we will explore this and other techniques to improve the math performance of children with mild disabilities. First, however, let's examine some of the factors that affect the achievement of these youngsters in mathematics.

✎ Factors Affecting Mathematics Performance

Students with learning disabilities, mild mental retardation, and/or behavioral disorders in the primary grades typically score below their same-aged peers on static tests of math achievement (Scruggs & Mastropieri, 1986). Moreover, adolescents with behavioral disorders appear to have more trouble with arithmetic than with reading, experiencing difficulty with basic skills and with time estimation (Epstein et al., 1989; Nelson, Smith, Dodd, & Gilbert, 1991). For students with mild disabilities of average intellectual ability, these deficits in mathematics may be related to the inefficient execution of arithmetic operations (Kirby & Becker, 1988).

Numerous factors may account for the problems experienced by children with mild disabilities in the mathematics curriculum. For example, deficits in reading or handwriting may impair math performance. The child may not be able to read directions and word problems in a math textbook or copy numbers legibly and align them properly. Similarly, if the youngster has difficulty attending to instruction or remembering number sequences, basic facts, or steps in complex operations like long division, math performance will suffer. In addition, language deficits may create difficulty for some youngsters in special education if teachers or textbooks use terms interchangeably (e.g., *subtract, less than, take away, minus*). Moreover, children with mild disabilities may have difficulty with both computation and problem solving (Cawley, Miller, & School, 1987), and they may not be able to devise effective mathematics strategies (Swanson & Rhine, 1985). Finally, as children get older, they may have a reduced motivation to practice basic mathematics skills, believing themselves to be low in math ability and math achievement (Montague, Bos, & Doucette, 1991). In fact, as students with mild disabilities exit school, they may have attained only a fifth- to a sixth-grade level of mathematics skill (Cawley, Kahn, & Tedesco, 1989).

A significant factor contributing to the poor math performance of youngsters with mild disabilities may be the mathematics curriculum itself. According to Porter (1989), regular classroom teachers vary greatly with respect to the amount of time they devote to teaching mathematics; moreover, they devote more time to instruction in computational skills than to concept and problem-solving development. Of the topics covered by mathematics textbooks, 70% receive under 30 minutes of instructional time (Porter, 1989). In addition, as noted by the National Council of Teachers of Mathematics (1989), the "spiral curriculum" of most mathematics series, in which concepts like fractional quantities are introduced in kindergarten or the first grade and repeated with increasing difficulty at each successive grade level, allows for only superficial coverage of most topics across grades. Thus, students do not have the opportunity to master skills before moving on to new concepts. Cawley and Parmar (1992) also agree with the National Council of Teachers of Mathematics that students with mild disabilities require opportunities to reason and problem solve, not just to practice isolated arithmetic skills.

Woodward (1991) argues that the mathematics curriculum for children with mild disabilities must be characterized by a full range of correct and incorrect examples of a given math concept, explicit instruction, and a "parsimonious" approach, in which seemingly unrelated concepts and skills are tightly linked. He maintains that the traditional spiral curriculum creates confusion in students with mild disabilities and communicates a subtle message that concepts come and go, and thus need not be remembered. Similarly, Engelmann, Carnine, and Steely (1991) describe six deficiencies in frequently used basal mathematics series:

1. Few provisions to ensure that students will recall relevant prior knowledge;

2. too rapid a rate for introducing new concepts;

3. lack of coherence in the presentation of general strategies;

4. lack of clear, concise instructional language;

5. inadequate guided practice to serve as a transition between initial teaching and independent student performance; and

6. inadequate review to ensure retention of what has been learned.

Given this mismatch between the instruction offered by the typical mathematics curriculum and the needs of learners with mild disabilities, it is not surprising that many of these youngsters exhibit deficits in math achievement. In the following section, we will present an overview of mathematics programs designed for students with mild disabilities. In addition, we will describe those skills that are critical for special education students to master if they are to function successfully and independently as adults.

✎ Mathematics Programs for Children with Mild Disabilities

Although some students with mild disabilities will complete the college preparatory mathematics curriculum, many of these youngsters require a math program that emphasizes essential skills necessary for adulthood. This means that teachers must provide systematic direct instruction not only in basic computational skills, but also in problem solving. Moreover, concepts of measurement, money, and time are also important in the lives of competent adults. Adults must use these skills, not only on the job, but also in routine tasks of daily life, including leisure-time activities. (See Table 12.1 for a list of essential concepts and skills for a mathematics curriculum.)

Today's children and youth also must master the use of calculators and computers if they are to meet the challenges of an increasingly technological world. Both are valuable tools that enable students to perform complex operations correctly and solve problems efficiently. Unfortunately, many teachers believe that using calculators interferes with learning basic skills and that children will become overly dependent on calculators. According to Hembree (1986), however, calculator use can increase basic-skill acquisition and result in higher achievement test scores. Importantly, for students with mild disabilities, calculators can also improve a child's attitude toward mathematics and provide a means by which to problem solve when he or she understands the necessary operations but makes computational errors (Horton et al., 1992). Similarly, the computer can become an instructional aid for group problem solving rather than merely a reinforcer for appropriate behavior or a means by which to gain independent drill and practice with basic skills (Malouf, Jamison, Kercher, & Carlucci, 1991). However, teachers must provide students with direct instruction in calculator or computer usage, including skills necessary to estimate and round answers.

Recently, several mathematics programs have been developed to teach essential math skills and concepts to students with mild disabilities. These

---

Table 12.1   A Mathematics Curriculum for Students with Mild Disabilities

---

Numeration

Counting:
- Counts by ones to 100.
- Counts cardinal and ordinal numbers.
- Counts in sequence by twos through tens.
- Counts by ones from a number through 999.
- Counts by ones from a number through 1,000,000.

Number Symbols and Place Value:
- Reads and writes numerals through 100.
- Writes the number of objects in a set.
- Aligns columns with 1-, 2-, and 3-digit numbers.
- Uses expanded place-value notation.
- Identifies equal, bigger, smaller numbers and sets.
- Expresses numbers using decimal notation to thousandths.

Fractions:
- States fractions represented by pictures/manipulatives.
- Illustrates fractions given orally or in written form.
- Identifies fractions equal to, greater than, and less than one.
- Identifies equivalent fractions.
- Reads and writes simple and mixed fractional numbers.

Computation

Addition:
- Adds using "counting-on" and "counting-on-from-larger" strategies.
- Computes all basic addition facts in column and horizontal form.
- Performs addition of two- by one-, two- by two-, two- by three-, and three-by three-digit numbers with no renaming.
- Adds three and four 1-digit numbers.
- Adds with renaming in the tens place.
- Adds with renaming in the hundreds place.
- Completes multidigit problems with three or more digits.
- Adds fractions with like and unlike denominators.
- Adds mixed-number fractions.

Subtraction:
- Computes basic subtraction facts in column and horizontal form.
- Subtracts a 1- or 2-digit number from a 2-digit number with and without renaming.
- Subtracts a 1-, 2-, or 3-digit number from a 3-digit number with renaming in the ones and tens columns.
- Subtracts a 1-, 2-, or 3-digit number from a 3-digit number with zeros in the ones and/or tens place.

(continued)

Table 12.1   (*Continued*)

- Subtracts single and multidigit numbers from 1,000 or larger numbers with or without renaming and with or without zeros.
- Subtracts fractions with like and unlike denominators.
- Subtracts mixed-number fractions.

Multiplication:
- Computes multiplication facts in column and horizontal form.
- Multiplies fractions with like and unlike denominators.
- Multiplies 1-digit by 2- or 3-digit numbers with and without carrying.
- Multiplies 1-digit by 2-, 3-, or 4-digit numbers with zeros in the ones, tens, or hundreds place.
- Multiplies two by two, two by three, or three by three 1-digit numbers.
- Multiplies multidigit numbers by multidigit numbers with or without zeros in the ones, tens, and hundreds place.

Division:
- Computes basic division facts using both division symbols.
- Divides 2- or 3-digit dividends by 1-digit divisors with or without remainders.
- Divides multidigit dividends by multidigit divisors with or without remainders.
- Rewrites improper fractions to whole or mixed numbers.
- Converts remainders to fractional numbers.
- Carries out quotients to decimal value.
- Converts fractions to decimal values.

Math for Daily Living

Story Problems:
- Expressses story problems as mathematical sentences.
- Solves simple, direct story problems.
- Solves indirect story problems.
- Solves story problems containing extraneous information.

Tools:
- Uses calculator to solve problems.
- Uses simple computer programs to solve problems.

Time:
- Tells time to the minute using a standard clock.
- Tells time to the minute using a digital clock.
- Writes time to the minute from a standard or digital clock.
- Computes time taken and uses time clock.
- Reads time schedules (e.g., TV, airplane).
- Uses the calendar.

Money:
- Identifies all coins and bills.
- States value of all coins and bills.

(continued)

Table 12.1   (*Continued*)

- Writes dollar and cents amounts using decimal notation.
- Adds money to make a purchase.
- Makes/counts correct change.
- Maintains bank records.
- Computes percentages to determine discounts and prices.
- Computes payroll deductions and taxes.

Geometry and Measurement:
- Uses linear measurements as whole and fractional or mixed amounts.
- Converts from one unit of linear measurement to another.
- Uses liquid measurements and expresses equivalent and mixed amounts.
- Uses measurements of weight and expresses equivalent and mixed amounts.
- Identifies basic geometric shapes.
- Computes perimeter and area of basic geometric shapes.
- Computes volume.
- Reads thermometer.
- Uses scales and other measuring devices.

Adapted with the permission of Merrill, an imprint of Macmillan Publishing Company, from Direct Instruction Math, *Second Edition, pp. 49–52, by J. Silbert, D. Carnine, and M. Stein. Copyright © 1981 by Bell & Howell Company.*

include DISTAR Arithmetic, Corrective Mathematics, Project Math, Real Life Math, the Strategic Math Series, and Touch Math.

DISTAR Arithmetic

DISTAR Arithmetic (Engelmann & Carnine, 1972, 1975, 1976) follows a rapid, highly sequenced, scripted direct instructional format. Available as kits at three different instructional levels, the program is designed to teach basic arithmetic skills to children in small groups at the elementary level. *DISTAR I* focuses on ordinal counting, addition and subtraction facts, simple word problems, and the concepts of greater than and less than. In *DISTAR II,* target skills include the remaining addition and subtraction facts, addition with regrouping, the multiplication facts, operations with fractions, and the concepts of time, money, and measurement. *DISTAR III* covers additional regrouping skills, column multiplication, long division, and story problems. (The reader may also wish to consult *Direct Instruction Mathematics,* 2nd ed., Silbert, Carnine, and Stein, 1990, for an excellent discussion of procedures for adapting the standard mathematics curriculum to a direct instructional format. *DISTAR Arithmetic* is available from Science Research Associates, 155 N. Wacker Dr., Chicago, Illinois 60606.)

Corrective Mathematics

The *Corrective Mathematics Program* (Engelmann & Carnine, 1982) is a remedial mathematics program for children in grades 3–12. The program is also appropriate for adults who have not yet mastered basic arithmetic skills. It uses a highly sequenced direct instructional format requiring only minimal reading skills. Included in the program are the addition, subtraction, multiplication, and division facts; regrouping concepts; and story problem solving. (Corrective Mathematics is available from Science Research Associates, 155 N. Wacker Dr., Chicago, Illinois 60606.)

Project MATH

Project MATH (Cawley, Fitzmaurice, Goodstein, Lepore, Sedlak, & Althaus, 1976) is a total mathematics curriculum for children in preschool through grade 6. The program is designed to teach mathematics skills to children with mild disabilities who might otherwise be hindered by their poor reading ability. Included within *Project MATH* is a screening device, the Mathematics Concept Inventory, helpful for assessing and placing students within the curriculum. The four kits of the program cover sets, patterns, numbers, operations, fractions, geometry, and measurement. In addition, LAB units introduce topics such as calculators, metrics, and telephone use. *Project MATH* individualizes instruction for learners by including a variety of options for teaching and responding to information. The program emphasizes mastery of basic mathematics skills and concepts and is adaptable for students at the secondary level. (See Cawley, Fitzmaurice-Hayes, and Shaw, 1988, for additional information on this curriculum.)

Real Life Math

The *Real Life Math Program* (Schwartz, 1977) teaches functional mathematics skills to students with learning problems aged 13–18. The program uses a unique role-playing format in which students set up businesses, handle billing, conduct transactions with a bank, and keep business-related records and files. The approach is quite motivating to older students with mild disabilities who must soon function independently as adults in the world of work. (*Real Life Math* is available through Pro-Ed, 8700 Shoal Creek Blvd., Austin, Texas 78758–6897.)

The Strategic Math Series

The *Strategic Math Series* (Mercer & Miller, 1992a) is a field-tested curriculum for basic computational skills. Students learn to solve and create word problems using the basic arithmetic facts. They also increase their computational speed, improve accuracy, and learn to generalize acquired mathematics skills. (The *Strategic Math Series* is available through Edge Enterprises, Lawrence, Kansas.)

Touch Math

Touch Math: The Touchpoint Approach for Teaching Basic Math Computations (Bullock, Pierce, & McClellan, 1991) is a field-tested program for teaching basic arithmetic skills to children at the elementary level. Children first learn the numerals and their values through "touchpoints" (see Figure 12.1). The child learns addition as a "counting-on," then later, a "counting-on-from-bigger-

---

Figure 12.1   Touch Math Touchpoints

Reprinted from Touch Math: The Touchpoint Approach for Teaching Basic Math Computation. *Fourth Edition, Revised and Enlarged. By permission of the author and publisher. The Touch Math Series was first published in 1976, second edition 1981, third edition 1986, fourth revised and expanded edition in 1991. Touch Math™ and Touch Point™ are trademarks of Innovative Learning Concepts, Inc., of Colorado Springs.*

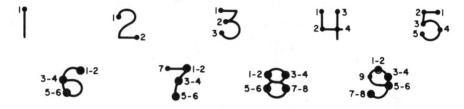

---

number'' strategy. (For example, when solving the problem 4 + 7 =, the child says the larger number, 7, and then counts on 8, 9, 10, 11, while touching each of the touchpoints on the numeral 4). Similarly, subtraction is introduced as a ''counting-off'' process. In addition, children learn to sequence count by ones, twos, threes, fours, fives, sixes, and so forth, in order to understand multiplication as a process of repeated addition. Later, multiplication and division are taught using ''count-by'' strategies, in which children count by the bottom number while touching the touchpoints on the top number during multiplication, or they count by the smaller number up to the larger number while making tally marks during division (see Figures 12.2 and 12.3). (*Touch Math* is available from Innovative Learning Concepts, 6760 Corporate Drive, Colorado Springs, Colorado 80919–1999.)

Figure 12.2   Touch Math Multiplication: Using the "Count-by" Strategy

---

Reprinted from Touch Math: The Touchpoint Approach for Teaching Basic Math Computation. *Fourth Edition, Revised and Enlarged. By permission of the author and publisher. The Touch Math Series was first published in 1976, second edition 1981, third edition 1986, fourth revised and expanded edition in 1991. Touch Math™ and Touch Point™ are trademarks of Innovative Learning Concepts, Inc., of Colorado Springs.*

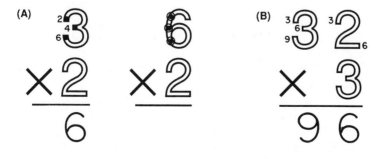

Students with mild disabilities need many opportunities to use manipulatives and to relate math skills to real life.

A Summary of Mathematics Programs

Teachers of children with mild disabilities must prepare their students to function successfully and independently as adults. Therefore, functional math skills and the use of calculators and computers as problem-solving tools are essential elements of the mathematics curriculum for children with mild disabilities. In addition, teachers may select from among several mathematics programs designed for special education students in order to meet individual needs. Let's turn now to a discussion of instructional procedures that are effective for teaching a wide range of mathematics skills to youngsters with mild disabilities, regardless of the mathematics curriculum followed.

✎ Generalizable Procedures for Teaching Mathematics

Children with mild disabilities must understand all critical mathematics concepts and be able to apply them successfully. This means that the special education teacher must minimize the amount of memorization required when learning basic facts and maximize the child's motivation to develop automaticity with basic skills. According to Lloyd and Keller (1989) and Mercer and Miller (1992b), mathematics instruction for children with mild disabilities should include:

1. curriculum-based assessment and error analysis to teach to mastery and control task difficulty;

2. concrete manipulatives to develop understanding of all important concepts;

Figure 12.3   Touch Math Division: Using the "Count-by" Strategy

Reprinted from Touch Math: The Touchpoint Approach for Teaching Basic Math Computation. *Fourth Edition, Revised and Enlarged. By permission of the author and publisher. The Touch Math Series was first published in 1976, second edition 1981, third edition 1986, fourth revised and expanded edition in 1991. Touch Math™ and Touch Point™ are trademarks of Innovative Learning Concepts, Inc., of Colorado Springs.*

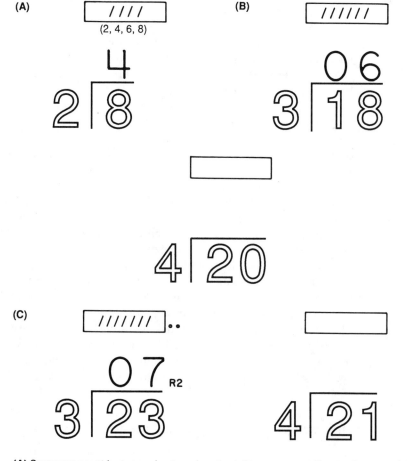

(A) Sequence count by two and get as close to eight as you can without going over eight.
(B) As you count, "2, 4, 6, 8," make a tally mark in the box above the problem as each number is stated.
(C) Count the tally marks. Record the answer (4).

3. direct instructional teaching techniques;

4. careful sequencing of skills and rule-based instruction to minimize memorization;

5. strategy instruction built into teaching sequences to minimize memorization and increase independent performance; and

6. motivational devices to enhance drill-and-practice sessions, including self-monitoring, peer tutoring, computer-assisted instruction, games, and real-life math tasks.

Curriculum-Based Assessment

Students learn best when they are given math tasks at their instructional level (i.e., when their success rate is approximately 70% to 90%) (Wilson & Wesson, 1991). Teachers can use criterion-referenced, curriculum-based measures that assess performance at each level of a mathematics-skills hierarchy to determine the skills children have mastered (performance at or above the 90% success level) and those still requiring additional instruction and practice. Performance below the 70% success rate indicates a task on the hierarchy at the frustration level—one that is currently too difficult for the child.

For example, Joey may know the subtraction facts with 100% accuracy, and he may be able to subtract a 2- or 3-digit number from a 3-digit number with no renaming. When given a similar problem requiring renaming, however, Joey's performance is likely to fall below the level for mastery. At this point, Ms. Lopez will need to analyze Joey's performance by carefully scrutinizing the errors he makes. Joey may be (a) renaming when not required, (b) having difficulty renaming in the hundreds but not the tens place, (c) having difficulty renaming when required in both the hundreds place and the tens place, (d) having difficulty renaming when zeros are involved, or (e) lacking understanding of place value. Ms. Lopez will need to teach or reteach the necessary skills to enable Joey to profit from instruction at this level of the hierarchy.

Through careful, ongoing assessment, teachers can provide children with tasks at the appropriate level of difficulty and teach skills to mastery. In addition, prompts and specific error-correction techniques, such as "slicing back" to reteach a lower skill on the task hierarchy based on observation of student errors, may also improve the child's success rate (Wilson & Wesson, 1991). In other words, student performance improves when component prerequisite skills are taught first to mastery rather than concurrently with a new skill (Carnine, 1980).

Concrete-to-Semiconcrete-to-Abstract Sequencing

In order to develop an understanding of mathematics concepts, children with mild disabilities need many opportunities to work with concrete manipulatives. Students can, for example, manipulate buttons, beans, or popsicle sticks to help them understand numeration or addition of sets (Paddock, 1992), or they can use base-10 blocks to help them understand place value and complex operations like long division. Travis and Joey, in the opening vignette for this chapter, for example, are able to understand the concept of division as forming equivalent subsets by manipulating base-10 blocks (see Figure 12.4).

Unfortunately, most mathematics textbooks begin at either the semiconcrete level, at which pictures are used to represent mathematical concepts, or at the abstract level, at which only numerals and other mathematics symbols are used. Students with mild disabilities learn concepts like place value best, however, when a concrete-to-semiconcrete-to-abstract sequence is followed (Peterson et al., 1988). That is, concepts are introduced first with concrete objects, later with pictorial representations, and finally with number symbols only. Students with mild disabilities require repeated opportunities to manipulate concrete objects in order to learn important concepts in mathematics.

In addition, teachers must take care to relate any manipulation of concrete objects or pictures immediately to the number symbols. This technique, called *parallel modeling,* enables youngsters with mild disabilities to make the transfer from the manipulatives or pictures to the actual number symbols. Ms. Lopez, for example, might place popsicle sticks on the table arranged in six rows of five sticks each:

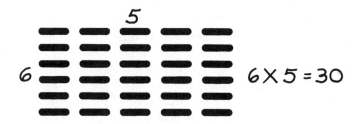

To illustrate multiplication as repeated addition of equal sets, she might ask "How many rows?" and "How many sticks in each row?" and write "6 × 5" immediately as the children give the answers. To answer the question, How many in all? (or 6 × 5 =?), Ms. Lopez may then help the children count by fives six times, writing the number 30 as the correct answer. Alternatively, Ms. Lopez could draw pictures to represent similar problems or use the number line to illustrate seven equal hops of three steps each. In each case, she would immediately use the number symbols necessary to express the concept illustrated: 7 × 3 = 21.

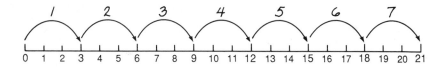

Direct Instructional Teaching Techniques

Students with mild disabilities learn best when instruction is focused, explicit, and interactive. Tasks are analyzed into appropriate substeps, clear examples are selected, questions are posed, and feedback is given to lead students to the correct response. Recall, for example, in Chapter 8, how Mr. Mathis taught his

Figure 12.4   Base-10 Blocks

Adapted from Mathematics with Manipulatives, Teacher's Guide, *copyright © 1988 by Cuisenaire Company of America, Inc., New Rochelle, NY 10602–5026. Adapted with permission.*

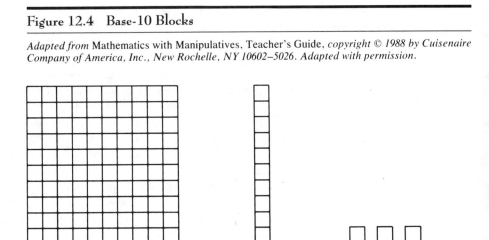

class to add decimal numbers with no regrouping required. He broke the task into three essential steps: (1) write the numbers, lining up the decimal points; (2) "bring down" a decimal point into the answer line; and (3) add the numbers together. These three steps became the focus for questions throughout the demonstration and guided-practice phase of the lesson.

In addition, following the demonstration of a skill or concept, teachers should provide a permanent model of the problem to be solved for students to refer to. Leaving on the chalkboard or on the top of a student's paper a clear example of the problem or a list of the steps to be followed improves student performance. Demonstration plus a permanent model is one simple teaching procedure that clearly improves the achievement of youngsters with mild disabilities in mathematics tasks (Smith & Lovitt, 1975).

Another procedure leading to a high success rate for students with mild disabilities is the time delay. Recall in Chapters 10 and 11 how a zero-second time delay was used to teach sight word vocabulary and spelling words. Cybriwsky and Schuster (1990) and Mattingly and Bott (1990) applied similar procedures to teach multiplication facts to students with learning problems. Initial instruction might begin, for example, with a zero-second delay between the presentation of the multiplication fact and the prompted answer. Later, the delay could be increased to a 3-, 4-, or 5-second interval.

Sequencing and Rule-Based Instruction

Some authorities suggest that teachers should not be afraid to resequence the skills and concepts presented in the mathematics textbook if the sequences in the text are not appropriate for the children in their special education programs (Silbert et al., 1990; Thornton & Toohey, 1985; Wilson & Wesson, 1991). Teachers may, for example, decide to work to mastery with all addition skills before moving on to subtraction. Similarly, within the addition-skills hierarchy, they may decide to teach the addition of "zero" facts early as a simple rule: Any number plus zero means the number stays the same. Usually, the addition of zero is taught as one of the last set of facts.

Rule-based instruction, like careful sequencing of skills, minimizes the amount of memorization children must do. Engelmann et al. (1991) characterize mathematics instruction for low-performing students as explicit instruction about important samenesses. If, for example, when children learn about fractions they are taught the rule: The bottom number tells how many parts are in each group and the top number tells how many parts you use, they will immediately be able to analyze fractions less than, equal to, or greater than one whole—provided that initial examples are used to clearly illustrate each of these possibilities. Similarly, teaching the commutative property of addition as a rule reduces the number of addition facts the child must memorize if he or she recognizes 3 + 5 = _____ and 5 + 3 = _____ as examples of the rule.

Using rule-based instruction does not negate or contradict the need to develop understanding of the mathematical concepts involved. That is, teachers can begin with concrete objects and parallel modeling to demonstrate concepts and rules. Once the child understands the concept, the rule may be presented explicitly, then practiced and applied using direct instructional teaching techniques.

Counters and number lines help students understand basic operations like subtraction.

Building Strategies into Teaching Sequences

Self-instructional and mnemonic strategies can be helpful to students with mild disabilities (Davis & Hajicek, 1985; Mastropieri, Scruggs, & Shiah, 1991). Teachers can provide strategies, when needed, to help children in special education programs complete math tasks independently. When incorporated into a direct instructional lesson, teachers can use these strategies to prompt students, thus improving their success rate. For example, the youngster might learn the "counting-on-from-bigger" strategy as an aid to completing addition problems independently (i.e., "Say the larger number and count up from that number, raising a finger each time you count until you have the other number of fingers raised") or a mnemonic, such as "Daddy, Mother, Sister, Brother" to remember the steps in a long division problem (i.e., "Divide, Multiply, Subtract, and Bring down").

Cullinan, Lloyd, and Epstein (1981) suggest a "count-by" strategy to teach multiplication facts:

1. Read the problem. $(2 \times 5 =)$

2. Point to a number you can count by.   (2)

Students can use concrete objects to recreate and solve word problems.

3. Make the number of marks indicated by the other number.   (//////)

4. Count by your number, touching a mark each time you count. Stop counting when you touch the last mark.   (2,4,6,8,10)

5. Write the last answer you said. $2 \times 5 = \underline{10}$

Such a strategy can easily be applied to forming a line of questioning for use during guided practice, providing a permanent model of task-completion steps to be left on the chalkboard or at the child's desk, and prompting the child when he or she is "stuck." Strategies of this type often provide a bridge between teacher-led and independent practice.

Similarly, Thornton and Toohey (1985) describe a strategy for teaching addition facts containing doubles. Children learn to associate pictures with the addition doubles facts, giving them a visual representation of the fact and a way for the teacher to visually or verbally cue a correct response if the youngster has not yet mastered the facts. For example, $2 + 2$ can become the "bunny ears" or the "car" fact. Depending upon the age level of the child, a picture of two bunnies or of a car with two front and two rear tires can be presented to teach and/or cue the answer "four." The fact $5 + 5 =$ can become the "hands" fact, $6 + 6 =$ can become the "egg-carton" fact, and so forth.

Some authorities are concerned that an overemphasis on teaching strategies such as "counting on" or "counting by" may interfere with learning when the child attempts more complex operations (Hasselbring, Goin, & Bransford, 1987). That is, if the child has only a very limited attentional capacity and he or she must devote a great deal of attention to arriving at the correct answer to a basic fact, the youngster will have only limited attention to devote to solving the complex operation. In other words, the efficient execution of lower level skills, such as basic math facts, enhances the performance of higher level skills, such as completing multistep long division problems.

Teachers must remember that strategy instruction should be used only when needed by an individual child. The youngster with a mild disability will need to practice basic facts and operations, including addition, subtraction, multiplication, and division, until these become automatic. Strategy instruction does not obviate the need for drill-and-practice activities for mastery and maintenance of skills. If a strategy "makes sense," however, within an instructional sequence, and if it will enable students to solve a wide range of sample problems, the teacher should consider its use to facilitate the transition between teacher-directed guided practice and independent practice (Silbert et al., 1990). Moreover, if the child experiences severe difficulty with rote memorization, strategies can become useful tools to enable problem solving with a greater degree of independence. One might argue that the use of strategy instruction is similar to the use of calculators. For some children, the strategy serves as a useful tool until basic facts can be recalled without hesitation or error. On the other hand, for some children with mild disabilities, the strategy may be a necessity if progress on more complex tasks is to be made.

Providing Motivation for Drill and Practice

In order to become proficient with mathematics skills, children must engage in multiple practice sessions. Unfortunately, as students with mild disabilities become older, or as they come to believe that they are not good at math, they are less motivated to participate in drill-and-practice activities. Sometimes simple procedures, such as including basic facts that are known among those to be practiced, can improve motivation. At other times, the teacher must be very creative in efforts to motivate students!

Games.   Traditional game formats, such as Bingo, War, or Concentration, can be adapted for active practice of basic mathematics skills by small groups of children (Wesson, Wilson, & Mandlebaum, 1988). For example, in Bingo, the teacher can present a math fact on a flash card. The children would then write the fact and the correct answer in one of the spaces on a laminated, washable Bingo card. When playing War, addition-fact flash cards can be divided equally between pairs of children. The two children would turn their cards over simultaneously, and the one with the higher sum would keep both cards if he or she correctly stated the sum. In the case of equal sums or incorrectly stated higher sums, both cards would be placed in a center pile to become an additional "kitty" for the next round of play. Concentration is played in the traditional manner; however, students would have to match a math fact to its answer in order to keep the cards.

If permitted by the school district, card games such as Blackjack may motivate older students to practice basic addition facts, such as adding to 21. Similarly, dice can be used to practice addition, subtraction, or multiplication facts. In addition, board games can be devised or adapted for practice of basic math skills. For example, the child would have to draw a card and state the correct product before moving that number of spaces on a game board, or the child would have to draw a card and state the correct quotient before moving a game piece in checkers or chess. Finally, many commercially available games encourage use of basic mathematics skills involving money—particularly games like Monopoly and Life.

When considering the use of games, teachers must ensure that the practice will be more important than the competition. Moreover, games can be used inappropriately to "fill time." They can also be overused or not enjoyed by some students. If used correctly, however, games can provide motivating practice opportunities for many children with mild disabilities. Even a "game" as simple as establishing a set of "fast facts" for the day (i.e., a small set of basic facts to be stated rapidly as a password before leaving the classroom or upon hearing the teacher say "fast facts") can give students additional motivating practice with essential skills (Hasselbring et al., 1987).

Relating math to real life.   Relating math skills to real life is another motivational technique useful for older students with mild disabilities. Youngsters can use the newspaper, for example, to find an affordable apartment given a particular "salary" and other living expenses. The newspaper can also be used to illustrate sales discounts, to calculate "best buys" on varying quantities of a given item, or to determine the average temperature in the community for a week. Math skills can also be linked to vocational-technical school training (e.g., understanding linear measurement, perimeter, area, or the pythagorean theorem as a means for producing a level tool shed of the proper size and with square corners). Telling time, reading bus and television schedules, and reading and recording calendar dates are also critical real-life skills required by older students with mild disabilities.

Self-Monitoring and Goal Setting

Students with mild disabilities can be taught to monitor the number of arithmetic problems they complete correctly (Reith, Polsgrove, McCleskey, Payne, & Anderson, 1978). For example, the child can count and then record or graph the number of problems correctly answered on a 3-minute division-fact probe. On the next day, the child may attempt to "beat" his or her previous record, correctly answering a greater number of problems.

Older students with mild disabilities may enjoy setting their own goals for the number of practice problems or pages to be completed when given a range of appropriate goals from which to choose. Schunk (1985), for example, improved the subtraction skills of sixth-grade students with learning disabilities by allowing each child to determine the number of daily practice pages to be completed, given a range of from 4 to 10 pages per day. Similarly, Fuchs, Bahr, and Rieth (1989) improved the math fluency of adolescents with learning disabilities by allowing each student to set an individual goal for the number of digits to be correctly written during 1-minute timed trials.

Cooperative learning and peer tutoring.   Both cooperative learning arrangements and peer tutoring may enhance mathematics practice for youngsters with mild disabilities. For example, Beirne-Smith (1991) trained cross-aged tutors to help elementary-level students with learning disabilities practice the basic addition facts. Tutors used either an explicit counting-on strategy or a rote memorization approach. In each case, addition-fact performance improved for the tutees. According to Kane and Alley (1980), peer tutoring is an effective method for providing additional interactive practice with computational mathematics for adolescent students with learning disabilities who have been incarcerated as juvenile delinquents.

Cooperative learning arrangements offer yet another way to increase interactive mathematics practice sessions in the special education classroom or in the mainstream (Maheady et al., 1987). The teacher forms mixed-ability cooperative learning groups within the class. Then, after the teacher has demonstrated new content, students within each group take turns as tutors and tutees. Tutors, for example, may present a set of multiplication facts to the tutees, checking their answers and giving them necessary feedback. Tutees earn points for their team for correct answers and bonus points from the teacher for appropriate practice behaviors. Tutors earn bonus points for giving corrective feedback to tutees. Such arrangements have been used successfully at both the elementary and secondary level (Maheady, Sacca, & Harper, 1987).

Computer-assisted instruction.   Drill-and-practice, tutorial, and educational-games software abound in the area of mathematics and can provide students with motivating practice opportunities. Teacher-directed instruction, in combination with drill-and-practice or tutorial software, may, therefore, enhance the math performance of students with mild disabilities (Howell, Sidorenko & Jurica, 1987; Trifiletti, Frith, & Armstrong, 1984). (See Table 12.2 for a list of tutorial and drill-and-practice mathematics software.)

When considering computer-assisted instruction, however, teachers must be sure that students have the prerequisite skills to make use of the software chosen and that the software employs appropriate options for branching to practice on critical, but weak, preskills. In addition, for students with selective

---

Table 12.2   Mathematics Computer Software for Drill and Practice

1. *Basic Skills in Math,* Love Publishing Co., Apple II.

   Designed for grades 1–6, but can be adapted for remedial math at the secondary level. Provides assessment and placement for basic operations. Rewards child with skill game after completing mastery tests. Provides numerical and visual representations of problems. Keeps records automatically.

2. *Computer Drill and Instruction: Mathematics,* Science Research Associates, Apple II and IBM.

   Covers all major skills in the math curriculum for grades 1–9. Features built-in assessment and placement and record-keeping systems, as well as interactive tutorial sessions to give help when needed. Provides teacher assistance for generating practice problems. Offers an additional program for solving word problems.

3. *Mathematics Problem Solving,* Media Materials, Apple II.

   Provides low-level reading programs with tutorial assistance for incorrect answers: "Shoot for Solutions" (word problems); "Home Run Logic" (averages, percents); "Dive into Data" (whole numbers, fractions, decimals, and word problems to find essential data); "Answer Matches" (money problems and rounding decimals); "On Your Mark—Go" (fractions and word problems with distance); "Score the Goal" (multiplication and division with whole numbers); "Chin Bars and Charts" (use of charts, tables, and graphs); "Run a Relay" (tables for rate and records); and "Stick to a Plan" (solving word problems).

4. *Math Sequences,* Milliken, Apple II.

   Designed for grades 2–8 and adaptable for older students. Covers all operations with whole numbers, fractions, and decimals. Includes measurement and percentages. Monitors skills mastery and advances or moves students back to proper levels.

attention problems, computer math games may provide too many distracting elements for the practice sessions to be beneficial (Christensen & Gerber, 1990).

A Summary of Generalizable Teaching Procedures

Mathematics instruction for children with mild disabilities begins with careful curriculum-based assessment and analysis of errors to determine appropriate tasks and student needs. Initial instruction proceeds using a concrete-to-semiconcrete-to-abstract sequence in order to maximize the child's understanding of new skills and concepts. In addition, a youngster's understanding of math increases when the teacher uses explicit and focused direct instructional techniques. Careful sequencing, rule-based instruction, and strategy training may help to minimize memorization and simplify mathematics learning for students with mild disabilities. Finally, teachers must provide children with many motivating practice opportunities if they are to become fluent and automatic with basic math skills.

✎ Procedures for Teaching Specific Skills and Concepts

Each of the procedures we have considered thus far is useful for teaching a wide range of mathematics tasks. The reader is encouraged to keep these firmly in mind as we turn to a discussion of instructional tips for teaching specific math skills and concepts.

Basic Number Concepts

Children with mild disabilities must understand basic information about numerals and their meanings. For example, they must develop an understanding of the relationship between numbers and objects (one-to-one correspondence) and they must be able to identify the numerals and their face value (numeration). In addition, an understanding of seriation (ordinal properties of objects) and place value is necessary if students are to perform complex operations.

One-to-one correspondence. One-to-one correspondence is a mathematics "readiness" skill included in all early childhood programs. Youngsters must understand that one object may be matched exactly to another object and that number words help us to identify this relationship and to count objects. Teachers should engage children in activities such as the following to develop this concept:

1. Have children pass out common classroom supplies, such as crayons, scissors, or paper, giving one item to each child. As children do this, say "That's one for Joey, and one for Travis. That's two crayons," and so forth.

2. Provide children with egg cartons or muffin tins and have children place one raisin or one bean in each hole. Count the raisins or beans with the children.

3. Use common nursery rhymes for counting (e.g., "One, two, buckle my shoe").

4. Give children counting sticks, such as popsicle sticks or plastic straws, or counters, such as checkers or buttons. Count these saying the numbers out loud with the children. Begin by moving each item away from the others as you say the number. Later, help the child to touch and move each counter as he or she says the numbers with you. You may need to use physical prompting at this stage for some youngsters.

5. If children have difficulty establishing a counting "rhythm," clap or tap the table as the child counts. Alternatively, hold the child's hands and control his or her clapping as you count the claps with the child. Children can also count with you as you bounce a ball or jump.

Numeration.   To help children understand cardinal numbers, teachers must provide opportunities for youngsters to identify numerals, recognize their value, and write them. Following are several suggestions for teaching numeration skills:

1. Give the child a card with a numeral or number word on it. Help the child place the correct number of blocks, buttons, or the like, on the card. Initially, you may need to begin with large dots on the card arranged in a recognizable pattern so that the child has a visual reference point for the number of items to be counted:

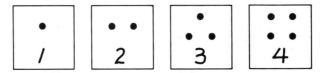

2. Give the child an egg carton, muffin tin, or set of paper cups with numerals written in the bottom of each. Have the child count the correct number of raisins, beans, buttons, or the like, to place in each.

3. Attach cards with numerals or number words to coat hangers. Have children place the correct number of clothespins on each hanger and hang each from a "clothesline" in a designated classroom space. Alternatively, have children clip cards containing sets of dots or sets of objects to the correct coat hanger.

4. Using the felt board, have children match numerals or number words to sets of objects and vice versa.

5. Use trading tasks with the children. Tell the student, "Give me four beans and I'll give you the numeral 4." Or, conversely, "Give me the numeral 4 and I'll give you four raisins."

6. Give each child a personal number line. For each numeral, 1 through 10, provide an illustration using patterns of dots (Mercer & Mercer, 1989):

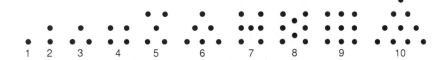

7. Teach children to write the numerals when they are learning the manuscript alphabet. Use the same procedures described in Chapter 11 for teaching handwriting skills. Provide children with the numerals 1 through 9 to trace, to trace over dots, and to copy from near point. Verbalize numerals and the strokes as they are formed. Use directional arrows and color cues if these are necessary.

8. Arrange sets of objects on the table. Have the child hold up a card with the correct numeral or number word written on it. Alternatively, have the child state or write the numeral that correctly represents the set. Be sure to arrange the sets in easily recognizable patterns and stress immediate recognition rather than counting of objects.

9. Place the numerals 1 through 9 on large cards. Have the children arrange the cards in correct sequence on the chalkboard tray or on the floor. Children may also enjoy holding the cards and arranging themselves in correct sequence.

10. Make self-correcting puzzles, each containing a numeral and a matching set of dots. Or, have children complete a number-sequence puzzle by placing the numerals in correct sequence. On the back of the puzzle, draw sets of dots to represent each numeral:

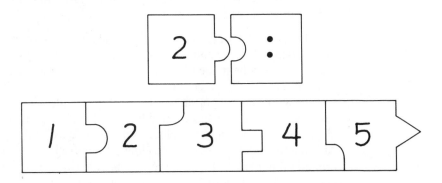

11. Teach the children the touchpoints for each numeral as used in *Touch Math* (Bullock et al., 1991).

Seriation.   Children must understand that objects can be arranged by attributes such as length, height, weight, and so forth. The ordinal property of objects and numerals is essential to developing such concepts as more than/less than/equal to. To develop these concepts, teachers should engage students in the following activities:

1. Give students objects such as Cuisenaire rods (Davidson, 1969) of varying lengths. Have the children arrange these in order from the shortest to the longest and from the longest to the shortest.

2. Fill jars with sand or water and have students arrange these in order (Bos & Vaughn, 1991).

3. Have students arrange themselves in order from the tallest to the shortest and vice versa.

4. Have children count their place in line as they line up during daily activities (e.g., first, second, third, and so forth).

Place value.   Place value is a difficult concept for many students with mild disabilities. It is an essential concept, however, if students are to progress to complex operations involving regrouping (i.e., "carrying" or "borrowing"). The following techniques are useful in developing an understanding of place value:

1. Bundle objects like popsicle sticks or pencils into groups of 10. Count the groups of 10 with students saying, "two 10s is 20, five 10s is 50," and so forth. Practice counting by 10s until students are firm with this skill.

2. Bundle objects like popsicle sticks or pencils into groups of 10. Keep 9 sticks or pencils loose to serve as 1s. Arrange groups of 10s and 1s on a large sheet of paper and have the children count the bundles of 10s and then the 1s with you. Write the numerals on the paper under the 10s and the 1s. Later, arrange the paper into columns headed "tens" and "ones." Repeat the preceding activity, placing the sticks over the proper heading. Write the numerals in the columns, stressing to the children that only one digit can be written in each position or place.

3. Use base-10 blocks such as those available from the Cuisenaire Company of America. (If your school cannot afford to purchase blocks, sets for each child can easily be made by purchasing contact shelf paper patterned with large squares. Fold the contact paper in half so that it sticks to itself and so that the same square pattern is visible on both sides. Then, cut out single squares, strips of 10 squares, and blocks of 100s squares.) Have children place the correct number of blocks on the table to form various numbers. Arrange the blocks under the headings, "hundreds," "tens," and "ones" printed on paper lined with three columns. Write the corresponding numerals in each column directly beneath the blocks. (See top of page 303.)

4. Place only numerals in columns headed by thousands, hundreds, tens, and ones. Have children identify the place value of each numeral. Later, write the numerals without the headings and have children again identify the place each numeral occupies. Later, write numbers like 3,333 and ask the student to identify the "3" that is worth the most and the "3" that is worth the least.

5. Ask children to write the number representing seven 1,000s, three 100s, two 10s, and four 1s and to read the number he or she has written. If

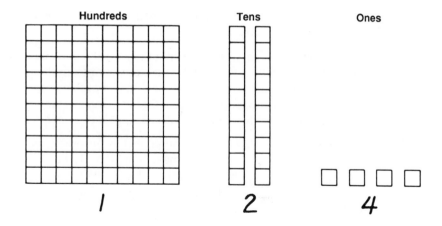

necessary, this can first be done using the headed column paper described in item 3.

6. Using the base-10 blocks, give children thirteen 1s and one 10-strip. Arrange these on column paper headed "tens" and "ones." Ask children to write the numerals to represent the number of blocks. Remind them that only one digit can be written in each place. Explain to the children that ten of the 1s blocks can be traded in for a 10-strip. Now, the child can write the numerals correctly (i.e., 23). Repeat this procedure until children have mastered trading 1s and 10s. Use the same procedure, later, for trading ten 10-strips for a 100s square.

7. Children also must understand that zero can be used as a place holder in addition to representing "nothing." Using the base-10 blocks and column paper, set up problems in which children must trade in ten 1s blocks for a 10-strip and have no 1s remaining (e.g., give students two 10-strips and ten 1s blocks). Arrange the blocks under the proper column headings and write the numerals to represent the number (i.e., 30). Explain to children that the zero is used as a place holder and remind children of the "three-10s-is-30" and counting-by-tens concept they have mastered. Later, arrange situations in which youngsters must trade in ten 10-strips for a 100s square and have zero in the tens place as a place holder.

8. Write numbers and have children identify incorrect zeros (e.g., 032, 0706, 05, 3070). This can be done initially on the column paper described earlier if necessary. Teach children the rule: Zero can never be the numeral farthest to the left in a whole number. Using the column paper, children can see that zero can be a numeral "in the middle" or the numeral "farthest to the right," serving as a place holder.

9. Give children dice of three different colors. Make each color represent one place value: 100s, 10s, and 1s. Children roll the dice and then write and/or read the number they roll. Column paper may be used as necessary. To change this practice into a game format, children may be paired and each child given his or her own set of dice. The children roll the dice, write/read

the number, and score a point for the larger of the two numbers if it is written/read correctly.

10. For older students, the concept of place value may be practiced using an odometer or numbers from student textbooks or from the newspaper (Bos & Vaughn, 1991). Alternatively, "money" and a cashier's drawer may be used to practice place value, particularly trading pennies (1s) for dimes (10s) and trading dimes (10s) for dollars (100s).

11. The abacus is also a time-honored means for practicing place value. Students can see that when they have more than 10 beads on a row, they must trade for 1 bead on the next row. Help children to form, write, and read numbers using the abacus as a concrete aid along with color-coded column paper if necessary.

Basic Facts and Operations

Proficiency with the basic facts and operations is as essential as understanding number concepts if students are to perform complex mathematics with ease. Automaticity with the basic addition, subtraction, multiplication, and division facts does not, of course, ensure that the student will be able to solve advanced problems easily; however, if they understand the operations and can immediately recall the basic facts, they will be better equipped to tackle more complex problems.

Addition.   Addition is a basic operation involving the joining of two or more sets. The sums through 18 are the essential addition facts for children to master. Following are several suggestions for teaching addition to students with mild disabilities:

1. Begin with counters or sticks. Place these on the table in two groups (e.g., three sticks and four sticks). Together with the child, count the sticks in each group and write the number on a sheet of paper beneath each group. Then, count all the sticks together and write the total number of sticks. Stress that 3 + 4 is another way to name 7. To move to the semiconcrete level, substitute tally marks or draw pictures to represent the number in each set.

2. Place patterns of dots on cards with numerals beneath each to represent addition facts from the 1s through the 5s. Place numerals on separate cards. Have children match the dots to the sums. Later, move to larger sums through 18.

3. Flexer (1989) suggests using 5- and 10-frames to enable children to visualize the basic addition facts. Once children recognize number patterns using the 5- and 10-frames (see Figure 12.5), they can use frames and counters to learn the addition facts. The child places frames on the table with counters, such as beans, to represent each addend. Counters are then moved from one frame to fill in any missing cells in the other frame, and the new configuration becomes the sum (see Figure 12.6).

Figure 12.5   The 5- and 10-Frames

From "Conceptualizing Addition," by R. J. Flexer, Teaching Exceptional Children, 21, 1989, *p. 23. Copyright © 1989 by the Council for Exceptional Children. Reprinted with permission.*

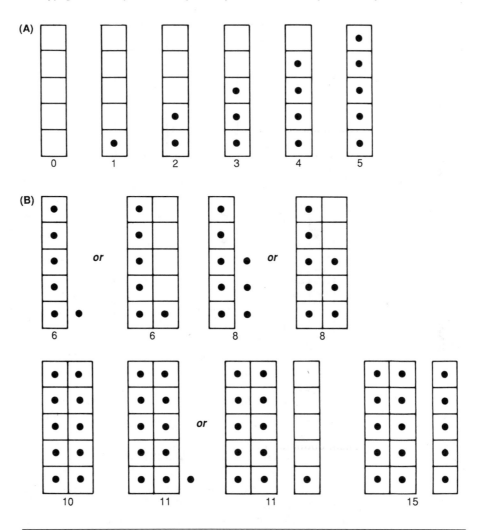

Jones, Thornton, and Toohey (1985) used a similar strategy to help children to remember the "harder" facts. For example, the children visualized the 10-frame and used the strategy "make 10 and add on" to complete difficult addition facts like 9 + 4 = _____ (see Figure 12.7).

4. Thornton and Toohey (1985) suggest that students with mild disabilities be given specific strategies for attacking unknown addition facts prior to drill. They also recommend using a teaching sequence based on the strategy for recalling the sum rather than the traditional sequence based on the size of

Figure 12.6   Addition with the 5- and 10-Frames

From "Conceptualizing Addition," by R. J. Flexer, Teaching Exceptional Children, *21, 1989, p. 24. Copyright © 1989 by The Council for Exceptional Children. Reprinted with permission.*

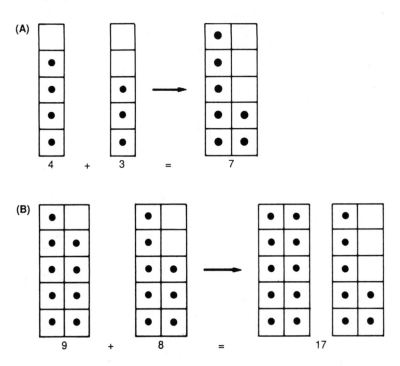

the sum. In the traditional sequence, "easy" facts are the 1s through the 5s because they sum to 9 or less; the "harder" facts sum to 18 (see Figure 12.8).

5. A program such as *Touch Math* (Bullock et al., 1991) can also be used to teach addition as "counting on" or "counting on from bigger." For example, students first touch the touchpoints on each numeral in turn while counting up. Later, children say the larger number while simultaneously crossing it out, then count on the remaining numerals by touching each touchpoint.

Figure 12.7   Using a 10-Frame for Difficult Addition Facts

From "A Multi-Option Program for Learning Basic Addition Facts: Case Studies and an Experimental Report," by G. A. Jones, C. A. Thornton and M. A. Toohey, 1985, Journal of Learning Disabilities, *18, p. 324. Copyright © 1985 by Donald D. Hammill Foundation. Reprinted with permission.*

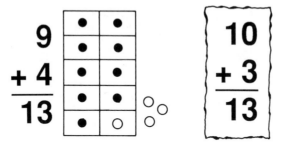

6. When students have mastered basic addition facts, they can practice column addition using three or four digits. Using the touchpoints and the "counting-on-from-bigger" strategy described in item 5 is helpful for computing column addition problems. In addition, teachers may draw blank lines to the side of column addition problems and cue children to break these into separate addition facts. For example:

$$\begin{array}{ll} 4 & \\ 3 & \underline{\;(7)\;} \\ +\,2 & \end{array} \qquad \begin{array}{ll} 2 & \\ 4 & \underline{\;(6)\;} \\ 3 & \\ +\,6 & \underline{\;(9)\;} \end{array}$$

7. Give students personal number lines to use for solving unknown addition facts. Begin with number lines 1–10 and advance to a line from 1–18. Teach children to find the larger addend on the line and count on the next addend, touching a number along the line each time they count. Thus, 3 + 4 = _____ is represented as "Find 4 and count on three more":

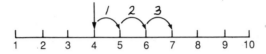

Similarly, 7 + 9 = _____ can become "Touch 9 and then count on seven more":

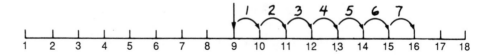

Figure 12.8 A Sequence for Teaching the Addition Facts: Grouping the Facts by Strategy for Recall

Adapted from "Basic Math Facts: Guidelines for Teaching and Learning" by C. A. Thornton and M. A. Toohey, Learning Disabilities Focus, 1, *1985, pp. 50–51. Copyright © 1985 by The Council for Exceptional Children. Adapted with permission.*

	Fact group	Examples	Most popular strategy for working out unknown answers	Sentence pattern (verbal prompt)
No fingers needed!	Count ons	(+1, +2, +3, facts)	"Feel" the count	Start BIG and count on.
No fingers needed!	Zero facts	(6 + 0, 0 + 4)	Show it	Plus zero stays the same.
No fingers needed!	Doubles	(4 + 4, 7 + 7)	Use pictures (e.g. 7 + 7 is the 2-week fact; 7 + 7 = 14)	Think of the picture.
No fingers needed!	10 sums	(especially 6 + 4)	Use 10-frame 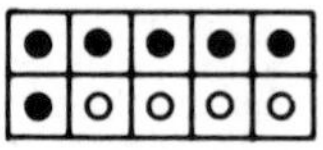	
No fingers needed!	9's	(4 + 9, 9 + 6)	Use pattern	What's the pattern?
No fingers needed!	Near doubles	(4 + 5, 7 + 8)	Relate to doubles (via pictures)	Think doubles to help.
	4 last facts	(7 + 5, 8 + 4, 8 + 5, 8 + 6)	Make 10, add extra 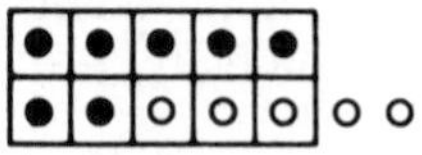	Use 10 to help.

Note: Turnarounds (cummutatives of facts within each group would be learned before moving to a different group of facts.)

For both addition and subtraction facts, Cohen and deBettencourt (1988) suggest a modified number line that highlights the size relationships among numbers (see Figure 12.9). For addition, the child places a marker under the smaller addend and then moves the marker down the number of spaces indicated by the larger addend. (Note: For subtraction, the child places the marker under the larger number and moves up.)

8. Students must also understand the concept of missing addends. Arrange addition problems in families and help children to find the addend.

2 + 3 = ____	2 + ____ = 5	____ + 3 = 5
3 + 2 = ____	3 + ____ = 5	____ + 2 = 5

Subtraction. Subtraction is relatively easy once students understand the operation of addition and know the basic addition facts. Teachers can, for example, help students to use the missing-addends concept as they learn the "fact families" (i.e., If 2 + 3 = 5 and 3 + 2 = 5, then 5 − 2 = 3 and 5 − 3 = 2). Following are several suggestions for teaching subtraction:

Figure 12.9   The "Triangle" Number Line

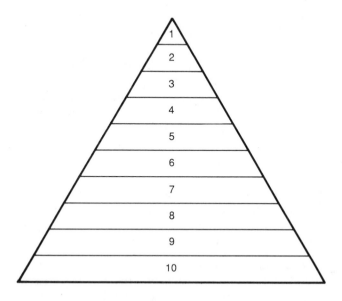

1. As with addition, begin with counters and move to pictures to establish an understanding of the subtraction operation. Be sure to tie each set of counters or set of pictures immediately to the number symbols.

2. Students may use number lines starting with the larger number (the minuend) and counting back the number of spaces indicated by the smaller number (the subtrahend) to find unknown differences. Similarly, the student can be taught to make tally marks for the minuend and then "minus" the number of tally marks indicated by the subtrahend. The difference is the number of tally marks remaining:

$$9 - 3 = 6$$

//////////

3. In *Touch Math* (Bullock et al., 1991), students learn to touch the touchpoints while "counting off." This means that students will first require practice counting in reverse from 10 to zero and then from 18 to zero:

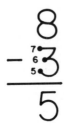

4. Thornton and Toohey (1986) suggest a way to help students with mild disabilities visualize subtraction facts and relate these to the addition facts. For example, pictures are used to illustrate subtraction doubles (see Figure 12.10) and a "counting-on" technique is used with number dot patterns (see Figure 12.11). In addition, Thornton and Toohey present a unique triangular-shaped flash card for practice of addition- and subtraction-fact families (see Figure 12.12).

Multiplication.   Multiplication is essentially a fast way to add the same number time and time again. This relationship can be stressed to youngsters with mild disabilities as they first learn the operation of multiplication. Consider, for example, the following activities:

1.   Arrange equal groups of counters in rows. Begin with simple groups and rows such as three rows of two. Count the number of counters in each group, then the number of rows, and write these numerals on paper. Count

---

Figure 12.10   Using Pictures to Teach Subtraction Doubles

From "Subtraction Hide-and-Seek Cards Can Help" by C. A. Thornton and M. A. Toohey, Teaching Exceptional Children, 19, 1986, p. 12. Copyright © 1986 by The Council for Exceptional Children. Reprinted with permission.

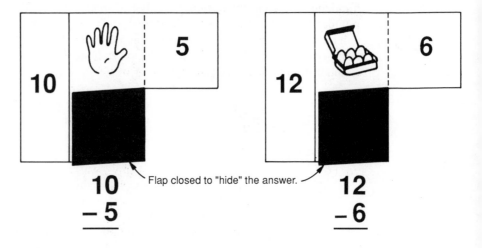

Figure 12.11   Using a "Counting-On" Strategy to Subtract

From "Subtraction Hide-and-Seek Cards Can Help" by C. A. Thornton and M. A. Toohey, Teaching Exceptional Children, 19, 1986, p. 12. Copyright © 1986 by The Council for Exceptional Children. Reprinted with permission.

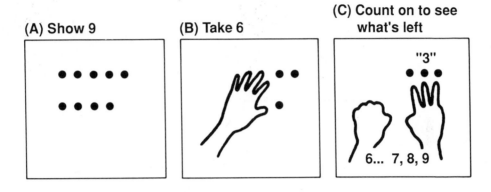

the total number of counters and write the product. Illustrate for the child how this is the same as the operation 2 + 2 + 2. Later, move to pictures to represent the multiplication problems.

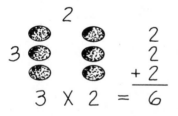

2. When children can sequence count, sometimes called "skip counting," by twos, threes, fours, fives, and so forth, they can learn the "count-by" strategy illustrated earlier in the chapter (pp. 294–95). In addition, programs like *Touch Math* (Bullock et al., 1991) use the "count-by" strategy to teach multiplication facts. (Refer to Figure 12.2.)

3. Mercer and Mercer (1989) suggest a sensible sequence for teaching the multiplication facts, in which the amount of memorization required by the student is minimized:

(a) Teach as a rule that zero times any number is always zero.

(b) Teach as a rule that 1 times any number is always that same number.

(c) Teach that 2 times any number means double that number. Emphasize that 2 times a number is the same as the doubles facts in addition, so these are not really new facts to learn.

(d) Teach the child to use the "count-by" strategy, particularly for the 3s, 4s, and 5s.

Figure 12.12   Triangle "Fact-Family" Flash Cards

From "Subtraction Hide-and-Seek Cards Can Help" by C. A. Thornton and M. A. Toohey, Teaching Exceptional Children, 19, 1986, p. 14. Copyright © 1986 by The Council for Exceptional Children. Reprinted with permission.

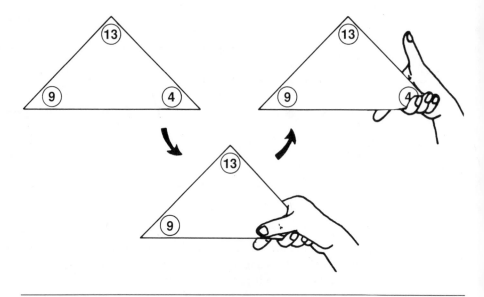

(e) Group the multiplication doubles facts (e.g., 3×3, 4×4) as a family for learning.

(f) Teach the child "tricks" for learning the 9s, such as the inverse trick or the 9s using fingers.

Inverse Trick

0	9	(1×9)
1	8	
2	7	
3	6	
4	5	
5	4	
6	3	
7	2	
8	1	
9	0	(10×9)

(Notice that the inverse-trick procedure also results in the sums to 9.)

Fingers Trick

The fingers are numbered 1 through 10 from left to right. To multiply any number by 9, count over on the fingers to that number and put that finger down. The fingers to the left are the 10s and the fingers to the right are the 1s. Thus, $3 \times 9 = 27$ is represented as follows:

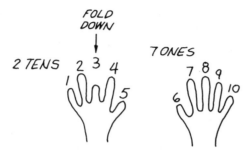

Division. Division is the inverse of multiplication. Frequently, division becomes the most difficult of the four operations for students with mild disabilities to master. The task can be made easier if the teacher uses the following strategies.

1. Begin with base-10 blocks, having students divide numbers into equal piles. For example, students could be given nine 1s blocks and asked to place these into piles containing the same number in each. The teacher would then write the symbols to illustrate that 9 can be divided into three equal groups (i.e., of three each). Later, the teacher can use tally marks drawn on paper and ask children to circle equal groups of marks and count the groups. For example, 30 divided by 6 can be illustrated as follows:

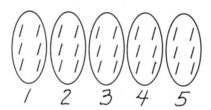

2. Teach the child to use a "count-by" strategy to solve unknown division facts, such as that used in *Touch Math* (Bullock et al., 1991).

3. Some youngsters can remember the "easy" division facts by using a number line through 25. Students begin at the larger number (the dividend) and then hop back along the number line to zero in equal jumps indicated by the smaller number (the divisor). Using laminated number lines that are washable, the child then counts his or her number of "hops" to find the answer (the quotient). Thus, 20 divided by 5 means start at 20 and hop back along the number line to zero in equal jumps of five (Silbert et al., 1990).

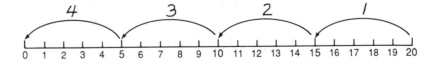

The relationship along the number line of division to equal subtractions is also sometimes helpful to youngsters with mild disabilities.

4. Make fact-family cards and worksheets so that students may practice multiplication and division families just as they did with addition and subtraction families.

Complex Operations and Algorithms

When students understand the basic operations and are automatic with basic facts, they are ready to learn more complex operations that involve step-by-step procedures. It should be emphasized, however, that to learn these procedures, or algorithms, students must first understand the concept of place value. In order to complete complex operations, regrouping (i.e., carrying and borrowing) is often required. In addition, the teacher should remember that more than one algorithm can be used to arrive at the correct answer. Although teachers must give students efficient and effective algorithms, they must also be "flexible" in selecting those that will best suit the needs of the individual child.

As students begin work performing complex operations, teachers may find it helpful to have the child state the operation involved before solving the problem. This procedure focuses student attention on the relevant symbol; therefore, the youngster is more likely to perform the correct operation (Lovitt & Curtiss, 1968). For children having difficulty aligning columns of numbers, a useful technique is to turn a sheet of notebook paper on its side. The lines then become columns to be used for writing numbers in their proper positions. Alternatively, graph paper with large squares is a helpful aid to some youngsters who must overcome alignment problems. Let's now examine some additional ways in which to teach complex operations involving regrouping.

Addition with regrouping.   If children with mild disabilities understand place value, they can easily learn to regroup for complex addition problems. Again, teachers must start with concrete manipulatives, such as base-10 blocks, to enable students to trade ten 1s for a 10-strip ten, ten 10-strips for a 100s square, and so forth. Moving these blocks across column paper and writing the numerals in the proper columns allows the child to "see" the operation performed. Some teachers also suggest that a small card be placed over the problem, uncovering only one column from right to left at a time. In this way, the child must focus on each vertical column of numbers for addition before moving on to the next column.

An alternative algorithm for addition with regrouping, useful as a transitional step for some youngsters with mild disabilities, is partial sums. In this algorithm, when the 1s digits are added together to produce a sum greater than 10, that sum is written *beneath* the proper columns. The 10s digits are then added using the verbalization "*x* 10s plus *x* 10s is ___." The sum for the "tens" column is then written underneath the sum for the "ones," with zero used as a place holder. The two partial sums are added with no regrouping required to find the actual sum for the problem.

```
      3 6
    +5 9
    ─────
      1 5      (six 1s + nine 1s)
      8 0      (three 10s + five 10s)
    ─────
      9 5
```

Subtraction with regrouping.   As with addition, subtraction with regrouping begins with base-10 blocks and trading of one 10-strip for ten 1s and, later, trading of one 100s square for ten 10-strips. Again, youngsters can ''see'' the regrouping necessary to complete the operation as the manipulatives are moved across columns headed ''hundreds,'' ''tens,'' and ''ones'' on lined paper and the corresponding numbers are written to represent each.

For complex regrouping involving one or more zeros, teach the child to recognize and name a quantity of 10s or 100s. Thus, in the problem $405 - 37 =$ _____, the child can verbalize: ''Forty 10s borrow one 10 is thirty-nine 10s,'' while crossing out the 4 and 0 and writing the 39 and ''borrowed'' 10 above the proper columns. Similarly, $4,005 - 378 =$ _____ becomes ''Four hundred 10s borrow one ten is three hundred ninety-nine 10s.''

$$
\begin{array}{r}
\overset{39}{\cancel{4}\cancel{0}5} \\
-\ 37 \\
\hline
368
\end{array}
\qquad
\begin{array}{r}
\overset{399}{\cancel{4}\cancel{0}\cancel{0}5} \\
-\ 378 \\
\hline
3627
\end{array}
$$

Multiplication.   Complex multiplication involving regrouping can be confusing for many youngsters with mild disabilities. A partial-products algorithm may be a useful transitional step for some children when learning to multiply a 2- or 3-digit number by a 1-digit number with regrouping required. The student multiplies each digit in the multiplicand in turn by the multiplier, immediately recording each partial product beneath the problem. The partial products may then be summed to produce the final product. An understanding of place value and of zero as a place holder is, of course, an essential prerequisite for a multiplication algorithm such as this.

$$
\begin{array}{r}
3\ 8 \\
\times\ \ 2 \\
\hline
1\ 6 \\
6\ 0
\end{array}
$$

(2 times eight 1s is sixteen 1s)
(2 times three 10s is six 10s)

Similarly,

$$
\begin{array}{r}
3\ 8 \\
3\ 8\ 6 \\
\times\ \ \ \ \ 3 \\
\hline
1\ 8 \\
2\ 4\ 0 \\
9\ 0\ 0 \\
\hline
1,\ 1\ 5\ 8
\end{array}
$$

(3 times six 1s is eighteen 1s)
(3 times eight 10s is twenty-four 10s)
(3 times three 100s is nine 100s)

Division.   Long division can be an extremely difficult skill for some students with mild disabilities to master. Providing children with a mnemonic or visual reminder of the steps to be performed is helpful; however, for many youngsters, extensive manipulation of concrete aids such as base-10 blocks may be necessary. For example, given the problem 537 divided by 4, Ms. Lopez might place five 100s squares, three 10-strips, and seven 1s blocks under the appropriate headings on column paper. Then, she might write the division problem and say, "I have to divide 537 into equal groups of four. I'll start with the 100s. I can make one group of four 100s squares, that's 400." At this point, Ms. Lopez has written the 1 in the quotient in the hundreds place and the 400 beneath the problem. "Now, I have one 100s square, three 10s, and seven 1s left over." She draws a line beneath the 400 and writes 137 as she talks. "Now I must divide the 10s into groups of four, but I can't do that unless I trade in the one leftover 100s square for ten 10-strips. Now I have thirteen 10-strips, and I can divide these into three groups of four each. That's twelve 10s I used up." Ms. Lopez writes the 3 in the quotient in the tens place and the twelve 10s, or 120, under the 137. Continuing, she says, "I now have one 10-strip and seven 1s left over." She draws the line and writes 17. "Now, 17 divided into equal groups of four. Oops! I'll have to trade in my one 10-strip first to make seventeen 1s. Now, I can divide into four groups of four each, that's sixteen 1s that I used, and I only have one 1s block left, so that's my remainder." She completes the problem, writing the 4 in the quotient, the 16 below the 17, and the remainder, 1.

$$\begin{array}{r} 1\;3\;4\ \text{R}1 \\ 4\,\overline{)5\;3\;7} \\ 4\;0\;0 \\ \hline 1\;3\;7 \\ 1\;2\;0 \\ \hline 1\;7 \\ 1\;6 \\ \hline 1 \end{array}$$

When students understand the long division process, they can learn the steps "divide, multiply, subtract, compare, and bring down." At this stage, some teachers also suggest that arrows be drawn straight down in the long division problem to help students keep numbers lined up in the appropriate columns when "bringing them down." Thus, in the preceding problem the lines and cues might look like this:

$$\begin{array}{r} 1\;3\;4\ \text{R}1 \\ \div\;4\,\overline{)5\;3\;7} \\ \times\quad4 \\ \hline -\;\;1\;3 \\ 1\;2 \\ \hline 1\;7 \\ 1\;6 \\ \hline 1 \end{array}$$

Other Essential Concepts and Skills

To function successfully as independent adults, students with mild disabilities must master fractions and decimals, as well as concepts of money, measurement, and time. Each of these skills may pose difficulty for learners in special programs.

Fractions. An understanding of fractions is necessary if students are to share items equally with one another, measure materials/ingredients for a hobby project or recipe, or solve a ratio problem. Kelly, Gersten, and Carnine (1990) maintain that the typical mathematics curriculum does not use essential design principles necessary for children with mild disabilities to master concepts like fractions. That is, mathematics textbooks often do not provide systemic practice in discriminating among related problem types (e.g., knowing when and when not to find a common denominator). Moreover, they fail to separate confusing elements or to give sufficient examples to illustrate concepts.

Similarly, Baroody and Hume (1991) argue that the typical mathematics curriculum fails to deliver instruction designed to ensure that youngsters with mild disabilities will understand fractional concepts. These authors argue that teachers should first develop an understanding of fractions as a part of so many equal-sized parts. Thus, the child must first use many different manipulatives to see that this relationship applies whether the "whole" refers to a single unit (e.g., a candy bar divided into four equal parts) or to a set of discrete things (e.g., four cookies shared equally by two children). Baroody and Hume offer the following suggestions for teaching fractions:

1. Have children explicitly define the whole and emphasize that a fraction is a part of so many equal-sized parts. Use many different types of manipulatives to illustrate this relationship.

2. Engage children in "fair-sharing" activities. Have children divide groups of objects like toys or crackers equally among themselves. Have them divide whole objects, such as a pizza, equally.

3. When children understand the concept of a fraction as a part of so many equivalent parts, introduce the formal symbolism to represent the fractional parts. Begin by labeling fractional parts such as 1/2, 1/3, and 1/4. Using manipulatives during this stage can help students compare fractions and "see" that 1/2 is larger than 1/3, 1/3 is larger than 1/4, and so forth. At this point, teachers can help children understand that we cannot compare fractions like 1/3 and 1/4 unless we identify the *whole* that is being defined.

4. When teaching youngsters to perform the four basic operations on fractional numbers, begin with concrete aids to develop an understanding of the concepts before teaching rules. For some youngsters with mild disabilities, rule-based instruction may ultimately be necessary; however, the teacher should first emphasize understanding. For example, the teacher can manipulate transparencies of different colors on the overhead projector to demonstrate the multiplication of fractions by shading in half the rows on a square grid and superimposing a similar square grid with columns shaded in to represent 3/4. The product of 1/2 × 3/4 is then shown by counting the total

number of blocks in the grid for the denominator and the number of blocks that overlap in the grid for the numerator. Paper strips can also be used to demonstrate addition of fractions with unlike denominators (see Figure 12.13).

5. Several programs and materials merit consideration for use in teaching fractions to children with mild disabilities. These include *Peatmoss Math: The Fraction Books* (Peck & Connell, 1990), Cuisenaire rods (Davidson, 1969), and, more recently, an interactive videodisc program entitled "Mastering Fractions" (Lubke, Rogers, & Evans, 1989; Systems Impact, 1985).

Decimals. Students learn decimals best when instruction begins with concrete manipulatives. Thus, they first develop an understanding that decimals repre-

---

Figure 12.13 Using Manipulatives to Teach Addition of Fractions with Unlike Denominators

---

From "Meaningful Mathematics Instruction: The Case of Fractions" by A. J. Baroody and J. Hume, 1991. Remedial and Special Education, *12, p. 65. Copyright © 1991 by PRO-ED, Inc. Reprinted with permission.*

The teacher can use a variety of manipulatives to teach difficult concepts like adding fractions with unlike denominators. Below is one example of how paper strips can be used to illustrate the problem $1/2 + 1/3 = 5/6$ in a concrete manner:

Step 1: Take a strip of paper.

Step 2: Fold in half and color 1/2.

Step 3: Fold in thirds and color 1/3.

Step 4: Fold paper into lengths equal to the shortest section.

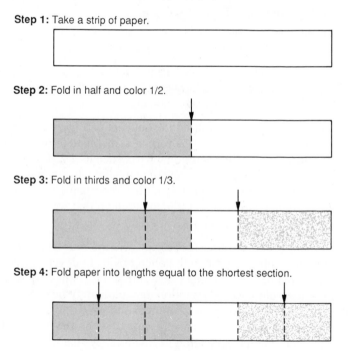

sent fractions with denominators of 10 or 100, or later, 1,000. Base-10 blocks can be used to illustrate this concept. That is, youngsters can place 1s blocks on a 10-strip to see the relationship between 1/10 (i.e., 1 part out of 10 equal parts) and 2/10 (i.e., 2 parts out of 10 equal parts), and so forth. Similarly, students can place 1s blocks on the 100s square to illustrate the concept of hundreths. Initially, the teacher might emphasize the concept that decimal numerals are less than one whole by placing the 10-strip or 100s block to the right of a large decimal point. Later, children can examine equivalent amounts by such activities as comparing twenty 1s blocks on the 100s square (i.e., 20 parts out of 100 equal parts) with two ten-strips on the 100s square (i.e., 2 parts out of 10 equal parts). Similarly, youngsters can easily see, by manipulating the blocks, the relative size of decimals (e.g., .32 is greater than .30, but .30 is greater than .03). Teachers can construct column paper with the appropriate headings for decimal numerals and teach children to read and write these numerals following a procedure similar to that described for teaching place value.

Money, measurement, and time.   Students with mild disabilities require numerous opportunities to work with money in real-life contexts. Students must practice counting coins and bills and making up equivalent amounts. For example, Ms. Lopez might challenge Joey to find all the ways he can make 36¢ given pennies, nickels, dimes, and quarters. Setting up a classroom store or using the newspaper to clip coupons and/or calculate purchases are two additional ways teachers can provide youngsters with real-life opportunities to practice money skills. For students having difficulty determining the amount of correct change, Mercer and Mercer (1989) suggest a "money card." Based on a $10 bill used to make a purchase, the student simply crosses out the purchase amount on the card. The remaining "money" on the card indicates the correct change. The change to be returned from a $10 bill, based on a purchase of $7.38, is determined as follows:

$10.00 Money card

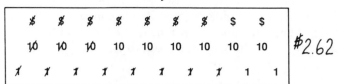

Youngsters in special education programs also need many opportunities to measure familiar objects. Begin with simple rulers, measuring only to the inch. Later, students can measure to the 1/2 inch, 1/4 inch, and so forth, to complete art or hobby projects or to determine their height. Similarly, students can measure the width of the classroom in feet or the length of the hall in yards. Measurement of liquids and solids can easily be practiced by following recipes calling for cups, pints, quarts, pounds, ounces, and so forth. Youngster also can weigh themselves or other objects, recording the weight in pounds and ounces. Concrete and realistic experiences with measurement are essential before children move to tasks involving comparisons and conversions of units of measure that require paper and pencil.

Children with mild disabilities also must understand the concept of time. The teacher can establish a basic understanding of time by sequencing events over the course of a class day or during a story and pointing out, for example, "We go to P.E. first at 11:15 and then we go to lunch." Students can begin to understand the passage of time and relative lengths of time through concrete activities; for example, naming which of two familiar events is longer, reading time or snack time, or naming which student jumps for the longest time. In addition, daily routines involving the calendar highlight the everyday importance of time. Teachers can, for example, ask youngsters to name the day of the week on which they watch a favorite TV show or the day of the week on which they have music activities.

Telling time can be a particularly difficult skill for some students with mild disabilities. Lipstreu and Johnson (1988) suggest that teachers use the "whole-clock" method rather than traditional methods. The latter often confuse children with mild disabilities because of the terminology used (e.g., "a quarter after six," "15 minutes before two"). To use the whole-clock method, students must be able to count by ones and by fives to 60 and identify the numerals 1 through 12. Children first learn to discriminate between the hour and minute hand and to tell time to the hour. At this step, teachers might choose to state the rule: When the minute hand is pointing to the 12 and the hour hand is pointing to a number, we say the number and o'clock. Next, students practice 5 minutes after each hour, then 10 minutes, 15 minutes, and so on, through 55 minutes after the hour. In this way, children can focus on the movement of the minute hand and see that every hour has the same 5-minute intervals. Sometimes the teacher may find it necessary to highlight the proper hour on the clock face with color to help children discriminate the correct times after the half hour. When students have mastered time in 5-minute intervals, they can learn to count on by ones up to the minute hand (e.g., 3:45, 3:46, 3:47), learning a predictable pattern for telling time.

This predictable pattern for telling time is also consistent with the use of digital clocks. Teachers can use this pattern as a starting point for direct instruction in telling time to the hour and to the minute with digital clocks (e.g., 4:00 or 4:37). When students master time to the hour and to the minute, teachers may explicitly teach alternative language forms, such as a "quarter before," a "quarter after," or "half past" 2.

Arithmetic Word Problems

One particularly difficult task for youngsters with mild disabilities is that of solving word problems. Cawley et al. (1987) suggest that much of this difficulty is due to mathematics textbooks that teach students to rely on "cue words" to solve simple, direct word problems. For example, the text may state: "Mary has two candies. Bob gives her two more candies. How many candies does Mary have *altogether?*" Rather than relying on cue words, these authors, among others, suggest that word problems about familiar subjects become the basis for learning computational skills in context from the first day of school (Cawley, Baker-Kroczynski, Urban, 1992; Cawley et al., 1987; Cawley & Parmar, 1992). Although instruction should begin with direct word problems using relatively

simple sentence structures, students need systematic instruction in more difficult word problems, including those having an operation inconsistent with the
"cue words," those requiring more than one step to solve (e.g., indirect problems such as "Mary had five candies after Bob gave her three. How many
candies did Mary have before Bob gave her some?") and those containing
extraneous information.

Cawley and Miller (1986) also suggest that teachers group story problems
around familiar themes and that they use a series of questions to focus attention
on the important information stated within the problem. Pictures and manipulatives can be used as aids to help children visualize and re-create the actions
within each word problem.

On the other hand, Stein (1987) applies the principles of effective instruction
to the teaching of word problems. She maintains that students must learn rules
and strategies for attacking word problems as teachers present carefully sequenced examples. According to Stein (1987), "Rule One" is to determine
whether or not the "big number" is given in the problem. If that number is not
given, the operation is either addition or multiplication. If the big number is
given, subtraction is used. Thus, in the problem, Doug has 3 dogs. He gives one
dog to his best friend, Pete. How many dogs does Doug have now? "three" is
the "big number" that is given, resulting in subtraction as the chosen operation.
Similarly, "Rule Two" is to multiply whenever a problem refers to the same
number of equal-sized groups over and over again.

Although controversy exists regarding whether or not to teach children with
mild disabilities to search for "cues" within word problems, numerous
strategies appear in the literature. We suggest that the teacher first emphasize
understanding the problem by re-creating it with concrete manipulatives or
pictures, or engaging children in the actions detailed in the story (Cawley &
Parmar, 1992). Additionally, teachers must prepare a line of questions designed
to elicit important information about the word problem as they transcribe information into the proper number symbols to represent the equation. Finally,
teachers can combine these techniques with strategies such as the following to
help learners with mild disabilities solve word problems independently:

1. Study the Question (Choate, 1990, p. 45)
   (a) Scan for clues.
   (b) Highlight the clues and the question.
   (c) Revise the question. (Turn it into a fill-in-the-blank statement.)
   (d) Read the statement and then reread the problem.

2. The SOLVE Strategy (Enright & Beattie, 1989, p. 58)
   (a) Study the problem.
   (b) Organize the facts.
   (c) Line up a plan.
   (d) Verify the plan/computation.
   (e) Examine your answer.

3. The Problem-Solving Prompt Card (Fleischner, Nuzum, & Marzola, 1987,
   p. 216)
   (a) READ: What is the question?

    (b) REREAD: What is the necessary information?
    (c) THINK: Putting together? (Add)
                      Taking apart? (Subtract)
                      Do I need all the information?
                      Is it a two-step problem?
    (d) SOLVE: Write the equation.
    (e) CHECK: Recalculate.
                      Label.
                      Compare.

✎ Summary

Children with mild disabilities are likely to have numerous deficits in mathematics. Related reading, handwriting, and language problems may hinder the child's progress when learning math skills and concepts. The spiral curriculum—the approach used by most of the major math textbook series—may also contribute to the difficulty youngsters with mild disabilities experience in mathematics, particularly with the automatic recall of basic facts and the efficient execution of operations.

Students with mild disabilities must master essential skills if they are to function as independent adults. In addition to the basic facts and operations using whole numbers, fractions, and decimals, children must master concepts of money, measurement, and time to be successful in later life. One other necessary skill, problem solving, is receiving increased emphasis in the mathematics curriculum for youngsters in special education. Several programs are available for teaching problem-solving skills to students with mild disabilities.

Some instructional procedures are useful for teaching a wide range of mathematics skills and concepts to youngsters. These include increasing the child's understanding of concepts through a concrete-to-semiconcrete-to-abstract sequence. Although teachers must help students achieve automaticity with basic facts and operations, they also must minimize rote memorization for children with mild disabilities. This can be accomplished through careful sequencing; explicit direct instruction of skills, identified by curriculum-based assessment and error analysis; and provision of useful strategies for independent problem solving.

Other instructional procedures are specific for particular math skills and concepts. These include suggestions for teaching basic number concepts, such as one-to-one correspondence, numeration, and place value, as well as tips for teaching basic facts and operations, complex operations and algorithms, and functional math skills.

✎ Application Exercises

1. Assume you are Mr. Abel participating in an IEP meeting for Susan.
   Justify including the following provisions on the IEP: Susan's use of a

calculator in her math class with Mr. Mathis and her use of the
calculator to complete a state-required competency test for graduation.

2. Examine two or three mathematics books used in nearby school districts.
   Explain the algorithms used to teach addition and subtraction with
   regrouping, complex multiplication, and long division. How could each
   of these algorithms be adapted and/or the instructional methods be
   changed to teach Joey and Travis these skills?

3. Make a set of base-10 blocks from paper. Illustrate how you might teach
   Joey and Travis to add and subtract with regrouping required. Illustrate
   the long division problem 648 divided by 6 with the base-10 blocks. How
   you would explain the zero as a place holder?

4. Given the following word problem, explain how you might use
   manipulatives to improve the performance of Joey and Travis: "Heather
   has eight cookies. If she has three friends, how many cookies can she
   give to each friend so that everyone has the same number of cookies?

Content Instruction
in the Regular Classroom

Chapter 13

Focus

As you read, think about the following questions:

  What adaptations are likely to be "acceptable" to regular
  classroom teachers?

  What essential skills must be mastered by students with mild
  disabilities if they are to succeed in content-area instruction in the
  regular classroom?

  How can instruction, textbooks, assignments, and tests be
  adapted to accommodate students with mild disabilities in the
  mainstream?

  What are some learning strategies and school survival skills that
  students with mild disabilities can use to enhance their
  performance in the regular classroom?

✎ Most low-achieving students, with or without identified disabilities, will complete much of their content-area instruction in the regular classroom. Often, special education teachers are not trained to teach vital content areas like science, social studies, or health. In fact, special educators, intent on teaching the basic reading, language arts, and mathematics skills, may overlook these important areas of the curriculum (Patton, Polloway, & Cronin, 1987).

Regular classroom teachers, on the other hand, may be certified to teach science, social studies, or other subject areas, but hesitant to accept students with learning and/or behavioral problems into large, heterogeneous classes. Regular educators may believe, for example, that students with mild disabilities require more instructional time than they are able to provide, given the size of many classrooms today (Martens, Peterson, Witt, & Cirone, 1986). Many regular educators also feel that they lack the instructional assistance necessary to support students with mild disabilities in the mainstream (Heron & Harris, 1987). Increasingly, special educators and regular classroom teachers must collaborate to ensure the full, successful participation of youngsters with mild disabilities in content classes. The following discussion between Mr. Abel and Mr. McNally illustrates the type of ongoing communication necessary to support one student, Robert, in geography class:

> Mr. McNally: *For Robert, Marcus, and my other students in world geography, the main concepts in Chapter 2 involve map and globe skills, as well as skill in interpreting charts and graphs. Many of my students—not just those in special education—have trouble understanding the vocabulary for this chapter.*
>
> Mr. Abel: *What are some of the important vocabulary terms the students need to know?*
>
> Mr. McNally: *Usually, I require the students to know all the terms listed in the "Keys to Understanding" section at the start of each chapter. In this chapter, the vocabulary words are on page 34, and students should especially know how to use latitude and longitude to cite locations. The new words are always in boldface type when they first appear in the chapter, but the definition sometimes precedes the actual word. When the definition comes before the word itself, that's difficult for some of my students.*
>
> Mr. Abel: *Robert does have difficulty with that type of text structure. I know you give students a study guide for each chapter. Would it be possible to list questions for the important terms and concepts in sequential order followed by a page number to serve as a student guide? For Robert, that would be very helpful. Also, I could teach the students a simple strategy to follow: Read the question; find the page given; find the clue (like words in boldface type or headings and subheadings); skim above and below the clue for the answer; and, finally, write the answer.*

Mr. McNally: *That sounds reasonable. Here's the study guide I've used before. I'll redo this using the page numbers.*

Mr. Abel: *Okay. You may want to put the steps of the strategy at the top of the study guide, too. When do you plan to begin the chapter?*

Mr. McNally: *I'll introduce the chapter Wednesday, but I won't use the study guide until Thursday. I think it's a good idea to put the steps of the strategy on the study guide as you suggested. I think I'll do that.*

Mr. Abel: *Okay. I'll start working with the students in class tomorrow on the study guide strategy.*

Regular classroom teachers, like Mr. McNally, may be quite willing to adapt instruction to accommodate the needs of students with mild disabilities in the mainstream *if* they believe that the suggested intervention is likely to be effective (Whinnery, Fuchs, & Fuchs, 1991). However, because of limited time and resources across grade levels, regular educators consider most adaptations to be more desirable than feasible. According to Schumm and Vaughn (1991), adaptations involving the mainstreamed student in *whole-class* activities with positive reinforcement and encouragement are, not surprisingly, viewed more favorably by regular classroom teachers than are adaptations requiring adjustment of long-range plans, materials, or scoring/grading criteria on an individual basis. Interventions that are the "least invasive"—involving the fewest changes in the regular classroom program while helping many students simultaneously—are those most likely to be embraced by teachers (Reisberg & Wolf, 1988). Thus, at both the elementary and secondary level, shortened assignments, preferential seating, and oral testing are examples of instructional modifications many classroom teachers find "reasonable" (Bacon & Schulz, 1991).

When recommending instructional modifications in the mainstreamed classroom, special education teachers must first understand the classroom teacher's view of the situation and what that teacher considers to be practical and possible (Margolis & McGettigan, 1988). Suggestions that are perceived by the regular educator as easy to employ, likely to work, and responsive to their needs are accepted with the least amount of resistance. Margolis and McGettigan (1988) offer the following guidelines to assist special educators when collaborating with regular classroom teachers on behalf of mainstreamed youngsters:

1. Ascertain the strengths and perceived needs of the classroom teacher by observing, asking open-ended questions, and listening empathetically.

2. Build upon what the teacher knows and does well.

3. Brainstorm alternatives with the teacher so that he or she becomes a central figure in the decision-making process and "owns" the modifications selected;

4. Provide support and feedback as instructional modifications are implemented;

5. Encourage teachers to make those changes and adaptations consistent with their teaching styles.

6. Give teachers positive recognition for their efforts.

(See Chapter 4 for additional suggestions for communicating with regular classroom teachers.)

According to Cohen and Lynch (1991), regular classroom teachers have a wide range of modification options from which to choose. These include modifying the physical and/or social environment of the classroom, altering the lesson structure or objective, selecting materials and activities to meet the needs of individual students, enlisting support staff to help in the classroom, and changing the classroom-management or evaluation procedures used. The task of the special education teacher is to assist the regular educator in determining whether or not a problem exists, in clearly defining the problem, and in selecting a modification that will be under the regular teacher's control and within his or her level of comfort (Cohen & Lynch, 1991). For example, Mr. McNally might select modifications pertaining to the problem he identified from a ''menu'' of options and then rate the ones selected according to their likelihood of being effective (see Tables 13.1 and 13.2). Later, after the modifications have been implemented, Mr. McNally would evaluate them along several dimensions, including degree of effectiveness, for future reference.

Special education teachers also must consider how their students feel about instructional modifications. Feedback from mainstreamed students with mild disabilities and their peers regarding the ''acceptability'' of various accommodation strategies may help the teacher select strategies and implement them to best advantage. As a matter of fact, Schumm and Vaughn (1991) report that students perceive teacher adaptations in instructional procedures, student grouping, and special assistance positively. On the other hand, they view adaptations in assignments, tests, and textbooks negatively. Students with mild disabilities want to be like their peers. If students and teachers are to use adaptations when appropriate in the content classroom, special educators must consider student preferences and needs, as well as those of the classroom teacher.

Finally, special education teachers must assess the student's ability to meet regular classroom demands, such as taking tests (Putnam, 1992a, 1992b). Asking Robert specific questions about how his teachers instruct and evaluate him in content classes and about how he prepares for and takes tests may give Mr. Abel valuable information for helping Robert perform successfully in those classes. Mr. Abel may ascertain, for example, the types of tests that are given and the relative importance of tests, notebooks, and assignments in determining grades. Moreover, informally analyzing Robert's notebook, his actual performance on tests, and his ability to use the textbook may provide Mr. Abel with data regarding effective strategies for learning that Robert may or may not be using (Wiener, 1991).

What are the essential skills needed by learners with mild disabilities if they are to succeed in the regular classroom? How can curriculum, instruction, materials, and assignments be modified to accommodate mainstreamed students? These questions are the focus for the remainder of this chapter.

Table 13.1   Modification Options for the Regular Classroom: A "Menu" for the Teacher

---

1. study carrels

2. room dividers

3. headsets to muffle noise

4. seat child away from doors/windows

5. seat near model (student or teacher)

6. time out area

7. rearrange student groups (according to instructional needs, role models, etc.)

8. group for cooperative learning

9. vary working surface (e.g. floor or vertical surface such as blackboards)

10. simplify/shorten directions

11. give both oral and written directions

12. have student repeat directions

13. have student repeat lesson objective

14. ask frequent questions

15. change question level

16. change response format (e.g., from verbal to physical: from saying to pointing)

17. provide sequential directions (label as first, seconds, etc.)

18. use manipulatives

19. alter objective criterion level

20. provide functional tasks (relate to child's environment)

21. reduce number of items on a task

22. highlight relevant words/features

23. use rebus (picture) directions

24. provide guided practice

25. provide more practice trials

26. increase allocated time

27. use a strategy approach

28. change reinforcers

(continued)

Table 13.1   *(Continued)*

29. increase reinforcement frequency

30. delay reinforcement

31. provide error drill

32. increase wait-time

33. use firm-up activities

34. use specific rather than general praise

35. have a peer-tutor program

36. provide frequent review

37. have student summarize at end of lesson

38. use self-correcting materials

39. adapt test items for differing response modes

40. provide mnemonic devices

41. provide tangible reinforcers

42. use behavioral contracts

43. establish routines for handing work in, heading papers, etc.

44. use timers to show allocated time

45. teach self-monitoring

46. provide visual cues (posters, desktop number lines, etc.)

47. block out extraneous stimuli on written material

48. tape record directions

49. tape record student responses

50. use a study guide

51. provide critical vocabulary list for content material

52. provide essential fact list

53. use clock faces to show classroom routine times

54. use dotted lines to line up math problems or show margins

55. use cloze procedure to test comprehension

56. provide transition directions

57. assign only one task at a time

(continued)

Table 13.1   (*Continued*)

58. provide discussion questions before reading

59. use word markers to guide reading

60. alter sequence of presentation

61. enlarge or highlight key words on test items

62. provide daily and weekly assignment sheets

63. post daily/weekly schedule

64. use graph paper for place value or when adding/subtracting 2-digit numbers or turn notebook paper horizontally

65. provide anticipation cues

66. establish rules and review frequently

67. teach key direction words

68. use distributed practice

69. pencil grips

70. tape paper to desk

71. shorten project assignment into daily tasks

72. segment directions

73. number (order) assignments to be completed

74. change far-point to near-point material for copying or review

75. put desk close to blackboard

76. incorporate currently popular themes/characters into assignments for motivation

77. repeat major points

78. use physical cues while speaking (1, 2, 3, etc.)

79. pause during speaking

80. use verbal cues ("don't write this down; this is important")

81. change tone of voice, whisper, etc.

82. use an honor system

83. collect notebooks weekly (periodically) to review student notes

84. reorganize tests to go from easy to hard

85. color code place value tasks

(*continued*)

Table 13.1   (*Continued*)

86. use self-teaching materials

87. do only odd- or even-numbered items on a large task sheet

88. use a primary typewriter or large print to create written material

89. provide organizers (cartons/bins) for desk material

90. teach varied reading rates (scanning, skimming, etc.)

91. provide content/lecture summaries

From "Effective Instruction: Principles and Strategies for Programs," by S. B. Cohen and D. K. Lynch. In Program Leadership for Serving Students with Disabilities, *by B. Billingsley (Ed.), 1993, pp. 201–203. Copyright © 1993 by the State Department of Education, Commonwealth of Virginia. Reprinted by permission of the author.*

Although much of our discussion will focus on students at the secondary level in science and social studies classes, we believe that elementary teachers may find many of the suggested modifications applicable to their children as well. In addition, most of the recommended procedures are also appropriate for content classes other than science and social studies.

✎ Factors Affecting Success in the Regular Classroom

Before making a decision to "mainstream" a student for content-area instruction, the IEP team must consider the demands of the regular classroom environment and the ability of the student to meet those demands. To be successful in the regular classroom, youngsters with mild disabilities must possess not only adequate academic skills but also certain "school survival skills" and learning strategies. In addition, the regular curriculum must be well organized and appropriate for students with mild disabilities.

School Survival Skills

Students with mild disabilities may lack many of the so-called school survival skills that seem to come naturally for "good" students. Many of these skills are nonacademic in nature. For example, in a survey of skills critical for school success (Schaeffer, Zigmond, Kerr, & Farra, 1980), principals, teachers, and students listed the following six items as most important:

1. going to class each day;

2. being on time to school;

3. bringing pencils, paper and books to class;

Table 13.2   A Modification Rating Scale

Directions: Rate the modification according to the value given for each item. Priority should be given to those items receiving the highest total scores.

1. In my estimation the potential impact of this modification is: (1 low–5 high)   1   2   3   4   5

2. In my experience the use of the modification has been successful: (1 seldom–5 often)   1   2   3   4   5

3. I feel comfortable in my ability to apply this modification: (1 strongly disagree–5 strongly agree)   1   2   3   4   5

4. The estimated time needed for this modification to be effective is (1 long–5 short)   1   2   3   4   5

5. The number of additional resources needed to implement this modification is (1 many–5 few)   1   2   3   4   5

Total score   _____

Modification:	Total Score	Ranking
_____	_____	_____
_____	_____	_____
_____	_____	_____
_____	_____	_____
_____	_____	_____

From "An Instructional Modification Process," by S. B. Cohen and D. K. Lynch, Teaching Exceptional Children, 23, 1991, p. 15. Copyright © 1991 by The Council for Exceptional Children. Reprinted with permission.

4. turning work in on time;

5. talking to teachers without using "backtalk"; and

6. reading and following directions.

Similarly, regular classroom teachers consider such nonacademic skills as asking for help when needed, interacting appropriately with peers and teachers, obeying classroom rules, following oral and written instructions, attending class, beginning tasks promptly, and working independently as vital for success in the mainstream. Employers, too, expect similar attitudes and behaviors from their employees. Unfortunately, special educators and regular educators sometimes differ in their perceptions of the degree to which students with mild disabilities possess these critical school survival skills (Downing et al., 1990). That is, a youngster may demonstrate these skills within the special education classroom, but fail to generalize or transfer them to the regular classroom.

Academic Skills and Learning Strategies

Although many special education students, particularly those with learning disabilities, may be able to get passing grades in their content-area classes, they may not learn or perform well in these classes. For example, Donahoe and Zigmond (1990) found that ninth-grade youngsters with learning disabilities received lower grades than did low-achieving peers in the same mainstreamed social studies and health classes. Both groups, however, received primarily below C-level grades in science. Astoundingly, 20% of the students with learning disabilities failed the ninth grade, while 79% earned a D or lower in social studies, 69% earned a D or below in science, and 63% earned a D or lower in health. These grades do not reflect the intelligence and potential for success of most youngsters with learning disabilities.

Apparently, many students with mild disabilities do exhibit academic deficits that impede their progress in the mainstream. Warner, Schumaker, Alley, and Deshler (1980) note that many students with learning disabilities plateau at about the fourth- to sixth-grade level in reading and mathematics by grade 10. These students may not be able to read content-area textbooks, listen and take notes in class, produce coherent written work, or take tests. Furthermore, students with mild disabilities may lack the experiences, vocabulary, and study strategies necessary for school success. Yet, Moran (1980) reports that teachers often rely on lectures, textbooks, and written tests as the primary means of delivering and evaluating instruction in content-area classrooms. Teachers expect students to read at grade level, obtain information from the textbook and lectures, and memorize this material for tests.

Donahoe and Zigmond (1990) suggest that the typical resource-room program at the high school level—one in which students receive remedial instruction in English, reading, or mathematics—may not be providing youngsters with the learning strategies they need to be successful in the regular curriculum. Moreover, classroom teachers may not be receiving the support they need to adapt the curriculum for their special learners. Of greater importance, however, is whether or not the "standard" curriculum is appropriate for students with mild disabilities and their low-achieving peers.

The Standard Curriculum and Instructional Approaches

Instruction in science, social studies, and other subject areas is dominated by daily use of the textbook (Armento, 1986). Critics argue that this traditional instructional approach is overly dependent upon curricular materials that are often poorly organized. When combined with administrative pressure to "cover" the curriculum during an academic year, the "textbook" approach results in superficial learning of isolated facts rather than a deeper understanding of the overall structure and related nature of the concepts involved (Kinder & Bursuck, 1991). Thus, students with mild disabilities may fail to see the "connectedness" of the many facts they learn, soon becoming disenchanted with the endless and, for them, difficult memorization of details.

In an attempt to promote higher order thinking and learning, some teachers adopt curricular materials that employ an inquiry or discovery approach to instruction. In this approach, the teacher serves as a facilitator, guiding children to ask questions, discover solutions, and formulate generalizations. Although inquiry approaches to instruction in science and social studies create more "student-directed" opportunities for learning, most youngsters with mild disabilities do not learn well inductively (Carnine, 1991). For these students, an inquiry approach may still result in the retention of isolated bits of information, with no understanding of how the information is connected.

Although a degree of rote learning of basic facts is necessary in any discipline, some authorities are calling for a reorganization of the "standard curriculum" to promote higher-order thinking skills for both students with low achievement and those with mild disabilities (Carnine, 1991). Whereas curricular materials currently in use often present content rapidly, superficially, and in a fragmented manner, a "smart" curriculum would highlight the organizational structure of a discipline so that facts always become connected for learners. As pointed out by Prawat (1989), Brophy (1990), and Carnine (1991), all of science involves the noting of similarities and the development of interwoven networks of knowledge rather than the memorization of unrelated bits of information. These authorities suggest that if teachers teach both facts and concepts "efficiently" to all youngsters in the regular classroom, students with mild disabilities may experience a reduced memory load as new knowledge is constantly connected to old (Carnine, 1991).

For example, Kinder and Bursuck (1991) describe a unified social studies curriculum in which students are first taught a strategy for analyzing historical events according to a "problem-solutions-effects" network (see Figure 13.1). Using this framework, youngsters can see how history revolves around human reactions to problems which lead to solutions which often lead to other problems. Moreover, these problems and solutions often involve similar issues, such as economics, religion, or human rights. Also within this curriculum, students make time lines for historical events, learn a strategy for defining vocabulary from the textbook, and are continually challenged by the question *why* to explain their statements.

Similarly, using two videodisc programs—"Earth Science" and "Understanding Chemistry and Energy"—both available from Systems Impact, Woodward and Noell (1991) illustrate how seemingly unrelated facts in science can become integrated as concepts for low-achieving students. For example, when students understand how convection cells work, they can apply this knowledge to understanding movement in the atmosphere, the ocean, or the Earth's mantle because the link is made explicit for them. Thus, youngsters with mild disabilities can be challenged to use higher-order thought processes to solve complex problems through deductive reasoning.

Although many students with mild disabilities can be challenged to demonstrate higher-order thinking skills, the reader must remember that a "connected" curriculum such as that just described will not be appropriate for all youngsters in special education programs. Moreover, such curricula are only now in the formative stages. Until "user-friendly" curricula are developed, special education teachers will need to help regular educators adapt textbooks, tests, instructional presentations, and assignments while simultaneously teaching students with mild disabilities those learning strategies and

Figure 13.1 Problems-Solutions-Effect Framework

From "The Search for a Unified Social Studies Curriculum: Does History Really Repeat Itself?," by D. Kinder and W. Bursuck, 1991, Journal of Learning Disabilities, 24, *p. 274. Copyright © 1991 by Donald D. Hammill Foundation. Reprinted with permission.*

CHAPTER 4 MAKING A LIVING
SECTION 2 COLONIAL TRADE

Problem	Solution	Effect
England was unhappy cause Dutch was getting all the money.	*The Navigation Acts* They started a thing called the Navigation acts they said. 1. The English ships had to carry all good 2. They had to sell the goods only to England 3. They put a tax on some good shipped from foreign colonies	The shipbuilding grew. They had to sell their goods for lower prices. Had to pay more for foreign goods.
The colonists had to pay more than what they got back.	They smuggled goods in and out of the USA.	Englands to far away to stop them.

school survival skills essential for their successful performance in a particular classroom environment.

✎ Adapting Instruction, Textbooks, Tests, and Assignments

After a decision has been made to mainstream a student with mild disabilities into the regular classroom for science, social studies, health, or any other content area, the special education teacher must not assume that instruction then becomes the sole responsibility of the classroom teacher. Although not all youngsters with mild disabilities will require modifications in order to achieve in the regular classroom, the special educator must ensure that those who do are given the special assistance they need. Moreover, special education teachers have an obligation to assist and support regular classroom teachers in providing necessary modifications to ensure that the quality of education received by *all* youngsters in the classroom will remain high. Teachers must, of course, be provided with adequate time to plan together, as well as individually, and they must specify their roles and responsibilities clearly (see Chapter 4).

Fortunately, those modifications designed to help students with mild disabilities perform successfully in the regular classroom often help other children as well. These include adapting the instructional presentation, adapting the textbook, and modifying assignments and/or tests.

Adapting Instruction

How teachers organize and present information in the content classroom profoundly affects student learning. Typically, teachers at the secondary level convey information through lectures, discussions, group projects, and videotapes or filmstrips. Each of the following suggestions may help classroom teachers adapt their instructional presentations to suit the needs of learners with mild disabilities.

Advance organizers.   Advance organizers refer to preteaching events that structure the learning situation (Ausubel & Robinson, 1969) and provide low-achieving students a framework for integrating new knowledge with old. Advance organizers can be visual reminders (e.g., a topical outline on the board) or verbal statements made by the teacher regarding the task or topic. They also can involve steps taken by students themselves to organize for learning. Teachers can provide structure for learning in numerous ways, some of which are listed in Table 13.3.

Lenz, Alley, and Schumaker (1987) used advance organizers to help secondary-level content-area teachers improve the quality of their instruction, as well as the performance of their students with learning disabilities. First, however, the students themselves had to be trained to recognize and use the advance organizers provided by their teachers. To train students, Mr. McNally might organize his geography lesson by placing a topical outline on an overhead transparency, by referring to previous learning and the topic for the current class session, and by saying, for example, "This is important" or using words like *first, next,* and *finally* throughout the discussion. In addition, Mr. McNally might write important vocabulary or concepts on the overhead as he talks and remind students to write these on their own copies of the outline. If Robert does not recognize these organizational cues, however, he cannot use them to facilitate learning. Thus, Mr. Abel might support Mr. McNally's instruction by teaching Robert the importance of the advance organizers used in his classes.

When teachers present well-organized lectures and discussions, student learning and note taking become easier. In addition to providing written outlines, teachers can improve their lecture effectiveness by preteaching vocabulary, writing important terms or directions on the chalkboard, varying their voice tone and position in the classroom as they make key points, raising questions to test comprehension, pausing periodically to allow students to ask questions or to write important information in their notes, and using pictures or diagrams to represent the relationships among key ideas and concepts.

Graphic organizers.   In our previous discussion regarding the science and social studies curriculum, we noted the importance of explicitly linking facts in

---

Table 13.3   Suggestions for Advance Organizers

Lenz, Alley, and Schumaker (1987) suggest that teachers use the following behaviors as advance organizers to structure learning for students in their content-area classrooms:

1. Tell students the purpose for the advance organizer.

2. Clarify the actions to be taken by the teacher.

3. Clarify the actions to be taken by the students.

4. Identify the topic for the learning task.

5. Identify the subtopics related to the learning task.

6. Provide essential background information.

7. State the concepts to be learned.

8. Clarify the concepts to be learned through examples, nonexamples, or cautions about possible errors.

9. Motivate students to learn by relating content to their lives.

10. Introduce and repeat new vocabulary.

11. Give students an organizational framework for the learning task, such as an outline, a list, or a general overview of the topic presented verbally or visually.

12. State the outcomes expected from the learning activity.

---

order to build concepts and promote higher-order thinking skills. One way to accomplish this task is through the use of graphic organizers (Anders & Bos, 1984). Graphic organizers sometimes take the form of *semantic maps* (Pearson & Johnson, 1978) or *concept diagrams* (Bulgren, Schumaker, & Deshler, 1988). They are visual displays clearly representing the relationships among the facts, vocabulary, and concepts to be developed (see Figures 13.2 and 13.3).

To prepare a graphic organizer, the teacher must first precisely state the concepts to be learned. Next, the teacher must list all vocabulary or facts that learners must know in order to understand the concept. McKeown and Beck (1988) suggest that teachers focus on important terms that are related not only to the specific concept, but also to other concepts and lessons within the discipline. For example, as illustrated in Figure 13.1, rather than learning about the Navigation Acts or the Stamp Act as separate facts or events, the student would gain an understanding of the larger concept: The basic problem leading to the American Revolution was that Great Britain wanted control of production, taxation, and navigation in order to benefit economically from the colonies (Kinder & Bursuck, 1991). The problem-solutions-effects framework serves as one vehicle for graphically representing this concept.

Figure 13.2   A Graphic Organizer on the Topic of Matter

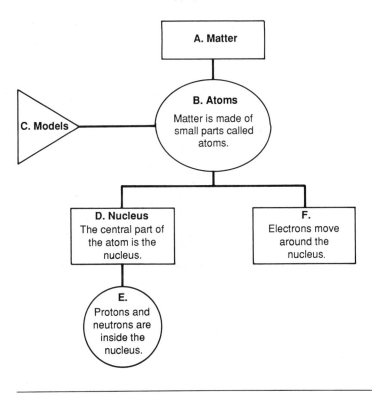

Once the teacher has selected the important concepts and related vocabulary, these are arranged visually to highlight their relationships. The teacher might, for example, construct a concept diagram illustrating characteristics that "always," "sometimes," and "never" relate to the concept of "democracy." The teacher might also state examples of democracy and compare and contrast other forms of government. Bulgren et al. (1988) improved the performance of high school students with learning disabilities in their content classes by using the concept diagram illustrated in Figure 13.4. When using this diagram, the authors suggest that teachers incorporate the following routine:

1. Provide the advance organizer.

2. Elicit from the students a list of key words from the chapter and write the words on the board.

3. Review the symbols on the concept diagram.

4. Name the concept.

Figure 13.3   A Graphic Organizer from Robert's Science Class

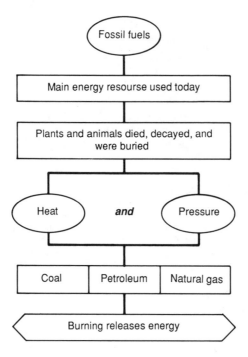

5. Define the concept.

6. Discuss the "always" characteristics.

7. Discuss the "sometimes" characteristics.

8. Discuss the "never" characteristics.

9. Discuss one example of the concept.

10. Discuss one nonexample of the concept.

11. Link the example to each of the characteristics.

12. Link the nonexample to each of the characteristics.

13. Test potential examples and nonexamples to determine whether or not they are members of the concept class.

14. Provide a postorganizer.

Secondary-level classroom teachers expressed satisfaction with the concept diagrams and concept teaching routines (Bulgren, Schumaker, & Deshler,

Computer software enhances science and geography lessons and gives the teacher a tool for producing study guides and test questions.

1988). When they completed blank concept diagrams on the chalkboard or on an overhead transparency as they progressed through the concept teaching routine, they facilitated notetaking by students who completed identical diagrams individually.

Bos and her colleagues also used an interactive teaching strategy, the semantic feature analysis, to improve the vocabulary and reading comprehension of high school students with learning disabilities in their special education social studies classes (Bos, Anders, Filip, & Jaffe, 1989). Teachers first listed key concepts and vocabulary from the text and arranged these on a relationship chart (see Figure 13.5). The superordinate concept became the name of the chart, the coordinate concepts (important ideas) became the column heads, and the subordinate concepts and terms (related vocabulary) formed the left-hand column, or stub.

To implement the interactive teaching strategy using the semantic feature analysis, Mr. Abel gave each of his students a copy of the relationship chart and also drew the chart on the chalkboard. He then introduced the chart by its title and helped his students define all important ideas and related vocabulary. As students defined the vocabulary, they predicted the relationship between

---

Figure 13.4   A Concept Diagram from Social Studies

From "Effectiveness of a Concept Teaching Routine in Enhancing the Performance of LD Students in Secondary Level Mainstream Classes," by J. Bulgren, J.B. Schumaler, and D.D. Deshler, 1988, Learning Disability Quarterly, 11, *p. 6. Copyright © 1988 by the Council for Learning Disabilities. Reprinted with permission.*

Concept name: Democracy

Definitions: A democracy is a form of government in which the people hold the ruling power, citizens are equal, the individual is valued, and compromise is necessary.

Characteristics present in the concept:

Always	Sometimes	Never
form of government	direct representation	king rules
people hold power	indirect representation	dictator rules
individual is valued		
citizens equal		
compromise necessary		

Example	Nonexample
United States	Cuba
Mexico	Iraq
Germany today	Germany under Hitler
Athens (about 500 B.C.)	Macedonia (under Alexander)

Figure 13.5   A Semantic Relationship Chart

From "The Effects of an Interactive Instructional Strategy for Enhancing Reading Comprehension and Content Area Learning for Students with Learning Disabilities," by C.S. Boss, P.L. Anders, D. Filip, and L.E. Jaffe, 1989, Journal of Learning Disabilities, 22, p. 386. Copyright © *1989 by the Donald D. Hammill Foundation. Reprinted with permission.*

IMPORTANT IDEAS

LEGEND:
+ = Positive relationship
− = Negative relationship
0 = No relationship
? = Uncertain

Important Ideas (columns): Citizen's right to privacy / **versus** / Society needs to keep law and order / Police search with a search warrant / Police search without a search warrant / Evidence allowed in court

RELATED VOCABULARY (rows):
- search and seizure
- unreasonable search and seizure
- probable cause to search
- your property and possessions
- absolute privacy
- you give consent
- hot pursuit
- moving vehicle
- stop-and-frisk
- plain view
- during an arrest
- evidence
- exclusionary rule

the vocabulary and each important idea as positive, negative, no relationship, or unknown. When the class achieved consensus on the relationship, it was recorded on the chart. Later, Mr. Abel's students read content-area passages to confirm or clarify predictions and amended their relationship charts.

According to Bos et al. (1989), students with learning disabilities who completed the semantic feature analysis evidenced superior performance on a multiple-choice comprehension test when compared with a group of peers who looked up the vocabulary words in a dictionary and wrote sentences using the terms. The authors suggested that the interactive nature of the strategy may help students with learning disabilities overcome their "passive" approach to learning, as well as facilitate storage and retrieval of information from memory.

Mnemonics.   Teachers can make use of various mnemonics to help learners with mild disabilities actively store information in memory and retrieve it. For example, Mr. McNally might give his students a first-letter acronym, HOMES, to help them remember the names of the Great Lakes (i.e., Huron, Ontario, Michigan, Erie, Superior). Similarly, Ms. Stone might give the students in her ninth-grade earth science class a first-letter acronym for remembering the planets by using the sentence "Mary's violet eyes make John stay up nights permanently." Although first-letter acronyms are well-known devices, other mnemonic strategies include the keyword method, reconstructive elaborations, and the pegword method.

In the *keyword method,* students form mental pictures in which new information to be learned is related in an unusual manner to known information in order to form an association for memory. The keyword is often an acoustic reconstruction. That is, a "sound-alike" word is used to form the mental image (Scruggs & Mastropieri, 1990). For example, to remember that *trace* means a narrow trail used by the pioneers, students might use the similar sounding but more familiar word *race* to form a mental image of pioneers racing on a narrow road, as shown in Figure 13.6 (Mastropieri & Scruggs, 1989b). Or, to remember that a herbivore is an animal that eats plants,

---

Figure 13.6   A Keyword Mnemonic Using an Acoustic Reconstruction

From "Mneumonic Social Studies Instruction: Classroom Applications," by M.A. Mastropieri and T.E. Scruggs, 1989, Remedial and Special Education, 10, *p. 43. Copyright © 1989 by PRO-ED, Inc. Reprinted with permission.*

TRACE (race)   **Narrow trail used by pioneers**

students might picture animals in herds (the keyword), eating only plants (Mastropieri, Emerick, & Scruggs, 1988).

For those terms or concepts more familiar to students, mimetic (literal representational) pictures can be used. Students may be familiar, for example, with concrete words like *soldier* and *trench*. Thus, to remember that during World War I many soldiers became ill or died from the unhealthy conditions resulting from living in the trenches over extended periods of time, students might simply be told to picture soldiers getting sick or dying in trenches (Mastropieri & Scruggs, 1988c). When information is more abstract, however, such *reconstructive elaborations* as symbolic representations might be more useful (e.g., students picture Uncle Sam as a symbolic representation of the United States looking over Europe and stating "It's not my war" in order to remember America's initial policy of neutrality during World War I).

King-Sears, Mercer, and Sindelar (1992) describe an interesting strategy for teaching students to produce keywords in science class. The authors use a first-letter acronym, IT FITS, to help students with mild disabilities recall the steps in the strategy:

<u>*I*</u> dentify the term.

<u>*T*</u> ell the definition of the term.

<u>*F*</u> Find a keyword.

<u>*I*</u> magine the definition doing something with the keyword.

<u>*T*</u> hink about the definition doing something with the keyword.

<u>*S*</u> tudy what you imagined until you know the definition.

Pegwords are helpful when students must remember ordered information or numbers associated with unfamiliar terms. To implement this mnemonic strategy, students first learn a rhyming poem in which familiar concrete objects are associated with numbers (e.g., one-sun or bun, two-shoe, three-bee or tree, four-door or floor, and so forth). Then, to produce the visual image, students picture the information to be remembered in association with the familiar object. For example, in Ms. Stone's earth science class, Robert might remember that wolframite is 4 on the Mohs hardness scale, is black in color, and is used for making light bulbs by picturing a wolf standing on a black *floor* (i.e., the pegword for *four*) surrounded by light bulbs, as shown in Figure 13.7 (Scruggs, Mastropieri, Levin, & Gaffney, 1985).

Although still requiring additional research, mnemonic strategy instruction appears to hold promise for students with mild disabilities in content-area classes (Mastropieri & Scruggs, 1988; Pressley, Scruggs, & Mastropieri, 1989). In particular, mnemonic instruction appears superior to the use of visual-spatial displays and/or direct instruction alone for enhancing the memory performance of youngsters with mild disabilities (Scruggs et al., 1985; Scruggs, Mastropieri, Levin, McLoone, Gaffney, & Prater, 1985). Keywords and pegwords do, however, require students to generate and remember complex images. Moreover, some abstract concepts may not lend themselves to meaningful images or pegwords likely to be retained by students. Teachers should use these strategies only when they facilitate learning for their students with mild disabilities.

Figure 13.7   Using a Pegword Mnemonic in Science

Technology.   Increasingly, teachers are using technology to improve instructional presentations. Traditional films or filmstrips, which can be rolled backward after viewing with pauses for questioning at appropriate frames to increase student interaction and active review of important information, are rapidly being replaced by modern technology in the form of videos, videodiscs, and computer software.

Carnine (1989) describes how such technology can incorporate essential features of instructional design and mastery learning to improve the performance of students with mild disabilities in science, health, chemistry, and other complex content areas. Using a laser videodisc in earth science, for example, Ms. Stone can "play" a video, but stop instantly to display any given video frame, enabling her students to focus on key ideas. At the touch of a remote-control button, she can move to a new section on the videodisc to review difficult concepts and to provide students with additional application exercises.

Experiments or demonstrations that may be too expensive or impractical to conduct in her classroom can be presented using the graphics and sound effects available on the laser videodisc.

Computer software is also used to produce study guides and corresponding test questions. Students with learning disabilities who make use of computerized study guide questions, answers, and corresponding multiple-choice tests do better on these tests than students who use standard note-taking procedures (Horton & Lovitt, 1989). Similarly, an advanced form of computer software, hypertext, allows teachers to link related information across several levels of computer "windows," analogous to laying several overhead transparencies one upon the other (see Figure 13.8). Study guides using hypertext are no more effective than teacher lectures; however, they do result in better test scores and retention than traditional lecture/study guide methods for students with mild disabilities and remedial students who require repeated exposure to all or part of the information presented in a lecture (Higgins & Boone, 1990).

Adapting Textbooks

Content-area textbooks are currently receiving much criticism. For example, according to Crabtree (1989) and Tyson and Woodward (1989), textbooks in history and social studies are poorly written and cover many topics superficially without providing analyses and connectives to tie events and concepts together for learners. Science textbooks, too, are densely packed with concepts and terms that are often not repeated, and they frequently assume considerable background knowledge that learners may or may not possess (Tyson & Woodward, 1989).

Teachers must not assume that textbooks prepared for a given grade level are at the appropriate reading level for students. Many factors other than sentence length and word length/difficulty affect the overall readability of a textbook. For example, well-organized texts contain clear headings, subheadings, introductory paragraphs, summary paragraphs, highlighted vocabulary or key concepts, marginal notes, and illustrative pictures, charts, and graphs. Moreover, key concepts are linked together through connective words and phrases in order to clarify relationships in the content.

In an attempt to provide students with mild disabilities relevant and age-appropriate content-area materials that are written at an appropriate reading level, some teachers use "high-interest, low-vocabulary" materials (see Table 13.4). For example, Mr. Abel might give Robert an earth science text written at the fifth-grade reading level but covering the same ninth-grade curriculum as Ms. Stone's normal textbook. Such an approach may be appropriate for some students with mild disabilities, particularly those in departmentalized special education content classes. Many adolescents with mild disabilities, however, prefer to use the same text as their peers. Furthermore, reducing the reading level of the text by decreasing the sentence length, sentence complexity, and vocabulary produces a fragmented text that is difficult to comprehend because important connective words and ideas have been eliminated.

To permit students with mild disabilities to read the textbook used in the regular classroom, some teachers tape-record the textbook or order prere-

Figure 13.8 A Geography Lesson with Hypertext

From "HyperText Computer Study Guides and the Social Studies Achievement of Students with Learning Disabilities, Remedial Students, and Regular Education Students," by K. Higgens and R. Boone, 1990, Journal of Learning Disabilities, 23, *p. 530. Copyright © 1990 by the Donald D. Hammill Foundation. Reprinted with permission.*

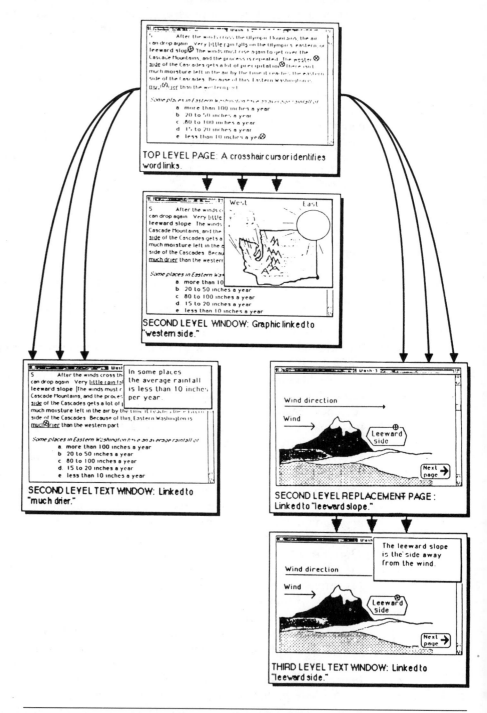

Table 13.4   Publishers of High-Interest/Low-Vocabulary Materials

Curriculum Associates
5 Esquire Road
North Billerica, MA 01862

Fearon/Janus/Quercus
500 Harbor Boulevard
Belmont, CA 94002

Follett Publishing Co.
1010 West Washington Blvd.
Chicago, IL 60607

Globe Book Company
4350 Equity Drive
P.O. Box 2649
Columbus, Ohio 43216

High Noon Books
Academic Therapy Publications
20 Commercial Boulevard
Novato, CA 94949

Modern Curriculum Press
13900 Prospect Road
Cleveland, OH 44136

Scholastic, Inc.
2931 E. McCarty Street
P.O. Box 7502
Jefferson City, MO 65102

Science Research Associates
155 North Wacker Drive
Chicago, IL 60606

Special Times
Cambridge Dev. Lab
214 Third Ave.
Walthan, MA 02154

Steck-Vaughn Company
P.O. Box 26015
Austin, TX 78755

---

corded versions of texts. Although recording services may require a nominal registration fee, they can provide copies of most major textbooks used in the schools or they can make copies of texts not in frequent use. Teachers must make advanced arrangements, though, if they are to receive textbooks for their students in a timely manner. (For information on one such service, write to Recording for the Blind, 20 Roszel Road, Princeton, New Jersey, 08540.)

Although tape recording may be a useful adaptation for some students with mild disabilities, the procedure can also be a time-consuming one for teachers. The following suggestions may be helpful for teachers who choose to tape-record textbooks for their students:

1. Enlist the aid of student, parent, or community volunteer groups as readers.

2. Use clear directions on the tape so that students will know when to move from one page to the next or from one paragraph/section to the next.

3. Use colors or symbols to highlight important information or to indicate movement through the text.

4. Periodically pause and insert questions to keep the listener actively engaged with the text.

5. Give students an advance organizer (i.e., a topical outline or study guide) to structure the reading selection.

Many effective "textbook adaptations" are really not modifications of the textbook at all. Rather, they are changes in the teacher's instructional presentation that enhance the student's involvement with the text (see also Chapter 10). Teachers can begin each new chapter or section of a textbook with a systematic overview. Mr. McNally, for example, might have students in his class page through a new chapter locating headings, subheadings, boldfaced or highlighted terms, and pictures, charts, or graphs. As students scan the text, Mr. McNally might ask, "What do you think this section will be about?" or "What do you think that word means?"

Following this structured overview, the students and Mr. McNally might take turns previewing (i.e., reading aloud) the text selection, with Mr. McNally interjecting questions between short segments. Students can be challenged to name as many facts as they can remember without looking back at the passage as Mr. McNally arranges these on the chalkboard to link related information and facilitate notetaking. Or, Mr. McNally might choose to use a cooperative learning strategy, such as Numbered Heads Together described in Chapter 9, to increase student involvement during textbook reading. Finally, Mr. McNally might use a pause procedure (Ruhl, Hughes, & Schloss, 1987), stopping periodically at logical points of a lecture or textbook selection while students work in pairs to clarify complex information or fill in notes or study guides.

Study guides or graphic organizers can help to structure textbook reading assignments and improve reading comprehension, just as they facilitate understanding during lectures or classroom discussions. Billingsley and Wildman (1988) improved the textbook comprehension of high school students with learning disabilities by giving them a structured visual overview of the major ideas in a passage prior to reading it. Similarly, Horton and Lovitt (1989) found that remedial students and youngsters with learning disabilities achieve higher social studies and science test scores when textbook reading is accompanied by study guides containing comprehension questions or graphics and visual/verbal clues, such as page numbers to locate answers (see Figure 13.9).

Adapting Assignments and Tests

Assignments can be modified in numerous ways to suit the needs of learners with mild disabilities. For example, teachers can post directions for assignments in a designated area of the classroom and use a consistent format for written work. Reducing the quantity of items to be completed, assigning a "study buddy" (i.e., a peer helper), and giving alternatives to written work (e.g., oral presentations, hands-on projects, tape-recorded answers) are also time-honored ways in which to modify assignments in the regular classroom. Additional suggestions for adapting assignments for students with mild disabilities include:

1. extending time for assignment completion;

2. breaking down long assignments into small chunks, reviewing the steps with students and posting them with a time line for later reference;

3. having students verbalize the necessary steps for assignment completion;

4. permitting the use of calculators, word processors, or other aids in assignment completion;

5. allowing some written assignments to be completed by cooperative groups; and

6. reducing the amount of written material to be copied; for example, by providing the student with a copy of the text page to write on instead of having him or her copy a problem from the text.

Similarly, teachers can vary the requirements of tests used to evaluate the outcome of instruction. Some teachers, for example, give frequent small tests, or practice tests, to alleviate "test anxiety" and review essential information. In addition, telling students the types of questions to expect on a test (e.g., true/false, multiple-choice, short-answer, matching, essay) and providing them with a study guide can help low-achieving students prepare for tests. Other suggestions that classroom teachers often find helpful and acceptable are as follows:

1. Use multiple-choice items with fewer choices (e.g., three instead of four or five alternatives).

2. Arrange matching items so that related information is grouped together with no more than five or six items in a group.

3. Provide a list of terms or phrases from which students can choose for short-answer tests.

4. Provide a partial outine for students to complete when giving essay tests.

5. Permit the student to tape-record answers to test questions.

6. Underline important directions or key words on the student's test paper.

7. Allow extended time for test taking.

A Summary of Adaptations

Special education teachers can help classroom teachers adapt their instructional presentations to assist students with mild disabilities in the regular classroom. Advance organizers and graphic organizers can be used to provide students with a framework by which to integrate new information with old. The use of mnemonics and technological aids may also improve the comprehension and retention of content-area information by special learners.

In addition, teachers can adapt textbooks to assist students who are having problems with reading. Often, effective textbook adaptations involve alterations in instructional procedures that increase active involvement with textbooks. Similarly, simple modifications in assignments or tests also can improve the content-area performance of youngsters with mild disabilities.

**Figure 13.9   Study Guide
Questions and Graphics**

*From "The Effectiveness of Textbook Applica-
tions in Life Science for High School Students
with Learning Disabilities," by D. Bergerud,
T. C. Lovitt, and S. Horton, 1988,* Journal of
Learning Disabilities, 21, *pp. 72–73. Copyright
© 1990 by the Donald D. Hammill Foundation.
Reprinted with permission.*

CIRCULATION

Directions: Answer the following questions with a
word or a phrase. Look for the answers
in the passage you just read.

1. What is the size of the human heart?

2. Where is the heart located in a human being?

3. How many chambers are there in a human heart?

4. At what rate does a person's heart beat?

5. What are the upper chambers of the heart called?

6. What are the lower chambers called?

7. How are the right and left halves of the heart separated?

8. How are the atria separated from the ventricles?

9. Name two points where the heartbeat can be detected in the body?

10. What is the throbbing called that can be felt at those points?

(continued)

✎ Teaching Learning Strategies and School Survival Skills

In major research projects conducted at the University of Kansas (Deshler & Schumaker, 1986) and the University of Pittsburgh (Zigmond, Kerr, Schaeffer, Brown, & Farrar, 1986), researchers examined the demands of secondary schools and the characteristics of adolescents with learning disabilities. Not surprisingly, findings indicated that adolescents with mild disabilities do not adjust well to such complex demands of the secondary school environment as meeting due dates for multiple assignments and demonstrating active interest or participation in various content classes (Kerr, Zigmond, Schaeffer, & Brown, 1986). Rather, these students are passive in their approach to learning and deficient in the study skills and strategies needed for success in secondary schools (Deshler, Schumaker, Alley, Warner, & Clark, 1982). Moreover, they do not seem to generalize the strategies and study skills learned in the special education setting to appropriate use in the regular classroom (Alley, Deshler, Clark, Schumaker, & Warner, 1983).

Deshler, Schumaker, and their colleagues at the University of Kansas (Alley & Deshler, 1979; Deshler & Schumaker, 1986) recommend that teachers use a learning-strategies approach to help their students with mild disabilities cope with the many demands of the secondary school. Learning strategies involve teaching students procedures or rules to help them "learn how to learn" and become more active and self-directed in their content classes. Immediately

Figure 13.9   *(Continued)*

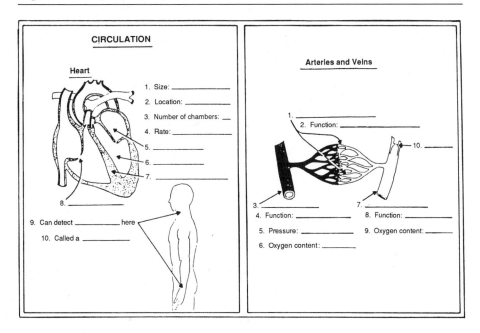

useful strategies for acquiring, storing, and expressing content-area information are the essential elements of a learning-strategies curriculum. (See Chapter 9 for a discussion of the learning-strategies curriculum and the Strategies Intervention Model.) For example, Mr. Abel might help his students learn specific strategies for completing their current assignments. Or, he might teach his students strategies to prepare for classes, take notes, read textbooks, or take various types of tests.

Not all students with mild disabilities will require new strategies in order to be successful in their content-area instruction. For those who do, however, Schumaker, Deshler, Alley, and Warner (1983) describe the following procedure as essential:

Step 1: Pretest the student and point out the student's strengths and weaknesses on the task for which a new learning strategy is being considered. Discuss with the student the need for a more effective strategy and *obtain the student's commitment to try a new method.*

Step 2: Break the strategy into separate parts. Describe each step of the strategy for the student, telling the student why each part is important and where the strategy might be useful.

Step 3: Model the new strategy for the student. Make overt and explicit all of the thought processes that are a part of the strategy by "thinking aloud."

Step 4: Require the student to rehearse each step of the strategy verbally until he or she can self-instruct without error.

Step 5: Have the student practice the new strategy using controlled materials that are closer to his or her current performance level than the regular classroom materials. Provide the student with positive and corrective feedback throughout the practice trials until he or she performs to a specified criterion level.

Step 6: Increase the difficulty level of the practice materials until they approximate that of the regular classroom. Require the student to perform to a specified criterion level each time before moving to harder practice materials.

Step 7: Posttest the student and state specific information regarding performance gains.

Step 8: Help the student generalize the strategy to the regular classroom. This step requires careful planning and monitoring by the teacher, including:
  • helping the student to verbalize where and under what conditions the strategy might be useful in his or her content-area classes;
  • encouraging the student to use the strategy in the regular classroom and, if appropriate, informing the regular classroom teacher of the strategy so that he or she can privately reward the student for using it; and
  • continuing with periodic follow-up to make sure that the strategy is still appropriate, that the student is still using it correctly, and that the student is setting personal goals for strategy use.

Several cautions are in order when teaching learning strategies. First, steps 1 through 3 are critical for student success. Of particular importance is obtaining the student's commitment to try a potentially useful new approach (see Box 13.1). Steps 4 through 7 may vary depending upon the skill and maturity level of the individual student. Often, however, students require extensive controlled and grade-appropriate practice in order to master learning strategies. Second, the teacher must not assume that the student will automatically use the new strategy in his or her content classes. Generalization to the regular classroom is still problematic within the Strategies Intervention Model. Teachers must plan systematically for generalization if it is to occur as suggested in step 8. Finally, the teacher must refrain from teaching learning strategies to particular students if there is no need to do so. Learning strategies should never be taught merely for the sake of teaching a "new" and "different" curriculum.

In addition, the Strategies Intervention Model is receiving recent criticism on the grounds that is still teacher-directed rather than student-directed (Ellis, 1986). That is, some authorities argue that students are merely taught rote procedures for completing specific tasks, precluding their active involvement in the construction of knowledge (Poplin, 1988). Although the goal of learning-

Box 13.1   Mr. Abel Teaches Robert a Learning Strategy

Mr. Abel is about to introduce Robert to a "better way" to write sequence paragraphs in his content-area classes. First, Mr. Abel reviews Robert's current level of performance when writing sequence paragraphs and gives Robert a reason to learn a better way to write these. After obtaining Robert's commitment to learn the new strategy, Mr. Abel describes and then models the strategy for Robert using a "think-aloud" procedure. Let's listen to the conversation as Mr. Abel begins the learning-strategies teaching sequence:

Mr. Abel: *Remember yesterday in class you wrote a sequence paragraph similar to the ones you have to write for Mr. McNally and Ms. Stone.* [Placing Robert's paragraph on the desk] *Here's the paragraph you wrote. You used a nice topic sentence for your paragraph, but I had difficulty following the order of your thoughts. For example, I didn't see words or phrases to help me, as the reader, see how the events took place in a certain order. You know how Mr. McNally and Ms. Stone are always giving you low marks on tests and on the homework you turn in when you don't show things occurring in the proper order.*

Robert: *Yeah, sometimes I forget the order. But, I do know it lots of times. I just don't do good on written tests and homework.*

Mr. Abel: *I know a way to help you write better sequence paragraphs like this one for Mr. McNally and Ms. Stone. Would you like to give it a try?*

Robert: *Okay, I guess so.*

Mr. Abel: *Fantastic! The strategy goes like this. Write a topic sentence. Write three or four sentences about the topic and start these sentences with the words* first, next, then, *and* finally *in that order. End with a "clincher" sentence that says the same thing as the topic sentence but in different words.* [He writes the steps to the strategy on the board as he talks.]
    Topic Sentence
    First, . . .

Next, . . .
Then, . . .
Finally, . . .
Clincher Sentence.
It's important to use first, next, then, *and* finally *because these are the words that tell the reader the exact sequence in your paragraph.*

Robert: *That doesn't look too hard.*

Mr. Abel: *It's not. Watch me do an example. In earth science with Ms. Stone, you've been talking about convection. That process takes place in a certain sequence, so I can write a paragraph about that using the steps in this strategy.* [He "thinks aloud" as he writes the sample paragraph on the chalkboard.] *Let's see, I have to write a topic sentence. I know what convection means, so I'll use that in my topic sentence. "Convection is the movement of molecules caused by heating." Now, I have to write a sentence about the convection process that begins with the word* first. *"First, molecules are heated, move faster, and become less dense." Hmmm . . . now I need a sentence starting with* next. *"Next, these buoyant molecules move up, forming an area of high pressure." Let's see, now a sentence starting with* then. *"Then, the molecules move across the top from the area of high pressure to an area of low pressure." Now, I need a sentence using* finally. *"Finally, as the molecules move across the top, they cool and slow down, become less dense, and sink back down." Let's see, the last step is to write a clincher sentence. "Convection is one way to explain the movement of molecules."*

Robert: *The other day in class, we had to write an answer to tell about convection like that.*

Mr. Abel: *Yeah, I think you can use this strategy in earth science and in geography. You might be able to use it in health, too. You can use it any time you have to write a paragraph to explain how something happens*

(continued)

Box 13.1   *(Continued)*

in a specific order. Now, tell me the steps to follow when you write a sequence paragraph.

Mr. Abel moves the lesson to verbal rehearsal and guided practice with the steps in the strategy. Later, he will help Robert apply the strategy to write sequence paragraphs using curricular materials from Robert's earth science and geography classes. When Robert masters

this paragraph-writing strategy, Mr. Abel will help him plan and evaluate his independent use of the strategy in content classes.

Based on: Teaching a Paragraph Organization Strategy to Learning Disabled Adolescents *by M. Moran, J.B. Schumaker and A. Vetter, 1981. For additional information on Paragraph Writing Strategies please contact: The University of Kansas Institute for Research in Learning Disabilities, Lawrence, Kansas.*

---

strategies instruction is to produce students who function strategically and *independently* as learners in their content-area classes, it is the teacher who most often assumes the responsibility for evaluating and selecting appropriate strategies for use. To address this difficulty, Ellis, Deshler, and Schumaker (1989) designed an executive strategy procedure to enable students to produce their own strategies. Students learn to employ the SUCCESS strategy procedure, following the eight-step teaching sequence:

S = Sort out the most important demand or problem.

U = Unarm the problem by identifying the critical trouble spots.

C = Cash in on your old strategies, experiences, and observations of others.

C = Create a strategy for solving this problem that will work on all similar problems.

E = Echo your strategy (use substrategy ECHO):

    E = Evaluate the strategy as you try it.

    C = Change the strategy to make it work better for future use.

    H = Have another try and reevaluate it.

    O = Overlearn your strategy.

S = See how well your strategy works in different situations.

S = Save your strategy.

Although the effectiveness of strategy instruction requires further investigation, the technique appears promising for students with mild disabilities. "Good" strategy instruction is interactive in nature, involving ongoing dialogue and collaboration between students and their teachers to produce individualized strategies that meet specific needs of learners in their regular classes (Harris & Pressley, 1991). (Additional information about the Strategies Intervention Model and specific training in its use may be obtained from Institute for Research in Learning Disabilities, 3061 Dole Building, University of Kansas, Lawrence, Kansas 66045.) Although many of the strategies we will now discuss have been designed for adolescents with mild disabilities, some are also appropriate for elementary-level students.

Class-Preparation and Assignment-Completion Strategies

Robert constantly loses study guides, books, and assignments. He complains that he never has time to finish his homework and he frequently makes the excuse that he didn't know an assignment was due. Robert feels that his teachers pick on him. Like many students with mild disabilities, he has difficulty organizing himself in order to come to class prepared and complete the work required by Mr. McNally, Ms. Stone, and his other teachers.

Shields and Heron (1989) suggest that teachers have students use assignment logs or calendars. When assignments are given, students write down the present date, the nature of the assignment, its due date, and other pertinent information in columns on the assignment log. Similarly, students can use a weekly or monthly calendar and a "to do today" list. On these calendars, students note assignments with due dates, estimate time for assignment completion, and block out time in increments in order to complete both short- and long-range projects. First, however, they may need to complete a time log, monitoring exactly how they spend their time for a week, in order to see "where time goes."

Having a notebook with pockets large enough to hold standard notebook paper also enables students to keep track of work to be completed and work to be turned in during the day. Teachers who require students to keep notebooks and who spend time helping students organize them are using their time wisely. In addition, teachers are advised to check notebooks frequently and help students reorganize them periodically.

Students may also require specific strategies to ensure that they arrive in class with work completed, fully prepared to participate. Four specific strategies for classroom preparation and assignment completion are PREPARE, PREP, WATCh and HOW.

PREPARE.   PREPARE (Ellis & Lenz, 1987, p. 100) cues the student to bring both materials and a positive attitude to the class session. In addition, the student reminds himself/herself to review the previous day's lesson before class begins.

P = Plan locker visits.

R = Reflect on what you need and get it.

E = Erase personal needs.

P = PSYC (substrategy):

    P = Pause for an attitude check.

    S = Say a personal goal related to the class.

Y = Yoke in your negative thoughts.

C = Challenge yourself to good performance.

A = Ask yourself where class has been and where class is going.

R = Review notes and study guides.

E = Explore the meaning of the teacher's introduction.

PREP.   PREP (Ellis, 1989, p. 36) is a strategy designed to engage the student in thought about an upcoming lesson before the lesson actually begins. This strategy also ensures that the student will bring a positive attitude, as well as materials, to content-area classes.

P = Prepare materials.
Get notebook, study guide, pencil, and textbooks ready for class.
Mark difficult parts of the textbook, notes, and study guide.

R = Review what you know.
Read notes, study guide, and textbook cues and relate these to what you already know about the topic. List at least three things you know about the topic.

E = Establish a positive mind set.
Tell yourself to learn. Suppress "put downs" and make a positive statement.

P = Pinpoint goals.
Decide what you want to find out and note your participation goals.

WATCh.   WATCh (Glomb & West, 1990, p. 236) is a strategy designed to help students with behavior disorders complete their assignments neatly, accurately, and on time.

W = Write down the assignment, the due date, and any special requirements in an "assignment planner."

A = Ask yourself if you understand the assignment, and ask for clarification if necessary.

T = Task-analyze the assignment and schedule the task over the days available to complete the assignment.

Ch = Check each task as you do it with CAN (substrategy):

C = Completeness

A = Accuracy

N = Neatness

HOW.   HOW (Archer, 1988, p. 56; Archer & Gleason, 1989) is actually part of a larger strategy to help elementary-level students with mild disabilities complete content-area assignments accurately and on time. The strategy requires students to read directions and check assignments for neatness.

Step 1: Plan it.
> Read the directions and circle the words that tell you what to do.
> Get out the materials you need.
> Tell yourself what to do.

Step 2: Complete it.
> Do all the items.
> If you can't do an item, go to the next one or ask for help.
> Use HOW (substrategy for How should your paper look?):

> H = Heading.
> > Name, date, subject, page number.

> O = Organized.
> > On the front side of the paper, left and right margins, at least one blank line at the top and bottom, good spacing.

> W = Written neatly.
> > Words or numbers written neatly and on the lines. Neat erasing.

Step 3: Check it.
> Did you do everything?
> Did you get the right answers?
> Did you proofread?

Step 4: Turn it in.

Class-Participation Strategies

In addition to completing work and coming to class prepared, Robert must actively participate in his classes if he is to be successful. Class participation entails listening to the teacher and to class discussions, reflecting on what is being said, asking relevant questions or making comments in an appropriate manner, and taking notes. Three specific strategies for class participation are SLANT, RELATE, and WISE.

SLANT.   SLANT (Ellis, 1989, p. 37) is a strategy designed to help students with mild disabilities increase nonverbal "teacher-pleasing" behaviors in the content class.

> S = Sit up.

> L = Lean forward.

> A = Act like you're interested.

> N = Nod your head.

> T = Track the teacher with your eyes.

RELATE.   RELATE (Ellis, 1989, p. 37) gives students a specific strategy for verbal participation during a class session. Students learn, for example, how to listen for "alert" words that signal important information, such as reasons, examples, or comparisons, and for opportunities to contribute by asking questions or making comments (see Table 13.5).

R = Reveal reasons.
Listen for alert words and reasons. Paraphrase the reasons back to the teacher.

E = Echo examples.
Listen for alert words and examples. Paraphrase the examples back to the teacher.

L = Lasso comparisons.
Listen for alert words and comparisons. Paraphrase the similarities and/or differences back to the teacher.

A = Ask questions.
Ask yourself if the information makes sense. If not, ask a question at an appropriate pause.

T = Tell the main idea.
Listen for alert words. Listen for a main-idea statement. Paraphrase the main idea.
      Or,
Tell what you think the main idea is and see if others agree with you.

E = Examine importance.
Ask the teacher to say what is most important.
      Or,
Decide what you think is most important. Tell what you think is most important and see if others agree with you.

WISE.   WISE (Ellis, 1989, p. 37) is a strategy to help students "think back on" class sessions to monitor their learning and remember information.

W = Were goals met?
Did you learn what you wanted to learn? Did you meet your participation goals?

I = Itemize important information.
Review the study guide, notes, or the textbook and mark key information.

S = See how information can be remembered.
Draw graphic displays, create study cards, or make up mnemonics.

E = Explain what was learned to somebody.
Use your notes to teach somebody about the topic.

Table 13.5 Alert Words for Classroom Discussions

Alert words that may be signaling that reasons are being offered:

because   deduct   effect   explanation   purpose   reasons   since   therefore

Alert words that may be signaling that examples of things/ideas are being offered:

example   instance   model   pattern   sample   type

Alert words and phrases that may be signaling that things/ideas are being compared:

associated   contrast   differences   with relation to . . .   opposite   parallel

resemblance   similarities   on the other hand . . .

Alert words and phrases that may be signaling that main-idea statements are being offered:

basically . . .   driving at . . .   drift is . . .   in essence . . .

in conclusion . . .   in summary . . .   key point . . .

significance of this is . . .   the gist is . . .   the most important . . .

Alert words that may be signaling that lists of important information are being offered:

categories   characteristics   classes   divisions   features   first, second, etc.

groups   kinds   many   members   parts   roles   steps   stages   ways

---

From "A Metacognitive Intervention for Increasing Class Participation," by E.S. Ellis, Learning Disabilities Focus, 5, (1), 1989, p. 38. Copyright © 1989 by The Council for Exceptional Children. Reprinted with permission.

Teachers may need to model, or have other students model, appropriate ways to ask questions and make comments in the regular classroom. Modeling how to ask and/or answer questions and providing students with practice opportunities and specific feedback may enhance the generalization of this essential skill to the regular classroom (Knapcyzk, 1991). Moreover, teachers may need to demonstrate and give students practice using different formats for taking notes in content classes. To implement instruction, teachers must first use controlled lectures so that students have an opportunity to listen for clue words in well-organized presentations and to practice varying note-taking formats. Later, the teacher may use videotaped or audiotaped sessions from actual content-area classes to increase speed and proficiency.

Two note-taking formats are particularly useful to secondary-level students with mild disabilities. In the two-column format, Devine (1987) recommends that students write the date and topic at the top of the notebook page and divide the page into two columns. Writing only on the front of the page, students take notes in simple outline form during class in the right-hand column and then later label the key ideas in the left-hand column. The student follows a similar procedure using the three-column format; however, the third column (i.e., now the one on the far right) permits the student to return and add related notes from the textbook next to the corresponding information from class sessions.

Bos and Vaughn (1991) suggest that students use the following techniques to become proficient note-takers:

1. Skip lines in notes to indicate changes in ideas.

2. Write ideas or key phrases rather than complete sentences.

3. Use pictures and diagrams.

4. Use abbreviations or symbols consistently.

5. Underline or asterisk information stressed by the teacher.

6. Include in notes any information written on the chalkboard or shown on an overhead transparency.

7. If you miss an idea or fact, draw a blank line so that you can fill it in later. Look up the information in the textbook or ask about it later.

8. If you can't remember how to spell a word, spell it the way it sounds or the way you think it looks. Look the word up or ask about it later.

9. Review your notes as soon as possible after a class session.

Textbook Strategies

Students with mild disabilities often have difficulty reading and comprehending their content-area textbooks. At the same time, they are expected to study their texts to prepare for tests. In addition to adapting the textbook, the strategies we will next describe may help youngsters obtain important information from their texts. The reader also may wish to review the comprehension strategies discussed in Chapter 10: RAM (Clarke et al., 1984), RAP (Ellis & Lenz, 1987), and RIDER (Ellis & Lenz, 1987).

FIST.   In the FIST strategy (Ellis & Lenz, 1987, p. 98), students cue themselves to self-question while reading textbook passages in order to improve their comprehension.

F = First sentence in the paragraph is read.

I = Indicate a question based on information in the first sentence.

S = Search for the answer to the question.

T = Tie the answer to the question with a paraphrase.

Chapter-question strategy.   Archer and Gleason (1989) suggest a strategy to help students with mild disabilities answer specific questions from a textbook chapter or from a study guide. First, students practice turning a question into a statement containing part of the answer. For example, if the question is "What is latitude?" Robert might state, "Latitude means . . .". Next, students practice locating the section of the chapter in which the answer is likely to be found. These two steps force students to "think about" what exactly the question is asking and the type of information to be given in the answer (e.g., a name, event, date, place, etc.) *before* attempting to answer the question. Finally, students learn the complete strategy:

Step 1: Read the question carefully.

Step 2: Change the question into part of the answer.

Step 3: Locate the section of the chapter that discusses the topic.

Step 4: Read the section of the chapter until you find the answer.

Step 5: Complete the answer.

Other strategies give students with mild disabilities procedures for reading content-area textbooks while extracting and organizing important information for note taking. These strategies also use the familiar techniques of paraphrasing, self-questioning, and forming first-letter acronyms.

LISTS.   LISTS (Ellis & Lenz, 1987, p. 99) gives students a specific technique for taking notes while reading content-area textbooks. The strategy focuses student attention on textual clues that signal important information and provides a first-letter acronym for arranging the information in a format to promote study and memorization.

L = Look for clues.

I = Investigate the items. (Be sure they all relate to the topic and are parallel.)

S = Select a mnemonic using FIRST (substrategy):

   F = Form a word.

   I = Insert letters to form a word.

   R = Rearrange the letters to form a word.

   S = Shape a sentence.

   T = Try combinations.

T = Transfer information to a card.

S = Self-test.

The self-questioning summarization strategy.   The self-questioning summarization strategy (Wong, Wong, Perry, & Sawatsky, 1986, pp. 24–26) consists of a series of questions used as prompts for finding the main idea of a textbook paragraph and rewriting it.

1. In this paragraph, is there anything I don't understand?

2. In this paragraph, what's the most important sentence (main-idea sentence)? Let me underline it.

3. Let me summarize the paragraph. To summarize, I rewrite the main-idea sentence and add important details.

4. Now, does my summary statement link up with the chapter subheading?

5. When I have written summary statements for a whole subsection:

   (a) Let me review my summary statements for the subsection. (A subsection consists of several paragraphs under the same subheading.)

   (b) Do my summary statements link up with each other?

   (c) Do they all link up with the subheading?

6. At the end of an assigned reading section, let me see if I am aware of all of the themes. If I am, let me predict the teacher's test question on this section. If I'm not, let me go back to item 4.

Columnar note taking with tip sheets. In a technique devised by Horton, Lovitt, and Christensen (1991), middle school and high school students with mild disabilities improved in their ability to take notes from their social studies and science textbooks. In this form of note taking, four columns are used: "Heading," "What," "Special Terms," and "Facts" (see Figure 13.10). In the "Heading" column, students write each of the headings and subheadings from the chapter. To complete the "What" column, students formulate a main-idea statement for each paragraph. In order to find main ideas, they learn four specific strategies:

Level 1: Use the first sentence of the paragraph if it does a good job of describing the main point of the paragraph. If it doesn't, try level 2.

Level 2: Use the first sentence of the paragraph and add other information from the paragraph to it to make a "what" statement. It should still be one sentence. It helps sometimes to join sentences by using the word *and*. If this doesn't work, go to level 3.

Level 3: Look for a sentence other than the first sentence that describes the main point of the paragraph and use it as your "what" statement. If this doesn't work, try level 4.

Level 4: Use your own words to make a "what" statement.

Special terms are defined as any unusual words and their definitions. Students, for example, look for words that are written in boldfaced, italicized, or colored print. The "Fact" column consists of any items that support the main-idea statement. Students cue themselves to write at least one fact for each paragraph, but never more than three facts.

Figure 13.10   Columnar Note Taking from Textbooks

From "Notetaking from Textbooks: Effects of a Columnar Format on Three Categories of Secondary Students," by S. V. Horton, T. C. Lovitt and C. C. Christensen, 1991, Exceptionality, 2, *p. 25. Copyright © 1991 by Springer-Verlag. Reprinted with permission.*

Name: _____ **Period:** _____ **Date:** _____

WHAT: One statement of the main point of the paragraph.

SPECIAL TERMS: Unusual words and their definitions.

FACTS: Up to three short pieces of important information.

Heading	WHAT	SPECIAL TERMS	FACTS
	During the early 1500s: The conquistadores won for Spain control of much of Latin America	N/A	–the Spanish language and Christianity were imposed on all who lived there –the economic policies were Spanish, as were the social and political ideas
The Spanish Colonies	Thousands of Spanish colonists came to the New World after the conquistadores opened the lands for settlement	Colony: An area ruled by a foreign country	–settlers or colonists from the ruling country came to live in the colony –the King gave land grants to nobles, army officers, and priests
Towns	Spanish settlers built towns in the New World patterned after Spanish towns	Plaza: Central square in the center of each town	–Spanish settlers brought their customs and traditions to the New World –plaza was the center of the town's business and religious life –Catholic church and government buildings were on the plaza

A note-taking strategy using index cards.   Rooney (1988) describes a similar strategy for note taking from content-area textbooks. In her strategy, however, students place their notes on index cards using the following steps:

Step 1: Read the subtitle and the section under the subtitle. While reading, write on *separate* index cards names of people and places, important numbers, and important terms. Write only two or three words per card. Do this for each paragraph in the section.

Step 2: Go back to the subtitle and turn it into the best test question you can. Write this question on one side of an index card and the answer on the other side. You now have a set of main-idea and detail cards from a chapter section.

Step 3: Repeat steps 1 and 2 for all the sections to be covered.

Step 4: Study the cards by looking at them one at a time. For detail cards, ask yourself, How is this related to the material? Try to answer the main-idea question cards from memory.

Study and Test-Taking Strategies

Closely related to the preceding strategies are several others designed to help youngsters with mild disabilities study for and take tests in their content classes. When students in special programs receive instruction on how to take specific types of tests, their performance in the regular classroom improves (Scruggs & Marsing, 1987).

EASY.   EASY (Ellis & Lenz, 1987, p. 99) is a relatively straightforward strategy to enable students with mild disabilities to prepare for tests systematically, for example, by organizing and then prioritizing the information for study.

E = Elicit "WH" questions to identify important information (e.g., who, what, when, where, why).

A = Ask yourself which information is the least troublesome.

S = Study the easy parts first and the hardest parts last.

Y = Say *yes* to self-reinforcement.

SPLASH.   SPLASH (Simmonds, Luchow, Kaminsky, & Cottone, 1989, p. 101) offers a systematic method for taking tests.

S = Skim the entire test. Note easy and hard parts, directions, and point values so that you can best allocate the available time.

P = Plan your strategy once you have a general idea of the test.

L = Leave out difficult questions in a planned manner. (Teachers may want to cue students to mark items skipped over with an asterisk.)

A = Attack immediately those questions you know.

S = Systematically guess after exhausting other strategies. (Here teachers must first instruct students to look for clues and answers on the test to help answer unknown questions. If there is no penalty for guessing, students should be told to guess the best choice after eliminating incorrect choices.)

H = House cleaning. (Leave 5%–10% of your allotted time to making sure all answers are filled in, cleaning up erasures, and checking answers.)

PIRATES.   Hughes, Schumaker, Deshler, & Mercer (1987) describe a similar test-taking strategy called PIRATES. Using this strategy, students establish a positive mindset for the test and read the instructions and look for clues systematically.

P = Prepare to succeed.
Put the acronym PIRATES and your name on the test. Prioritize test sections and allot time. Say something positive and start within 2 minutes.

I = Inspect the instructions.
Read all of the instructions and underline how and where to answer. Also, notice any special requirements.

R = Read, remember, reduce.
Read the whole question. Remember it with memory strategies and reduce your alternatives.

A = Answer or abandon.
If you know the answer, write it. If you're not sure, abandon the question for the moment.

T = Turn back.
Go back to abandoned items at the end of the test and tell yourself to earn more points.

E = Estimate.
Estimate unknown answers using the substrategy ACE:

A = Avoid absolutes (e.g., ''All'').

C = Choose the longest or most detailed alternative.

E = Eliminate identical alternatives.

S = Survey.
Survey the test to be sure all items are answered and switch answers only if you are sure they are wrong.

Teachers can give students practice tests of various types, gradually increasing the difficulty level, as students learn strategies like SPLASH. In addition, students can apply several important general rules when taking tests so as to improve performance:

1. When taking true/false tests, look for clue words like *always, never, none, no,* and *all*. These words frequently signal an item that is false. Conversely, words like *sometimes* and *usually* may signal items that are true. Although clue words are not foolproof, they may improve your odds to greater than chance if you do not know the correct answer.

2. On multiple-choice tests, one or two alternatives for each item are usually clearly incorrect. Eliminate these by marking them. In addition, learn to look for and underline key words like *except* and *not* on multiple-choice tests and always read all the alternatives before attempting an answer.

3. Essay tests contain directional words like *compare, contrast, describe, explain, evaluate,* or *illustrate*. Be sure that you know what these words mean and underline them before taking essay tests. In addition, you may find it helpful to sketch a simple outline on your test paper before beginning to write answers to essay items.

4. Never change your answers unless you are certain they are incorrect. If you must guess, go with your first instinct after exhausting all possible clues. Unless there is a penalty for guessing, never leave items unanswered.

5. Write down information that you are likely to forget immediately upon receiving your test paper. For example, you can write a first-letter acronym in a margin of the test paper before you begin the test.

A Summary of Strategies

A number of strategies have proven effective in helping students succeed in their content-area classes. These strategies may not turn students with mild disabilities into ''star pupils''; however, they may make the difference between an F or D and a passing grade. Teachers must remember to teach only those strategies that are needed by an individual student and to elicit the student's commitment to learn the strategy before proceeding. In addition, teachers must follow the critical steps for teaching learning strategies, including those for generalization to the regular classroom.

✎ Summary

Many students with mild disabilities will complete their content-area instruction in the regular classroom. Increasingly, special education teachers are collaborating with regular educators in an effort to adapt instructional presentations to suit the needs of special learners. Advance organizers, graphic organizers, planned mnemonic devices, and technological aids all may be employed in the regular classroom to enhance the learning of youngsters with mild disabilities. In addition, the teacher may adapt textbooks, assignments, and tests to improve student performance. Content-area teachers are often willing to make such modifications if they are likely to benefit many students simultaneously and if the necessary support from special education personnel is available.

Teachers also must make sure that students with mild disabilities have the school survival skills essential for success in the regular classroom. Many learning strategies are available to teach youngsters how to organize and prepare for class, how to participate in class, and how to complete assignments, take notes, read textbooks, study, and take tests. These learning strategies may be effective in helping many youngsters cope with the complex demands of the content classroom from the elementary level through the secondary grades.

✎ Application Exercises

1. Examine textbooks at two different grade levels in a nearby school district. Choose one social studies text at each level and one science text at each level. Describe how each text is organized. Describe the vocabulary and concept load, using specific examples. Then, state whether or not each text will be difficult for students with mild disabilities to read and comprehend. Justify your opinion. Give at least five ways in which each textbook could be adapted to improve student performance.

2. Interview a special education teacher and a regular classroom teacher at a chosen grade level who ''share'' students. What adaptations are typically used to assist students with mild disabilities in the content class. Are there any differences between suggestions made by the special educator and those made by the regular educator? If so, how would you account for the differences?

3. Assume you are Mr. Abel assisting Robert in his geography class with Mr. McNally. What learning strategies would you recommend for Robert in this class? Justify your recommendations.

4. Using a textbook from a chosen grade level, analyze the content of one chapter for important concepts, ideas, and vocabulary. Then, prepare a graphic organizer to illustrate the relationship among the key concepts and ideas you identified in your analysis.

5. Ms. Stone says, ''Robert never seems to listen in earth science. He doesn't take notes, and his test grades are low.'' Assume you are Mr. Abel. What information do you need to gather? How will you obtain it?

Instruction in Social and Independent Living Skills

Chapter 14

Focus

As you read, think about the following questions:

Why is instruction in social skills an important component of the curriculum for students with mild disabilities?

What are several effective ways to teach social skills?

What is meant by transition planning?

How can teachers help their students with mild disabilities prepare to live independently as adults?

✎ Students with mild disabilities often lack the social and independent living skills they need in order to function as productive members of their mainstreamed classrooms and contributing citizens during adulthood. Regular classroom teachers, for example, report that students with mild disabilities do not demonstrate the social behaviors that are necessary for success in their classes (Fad, 1990). Special educators must focus educational programming on critical skills enabling students with mild disabilities to function independently in the school and community. Let's take a look at how Ms. Lopez and Mr. Abel deal with these concerns.

Ms. Lopez evaluates Joey's recent performance in the classroom. Although Joey is now remaining in his seat for longer periods at a time, he still calls out the moment he has a question. If Ms. Lopez ignores Joey's rudeness, he becomes even more disruptive in attempting to gain attention. Ms. Lopez decides that Joey may not know how to gain teacher attention appropriately. She defines "Getting the Teacher's Attention the Right Way" as a three-step process: (1) Raise your hand, (2) Wait quietly for the teacher to call on you, and (3) Ask a question using a polite tone of voice. Ms. Lopez writes these steps on a small card, demonstrates each step for Joey, and asks him to practice each step. Then, she rewards Joey with points and specific praise each time he gets the teacher's attention the right way.

Mr. Abel knows that Susan will need assistance if she is to live independently as an adult. Susan has no marketable job skill, poor personal hygiene, and little self-confidence. She has no idea of what type of job she might enjoy after leaving school. Because Susan will turn 14 in 1 month, Mr. Abel discusses his concerns with Mrs. Friend, Susan's guidance counselor and the chair of her IEP team. Mrs. Friend will obtain permission for Susan to have a thorough evaluation of her vocational interests and abilities at a nearby vocational evaluation center. In addition, Mrs. Friend suggests that it might be useful for the local representative from the state's vocational rehabilitation agency to join the IEP team as Susan moves to the high school in an effort to plan appropriate goals and objectives for her transition to postsecondary services and/or employment.

Students with mild disabilities like Joey and Susan often lack social skills, daily living skills, or vocational skills. Without appropriate social skills, Joey will not be successful in the regular classroom. Moreover, if he fails to learn how to follow directions, accept criticism, or make requests politely, he may have problems finding and keeping a job once he has left school. In addition, if Susan does not receive instruction in the daily living and vocational skills necessary for her adulthood, it is unlikely that she will be able to earn an adequate income or live independently.

In this chapter, we will first examine the social behavior of students with mild disabilities. Next, we will explore effective instructional methods and programs for teaching critical social skills to special children and youth. Finally, we will discuss instruction in independent living skills and the transitioning of students with mild disabilities into postsecondary settings.

Social Skills and Students with Mild Disabilities

Students with mild disabilities often spend the majority of their school day in the regular classroom. Therefore, how teachers and peers view them with respect to social skills may be critical to their classroom success. For example, teachers rate the ability to cope with failure and to function independently as essential for classroom success (Kauffman, Wong, Lloyd, Hung, & Pullen, 1991). (See Table 14.1 for specific social skills identified by regular education teachers as necessary for success in the mainstream.)

Despite the importance of adequate social skills, students with mild disabilities often demonstrate numerous inappropriate behaviors. According to Center and Wascom (1987), regular classroom teachers perceive students with behavioral disorders as exhibiting more antisocial behaviors and fewer prosocial behaviors than normal peers. Students with learning disabilities are also rated by teachers as demonstrating fewer appropriate social skills (Bursuck, 1989); greater pragmatic language deficits (Lapadat, 1991); and increased levels of off-task behavior, conduct disorders, distractibility, and shyness (Bender & Smith, 1990; McKinney, 1989) when compared with same-age peers. Moreover, teachers rate children and youth with learning disabilities, mild mental retardation, and behavior disorders alike as below peers in almost all critical social skills (Gresham, Elliott, & Black, 1987).

The teacher's perceptions of the classroom behavior of mainstreamed students with mild disabilities also may be an important factor affecting the educational placement, social status, and achievement levels for these youngsters (Roberts & Zubrick, 1992). For example, the perceived "teachability" of students with mild disabilities may have a bearing on instructional opportunities and long-term academic outcomes (Osborne, Schulte, & McKinney, 1991). That is, children who exhibit more off-task, distractible, dependent, maladaptive classroom behaviors may receive different amounts or types of instruction as compared with peers (McKinney, 1989). This difference in instruction may, in turn, contribute to the low academic achievement of students in the mainstream, as well as those who remain in resource-room special education programs (Osborne et al., 1991).

Students with mild disabilities may also experience lower social status when compared with same-age peers. Students with behavioral disorders and mild mental retardation are often rejected by their peers in the regular classroom (Sabornie, Kauffman, & Cullinan, 1990). Moreover, children and youth with behavioral disorders are likely to reject their peers (Sabornie, 1987). On the other hand, studies examining the social acceptance of students with learning disabilities have yielded mixed results. According to some authorities, children with learning disabilities form fewer friendships (Bursuck, 1989) and experience more social rejection or neglect (Stone & La Greca, 1990) than do their same-aged peers. Other researchers, however, argue that some students with learning disabilities may form appropriate peer relationships, particularly in regular classroom settings (for example, Madge, Affleck,

Table 14.1 Essential Social Skills as Identified by Regular Classroom Teachers

Teachers identify many social skills as critical for success in the regular classroom. The following list does not imply a particular hierarchy of skills; however, it does illustrate those skills considered by regular educators to be important in their classrooms.

Coping Skills

1. Is able to express anger without physical aggression or yelling.
2. Copes appropriately if someone insults him or her.
3. Copes in an acceptable way if someone takes something that belongs to him or her.
4. Copes in an acceptable way when someone gives orders or bosses him or her around.
5. Avoids an argument when another student is provoking one.
6. Can handle being lied to.
7. Copes with being blamed for something he or she did not really do.
8. Can cope appropriately if someone is upset with him or her.
9. Copes with aggression in an appropriate way (walking away, seeking assistance, or defending himself or herself).
10. Is able to cope with someone calling him or her a name.

Work Habits

1. Completes homework assignments on time.
2. Completes classwork on time.
3. Is on task most of the time.
4. Pays attention during class discussions.
5. Uses class time efficiently.
6. Listens carefully to teacher directions.
7. Listens carefully during direct instruction.
8. Follows written directions.
9. Is an independent worker.
10. Promptly follows teachers requests.

Peer Relationships

1. Knows how to join a group activity already in progress.
2. Develops and maintains individual friendships with more than one significant peer.
3. Maintains friendships over an extended period of time.
4. Interacts with a variety of children on a regular basis.
5. Shares laughter and jokes with peers.
6. Will initiate conversations with peers.
7. Initiates play activities with other children.
8. Can express feelings of affection or friendship toward peers.
9. Appears to make friends easily.
10. Regularly compliments others.

From "The Fast Track to Success: Social-Behavioral Skills" by K. S. Fred, 1990, Intervention in School and Clinic, 26(1), p. 41. Copyright © 1990 by PRO-ED, Inc. Reprinted with permission.

& Lowenbraun, 1990; Sabornie et al., 1990). When students with learning disabilities drop out of school, however, they often cite feelings of social alienation toward classmates and teachers as a factor in their decision to leave (Seidel & Vaughn, 1991).

Not all children and youth with mild disabilities will require assistance with social skills. For those students who possess age-appropriate verbal and nonverbal skills enabling them to interact successfully with others, social-skills instruction is, of course, unnecessary. However, for many youngsters, specific instruction is essential if they are to be accepted by peers and teachers, grow in their self-confidence, and succeed at school and/or on the job.

Teaching Social Skills

As we have stated, not every student with a mild disability will require instruction in social skills. Moreover, some students will require less intensive instruction and practice than others. All students who do need social-skills instruction, however, will require a systematic program. Although social-skills training programs vary in the specific skills taught, most incorporate the following teaching procedures (Morgan & Jenson, 1988; Zaragoza, Vaughn, & McIntosh, 1991):

1. Select for instruction only those skills that will maximize the child's success. That is, teach age- and situation-appropriate skills observed and validated as critical for success (Meadows, Neel, Parker, & Timo, 1991). Educators may determine skills likely to impact positively on valued social outcomes through a combination of ratings by peers and/or teachers using social-skills checklists or rating systems (e.g., *The Social Skills Rating System* developed by Gresham and Elliott, 1990, available through American Guidance Services); direct observation in natural settings or during role playing; by sociometric techniques, such as peer nomination; or interviews (Maag, 1989).

2. Provide clear statements regarding the skill to be learned and the importance of learning this skill to improve interaction with peers and teachers. For example, Ms. Lopez might tell Joey, "Today, we are going to learn how to get the teacher's attention the right way. When you get the teacher's attention the right way, your teachers will know that you want help and that you know how to ask for help politely. Getting the teacher's attention the right way means raising your hand, waiting quietly for the teacher to call on you, and asking your question using a polite tone of voice." Ms. Lopez might also ask Joey to state why this skill might be important.

3. Model the new skill for the student. Modeling may be conducted using videotapes, audiotapes, or live demonstrations by peers or teachers. To increase the probability of success, the model must be of high or expert status and of the same age/sex/race as the learner. In addition, the model must appear to receive reinforcement for engaging in the modeled skill

(Goldstein, 1981). Moreover, demonstration sequences must be clear, detailed, and well sequenced.

4. Provide numerous examples and nonexamples of the social skill. For example, Ms. Lopez might demonstrate for Joey several instances of getting the teacher's attention appropriately and inappropriately. Then, she might ask Joey to identify several additional examples as either appropriate or inappropriate "teacher-attention-getting."

5. Construct role-playing and practice opportunities in which the student can receive teacher coaching and feedback regarding the correct use of the social skill. During role playing and practice, the teacher must be specific as to the steps students perform correctly and the ways in which to correct those performed incorrectly. For example, Ms. Lopez might ask a student to play the role of a teacher and ask Joey to practice getting the teacher's attention the right way. She might tell Joey, "You did a good job of raising your hand and waiting quietly until you were called on. But you need to remember to use a polite tone of voice. Now, watch me do it." After demonstrating, Ms. Lopez might ask Joey to practice the skill with her and then repeat the role play again with his peer.

6. Provide reinforcement contingent on successful demonstration of each skill during practice and in the classroom.

Although students with mild disabilities can learn appropriate social skills through direct systematic instruction, social-skills training is not a panacea for all of the behavioral and social difficulties experienced by youngsters outside their special education classrooms (Berler, Gross, & Drabman, 1982). One criticism often leveled at social-skills programs is that students will demonstrate appropriate social skills in the controlled context of role playing within the special class, but they may not use these skills when necessary in other classrooms or settings (Schloss, Schloss, Wood, & Kiehl, 1986).

Special education teachers must plan carefully for generalization if they are to help their students learn to use newly acquired social skills appropriately in the regular classroom (Blackbourn, 1989; Stokes & Baer, 1977). The following suggestions may help teachers promote the transfer of social skills outside the special class:

1. Target skills and select role-playing examples that are relevant for individual youngsters. Elicit from students, parents, and teachers necessary social skills and examples for realistic role-playing activities. Require students to demonstrate mastery with each skill in controlled settings before teaching for transfer (Morgan & Jenson, 1988).

2. Inform parents, teachers, and other school personnel of the trained social skill. Involve parents and teachers in role-playing and practice activities whenever possible. Ask for their assistance in prompting and reinforcing the student's appropriate use of the skill outside the special education setting.

3. Encourage peer support for social skills. Peers can participate in role-playing activities and learn to initiate interactions with children with

mild disabilities so that targeted students will experience increased opportunities to practice and receive reinforcement for appropriate social skills, such as sharing, participating in play, and offering assistance in naturally occurring contexts (Strain & Odom, 1986).

4. Require students with mild disabilities to complete "homework assignments" in which they document their use of new social skills (Armstrong & McPherson, 1991). These homework assignments might take the form of logs, diaries, journals, checklists of skills used on a particular day, or self-monitoring forms. For example, Ms. Lopez might provide Joey with a self-monitoring form on which to list each instance of getting the teacher's attention the right way in Ms. Kirk's classroom (see Figure 14.1). Structured teaching sessions, combined with self-recording techniques, appear to hold promise for helping children generalize social skills to new situations and people (Sasso, Melloy, & Kavale, 1990).

Social-Skills Programs

Numerous programs are now available for teaching social skills to children and youth with mild disabilities. Carter and Sugai (1989) and Sugai and Fuller (1991) offer excellent suggestions for choosing an appropriate social-skills curriculum. For example, they suggest that teachers examine commercially available curricula to determine whether or not (a) structured teaching procedures are used, (b) the social skills included are relevant, (c) assessment procedures and social validation data are included, and (d) strategies for maintenance and generalization of skills are included. In addition, teachers must consider the cost of the materials and the time required to learn and implement the curriculum.

Several commercially available social-skills curricula meet most of the aforementioned criteria. These include *Skillstreaming* (Goldstein, Sprafkin, Gershaw, & Klein, 1980; McGinnis & Goldstein, 1984); *The Walker Social Skills Curriculum* (Walker, McConnell, Holmes, Todis, Walker, & Golden, 1983; Walker, Todis, Holmes, & Horton, 1988), and *Getting Along with Others* (Jackson, Jackson, & Monroe, 1983).

Skillstreaming.   Skillstreaming is available for the young child, the elementary school youngster, and the adolescent. At the elementary level, McGinnis and Goldstein (1984) provide teachers with a checklist with which to form structured learning groups containing children with similar social skills and needs across five skills clusters (see Table 14.2) Each social skill is broken down into small steps and then taught through modeling, role playing, and specific performance feedback. In addition, children are given homework assignments enabling them to practice newly learned social skills in context.

With adolescents, teachers are again encouraged to group youngsters by need. Goldstein et al. (1980) list six skills clusters and 50 social skills for adolescents. Modeling, role playing, performance feedback, and structured homework assignments remain as key elements of the approach (see Table

Figure 14.1   Joey's Homework Form

Name: Joey   Date: January 14, 1993

Skill: Getting the Teacher's Attention the Right Way

My homework assignment is to practice: Getting my teacher's attention the right way. Each time I get Ms. Kirk's attention the right way today, I will write down the period when it happened, what I did, and what happened next.

Getting the Teacher's Attention the Right Way means:

1. Raise my hand.
2. Wait quietly in my seat for the teacher to call on me.
3. Ask for assistance using a polite voice tone.

What Class Period?   What Did I Do?   What Happened?

How Did I Do? _____

_____

_____

_____

14.3). (The *Skillstreaming* program may be obtained from Research Press, 2612 N. Mattis Ave., Champaign, Illinois 61821.)

The Walker Social Skills Curriculum.   This curriculum is available at two levels appropriate for students with mild disabilities. *The ACCEPTS* (i.e., A Curriculum for Children's Effective Peer and Teacher Skills) *Program* (Walker et al., 1983) is designed for elementary-aged youngsters. Five skill areas are included in the program: classroom skills, basic interaction skills, getting along, making friends, and coping skills. A pretest, teaching scripts, a behavior-management system, and optional videotapes are components of the curriculum. Modeling and role playing are, again, the key instructional features of this curriculum.

The ACCESS (i.e., Adolescent Curriculum for Communication and Effec-

Table 14.2   Skillstreaming the Elementary School Child: Grouping Chart

	Student name					Student name			
I. Classroom survival skills					**III. Skills for dealing with feelings (cont.)**				
1. Listening					31. Dealing with your anger				
2. Asking for help					32. Dealing with another's anger				
3. Saying thank you					33. Expressing affection				
4. Bringing materials to class					34. Dealing with fear				
5. Following instructions					35. Rewarding yourself				
6. Completing assignments					**IV. Skill alternatives to aggression**				
7. Contributing to discussions					36. Using self-control				
8. Offering help to an adult					37. Asking permission				
9. Asking a question					38. Responding to teasing				
10. Ignoring distractions					39. Avoiding trouble				
11. Making corrections					40. Staying out of fights				
12. Deciding on something to do					41. Problem solving				
13. Setting a goal					42. Accepting consequences				
II. Friendship-making skills					43. Dealing with accusation				
14. Introducing yourself					44. Negotiating				
15. Beginning a conversation					**V. Skills for dealing with stress**				
16. Ending a conversation					45. Dealing with boredom				
17. Joining in					46. Deciding what caused a problem				
18. Playing a game					47. Making a complaint				
19. Asking a favor					48. Answering a complaint				
20. Offering help to a classmate					49. Dealing with losing				
21. Giving a compliment					50. Showing sportsmanship				
22. Accepting a compliment					51. Dealing with being left out				
23. Suggesting an activity					52. Dealing with embarrassment				
24. Sharing					53. Reacting to failure				
25. Apologizing					54. Accepting no				
III. Skills for dealing with feelings					55. Saying no				
26. Knowing your feelings					56. Relaxing				
27. Expressing your feelings					57. Dealing with group pressure				
28. Recognizing another's feelings					58. Dealing with wanting something that isn't mine				
29. Showing understanding of another's feelings					59. Making a decision				
30. Expressing concern for another					60. Being honest				

From Skillstreaming the Elementary School Child: A Guide for Teaching Prosocial Skills *(pp. 43–44) by E. McGinnis and A.P. Goldstein, 1984, Champaign IL: Research Press. Copyright 1984 by the authors. Reprinted by permission.*

tive Social Skills) *Program* (Walker et al., 1988) provides teachers with role-playing activities and structured homework assignments appropriate for middle school and high school students. Peer, adult, and self-related skills are the focus of 31 lessons in *ACCESS*. In addition, a placement test and student contracts are helpful features of the curriculum. (*The Walker Social Skills Curriculum* is available through Pro-ED, 8700 Shoal Creek Blvd., Austin, Texas 78758.)

Table 14.3   Skillstreaming for the Adolescent

Group I. Beginning social skills
1. Listening _____
2. Starting a conversation _____
3. Having a conversation _____
4. Asking a question _____
5. Saying thank you _____
6. Introducing yourself _____
7. Introducing other people _____
8. Giving a compliment _____

Group II. Advanced social skills
9. Asking for help _____
10. Joining in _____
11. Giving instructions _____
12. Following instructions _____
13. Apologizing _____
14. Convincing others _____

Group III. Skills for dealing with feelings
15. Knowing your feelings _____
16. Expressing your feelings _____
17. Understanding the feelings of others _____
18. Dealing with someone else's anger _____
19. Expressing affection _____
20. Dealing with fear _____
21. Rewarding yourself _____

Group IV. Skill alternatives to aggression
22. Asking permission _____
23. Sharing something _____
24. Helping others _____
25. Negotiation _____
26. Using self-control _____
27. Standing up for your rights _____
28. Responding to teasing _____
29. Avoiding trouble with others _____
30. Keeping out of fights _____

Group V. Skills for dealing with stress
31. Making a complaint _____
32. Answering a complaint _____
33. Sportsmanship after the game _____
34. Dealing with embarrassment _____
35. Dealing with being left out _____
36. Standing up for a friend _____
37. Responding to persuasion _____
38. Responding to failure _____
39. Dealing with contradictory messages _____
40. Dealing with an accusation _____
41. Getting ready for a difficult conversation _____
42. Dealing with group pressure _____

Group VI. Planning skills
43. Deciding on something _____
44. Deciding what caused a problem _____
45. Setting a goal _____
46. Deciding on your abilities _____
47. Gathering information _____
48. Arranging problems by importance _____
49. Making a decision _____
29. Avoiding trouble with others _____
50. Concentrating on a task _____

From Skillstreaming the Elementary School Child: A Guide for Teaching Prosocial Skills *(pp. 73–74) by A.P. Goldstein, R.P. Sprafkin, N.J. Gershaw, and P. Klein, 1980. Champaign, IL: Research Press. Copyright 1980 by the authors. Reprinted by permission.*

Getting Along with Others. Although originally intended for elementary school children, Getting Along with Others is adaptable for students with mild disabilities at the middle school level. Scripted social-skills lessons, role-playing activities, relaxation exercises, and homework assignments are components of the program. The curriculum also provides teachers with excellent strategies, or "teaching interactions," for teaching social skills continuously within the classroom once students learn the steps for a specific social skill (Jackson et al., 1983). These interactions can easily be used along with any structured curriculum for teaching social skills.

    The first teaching interaction, called "effective praise," serves two purposes: to inform students about appropriate behaviors that should be repeated and to reward them for correct behavior. Effective praise begins with an expression of affection (e.g., smiling or saying the child's name) and ends with a specific statement of praise telling the student exactly what he or she did correctly. For example, Ms. Lopez might praise Joey for getting the teacher's attention appropriately by saying, "Joey" (an expression of affection), "that was a good job of getting my attention the right way. You raised your hand, waited quietly for me to call on you, and used a polite tone of voice" (specific praise). "You may certainly be line leader today."

The second strategy, called the "teaching interaction," is used to interrupt a student's inappropriate behavior and to prompt the student to practice the appropriate social skill (Jackson et al., 1983). The teaching interaction begins with an expression of affection in order to start the instructional episode on a positive note. Often, this expression of affection is either a statement of empathy or one of initial praise for something the student has done properly. This is followed by a description of the inappropriate behavior and then an explanation of the appropriate social behavior. Finally, the student is requested to practice the social skill and is given general praise for doing so.

The goal of this second strategy is to take positive action in order to teach the child the appropriate behavior when it is actually needed in a specific situation. In the previous example, if Joey were to leave his seat and start toward the classroom door, Ms. Lopez might interrupt his inappropriate behavior by stating, "Joey, I understand that you want to be line leader for lunch today" (an expression of affection and empathy), "but you just forgot to get my attention the right way" (a description of the inappropriate behavior). "What you need to do is stay in your seat, raise your hand and wait for me to call on you" (a description of the appropriate behavior). "Please go back to your seat, raise your hand, and wait quietly for me to call on you" (a request for practice of the appropriate social skill). When Joey returns to his seat, Ms. Lopez will give him general praise by stating, "Thank you, Joey. That was a good job of getting my attention the right way!"

Whenever a teacher enters a teaching interaction with a student and the student becomes argumentative, begins to display his or her temper, or begins to balk, the teacher initiates the third strategy. The "direct prompt" (Jackson et al., 1983) is a short statement telling the student exactly what he or she must do in order to behave appropriately. Here, the teacher calmly issues a "You need to . . ." statement. If the student complies, the teacher delivers effective praise. However, if the student continues to display inappropriate behavior, the teacher issues an "If . . . then . . ." statement and follows through with the consequence for noncompliance if necessary. The consequences for noncompliance must, of course, be preestablished and clearly explained to students before they are used.

Ms. Lopez, in the previous example, might enter a teaching interaction with Joey by stating, "Joey, I understand that you want to be line leader for lunch today, but you just forgot to get my attention the right way." Joey, however, continues to march toward the door mumbling, "It's my turn for line leader. You never let me be line leader and it's my turn!" At this point, Ms. Lopez issues a direct prompt saying, "You need to return to your seat, raise your hand, and wait for me to call on you to be line leader." If Joey complies, Ms. Lopez might deliver effective praise along with a point loss and gain: "Joey, that was excellent. You followed my instructions by returning to your seat and waiting for me to call on you. You lost 100 points for forgetting to get

my attention appropriately, but you've earned 75 points for following my instructions." If Joey were to fail to comply following the direct prompt,
however, Ms. Lopez might state, "Joey, if you do not return to your seat and
get my attention appropriately, then you will choose to lose 100 points." Ms.
Lopez must, of course, follow through with the point loss for continued noncompliance. (The teaching interactions are described in *Getting Along with
Others,* available through Research Press, 2612 N. Mattis Ave., Champaign,
Illinois 61821.)

A Summary of Social-Skills Instruction

Special education teachers must provide social-skills instruction for many of
their students. Although such instruction is not necessary for every child,
several fine social-skills curricula do exist for those youngsters requiring practice in this area. Teachers must take care to choose curricula using direct,
systematic teaching procedures, such as modeling, role playing, and specific
feedback. In addition, planned activities to promote the generalization of social skills are essential for the successful performance of these behaviors in
natural settings.

✎ Independent Living Skills

Recall, at the beginning of this chapter, Mr. Abel's concern for Susan's ability
to live independently as an adult. Like Susan, many students in special education programs do not have the basic daily living and vocational skills necessary for adult functioning. As a matter of fact, some authorities suggest that
children like Susan who are currently in programs for students with mild mental retardation have more serious deficits than those identified a decade ago
(Patton et al., 1990). These students require intensive instruction in functional
daily living, vocational, and social skills.

Recent reports to Congress (U.S. Department of Education, 1991) indicate
that 26.6% of students with disabilities over the age of 14 drop out of school.
Another 17.3% exit with "unknown" status. That is, these students stop attending school but are not known to have enrolled in a new school district.
Only 43.9% of all students in special education programs complete high
school, graduating with an actual diploma.

Other reports suggest that when students with disabilities leave school,
either with or without a high school diploma, they remain unemployed or work
at part-time jobs or at jobs that offer little opportunity for advancement more
often than their peers (Edgar, 1987; Wagner, 1989). Data in a massive longitudinal study of 8,000 youngsters aged 13 to 23 who were enrolled in special
education programs in the 1985–86 school year, for example, indicate that
only 29% of these former students were employed full-time 1 year after exiting
school (Wagner, 1989). Moreover, only 17% were working part-time, and
fewer than 15% were participating in any type of postsecondary education or
training. According to Edgar (1987), among special education graduates only
18% were earning at least minimum wage. Clearly, teachers must plan ways to

help their students with mild disabilities stay in school and learn those skills essential for adulthood.

In 1984, as a result of such dismal statistics as those just mentioned, transitioning became a national priority (Will, 1984). In 1990, with the reauthorization of PL 94-142—the Individuals with Disabilities Education Act, or PL 101-476—transitioning became a national mandate (U.S. Congress, 1990). According to PL 101-476, transitioning refers to coordinated and outcome-oriented activities that promote movement from school to postsecondary education or vocational training, to employment, to adult service agencies, to independent living, or to community participation. School districts are now adopting models for teaching critical life skills to youngsters while they are still in special education programs and are involving other appropriate service agencies in planning for the postsecondary needs of these youth before they actually leave school.

Individualized Transition Plans

One requirement of the Individuals with Disabilities Education Act is a statement of needed transition services for students in special education programs no later than age 16, and before the age of 14, whenever appropriate. This Individual Transition Plan (ITP) becomes a part of the student's IEP and describes interagency linkages and responsibilities if necessary. For example, the ITP promotes collaboration between special educators and state vocational rehabilitation counselors. Establishing early links to adult service agencies may be critical if students with mild disabilities are to make use of these agencies upon leaving school (Smith, 1992).

Whereas the IEP details educational or social goals, objectives, and services, the ITP must describe essential skills and services the student will require when he or she is no longer in school. Therefore, the ITP should include goals and objectives designed to help students succeed on the job, at home, or in the community. Using leisure time wisely, managing money, getting along with co-workers, traveling about the community, and home maintenance are representative skills that might be included on the ITP. Moreover, involvement of appropriate adult service agencies to document responsibilities for job training, placement, and follow-up services is a vital part of the ITP process. (See Figure 14.2 for a sample ITP designed for Susan.)

Appropriate goals and objectives for the ITP planning process may be developed through both formal and informal assessments. For example, special education teachers can gather much career-relevant information from the cumulative files (e.g., attendance data, health status, parental occupations) and from the confidential files (e.g., educational performance levels, family responsibilities and leisure-time interests) that are kept for each child in a special program. In addition, adaptive behavior scales such as those described in Chapter 6 offer teachers valuable information about social and independent living skills requiring instruction. Moreover, teachers can use criterion-referenced measures such as the *Brigance Diagnostic Inventory of Essential Skills, Red Level,* available from Curriculum Associates, to assess important life skills, such as completing checks, filling out job applications, or perform-

Figure 14.2   Representative Goals from Susan's Individualized
Transition Plan

Name: *SUSAN*   Date: *SEPTEMBER 2, 1993*
Current age: *13*   Expected date of graduation: *6/2000*

Transition service areas	Person responsible	Date begun
Occupational preparation goals:		
To obtain part-time work experience in food services (unpaid).	Cafeteria staff in the Middle School with assistance from Mr. Abel.	
Daily living goals:		
To demonstrate good habits of personal hygiene.	Mr. Abel Home Economics teacher P.E. teacher	
Personal living goals:		
To work independently.	Mr. Abel Mrs. Friend	
Recreation/leisure goals:		
To participate in Saturday outdoor recreation program sponsored by Apple County.	Mrs. Friend Apple County Recreation Department	

Signed:

Name	Title	Date
MR ABEL	TEACHER	9-2-93
Martha Moyler	Mother	9/2/93
Susan Moyler		9/2/93
Sandra Friend	Counselor	9-2-93

ing successfully during a job interview (Brigance, 1980). Other measures can help students to determine potential career interests (e.g., the *Reading Free Vocational Interest Inventory,* Becker, 1987). Finally, teachers may wish to conduct an "ecological inventory." That is, critical skills needed to function independently in the local community can be determined through systematic observation. Once these skills are identified, task analyses may be conducted and the resulting lists used to pinpoint instructional needs for individual students like Susan.

Independent-Living-Skills Instruction

Teachers must prepare their students to function independently as adults. This preparation must include more than just attaining a particular vocational or occupational skill. As Brolin (1986) suggests, career education must emphasize all roles and responsibilities of adulthood, both paid and unpaid work responsibilities and family, civic, and leisure-time roles. Furthermore, career education must begin early in special education programs, preferably during the primary grades, if youngsters are to gain the necessary skills, habits, and experiences they will need later in life. When teachers wait until students enter middle school or become eligible for high school vocational or technical programs to begin career education, many opportunities for discovering work interests and for establishing work-oriented values and attitudes are lost.

Often, special education programs are oriented toward academic achievement alone, despite the student's need for a more functional curriculum. Teachers can and should make academic-skills instruction relevant and meaningful for students by providing a career orientation to subject-area instruction. For example, Mr. Abel might help Susan relate measurement skills in mathematics to following cooking recipes or making patterns for sewing in her home economics class. He might also extend Susan's learning activities to include exploration of potential occupations that would require the use of measurement skills.

To integrate or infuse career education skills into subject-area instruction in school is an effective way of helping students learn independent living skills. Systematic planning is critical, however, if all essential skills are to be mastered.

In addition, teachers must involve students with special needs in *community-based instruction*. Community-based instruction requires teachers to identify relevant independent living skills in the local community and then teach these skills in the community setting. For example, Mr. Abel might determine that Susan needs instruction in making purchases and counting her change. In addition to instruction and practice in the classroom and school environments, such as the school store or cafeteria, Mr. Abel might arrange for opportunities to accompany Susan to local stores to give her supervised practice in making purchases and counting change in her community.

For those students requiring extended assistance in obtaining a job in the community, schools sometimes employ a job coach. That is, a professional might train Susan on the job, guaranteeing to her employer that the job will be performed satisfactorially during the training period. As Susan performs her job with increasing competence, her coach slowly fades from the job site while making systematic follow-up contacts to see that Susan's performance remains up to par.

Several career-education models also exist to help teachers provide students with the necessary skills for a successful transition to adult life.

These include the Adult Performance Level Curriculum, Life-Centered Career Education, and School-Based Career Development and Transition Education.

The Adult Performance Level Curriculum. The Adult Performance Level Curriculum (Adult Performance Level Project, 1975) is designed to teach low-performing students the competencies and skills needed for survival in common situations. Within the curriculum, basic reading, writing, listening/speaking, computation, problem solving, and interpersonal skills are applied to such content areas as consumer economics, health, occupational knowledge, community resources, and government/law. A total of 42 life skills make up the APL curriculum (see Figure 14.3).

Figure 14.3   Adult Performance Level Curriculum: Life Skills

From "Applying Curriculum for the Instruction of Life Skills," by M. E. Cronin. In G. A. Robinson, J. R. Patton, E. A. Polloway, and L. R. Sargent (Eds.), Best Practices in Mental Disabilities: Volume Two, *1988, p. 47. Copyright © 1988 by the Iowa Department of Education Bureau of Special Education, Des Moines, Iowa 50319.*

I. *Consumer Economics*
1. Counting and Converting
2. Consumer Fraud
3. Money Management
4. Income Tax
5. Care/Upkeep of Personal Possessions
6. Comparison Shopping
7. Catalog Ordering
8. Advertising Techniques
9. Ordering Food
10. Housing/Utilities
11. Car Buying/Maintenance
12. Insurance
13. Using Credit
14. World Resource
15. Banking Services
16. Measuring and Metrics

II. *Community Resources*
17. Public Assistance Program
18. Recreation
19. Information and Aid
20. Mass Media/Public Opinion
21. Driving
22. Transportation

III. *Health*
23. Safety Measures/Emergencies and First Aid
24. Preventive Care and Health Maintenance
25. Drug Control/Drug Abuse
26. The Adolescent
27. Self
28. Marriage and the Family
29. Parenting and Family Planning
30. Pregnancy and Childbirth
31. Child Rearing
32. Nutrition/Food Preparation

IV. *Occupational Knowledge*
33. Job Selection and Satisfaction
34. Sources of Employment
35. Job Applications and Interviews
36. Employment Agencies
37. Effective Job Behavior
38. Financial and Legal Aspects of Employment

V. *Government and Law*
39. Government Structure and Function
40. Citizen Rights and Duties
41. Criminal and Civil Law
42. Legal Documents

Concrete activities and tasks for attaining life skills at the elementary level include, for example, applying writing skills to the content area of community resources by filling out an application to play on a little league team. Similarly, at the middle school or junior high school level, youngsters apply interpersonal skills in the area of consumer economics by asking a salesperson for help when making a particular purchase. Appropriate high school tasks include using reading skills in the area of health to interpret directions on a bottle of cough syrup. (See Figure 14.4 for additional functional tasks across the grade levels.) The authors of this curriculum encourage school personnel to adapt the program to respond to technological advances and to current needs and resources of the local community.

Life-Centered Career Education. Life-Centered Career Education (LCCE) (Brolin, 1986) is a competency-based model that has been adopted by numerous school districts across the United States. It has also received the support of the Council for Exceptional Children. Brolin views career education as a lifelong process, culminating in successful functioning in school, family, and community roles. He identifies 22 competencies and almost 100 subcompetencies across three major domains: daily living skills, personal/social skills, and occupational guidance and preparation. Competencies and subcompetencies are infused into the regular curriculum, whenever possible, as well as into practice activities at home and in the community. Two LCCE activity books, available from the Council for Exceptional Children, provide numerous suggestions for instructing students at both the elementary and secondary levels. (See Figure 14.5 on pp. 390–91 for a list of competencies within the LCCE curriculum.)

Berkell and Brown (1989) have expanded the notion of life-centered career education to encompass transitioning requirements. Their LCCE Transitioning Model, illustrated in Figure 14.6 (on p. 392), spans kindergarten through adulthood and focuses on the attainment of Brolin's (1986) competencies and subcompetencies. The authors suggest that successful career education and transition planning must be based on 12 propositions, as follows:

1. Early experiences are essential if students with disabilities are to develop a "work personality" (i.e., one's unique collection of abilities, needs, habits, and values with respect to work).

2. A career encompasses unpaid work and other productive pursuits at home and in the community.

3. Career development occurs across four stages from career awareness to career exploration to career preparation to career placement, follow-up, and continuing education.

4. In addition to daily living, personal/social, and occupational skills, such fundamental academic skills as reading, writing, and computing are essential for a successful, independent adulthood.

5. Career education should be infused into subject-area instruction rather than taught as separate courses or curricula.

6. Successful career development and transitioning depends on interrelated efforts of schools, parents, businesses, and community agencies rather than on school instruction alone.

7. Hands-on, real-life experiences are critical for instruction in the LCCE curriculum.

8. Mainstreaming and community integration are vital aspects of career development and transitioning.

9. Cooperative-learning methods can help students with disabilities achieve social and interpersonal skills necessary for successful participation in the classroom and in the community.

10. Both formal and informal career and vocational assessment play an important role in successful career development and transition planning.

Figure 14.4   The Adult Performance Level Curriculum: Examples of Tasks at Different Grade Levels

From "Applying Curriculum for the Instruction of Life Skills," by M.E. Cronin. In G.A. Robinson, J.R. Patton, E.A. Polloway, and L.R. Sargent (eds.) Best Practices in Mental Disabilities: Volume Two, *1988, pp. 44–46. Copyright © 1988 by the Iowa Department of Education Bureau of Special Education, Des Moines, Iowa 50319.*

ELEMENTARY SCHOOL

	CONSUMER ECONOMICS	OCCUPATIONAL KNOWLEDGE	HEALTH	COMMUNITY RESOURCES	GOVERNMENT AND LAW
READING	Look for ads in the newspaper for toys	Read books from library on various occupations	Read the school lunch menu	Find television listing in the TV Guide	Read road signs and understand what they mean
WRITING	Write prices of items to be purchased	Write the specific tasks involved in performing one of the classroom jobs	Keep a diary of food you eat in each food group each day	Complete an application to play on a little league	Write a letter to the mayor inviting him/her to visit your school
SPEAKING, LISTENING, VIEWING	Listen to bank official talk about savings accounts	Call newspaper in town to inquire about delivering papers in your neighborhood	View a film on brushing teeth	Practice the use of 911 emergency number	Discuss park playground improvements with the mayor
PROBLEM-SOLVING	Decide if you have enough coins to make a purchase from a vending machine	Decide which job in the classroom you do best	Role play what one should do if you have a stomach ache	Role play the times you would use a 911 emergency number	Find the city hall on the map. Decide whether you will walk or drive
INTER-PERSONAL RELATIONS	Ask for help finding items in a grocery store	Ask a student in the class to assist you with a classroom job	Ask the school nurse how to take care of mosquito bites	Call the movie theater and ask the performance times of a movie	Role play asking a policeman for help if lost
COMPUTA-TION	Compute the cost of a box of cereal using a coupon	Calculate how much you would make on a paper route at $3 per hour for 5 hours per week	Compute the price of one tube of toothpaste if they are on sale-3 for 1	Compute the complete cost of going to the movie (adm., food, transportation)	Compute tax on a candy bar

(continued)

Figure 14.4 (Continued)

JUNIOR HIGH SCHOOL

	CONSUMER ECONOMICS	OCCUPATIONAL KNOWLEDGE	HEALTH	COMMUNITY RESOURCES	GOVERNMENT AND LAW
READING	Read an ad for a sale locating name of store, location, phone #, and price of item	Read a job description	Locate poison-control numbers in phone book	Use phone book to locate recreational program in community	Locate and read list of state and U.S. congressman
WRITING	Fill out a magazine order form completely	Practice writing abbreviations for words	Write a menu for a balanced diet	Write a letter to TV station about a program they just cancelled	Fill out voters registration form
SPEAKING, LISTENING, VIEWING	Discuss saving versus spending money	Discuss reasons why we work	Listen to positive and negative feed-back on personal appearance	Call library to find out if they have a certain book	Discuss why we need to vote
PROBLEM SOLVING	Given $10 for the evening, choose an activity: movies bowling, or pizza	Decide on job environment. . . inside, outside, desk, travel, etc.	Role play appropriate be-havior for various places (movies, church, restaurant)	Locate the skating rink on a city map and decide the best way to get there	Decide what items have state and/or local tax
INTER-PERSONAL RELATIONS	Ask sales person for help in purchasing jeans	List questions to ask in job interview	Discuss honesty, trust, and promise. Define each	Call skating rink to inquire about hours	Call to find out what precinct you live in
COMPUTA-TION	Compute the sales tax on a pair jeans	Compute net income	Calculate and compare the prices of hair washing products	Calculate bus fare to and from the teen center	Calculate the cost of getting a driver's license (fee, gas)

SENIOR HIGH SCHOOL

	CONSUMER ECONOMICS	OCCUPATIONAL KNOWLEDGE	HEALTH	COMMUNITY RESOURCES	GOVERNMENT AND LAW
READING	Read and compare prices of grocery store ads	Read a job description and qualifications	Read directions on cough-syrup bottle	Read a movie schedule	Obtain and read a sales tax sheet for your county/state
WRITING	Write a check for amount of purchase	Complete a job application	Write a grocery list for the week, including all the food groups	List government and community employment agencies from phone book	Apply for a work permit
SPEAKING, LISTENING, VIEWING	Explain the difference between charge, check, and cash purchases	Role play calling your boss when ill	Practice calling a doctor's office for an appointment	Listen to a state patrolman talk about highway driving	Decsribe an accident
PROBLEM-SOLVING	Decide what amount you can afford to rent an apartment	Decide what to wear to a job interview	Decide whether you should go to community clinic or hospital for an injury	Role play what you would do if your car broke down	Decide which candidate to vote for
INTER-PERSONAL RELATIONS	Ask salesperson if they have a layaway and the costs involved	Role play a mock interview	Ask pharmacist about a prescription	Ask directions to a video store	Call legal aid and ask what services are available
COMPUTA-TION	Calculate and compare savings on items from different stores	Calculate paycheck deductions	Decide how many times a day to take a pill	Compute cost of doing laundry in a laundromat vs. home	Calculate the cost of a speeding ticket

Figure 14.5 Life-Centered Career Education: Competencies and Subcompetencies

From Life-Centered Career Education: A Competency-Based Approach, *by D.E. Brolin. Copyright © 1986 by The Council for Exceptional Children. Reprinted with permission.*

CURRICULUM AREA	COMPETENCY	SUBCOMPETENCIES		
Daily living skills	1. Managing family finances	1. Identify money and make change	2. Make wise expenditures	
	2. Selecting, managing and maintaining a home	6. Select adequate housing	7. Maintain a home	
	3. Caring for personal needs	10. Dress appropriately	11. Exhibit proper grooming and hygiene	
	4. Raising children, enriching family living	14. Prepare for adjustment to marriage	15. Prepare for raising children (physical care)	
	5. Buying and preparing food	18. Demonstrate appropriate eating skills	19. Plan balanced meals	
	6. Buying and caring for clothing	24. Wash clothing	25. Iron and store clothing	
	7. Engaging in civic activities	28. Generally understand local laws and government	29. Generally understand Federal Government	
	8. Utilizing recreation and leisure	34. Participate actively in group activities	35. Know activities and available community resources	
	9. Getting around the community (mobility)	40. Demonstrate knowledge of traffic rules and safety practices	41. Demonstrate knowledge and use of various means of transportation	
Personal-social skills	10. Achieving self awareness	43. Attain a sense of body	44. Identify interests and abilities	
	11. Acquiring self confidence	48. Express feelings of worth	49. Tell how others see him/her	
	12. Achieving socially responsible behavior	53. Know character traits needed for acceptance	54. Know proper behavior in public places	
	13. Maintaining good interpersonal skills	58. Know how to listen and respond	59. Know how to make and maintain friendships	
	14. Achieving independence	62. Understand impact of behavior upon others	63. Understand self organization	
	15. Achieving problem solving skills	66. Differentiate bipolar concepts	67. Understand the need for goals	
	16. Communicating adequately with others	71. Recognize emergency situations	72. Read at level needed for future goals	
Occupational guidance and preparation	17. Knowing and exploring occupational possibilities	76. Identify the personal values met through work	77. Identify the societal values met through work	
	18. Selecting and planning occupational choices	82. Identify major occupational needs	83. Identify major occupational interests	
	19. Exhibiting appropriate work habits and behaviors	87. Follow directions	88. Work with others	
	20. Exhibiting sufficient physical-manual skills	94. Demonstrate satisfactory balance and coordination	95. Demonstrate satisfactory manual dexterity	
	21. Obtaining a specific occupational skill			
	22. Seeking, securing, and maintaining employment	98. Search for a job	99. Apply for a job	

(continued)

Figure 14.5 *(Continued)*

3. Obtain and use bank and credit facilities	4. Keep basic financial records	5. Calculate and pay taxes		
8. Use basic appliances and tools	9. Maintain home exterior			
12. Demonstrate knowledge of physical fitness, nutrition, and weight control	13. Demonstrate knowledge of common illness prevention and treatment			
16. Prepare for raising children (psychological care)	17. Practice family safety in the home			
20. Purchase food	21. Prepare meals	22. Clean food preparation areas	23. Store food	
26. Perform simple mending	27. Purchase clothing			
30. Understand citizenship rights and responsibilities	31. Understand registration and voting procedures	32. Understand Selective Service procedures	33. Understand civil rights and responsibilities when questioned by the law	
36. Understand recreational values	37. Use recreational facilities in the community	38. Plan and choose activities wisely	39. Plan vacations	
42. Drive a car				
45. Identify emotions	46. Identify needs	47. Understand the physical self		
50. Accept praise	51. Accept criticism	52. Develop confidence in self		
55. Develop respect for the rights and properties of others	56. Recognize authority and follow instructions	57. Recognize personal roles		
60. Establish appropriate heterosexual relationships	61. Know how to establish close relationships			
64. Develop goal seeking behavior	65. Strive toward self actualization			
68. Look at alternatives	69. Anticipate consequences	70. Know where to find good advice		
73. Write at the level needed for future goals	74. Speak adequately for understanding	75. Understand the subtleties of communication		
78. Identify the remunerative aspects of work	79. Understand classification of jobs into different occupational systems	80. Identify occupational opportunities available locally	81. Identify sources of occupational information	
84. Identify occupational aptitudes	85. Identify requirements of appropriate and available jobs	86. Make realistic occupational choices		
89. Work at a satisfactory rate	90. Accept supervision	91. Recognize the importance of attendance and punctuality	92. Meet demands for quality work	93. Demonstrate occupational safety
96. Demonstrate satisfactory stamina and endurance	97. Demonstrate satisfactory sensory discrimination			
100. Interview for a job	101. Adjust to competitive standards	102. Maintain postschool occupational adjustment		

Figure 14.6   The LCCE Transitioning Model

From Transition from School to Work for Persons with Disabilities, *edited by Dianne E. Berkell and James M. Brown. Copyright © 1989 by Longman Publishing Group.*

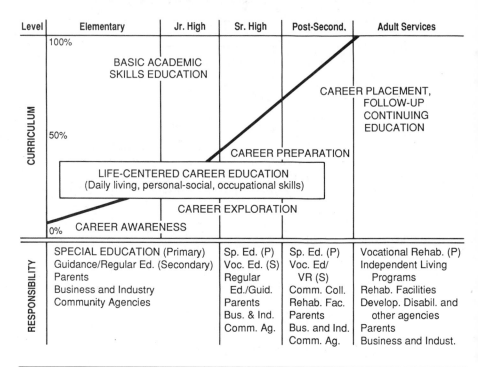

11. Local transition teams, including special and vocational educators and vocational rehabilitation counselors, must monitor and carry out career and transition programs.

12. Interagency agreements and cross-agency inservices are necessary to ensure that all appropriate personnel will be involved in career education and transitioning.

Stowitschek and Salzberg (1987) also provide special education teachers with ways to integrate the teaching of social skills with the LCCE competencies. In their social-protocol curriculum, available through the Council for Exceptional Children, 22 behaviors that are essential for success in a work environment are identified and scripted for instruction in both work-at-school and competitive-employment examples.

In all, 23 of Brolin's (1986) competencies and subcompetencies are directly addressed through this supportive social-protocol curriculum (Stowitschek & Salzberg, 1987). For example, Brolin lists accepting criticism as an important subcompetency within the domain of personal/social skills. In the social-protocol curriculum, students might be taught in a work-at-school situation to respond appropriately to criticism from teachers regarding such tasks as washing the blackboard. At work, they might be taught how to respond to criticism from supervisors concerning job-related tasks or responsibilities. Later, accepting criticism could be applied to specific occupational examples, from fast-food worker to motel maid.

School-Based Career Development and Transition Education.   This career-education model (Clark & Kolstoe, 1990) also infuses career-education concepts and skills into the special and/or regular curriculum (see Figure 14.7). Beginning in the preschool years and continuing throughout adulthood, the following areas are given special emphasis:

1. values, attitudes, and habits essential for work;

2. human relationships on the job, in the family, and in the community;

3. occupational information, including various occupational roles, occupational vocabulary, occupational alternatives, and basic realities about the world of work; and

4. job-acquisition and daily living skills appropriate for current and future needs.

A Summary of Independent-Living-Skills Instruction

Currently, most effective programs for career education, transition planning, or instruction in independent living skills have several features in common. They emphasize collaboration among professionals, coordination of services, and early planning as essential elements. In addition, effective programs infuse instruction across the curriculum and include instruction in community settings.

Like social-skills instruction, however, career education and transition planning are not panaceas for all students with disabilities. As Halpern (1992) cautions, we still have a long way to go to improve what we teach, how we teach, and where we teach students with disabilities. Frequently, career education and instruction in independent living skills are offered only within the confines of the classroom. Unfortunately, too, transition planning for some school districts means little more than choosing a career goal to write on a student's IEP. Such approaches are not likely to result in important and lasting benefits for youngsters in special education programs.

✎ Summary

Like Joey and Susan, many students in special education programs require social-skills instruction if they are to engage in successful interpersonal relationships with peers and teachers. Direct, systematic instructional techniques, using modeling, role playing, and specific feedback, are the most effective methods for teaching social skills. Teachers may choose from among several social-skills programs based on these methods. In addition, special educators must plan for the generalization of social skills to natural settings by using

Figure 14.7   School-Based Career Development and Transition Education

From Gary M. Clark and Oliver P. Kolstoe, Career Development and Transition Education for Adolescents with Disabilities. *Copyright © 1990 by Allyn & Bacon. Reprinted by permission.*

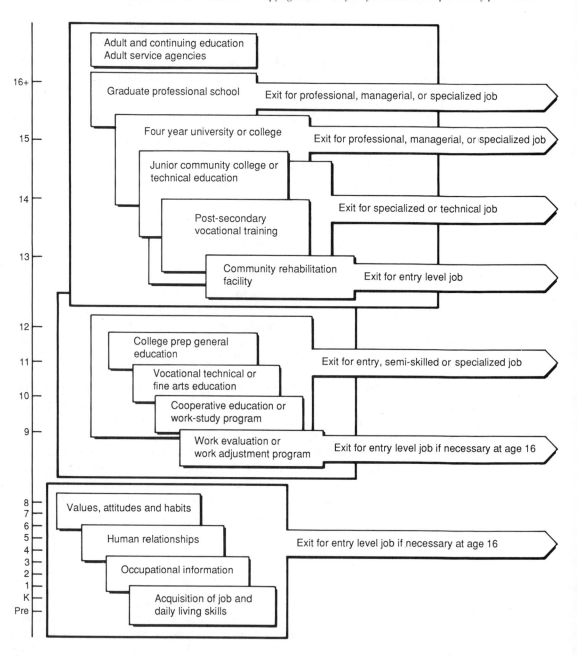

realistic role-playing scenarios and by giving students self-monitoring sheets or other relevant homework assignments.

Transition planning and instruction in independent living skills are two related areas requiring attention by special educators. If students in special programs are to learn those life skills necessary for successful performance on the job, in the home, and in the community, career education must begin during the preschool years. Moreover, appropriate personnel from adult service agencies must become a part of the IEP/ITP process while students are still in school in order to plan and coordinate appropriate goals, objectives, and services for these youngsters.

✎ Application Exercises

1. Examine the social-skills curriculum used by your local school district. Does this curriculum include the techniques of modeling, role playing, providing specific feedback, and planning for the transfer of skills learned?

2. Ms. Kirk gives Joey 10 math problems and asks him to complete them in the next 15 minutes before lunch. Assume Joey begins the assignment immediately. If you were Ms. Kirk, how would you give Joey effective praise? Now assume that Joey does not follow your instructions right away. How would you phrase a teaching interaction with Joey? (Hint: You will first need to define following your instructions!) Suppose Joey becomes argumentative during your teaching interaction. How would you issue a direct prompt?

3. Examine an ITP for a student in a local school district. What are the stated goals, objectives, and services? Be sure to obtain permission to examine the document and to protect the confidentiality of the information.

4. Assume you are Mr. Abel participating in the IEP/ITP process on behalf of Robert. What would you suggest as appropriate independent living goals and objectives for Robert? What adult services might Robert need after he leaves school?

Appendix A

✎ Psychoeducational Assessment for Travis

Name: Travis Johnson

School: Oak Hill Elementary

Date of Birth: 3-20-84

Date(s) of Evaluation: 11-14-92, 11-17-92

Chronological Age: 8-8

Current Grade Placement: 3.3

Examiners: Deborah Detail, School Psychologist; George Skillfull, Educational Diagnostician; Susan Lopez, Special Education Resource Teacher

Tests Administered: *Wechsler Intelligence Scale for Children-III; Woodcock–Johnson Revised Tests of Achievement, Standard Battery; Woodcock Reading Mastery Tests—Revised; KeyMath—Revised*

Other Evaluative Information: Student work samples, classroom behavioral observations, teacher and parent interviews

Background Information and Referral

Travis was referred for psychoeducational assessment by his third-grade teacher after several weeks of intervention strategies had been employed. According to his teacher, Travis is a bright youngster, but he has a difficult time in all areas of language arts and basic math skills. Travis's teacher feels that he does not pay attention to much of the group instruction and seems to work better in small groups or in a one-on-one situation.

Travis lives in an environment that appears to be warm and supportive. His mother, Mrs. Johnson, is concerned that Travis does not seem to be making progress in school and that he has a more difficult time with his studies than did his two older sisters. Mrs. Johnson believes that Travis is as smart as his sisters, but that he is sometimes forgetful. She also reports that Travis does not always finish what he begins at home, such as chores, games, or homework. He typically starts something new before finishing the original task. Mrs. Johnson also reports that Travis is not as neat and organized as his sisters. She believes that education is important and states that she will do whatever it takes to help her son achieve in school.

Test Results

Wechsler Intelligence Scale for Children-III

Verbal IQ:	102
Performance IQ:	127
Full Scale IQ:	119

Woodcock–Johnson Revised Tests of Achievement: Standard Battery

Subtest	Grade Equivalent	Standard Score	Percentile Rank
Letter-word identification	1.9	83	13
Passage comprehension	2.0	87	20
Calculation	2.2	85	16
Applied problems	1.8	84	15
Dictation	1.8	84	15
Writing samples	1.5	67	1
Science	3.1	98	43
Social studies	3.7	104	61
Humanities	3.2	100	50

Standard Battery Clusters	Grade Equivalent	Standard Score	Percentile Rank
Broad reading		85	15
Broad mathematics		82	12
Broad written language		77	12
Broad knowledge		100	50
Skills		80	9

Woodcock Reading Mastery Tests—Revised

Subtest	Grade Equivalent	Standard Score	Percentile Rank
Visual-auditory learning	1.8	91	26
Letter identification	2.6	88	20
Word identification	1.7	68	2
Word attack	1.2	65	1
Word comprehension	1.7	73	4
Passage comprehension	1.9	78	7
Readiness cluster	2.8	84	14
Basic skills cluster	1.5	66	1
Reading comp. cluster	1.8	73	4
TOTAL READING CLUSTER	1.6	70	2

KeyMath—Revised

Subtest	Scaled Scores	Percentile Rank
Numeration	8	25
Rational numbers	—	—
Geometry	4	2
Addition	8	25
Subtraction	9	37
Multiplication	7	16
Division	10	50
Mental computation	9	37
Measurement	5	5
Time and money	9	37
Estimation	9	37
Interpreting data	8	25
Problem solving	7	16

	Grade Equivalent	Standard Score	Percentile Rank
Basic concepts area	1.4	77	6
Operations area	2.8	93	32
Applications area	2.1	84	14
TOTAL TEST	2.2	84	14

Analysis of Test Results

According to measures of intellectual ability, Travis is currently functioning in the above-average range. The discrepancy between his Verbal and Performance IQ scores may be significant. Analysis of subtest scores reveals that Travis seems to have significant weaknesses in attention skills and short-term auditory memory. Travis has relative strengths in the areas of visual memory, nonverbal skills, and general intellectual ability according to his performance on the WISC-III. The low score obtained on the coding subtest may indicate difficulty in fine-motor skills.

Travis is currently functioning one to two grade levels below expectancy for his age in word-attack skills, word identification, and areas of comprehension according to his performance on the Woodcock Reading Mastery Tests—Revised and subtests of the Woodcock–Johnson Revised Tests of Achievement.

Travis's performance on the KeyMath indicates that he has the basic understanding of math concepts necessary to perform everyday math, as measured by skills on the Time and Money, Measurement, and Estimation subtests. He also has a basic understanding of elementary geometry. He exhibits weaknesses on the Operations subtests on items that require regrouping, algorithms, and multiple-step operations. In addition, he has difficulty retaining the data provided in order to answer some of the orally presented items of the Problem Solving and Interpreting Data subtests.

Summary and Recommendations

Although Travis is currently functioning within the above-average range of intellectual ability, he continues to struggle with grade-level school work. Travis seems to have academic weaknesses in the areas of reading, handwriting, and mathematics. His reading and math achievement may be influenced by significant deficits in attention and auditory memory. Classroom observations reveal that Travis finds it hard to pay attention and to follow directions.

Travis also has problems with the fine-motor skills necessary for handwriting. Student work samples display evidence of this difficulty. His weak organizational skills may influence his ability to complete assignments effectively.

The following recommendations are suggested to promote a successful academic experience for Travis:

1. Resource-room support is recommended for language arts and math. Travis will benefit from small-group instruction and the classroom environment of the resource room.

2. Travis will benefit from direct instruction of organizational skills and a management program that promotes self-monitoring of organizational skills. Behavior management to increase time on task in the resource room and the regular classroom should begin as soon as possible. These efforts will help to preserve Travis's healthy self-esteem.

3. Travis may need additional time and support to master handwriting skills. In the computer lab, he should receive instruction in typing and word processing. The resource-room teacher should determine when Travis is ready to begin this process and may wish to allow a majority of Travis's work to be typed once he feels comfortable with the computer.

Classroom Observation 1

Name of Student: Travis Johnson

Name of Observer: Deborah Detail

Date: 11-10-92

Time: 9:00 a.m.

Class: Language Arts

Teacher: Mrs. Smith

Grade: 3.3

Travis is seated with five other students in his reading group. Mrs. Smith calls on individual students to read short sentences of the story. Travis is unable to read when asked to do so. When Mrs. Smith verbally prompts him by providing the initial consonant sounds of the words, Travis is able to orally decode two of the five words in his sentence. He seems to be somewhat frustrated with the task and expresses relief when Mrs. Smith calls on another student to read. As the students alternate reading sentences, Travis looks around the room rather than following along in his book. He turns to the next page only after he notices that the other students have already done so. Travis quickly jumps up from his chair when Mrs. Smith announces that reading time is over for the day.

The students return to their desks and most make the transition to the handwriting activity fairly easily. Other students in the class get their handwriting tablets from beneath their desks when Mrs. Smith gives the visual cue of writing the letters for the day on the chalkboard. Travis spends more time looking beneath his desk, which has several ragged-edge papers sticking out of it. After several minutes, he is able to locate his tablet. The other students are well into copying the letters from the board as Travis labors over the first letter. He seems to be concentrating very hard. As he finishes the first letter, his pencil lead breaks and he hops up to the pencil sharpener. He churns away at the sharpener until Mrs. Smith asks him to return to his seat, assuring him that his pencil is sharp enough for the task. Travis struggles with the second letter and is not quite able to copy it satisfactorily. He erases the letter and begins again, but this effort, too, is not satisfactory. Finally, he erases too hard and tears the paper. Mrs. Smith walks over to Travis's desk and quietly calms him by placing her hand on his shoulder. She turns to a clean page in the tablet and instructs him to start again.

Classroom Observation 2

Name of Student: Travis Johnson

Name of Observer: Deborah Detail

Date: 11-11-92

Time: 1:15

Class: Math

Teacher: Mrs. Smith

Grade: 3.3

The students sit quietly as Mrs. Smith reviews the lesson from the previous day. Travis attends to Mrs. Smith initially but seems to be somewhat distracted by activities outside the window (another class is playing ball). Mrs. Smith asks a question that involves a 2-digit addition problem with regrouping. Travis raises his hand, along with several other students. Mrs. Smith calls on Travis and he responds incorrectly. Mrs. Smith reminds him that the number must be brought over to the tens column in this particular problem. Travis looks a little puzzled. Mrs. Smith begins the next problem on the chalkboard. Travis turns his head toward the window again and watches the other students outside.

Behavioral Observation

Name of Student: Travis Johnson   Teacher: Mrs. Smith

Name of Observer: Deborah   Grade: 3.3
   Detail

Date: 11-12-92

Time: 1:30

Class: Math

Behavior Observed: On task

Intervals: 30 seconds

1	2	3	4	5	6	7	8	9	10	11	12	13	14	15	16	17	18	19	20
+	+	−	−	+	−	+	−	−	+	−	−	+	−	+	+	−	+	+	−

10 / 20   50% time on task

Date: 11-13-92

Time: 9:45

Class: Language Arts

Behavior Observed: On task

Intervals: 30 seconds

1	2	3	4	5	6	7	8	9	10	11	12	13	14	15	16	17	18	19	20
+	+	+	−	−	−	+	+	+	−	+	−	+	+	+	−	−	+	+	−

12 / 20   60% time on task

Date: 11-13-92

Time: 11:00

Class: Science

Behavior Observed: On task

Intervals: 30 seconds

1		3	42	5	6	7	8	9	10	11	12	13	14	15	16	17	18	19	20
−		−	+−	+	−	+	+	+	+	+	+	+	+	−	+	−	+	−	−

13 / 20   65% time on task

Teacher Interview

Name of Student: Travis Johnson

Name of Interviewer: George Skillfull

Teacher: Mrs. Smith

Q: In what areas does Travis have difficulty?

A: Reading—especially reading new words. Mrs. Smith feels that Travis doesn't read well enough to comprehend sentences or remember details or story sequence. He also has difficulty with handwriting. Travis has been able to learn to spell and recognize a few short sight words. He hasn't yet mastered regrouping in addition or subtraction, although he does know his basic math facts 1 through 10.

Q: What are Travis's strengths?

A: Travis likes science and social studies best. He makes his highest grades in science. He likes math, but he hasn't yet mastered the organizational skills he needs to compute the more complex math problems.

Q: Describe Travis's typical behavior during a school day.

A: Travis likes school and he likes his peers. He seems to be eager to begin each day and he volunteers to answer questions from time to time, although he doesn't always answer correctly. He has a real interest in science, especially now that the class has begun to study a unit on insects. Travis brought some bugs to school in a container and he enthusiastically explained to the class how he caught each bug. When Mrs. Smith informed the class that they would next study a unit on fish, Travis volunteered that his family had an aquarium and several books on tropical fish.

Travis seems to have difficulty attending to large-group instruction. He does better in smaller groups or in one-on-one instruction. He becomes frustrated with some of his seatwork assignments, especially handwriting activities.

Mrs. Smith reports that Travis does not display any aggressive or acting-out behaviors. He is able to quietly resolve any conflicts he may have with peers and is generally well liked. Travis occasionally gets reprimanded for not following instructions or for not paying attention.

✎ Psychoeducational Assessment for Joey Greenhill

Name: Joey Greenhill

School: Oak Hill Elementary

Date of Birth: 9-4-83

Date(s) of Evaluation: 10-1-93, 10-4-93

Chronological Age: 10-1

Current Grade Placement: 4.2

Examiners: Deborah Detail, School Psychologist; George Skillfull, Educational Diagnostician; Susan Lopez, Special Education Resource Teacher

Tests Administered: *Wechsler Intelligence Scale for Children-III; Woodcock–Johnson Revised Tests of Achievement; Behavior Rating Profile: Parent, Teacher, Student*

Other Evaluative Information: Classroom behavioral observations

Background Information and Referral

Joey began receiving special education services in the first grade. The comprehensive reevaluation was completed to review his progress and to determine whether Joey is receiving appropriate services.

Joey's teachers feel that he has made some progress; however, they believe that he continues to need the support services provided through the special education resource teacher. Joey's teachers report that he needs support services in order to maximize both academic and behavioral skills.

During Joey's initial evaluation and subsequent eligibility meeting it was determined that he would benefit from placement in the regular classroom for science, social studies, health, music, art, and P.E., and that he should receive resource-room support for reading and math. Support for the development of social skills and a behavior-management strategy would also be provided in the resource room.

Ms. Kirk, Joey's regular fourth-grade teacher, reports that he continues to have difficulty controlling his acting-out behaviors. He has had some episodes of aggressive behavior, including fighting and calling names. He may also react to conflict by crying.

Test Results

Wechsler Intelligence Scale for Children-III

Verbal IQ:	102
Performance IQ:	109
Full Scale IQ:	105

Woodcock–Johnson Revised Tests of Achievement

	Grade Equivalent	Standard Score	Percentile Rank
Letter-word identification	2.3	76	5
Passage comprehension	2.4	82	12
Calculation	2.2	63	1
Applied problems	2.3	81	11
Dictation	2.6	83	13
Writing samples	2.2	82	12
Science	2.5	86	18
Social studies	2.5	85	15
Humanities	2.8	90	24
Broad reading	2.3	79	8
Broad mathematics	2.3	70	2
Broad written language	2.1	77	6
Broad knowledge	2.5	85	16

Behavior Rating Profile

	Standard Score	Percentile Rank
Student rating scale	6	9
	4	2
	4	2
Teacher rating scale	5	4
Parent rating scale	3	1

Joey's regular education teacher, Ms. Kirk, and his mother both rated the following behaviors as very typical of Joey's behavior:

- Is verbally aggressive
- Doesn't follow directions
- Doesn't follow rules

In addition, Ms. Kirk feels that he does not respect the rights of others, disrupts the classroom, and bullies other children. He says that other children don't like him. Ms. Kirk reports that Joey has no friends among his classmates. She rates him as overactive, restless, and an academic underachiever. Joey is considered to be "messy" in his personal space and he lacks organizational skills.

Joey's mother, Mrs. Greenhill, feels that he is sometimes verbally abusive to his parents and that he lies to avoid punishment. He obeys them only with reluctance. Furthermore, Mrs. Greenhill reports that Joey demands immediate gratification, is overly sensitive to teasing, makes "put-down" remarks about himself, and demands excessive parental attention. Among his peers, he is not a leader.

Joey completed the student version of the Behavior Rating Profile. His responses indicate that he is low in self-esteem. He is aware that he is argumentative and that he is not liked by others at school. He admits that he tries to avoid his chores at home and breaks rules, but he believes that his parents treat him like a baby and do not allow him enough freedom. His responses indicate that he has difficulty concentrating in class and that he is really not interested in what his teachers have to say to him.

Summary and Recommendations

Joey's mother, teacher, and Joey himself are in general agreement that Joey is neither a popular student nor a strong one academically. He responds inappropriately to everyday occurrences and does not follow rules or instructions. In addition, his self-esteem is low. Joey is currently functioning within the average range of intellectual ability according to his performance on the WISC III. His academic functioning continues to be somewhat depressed in terms of his intellectual potential. Based on these results, as well as his current educational functioning, it is recommended that he continue placement in the resource room and regular classroom with the same schedule. It is further recommended that appropriate behavior-management strategies be implemented in all school situations. Joey's parents may wish to meet with the school psychologist and guidance counselor to develop a home/school behavior-management plan.

Individual and/or group therapy with the school psychologist or guidance counselor is an additional strategy that may help Joey develop a more positive self-concept.

Parent Interview

Name of Student: Joey Greenhill

Name of Interviewer: Deborah Detail

Date: 10-3-93

Joey's mother reports that he seems to be doing somewhat better since he has been receiving help in the special class. Joey's grades continue to fluctuate, but he has not failed any subjects in about a year, and she is pleased with this progress.

Joey's mother does not feel that he has made much progress in developing appropriate social skills. She is aware that Joey's behaving a little better in some school situations, but he has not been able to improve much at home. (See the Behavior Rating Profile, Parent Rating Scale, for further details.)

Mrs. Greenhill wants Joey to be happy and wants very much to have a normal home environment. She stated that at times the entire household seems to revolve around Joey's behavior. If Joey is having a "bad day," all family schedules and events may have to be changed. She would like more guidance about how to handle Joey.

Student Interview

Name: Joey Greenhill

Name of Interviewer: Deborah Detail

Date: 10-2-93

Joey was asked to comment on his feelings about school prior to completing the Behavior Rating Profile. He remarked that he thought school was "okay," but that he would rather be at home. He said that he didn't like the kids in his class and that he wasn't interested in any particular subject.

During the interview, Joey spoke quietly with his head lowered. He did not maintain much eye contact. He was eager to begin the BRP questionnaire rather than continue answering questions posed by the examiner.

✎ Individualized Education Programs for Travis, Joey, Robert, and Susan

On the following 16 pages you will find the Individualized Education Programs (IEPs) for Travis, Joey, Robert, and Susan.

INDIVIDUALIZED EDUCATION PROGRAM

School Year 1992-93

Confidential Information

Name _Travis Johnson_ DOB _3-20-84_

School _Oak Hill Elementary_ Grade _4th_

Handicapping condition _Specific Learning Disability_

Date of IEP meeting _9-7-92_ Notification to parent _9-1-92_
M-D-Y   M-D-Y

Initiation and anticipated duration of services _9-8-92_ to _9-7-93_ Eligibility/Triennial _9-7-93_
M-Y   M-Y   M-Y

Plan to be reviewed no later than _11-21-92/11/95_ _9-7-93_
M-D-Y   M-Y

Educational/Vocational Program

Special Education Services

Resource Room Instruction with Mrs. Gray
for reading and mathematics

Regular Education Services

All other instruction in regular
4th grade classroom

Total Amount Times/Wk. _5 days/week_ Hrs./Day _2 hours/day_

Total Amount Times/Wk. _5 days/week_ Hrs./Day _4½ hours/day_

Related Services

Type	Amount
None	

Physical Education

Adapted Class Amount _N/a_

Regular Class Amount _2 days/week_

Transportation

Special _____ Regular _✓_

Participants in Plan Development

Name	Title
Susan Lopez	_IEP Teacher_
Mrs. Dirks	_4th grade Teacher_
Mr. Geier	_Principal_
Wm L. Johnson	_Mother_

Current Level of Performance

READING (Woodcock Reading Mastery (Revised)	G.E.
Word identification	1.7
Word attack	1.2
Word comprehension	1.7
Passage comprehension	1.9
Readiness cluster	2.8
Basic Skills cluster	1.5
Reading comprehension	1.9

MATH (Key math - Revised)	G.E.
Basic concepts	1.4
Operations	2.8
Applications	2.1

For High School Students ONLY (to be initially completed at 9th grade IEP meeting and reviewed annually).

This student is a candidate for: High School Diploma ____ ; Special Ed. Certificate ____ ; GED Equivalency Diploma ____

INDIVIDUALIZED EDUCATION PROGRAM

School Year __1992-93__

ANNUAL GOAL: The student __Travis__ will: __write the sum for 2-digit plus 2-digit addition problems with regrouping__

PROGRESS REPORTS

SHORT TERM OBJECTIVES	Grading Periods	COMMENTS
Objective: *Given a probe with 50 2-digit plus 2-digit addition problems with no regrouping, Travis will write the sum with 100% accuracy within 3 minutes.*	1. ✓	*mastered objective 9/22/92*
	2.	
Beginning Skill Level: *65% accuracy in 3 minutes on teacher made probe sheet.*	3.	
Date Initiated: *9-9-92*	4.	
Objective: *Given two ten blocks and any 2-digit plus 2-digit addition problem requiring regrouping from the ones to the tens, Travis will solve the problem by one time block correctly within 30 seconds.*	1. ✓	*mastered objective 10/3/92*
	2.	
Beginning Skill Level: *Unable to complete task w/o teacher assistance*	3.	
Date Initiated: *9-23-92*	4.	
Objective: *Given a probe sheet with 50 2-digit plus 2-digit addition problems with regrouping only from the tens column, Travis will write the sums with 100% accuracy within 3 minutes.*	1. ✓	*mastered objective 10/9/92*
	2.	
Beginning Skill Level: *30% accuracy within 3 minutes on teacher made probe.*	3.	
Date Initiated: *10-4-92*	4.	
Objective: *Given a probe sheet with any 2-digit plus 2-digit addition problem, Travis will write the sums with at least 90% accuracy within 3 minutes.*	1. ✓	
	2.	P
Beginning Skill Level: *45% accuracy within 3 minutes (≈½ of problems in teacher made probe required regrouping twice.*	3.	
Date Evaluated: *10-10-92*	4.	

Evaluation Procedures: Annual goals will be evaluated during the annual review. Short term objectives will be monitored at each nine week marking period. Beginning skill level indicates the student's performance prior to instruction.

Progress Key: No mark – Objective not initiated   P – Progressing on the objective

M – Objective mastered   D – Having difficulty with the objective (comment to describe difficulty)

M/R – Objective mastered, but needs review to maintain mastery

INDIVIDUALIZED EDUCATION PROGRAM

School Year 1992-93

ANNUAL GOAL: The student _Travis_ will: _write the product for multiplication facts through the nines._

PROGRESS REPORTS

SHORT TERM OBJECTIVES	Grading Periods	COMMENTS
Objective: Given a probe with multiplication facts through the nines presented in random order, Travis will write the products with 100% accuracy within 2 minutes.	1. ✓	not yet initiated
	2. ✓	not yet initiated
Beginning Skill Level: unable to complete any items on the probe	3.	
Date Initiated:	4.	
Objective: Given a probe with multiplication facts through the nines presented in random order, Travis will write the products with 100% accuracy within 2 minutes.	1. ✓	not yet initiated
	2. ✓	not yet initiated
Beginning Skill Level:	3.	
Date Initiated:	4.	
Objective:	1.	
	2.	
Beginning Skill Level:	3.	
Date Initiated:	4.	
Objective:	1.	
	2.	
Beginning Skill Level:	3.	
Date Initiated:	4.	

Evaluation Procedures: Annual goals will be evaluated during the annual review. Short term objectives will be monitored at each nine week marking period. Beginning skill level indicates the student's performance prior to instruction.

Progress Key: No mark – Objective not initiated   P – Progressing on the objective   D – Having difficulty with the objective (comment to describe difficulty)
          M – Objective mastered   M/R – Objective mastered, but needs review to maintain mastery

INDIVIDUALIZED EDUCATION PROGRAM

School Year ___1992-3___

ANNUAL GOAL: The student ___Travis___ will: ___complete the second level reader by the end of the academic year.___

PROGRESS REPORTS

SHORT TERM OBJECTIVES	Grading Periods		COMMENTS
Objective: Given 100 new vocabulary words from the 2nd level reader presented randomly in phrase copied from stories in the text, Travis will orally decode the words with at least 90% accuracy by February.	1. ✓	P	
	2. ✓	P	
	3.		
	4.		
Beginning Skill Level: 15% accuracy on untimed phrase reading list from text over 2nd reader.			
Date Initiated: 9-1-92			
G.E. 1.9 passage comprehension on W.R.M.			
Objective: Given 5 comprehension questions at the literal level following each story in the 2nd reader, Travis will orally answer the questions with at least 90% accuracy by January.	1. ✓	P	
	2. ✓	P	
	3.		
	4.		
Beginning Skill Level: G.E. 1.9 passage comprehension on W.R.M.			
Date Initiated: 9-1-92			
Objective: Given a story read silently from the 2nd reader, Travis will state the main idea of the story correctly with no teacher assistance.	1. ✓	P	
	2. ✓	P	
	3.		
	4.		
Beginning Skill Level: G.E. 1.9 Reading comprehension on W.R.M.			
Date Initiated: 9-1-92			
Objective: Given 100 new vocabulary words from the 2nd level reader presented randomly in phrases copied from stories in the text, Travis will orally decode the words with at least 90% accuracy by June.	1. —	not yet initiated	
	2. —	not yet initiated	
	3.		
	4.		
Beginning Skill Level:			
Date Initiated:			

Evaluation Procedures: Annual goals will be evaluated during the annual review. Short term objectives will be monitored at each nine week marking period. Beginning skill level indicates the student's performance prior to instruction.

Progress Key: No mark – Objective not initiated P – Progressing on the objective D – Having difficulty with the objective (comment to describe difficulty)

M – Objective mastered M/R – Objective mastered, but needs review to maintain mastery

Confidential Information

INDIVIDUALIZED EDUCATION PROGRAM

School Year 1992-93

Name *Joey Trumbull*   DOB 9-4-83   School *Oak Hill Elementary*   Grade 4th

Handicapping condition *Emotional Disturbance/Behavior Disorder*

Date of IEP meeting 9-8-92 (M-D-Y)   Notification to parent 9-1-92 (M-D-Y)

Initiation and anticipated duration of services 9-8-92 to 9-8-93 (M-Y)   Eligibility/Triennial 10-8-91/10-94 (M-Y)   Plan to be reviewed no later than 9-7-93 (M-Y)

Educational/Vocational Program

Special Education Services

Resource Room Instruction with Mr. Lopez for reading, mathematics, and social skills instruction

Regular Education Services

All other instruction in regular 4th grade classroom

Total Amount   Times/Wk *5 days/week*   Hrs./Day *2½ hours/day*

Total Amount   Times/Wk *5 days/week*   Hrs./Day *4 hours/day*

Related Services

Type	Amount
None	

Physical Education

Adapted Class   Amount *n/a*

Regular Class   Amount *2 days/week*

Transportation   Special ____   Regular ✓

Participants in Plan Development

Name	Title
Susan Lopez	*LD Teacher*
Mr. Kent	*4th Grade Teacher*
Mr. Grief	*Principal*
Mrs. Joan Hill	*Joey's Mother*

Current Level of Performance

ACHIEVEMENT (Woodcock-Johnson) - G.E.
- Passage comprehension — 2.2
- Calculation — 3.0
- Applied Problems — 2.5
- Dictation — 2.6
- Writing samples — 2.2
- Broad reading — 2.3
- Broad math — 2.3
- Broad written language — 2.1

BEHAVIOR (Behavior rating Profile) S.S.
- Student rating scale 6,4,4
- Teacher rating scale 5
- Parent rating scale 3

For High School Students ONLY (to be initially completed at 9th grade IEP meeting and reviewed annually).

This student is a candidate for: High School Diploma _____; Special Ed. Certificate _____; GED Equivalency Diploma _____.

INDIVIDUALIZED EDUCATION PROGRAM

School Year __1992-93__

ANNUAL GOAL: The student __Troy Treadhill__ will: __complete the third grade__ __reader by the end of the academic year.__

PROGRESS REPORTS

SHORT TERM OBJECTIVES	Grading Periods	COMMENTS
Objective: Given 100 new vocabulary words from the first level 3rd grade reader shown randomly in written phrases, Troy will verbally decode the words with at least 90% accuracy by January.	1. ✓	P
	2. ✓	P
Beginning Skill Level: 30% accuracy on untimed phrase reading list from Brigance third grade reader, W.I.	3.	
	4.	
Date Initiated: 9-9-92		
Objective: Given 5 comprehension questions following each story in the first level 3rd grade reader Troy will verbally answer the questions with at least 90% accuracy by January.	1. ✓	P Has no difficulty with comp questions at literal level. Inferential question problems.
	2. ✓	P
Beginning Skill Level: G.E. 2.4 on Woodcock-Johnson	3.	
	4.	
Date Initiated: 9-10-92		
Objective: Given 100 new vocabulary words from the 3² reader shown randomly in written phrases, Troy will verbally decode the words with at least 90% accuracy by June.	1. —	not yet initiated
	2. —	not yet initiated
Beginning Skill Level:	3.	
	4.	
Date Initiated:		
Objective: Given 5 comprehension questions following each story in the 3² reader, Troy will orally answer the questions with at least 80% accuracy by May.	1. —	not yet initiated
	2. —	not yet initiated
Beginning Skill Level:	3.	
	4.	
Date Initiated:		

Evaluation Procedures: Annual goals will be evaluated during the annual review. Short term objectives will be monitored at each nine week marking period. Beginning skill level indicates the student's performance prior to instruction.

Progress Key: No mark – Objective not initiated   P – Progressing on the objective   D – Having difficulty with the objective (comment to describe difficulty)

M – Objective mastered   M/R – Objective mastered, but needs review to maintain mastery

INDIVIDUALIZED EDUCATION PROGRAM

School Year 1992-93

ANNUAL GOAL: The student _Troy_ will: _subtract 3-digit minus 3-digit numbers requiring regrouping twice._

SHORT TERM OBJECTIVES	Grading Periods	PROGRESS REPORTS COMMENTS
Objective: Given a probe containing 50 2-digit minus 2-digit problems requiring regrouping only, Troy will fill the sheet with 100% accuracy within 3 minutes.	1. M	Mastered 10-1-92
	2.	
Beginning Skill Level: 50% accuracy on teacher made work sheet	3.	
Date Initiated: 9-8-92	4.	
Objective: Given a probe containing 50 3-digit minus 3-digit problems requiring regrouping only from the tens to the ones, Troy will write the difference with 100% accuracy within 3 minutes.	1. M	Mastered 10-18-92
	2.	
Beginning Skill Level: unable to complete teacher made probe w/o teacher assistance.	3.	
Date Initiated: 10-2-92	4.	
Objective: Given a probe containing 50 3-digit minus 3-digit numbers requiring regrouping twice, Troy will write the difference with 100% accuracy within 3 minutes.	1. ✓	P
	2.	
Beginning Skill Level: unable to complete any items on teacher made probe sheet.	3.	
Date Initiated: 10-21-92	4.	
Objective:	1.	
	2.	
Beginning Skill Level:	3.	
Date Initiated:	4.	

Evaluation Procedures: Annual goals will be evaluated during the annual review. Short term objectives will be monitored at each nine week marking period. Beginning skill level indicates the student's performance prior to instruction.

Progress Key: No mark – Objective not initiated   P – Progressing on the objective   D – Having difficulty with the objective (comment to describe difficulty)
M – Objective mastered   M/R – Objective mastered, but needs review to maintain mastery

INDIVIDUALIZED EDUCATION PROGRAM

School Year __1992-93__

ANNUAL GOAL: The student _Trey_ will: _write the products for multiplication facts through the nines._

PROGRESS REPORTS

SHORT TERM OBJECTIVES	Grading Periods	COMMENTS
Objective: _Given a probe with multiplication facts through the nines presented in random order, Trey will write the products accurately within 2 minutes._	1. ✓	_not yet initiated_
	2. ✓	_not yet initiated_
	3.	
Beginning Skill Level: _unable to complete any items on the probe_	4.	
Date Initiated:		
Objective: _Given a probe with multiplication facts through the nines through the nines presented in random order, Trey will write the products with 100% accuracy within 2 minutes._	1. ✓	_not yet initiated_
	2. ✓	_not yet initiated_
	3.	
Beginning Skill Level:	4.	
Date Initiated:		
Objective:	1.	
	2.	
	3.	
Beginning Skill Level:	4.	
Date Initiated:		
Objective:	1.	
	2.	
	3.	
Beginning Skill Level:	4.	
Date Initiated:		

Evaluation Procedures: Annual goals will be evaluated during the annual review. Short term objectives will be monitored at each nine week marking period. Beginning skill level indicates the student's performance prior to instruction.

Progress Key: No mark – Objective not initiated   P – Progressing on the objective   D – Having difficulty with the objective (comment to describe difficulty)

M – Objective mastered   M/R – Objective mastered, but needs review to maintain mastery

INDIVIDUALIZED EDUCATION PROGRAM

School Year __1992-93__

ANNUAL GOAL: The student __Trey__ will: __demonstrate the first 3 social skills in the "Essential Social Skills" sequence by the end of the academic year.__

PROGRESS REPORTS

SHORT TERM OBJECTIVES	Grading Periods		COMMENTS
Objective: Given a request presented orally by Trey's teacher or another professional in the school, Trey will comply with the request 100% of the time within 1 minute by saying "okay" and beginning the task.	1. ✓	P	
Beginning Skill Level: Trey complies with requests of teachers and paraprofessionals on only 1 of 5 requests.	2. ✓	P	
	3.		
Date Initiated: 9-8-92	4.		
Objective: When Trey needs the teacher's attention, Trey will remain in his seat and raise his hand until the teacher acknowledges him 100% of the time.	1. ✓	P	
Beginning Skill Level: Trey calls out to the teacher 100% of the time, & on 2 out of 3 occurrences Trey is out of his seat to gain teacher attention.	2. ✓	P	
	3.		
Date Initiated: 9-15-92	4.		
Objective: When Trey makes a request he will say "please" 100% of the time.	1. ✓	P	
Beginning Skill Level: Trey doesn't say "please" on any occasion of making a request.	2. ✓	P	
	3.		
Date Initiated: 9-22-92	4.		
Objective:	1.		
	2.		
Beginning Skill Level:	3.		
Date Initiated:	4.		

Evaluation Procedures: Annual goals will be evaluated during the annual review. Short term objectives will be monitored at each nine week marking period. Beginning skill level indicates the student's performance prior to instruction.

Progress Key: No mark – Objective not initiated

M – Objective mastered

P – Progressing on the objective

M/R – Objective mastered, but needs review to maintain mastery

D – Having difficulty with the objective (comment to describe difficulty)

Confidential Information

INDIVIDUALIZED EDUCATION PROGRAM

School Year _1992-93_

Name _ROBERT RICHARDSON_ DOB _8-7-77_ School _APPLE COUNTY HIGH SCHOOL_ Grade _9TH_

Handicapping condition _SPECIFIC LEARNING DISABILITY_ Date of IEP meeting _9-8-92_ Notification to parent _9-1-92_
M-D-Y   M-D-Y

Initiation and anticipated duration of services _9-8-92_ – _9-7-93_ Eligibility/Triennial _9-31-85 / 9-31-44_ Plan to be reviewed no later than _9-7-93_
M-Y   to   M-Y   M-Y   M-Y

Educational/Vocational Program

Special Education Services

LD RESOURCE ROOM-FOR STUDY SKILLS INST.;

COMPUTER AVAILABLE FOR WRITTEN WORK;

MODIFICATIONS IN TESTING -- EXTENDED TIME; TESTS

READ ORALLY IN RESOURCE ROOM.

Total Amount _5 DAYS/WEEK_ Hrs./Day _1 PD/DAY_

Regular Education Services

ALL ACADEMIC COURSEWORK IN THE REGULAR

CLASSROOM FOR ENGLISH, GEOGRAPHY

HEALTH/P.E., AND EARTH SCIENCE. INDUSTRIAL

ARTS ELECTIVE.

Total Amount _5 DAYS/WEEK_ Hrs./Day _5 PDs/DAY_

Related Services

Type   Amount

NONE   ———

Physical Education

Adapted Class   Amount _N/A_

Regular Class   Amount _5 DAYS/WEEK_

Transportation

Special ———   Regular _✓_

Participants in Plan Development

Name   Title

Mr. ABEL   _Teacher_

Mrs. Church   _Principal_

Mrs. Wolfe   _Counselor_

Mr. Richardson   _Father_

Robert Richardson   _Student_

Current Level of Performance

ACHIEVEMENT (WOODCOCK-JOHNSON) - G.E.
   PASSAGE COMPREHENSION - 5.2
   CALCULATION   _- 6.4_
   APPLIED PROBLEMS _- 6.3_
   WRITING SAMPLES   _- 5.3_
   BROAD READING   _- 5.2_
   BROAD MATH   _- 6.2_
   BROAD WRITTEN LANGUAGE - 5.4
STUDY SKILLS--MAINSTREAMING CHECKLISTS INDICATE
ROBERT DOES NOT BRING NECESSARY MATERIALS TO CLASS ON A DAILY
BASIS. HE DOES NOT BUDGET TIME TO COMPLETE ASSIGNMENTS

For High School Students ONLY (to be initially completed at 9th grade IEP meeting and reviewed annually).
This student is a candidate for: High School Diploma _✓_; Special Ed. Certificate ———; GED Equivalency Diploma ———.

INDIVIDUALIZED EDUCATION PROGRAM

20. INSTRUCTIONAL AREA: *STUDY SKILLS*

Code:　I - Introduced (date)
　　　　P - Progressing
　　　　NP - No Progress
　　　　M - Mastered (date)

21. ANNUAL GOAL: *ROBERT WILL DEMONSTRATE APPROPRIATE STUDY SKILLS IN HIS GEOGRAPHY, HEALTH, P.E., ENGLISH, AND EARTH SCIENCE CLASSES.*

Student's Name　*ROBERT RICHARDSON*

Page　*2*

22. SHORT-TERM OBJECTIVES	23. EVALUATION PROCEDURES AND SCHEDULES	24. PROGRESS PERIODS					25. CONTINUATION AND/OR MODIFICATION
		PERIOD ENDING	PERIOD ENDING	PERIOD ENDING	PERIOD ENDING	PERIOD ENDING	
a) ROBERT WILL IDENTIFY THE MATERIALS NEEDED FOR EACH SUBJECT AND WILL ATTEND CLASS WITH THE NECESSARY MATERIALS 100% OF THE TIME.	WEEKLY MAINSTREAMING CHECKLIST TO ALL MAINSTREAM TEACHERS.	P	M				CONTINUE TO MONITOR.
b) GIVEN A ONE WEEK PLAN SHEET, ROBERT WILL PRIORITIZE TASKS AND ALLOCATE TIME IN ORDER TO COMPLETE ALL ASSIGNMENTS BY THE DEADLINE DATES.	WEEKLY MAINSTREAMING CHECKLIST; PLAN SHEET CHECKED WEEKLY BY MR. ABEL.	P	P				CONTINUING
c) GIVEN INSTRUCTION IN STRATEGIES FOR TAKING TESTS AND STUDYING FOR TESTS, ROBERT WILL APPLY THE STRATEGIES IN GEOGRAPHY AND E.S. IN ORDER TO EARN A GRADE OF AT LEAST A "C" ON WEEKLY TESTS.	WEEKLY MAINSTREAMING CHECKLISTS; WEEKLY QUIZ GRADES; MID-GRADE ESTIMATES.	P	P				CONTINUING— HAS DIFFICULTY USING STRATEGY FOR OBJECTIVE TESTS.

INDIVIDUALIZED EDUCATION PROGRAM

Page ___3___

Student's Name *ROBERT RICHARDSON*

20. INSTRUCTIONAL AREA: *STUDY SKILLS*

Code: I - Introduced (date)
P - Progressing
NP - No Progress
M - Mastered (date)

21. ANNUAL GOAL: *ROBERT WILL DEMONSTRATE APPROPRIATE STUDY SKILLS IN HIS GEOGRAPHY, HEALTH/ P.E., ENGLISH, AND EARTH SCIENCE CLASSES.*

24. PROGRESS PERIODS

22. / 23. SHORT-TERM OBJECTIVES	EVALUATION PROCEDURES AND SCHEDULES	PERIOD ENDING	PERIOD ENDING	PERIOD ENDING	PERIOD ENDING	PERIOD ENDING	25. CONTINUATION AND/OR MODIFICATION
1.) GIVEN A WORD PROCESSING PROGRAM AND COMPUTER AVAILABLE IN THE RESOURCE ROOM, ROBERT WILL WRITE A COHERENT PARAGRAPH CONTAINING A TOPIC SENTENCE, 4-5 SUPPORTING SENTENCES RELATED TO THE TOPIC, AND NO MORE THAN ONE SPELLING ERROR.	WEEKLY MAINSTREAMING CHECKLISTS; WRITTEN SAMPLES WEEKLY FROM ENGLISH 9; MID-GRADE ESTIMATES.	P	P				

Confidential Information

INDIVIDUALIZED EDUCATION PROGRAM

School Year __1992-93__

Name __SUSAN MOYLER__ DOB __10-5-79__ School __APPLE COUNTY MIDDLE SCHOOL__ Grade __6__

Handicapping condition __MILD MENTAL RETARDATION__ Date of IEP meeting __9-8-92__ Notification to parent __9-1-92__
M-D-Y　　　　　　　　　　　　M-D-Y

Initiation and anticipated duration of services __9-8-92__ to __9-7-93__ Eligibility/Triennial __11-10-88 / 11-94__ Plan to be reviewed no later than __9-7-93__
M-Y　　　M-Y　　　　　　　　　　M-D-Y　　　　　　　　　　　　M-Y

Educational/Vocational Program

Special Education Services　　　　　　　　　　　　　　　Regular Education Services

RESOURCE ROOM INSTRUCTION IN READING　　　　SOCIAL STUDIES, LANGUAGE ARTS, AND

AND SOCIAL SKILLS, ASSISTANCE IN　　　　　　　GENERAL MATHEMATICS

RESOURCE ROOM FOR MATH.

Total Amount Times/Wk __5 DAYS/WEEK__ Hrs./Day __2 HOURS/DAY__   Total Amount Times/Wk __5 DAYS/WEEK__ Hrs./Day __3½ HOURS/DAY__

Related Services

Type	Amount
NONE	—

	Physical Education
Adapted Class Amount	5 DAYS/WEEK
Regular Class Amount	1 PD/DAY

HYGIENE & WEIGHT
CONTROL PROGRAM

Transportation	
Special	Regular ✓

Current Level of Performance

READING (WOODCOCK READING MASTERY-REVISED) - G.E.
　　WORD IDENTIFICATION　　2.9
　　WORD ATTACK　　　　　　2.4
　　WORD COMPREHENSION　　3.3
　　PASSAGE COMPREHENSION　2.3
　　READINESS CLUSTER　　　2.9
　　BASIC SKILLS CLUSTER　　2.3
　　READING COMPREHENSION　2.2

MATH (KEY-MATH-REVISED) - G.E.
　　BASIC CONCEPTS　　3.5
　　OPERATIONS　　　　4.3
　　APPLICATIONS　　　4.1

SOCIAL SKILLS
　　CHECKLIST INDICATES
　　PERSONAL APPEARANCE
　　AND SELF CONFIDENCE ARE PROBLEM AREAS.

Participants in Plan Development

Name	Title
MR. ABEL	TEACHER
MRS. FRIEND	COUNSELOR
SUSAN MOYLER	STUDENT
MARTHA MOYLER	MOTHER

For High School Students ONLY (to be initially completed at 9th grade IEP meeting and reviewed annually).
This student is a candidate for: High School Diploma ____; Special Ed. Certificate ____; GED Equivalency Diploma ____

INDIVIDUALIZED EDUCATION PROGRAM

20. INSTRUCTIONAL AREA: READING SKILLS

Code: I - Introduced (date)
P - Progressing
NP - No Progress
M - Mastered (date)

Student's Name SUSAN MOYLER

Page 2

21. ANNUAL GOAL: SUSAN WILL DEMONSTRATE MEASURABLE PROGRESS IN ORAL READING RATE AND PASSAGE COMPREHENSION.

22. SHORT-TERM OBJECTIVES	23. EVALUATION PROCEDURES AND SCHEDULES	24. PROGRESS PERIODS					25. CONTINUATION AND/OR MODIFICATION
		PERIOD ENDING	PERIOD ENDING	PERIOD ENDING	PERIOD ENDING	PERIOD ENDING	
a.) GIVEN A 200 WORD PASSAGE WRITTEN AT THE 3RD GRADE LEVEL, SUSAN WILL ORALLY READ THE PASSAGE AT A RATE OF 150 WORDS PER MINUTE WITH FEWER THAN 2 ERRORS.	TIMED READING PROBES ON DAILY BASIS FROM 3RD LEVEL HIGH INTEREST/ LOW VOC. MATERIAL. BEGINNING LEVEL 9/8/92 30 WPM, 3 ERRORS.	P	P				
b.) GIVEN A PASSAGE WRITTEN AT THE 3RD GRADE LEVEL, SUSAN WILL ORALLY ANSWER COMPREHENSION QUESTIONS AT THE LITERAL LEVEL, AFTER SILENTLY READING THE PASSAGE, WITH AT LEAST 80% ACCURACY.	DAILY PASSAGES FROM 3RD LEVEL MATERIAL - ANSWERS LITERAL QUESTIONS WITH 20% ACCURACY (1 OUT OF 5).	P	P				
c.) GIVEN A PASSAGE WRITTEN AT THE 3RD GRADE LEVEL, READ SILENTLY, SUSAN WILL STATE THE MAIN IDEA CORRECTLY WITHOUT TEACHER ASSISTANCE.	DAILY PASSAGE FROM 3RD LEVEL MATERIAL - MAIN IDEA STATED IN TEXT SUSAN REQUIRES TEACHER ASSISTANCE.	P	P				

INDIVIDUALIZED EDUCATION PROGRAM

Code: I - Introduced (date)
          P - Progressing
        NP - No Progress
        M - Mastered (date)

Page ___3___

Student's Name _SUSAN MOYLER_

20. INSTRUCTIONAL AREA: SOCIAL SKILLS

21. ANNUAL GOAL: SUSAN WILL IMPROVE PERSONAL APPEARANCE.

22.

23.

24. PROGRESS PERIODS

25.

SHORT-TERM OBJECTIVES	EVALUATION PROCEDURES AND SCHEDULES	PERIOD ENDING	PERIOD ENDING	PERIOD ENDING	PERIOD ENDING	PERIOD ENDING	CONTINUATION AND/OR MODIFICATION
a.) GIVEN A WEIGHT CONTROL AND EXERCISE PROGRAM IN ADAPTED HEALTH/P.E., SUSAN WILL OTTAIN THE APPROPRIATE WEIGHT FOR HER HEIGHT AND BUILD AND WILL MAINTAIN THAT WEIGHT.	DAILY WEIGH-IN IN ADAPTED P.E.; SOCIAL SKILLS CHECKLIST COMPLETED ON WEEKLY BASES.	P	P				
b.) SUSAN WILL SHOWER USING WARM WATER AND SOAP AND SHAMPOO ON A DAILY BASIS, APPLYING SOAP TO ALL BODY AREAS AND THOROUGHLY RINSING ALL AREAS.	DAILY CHECK BY HOMEROOM TEACHER (SUSAN'S ADAPTED P.E. TEACHER.)	P	M 1/9/83				CONTINUE TO MONITOR WEEKLY.
c.) SUSAN WILL APPLY DEODORANT ON A DAILY BASIS IMMEDIATELY AFTER SHOWERING.	DAILY CHECK BY HOMEROOM - ADAPTED P.E. TEACHER.	P	P				

INDIVIDUALIZED EDUCATION PROGRAM

Code: I - Introduced (date)
P - Progressing
NP - No Progress
M - Mastered (date)

Page _4_

Student's Name _SUSAN MOYLER_

20. INSTRUCTIONAL AREA: _SOCIAL SKILLS_

21. ANNUAL GOAL: _SUSAN WILL COMPLETE ASSIGNMENTS INDEPENDENTLY._

22. SHORT-TERM OBJECTIVES	23. EVALUATION PROCEDURES AND SCHEDULES	24. PROGRESS PERIODS					25. CONTINUATION AND/OR MODIFICATION
		PERIOD ENDING	PERIOD ENDING	PERIOD ENDING	PERIOD ENDING	PERIOD ENDING	
a.) GIVEN A SEATWORK ASSIGNMENT AT THE APPROPRIATE LEVEL AND ORAL AND WRITTEN DIRECTIONS/ DEMONSTRATION BY THE TEACHER, SUSAN WILL COMPLETE THE ASSIGNMENT WITH NO MORE THAN ONE REQUEST FOR ASSISTANCE BY THE TEACHER.	MAINSTREAMING CHECKLIST COMPLETED BY CLASSROOM TEACHERS ON A WEEKLY BASIS.	P	P				

Appendix B

✎ Materials

Academic Therapy
Publications
20 Commercial Boulevard
Novato, CA 94949
1-800-422-7249

American Guidance Service
4201 Woodland Road #1279
Circle Pines, MN 55014
1-800-328-2560

Apple Office of Special
Education Programs
20525 Mariani Avenue
MS 23-D
Cupertino, CA 95014
408-996-1010

Barnell Loft
958 Church Street
Baldwin, NY 11510

Communication Skill Builders
P.O. Box 42050-D
Department 62
Tucson, AZ 85733
602-323-7500

Conover Company
Box 155
Omro, WI 54963
1-800-933-1933

Creative Publications
3977 E. Bayshore Road
Palo Alto, CA 94303

Cuisenaire Company of
America
12 Church Street
New Rochelle, NY 10805

Curriculum Associates
5 Esquire Road
N. Billerica, MA 01862
1-800-225-0248

Developmental Learning
Materials
One DLM Park
P.O. Box 4000
Allen, TX 75002

Ebsco Curriculum Materials
Box 11542
Birmingham, AL 35202

Edmark Associates
P.O. Box 3903
Bellevue, WA 98009-3903

Educators Publishing Service
75 Moulton Street
Cambridge, MA 02138
1-800-225-5750

Fearon/Janus/Quercus
500 Harbor Boulevard
Belmont, CA 94002
1-800-877-4283

Ginn and Company
191 Spring Street
Lexington, MA 02173

Globe Book Company
4350 Equity Drive
P.O. Box 2649
Columbus, OH 43216
1-800-848-9500

Houghton Mifflin Company
One Beacon Street
Boston, MA 02107

Love Publishing Company
1777 South Bellaire Street
Denver, CO 80222

Media Materials
2936 Remington Avenue
Baltimore, MD 21211

Milliken
100 Research Boulevard
St. Louis, MO 63132

Modern Curriculum Press
13900 Prospect Road
Cleveland, OH 44136
1-800-321-3106

Open Court Publishing
Company
1039 Eighth Street
Box 599
LaSalle, IL 61301

Pro-ED
8700 Shoal Creek Boulevard
Austin, TX 78758
512-451-3246

Psychological Corporation
555 Academic Court
P.O. Box 9954
San Antonio, TX 78204

Research Press
Box 3177, Dept. B
Champaign, IL 61826
217-352-3273

Scholastic, Inc.
2931 E. McCarty Street
P.O. Box 7502
Jefferson City, MO 65102
1-800-325-6149

Scott, Foresman, & Company
1900 E. Lake Avenue
Glenview, IL 60025

Special Times
Cambridge Development Lab
214 Third Avenue
Waltham, MA 02154
1-800-637-0047

SRA (Science Research
Associates)
Macmillan/McGraw-Hill
860 Taylor Station Road
P.O. Box 543
Blacklick, OH 43004
1-800-621-0476

Steck-Vaughn
P.O. Box 26015
Austin, TX 78755
1-800-531-5015

The Education Center, Inc.
The Mailbox
1607 Battleground Avenue
P.O. Box 9753
Greensboro, NC 27429
1-800-334-0298

✎ Organizations

American Association on
    Mental Retardation
1790 Kalorama Road, N.W.
Washington, DC 20009
202-387-1968

American Psychological
    Association
1400 N. Uhle St.
Arlington, VA 22201
703-247-7705

American Vocational
    Association
2020 N. 14th Street
Arlington, VA 22201

Association for Supervision
    and Curriculum Development
1250 N. Pitt Street
Alexandria, VA 22314
703-549-9110

The Clearinghouse
Switzer Building, Room 3132
Washington, DC 20202
202-732-1245

Council for Exceptional
    Children/
Council for Children with
    Behavior Disorders/
Division for Learning
    Disabilities/
Division on Career
    Development/
Division on Mental
    Retardation/
Division on Research,
Technology and Media
1920 Association Drive
Reston, VA 22091
703-620-3660

Council for Learning
    Disabilities
P.O. Box 40303
Overland Park, KS 66204
913-492-8755

Federation of Families for
    Children's
    Mental Health
1021 Prince Street
Alexandria, VA 22314

International Reading
    Association
800 Barksdale Road
Newark, DE 19711

Learning Disabilities
    Association of America
5255 Grace Street
Pittsburgh, PA 15236
412-341-1515

Learning Disabilities Council
P.O. Box 8451
Richmond, VA 23226
1-800-394-7940

National Association for
    Retarded Citizens
2709 Avenue East
P.O. Box 6109
Arlington, TX 76005
817-640-0204

National Council of Teachers
    of Mathematics
1906 Association Drive
Reston, VA 22091

National Education
    Association
1210 16th Street, N.W.
Washington, D.C. 20036

Orton Dyslexia Society
724 York Road
Towson, MD 21204
410-296-0232

University of Kansas
Institute for Research on
    Learning Disabilities
P.O. Box 972
Lawrence, KS 66045

References

Abramson, L.Y., Seligman, M.E.P., & Teasdale, J. (1978). Learned helplessness in humans: Critique and reformulation. *Journal of Abnormal Psychology, 87,* 49–74.

Adams, M.J. (1990). *Beginning to read: Thinking and learning about print.* Cambridge, MA: MIT Press.

Adult Performance Level Project (APL). (1975). *Adult functional competency.* Austin: University of Texas Office of Continuing Education.

Affleck, J.Q., Madge, S., Adams, A., & Lowerbraun, S. (1988). Integrated classroom versus resource model: Academic viability and effectiveness. *Exceptional Children, 54,* 339–348.

Airasian, P.W. (1991). *Classroom assessment.* New York: McGraw-Hill.

Alberto, P.A., & Troutman, A.C. (1990). *Applied behavior analysis for teachers.* Columbus, OH: Merrill.

Algozzine, B., & Korinek, L. (1985). Where is special education for students with high prevalence handicaps going? *Exceptional Children, 51,* 388–394.

Alley, G.R., & Deshler, D.D. (1979). *Teaching the learning disabled adolescent: Strategies and methods.* Denver, CO: Love.

Alley, G.R., Deshler, D.D., Clark, F. L., Schumaker, J.B., & Warner, M.M. (1983). Learning disabilities in adolescent and adult populations: Research implications (Part II). *Focus on Exceptional Children, 15*(9), 1–14.

American Association on Mental Retardation. (1993). Mental retardation: Definition, classification, and systems of supports. 9th ed. Washington, DC: Author.

American Psychiatric Association. (1987). *Diagnostic and statistical manual of mental disorders* (3rd ed., revised). Washington, DC: Authur.

Anders, P.L., & Bos, C.S. (1984). In the beginning: Vocabulary instruction in content classrooms. *Topics in Learning and Learning Disabilities, 3*(4), 53–65.

Anderson, L.W., & Pellicer, L.O. (1990). Synthesis of research on compensatory and remedial education. *Educational Leadership, 48,* 10–16.

Anderson, R.C., Hiebert, E.H., Scott, J.A., & Wilkinson, I.A.G. (1985). *Becoming a nation of readers.* Champaign, IL: Center for the Study of Reading.

Archer, A.L. (1988). Strategies for responding to information. *Teaching Exceptional Children, 20,* 55–57.

Archer, A.L., & Gleason, M. (1989). *Skills for school success.* Billerica, MA: Curriculum Associates.

Armento, B. (1986). Research on teaching social studies. In M. Witrock (Ed.), *Handbook of research on teaching* (3rd ed. pp. 942–951). New York: Macmillan.

Armstrong, S.W., & McPherson, A. (1991). Homework as a critical component in social skills instruction. *Teaching Exceptional Children, 24,* 45–47.

Aronson, E., Blaney, N., Stephan, C., Sikes, J., & Snapp, M. (1978). *The jigsaw classroom.* Beverly Hills, CA: Sage.

Ausubel, D.P., & Robinson, F.G. (1969). *School learning: An introduction to educational psychology.* New York: Holt, Rinehart, & Winston.

Bacon, E.H., & Schulz, J.B. (1991). A survey of mainstreaming practices. *Teacher Education and Special Education, 14,* 144–149.

Baker, J., Young, M., & Martin, M. (1990). The effectiveness of small-group versus one-to-one remedial instruction for six students with learning disabilities. *Elementary School Journal, 91*(1), 65–76.

Barbe, W., Milone, M., & Wasylyk, T. (1983). Manuscript is the "write" start. *Academic Therapy, 18,* 397–406.

Barnett, D., Zins, J., & Wise, L. (1984). An analysis of parental participation as a means of reducing bias in the education of handicapped children. *Special Services in the Schools, 1,* 71–84.

Baroody, A.J., & Hume, J. (1991). Meaningful mathematics instruction: The case of fractions. *Remedial and Special Education, 12,* 54–68.

Bateman, B. (1992). Learning disabilities: The changing landscape. *Journal of Learning Disabilities, 25,* 29–36.

Beale, A., & Beers, C.S. (1982). What do you say to parents after you say hello? *Teaching Exceptional Children, 15*(1), 34–38.

Beck, I.L., & Roth, S.F. (1984a). *Construct a word teacher's manual.* Allen, TX: Developmental Learning Materials.

Beck, I.L., & Roth S.F. (1984b). *Hint and Hunt teacher's manual.* Allen, TX: Developmental Learning Materials.

Becker, R.L. (1987). *Reading-Free Vocational Interest Inventory.* Monterey, CA: Publishers Test Service.

Beirne-Smith, M. (1991). Peer tutoring in arithmetic for children with learning disabilities. *Exceptional Children, 57,* 330–337.

Bender, W.N., & Smith, J.K. (1990). Classroom behavior of children and adolescents with learning disabilities: A meta-analysis. *Journal of Learning Disabilities, 23,* 298–305.

Bennett, N., & Desforges, C. (1988). Matching classroom tasks to students' attainments. *Elementary School Journal, 88*(3), 221–234.

Bennett, R.E. (1982). Cautions for the use of informal measures in the educational assessment of exceptional children. *Journal of Learning Disabilities, 15,* 337–339.

Bereiter, C., & Engelmann, S. (1966). *Teaching disadvantaged children in the preschool.* Englewood Cliffs, NJ: Prentice-Hall.

Bereiter, C., & Scardamalia, M. (1982). From conversation to composition: The role of instruction in a developmental process. In R. Glaser (Ed.), *Advances in instructional psychology,* (Vol. 2, pp. 1–64). Hillsdale, NJ: Erlbaum.

Bergerud, D., Lovitt, T.C., & Horton, S. (1988). The effectiveness of textbook adaptations in life science for high school students with learning disabilities. *Journal of Learning Disabilities, 21,,* 70–76.

Berkell, D.E., & Brown, J.M. (1989). *Transition from school to work for persons with disabilities.* White Plains, NY: Longman.

Berler, E.S., Gross, A.M., & Drabman, R.S. (1982). Social skills training with children: Proceed with caution. *Journal of Applied Behavior Analysis, 15,* 41–53.

Berliner, D.C. (1984). The half-full glass: A review of research on teaching. In P.L. Hosford (Ed.), *Using what we know about teaching* (pp. 51–77). Alexandria, VA: Association for Supervision and Curriculum Development.

Billingsley, B.S., & Wildman, T.M. (1988). The effects of prereading activities on the comprehension monitoring of learning disabled adolescents. *Learning Disabilities Research, 4,* 36–44.

Billingsley, F.F. (1984). Where are the generalized objectives? An examination of instructional objectives. *Journal of the Association for Persons with Severe Handicaps, 9,* 186–192.

Billingsley, F.F., Burgess, D., Lynch, V.W., & Matlock, B.L. (1991). Toward generalized outcomes: Considerations and guidelines for writing instructional objectives. *Education and Training in Mental Retardation, 26,* 351–360.

Blackbourn, J.M. (1989). Acquisition and generalization of social skills in elementary-aged children with learning disabilities. *Journal of Learning Disabilities, 22,* 28–34.

Blackhurst, A.E. (1989). Using *AppleWorks* to improve personal productivity. *Teaching Exceptional Children, 21,* 68–70.

Bloom, B.S., Englehart, M.B., Furst, E.J., Hill, W.H., & Krathwohl, O.R. (1956). *Taxonomy of educational objectives: The classification of educational goals. Handbook I: The cognitive domain.* New York: Longman.

Boehnlein, M. (1987). Reading intervention for high-risk first-graders. *Educational Leadership, 44,* 32–37.

Boomer, L.W. (1980). Special education paraprofessionals: A guide for teachers. *Teaching Exceptional Children, 12,* 146–149.

Boomer, L.W. (1981). Meeting common goals through effective teacher-paraprofessional communication. *Teaching Exceptional Children, 13*, 51–53.

Boomer, L.W. (1982). The paraprofessional: A valued resource for special children and their teachers. *Teaching Exceptional Children, 14*, 194–197.

Bos, C.S. (1982). Getting past decoding: Using modeled and repeated readings as a remedial method for learning disabled students. *Topics in Learning and Learning Disabilities, 1*, 51–57.

Bos, C.S. (1988). Process-oriented writing: Instructional implications for mildly handicapped students. *Exceptional Children, 54*, 521–577.

Box, C.S., Anders, P.L., Filip, D., & Jaffe, L.E. (1989). The effects of an interactive instructional strategy for enhancing reading comprehension and content area learning for students with learning disabilities. *Journal of Learning Disabilities, 22*, 384–390.

Bos, C.S., & Vaughn, S. (1991). *Strategies for teaching students with learning and behavior problems* (2nd ed.). Boston: Allyn & Bacon.

Bower, E.M. (1981). *Early identification of emotionally handicapped children in school* (3rd ed.). Springfield, IL: Charles C Thomas.

Brantlinger, E. (1987). Making decisions about special education placement: Do low income parents have the information they need? *Journal of Learning Disabilities, 20*, 94–101.

Brigance, A.H. (1977). *Brigance diagnostic inventory of basic skills*. North Billerica, MA: Curriculum Associates.

Brigance, A.H. (1978). *Brigance diagnostic inventory of early development*. North Billerica, MA: Curriculum Associates.

Brigance, A.H. (1980). *Brigance Diagnostic Inventory of Essential Skills, Red Level*. North Billerica, MA: Curriculum Associates.

Brigance, A.H. (1981). *Brigance diagnostic inventory of essential skills*. North Billerica, MA: Curriculum Associates.

Brolin, D.E. (1986). *Life-Centered Career Education: A competency-based approach (rev. ed.)*. Reston, VA: Council for Exceptional Children.

Brooks, P.H., & McCauley, C. (1984). Cognitive research in mental retardation. *American Journal of Mental Deficiency, 88*, 479–486.

Brophy, J. (1990). Teaching social studies for understanding and higher-order applications. *Elementary School Journal, 90*, 351–417.

Brophy, J., & Good, T.L. (1986). Teacher behavior and student achievement. In M.C. Wittrock (Ed.), *Handbook of research on teaching*. New York: Macmillan.

Browder, D.M., Hines, C., McCarthy, L.J., & Fees, J. (1984). A treatment package for increasing sight word recognition for use in daily living skills. *Education and Training of the Mentally Retarded, 19*, 191–200.

Brown, A.S. (1988). Encountering misspellings and spelling performance: Why wrong isn't right. *Journal of Educational Psychology, 80*, 488–494.

Brown, D.S. (1988). Twelve middle-school teachers' planning. *Elementary School Journal, 89* (1), 69–87.

Brown, L.L., & Hammill, D.D. (1983). *Behavior rating profile*. Austin, TX: Pro-Ed.

Bryan, T.H. (1986). Self-concept and attributions of the learning disabled. *Learning Disabilities Focus, 1*, 82–89.

Bryan, T.H., Donahue, M., & Pearl, R. (1981). Studies of learning disabled children's pragmatic competence. *Topics in Learning and Learning Disabilities, 1*, 29–41.

Bryant, N.D., Drabin, I.R., & Gettinger, M. (1981). Effects of varying unit size on spelling achievement in learning disabled children. *Journal of Learning Disabilities, 14*, 200–203.

Bulgren, J., Schumaker, J.B., & Deshler, D.D. (1988). Effectiveness of a concept teaching routine in enhancing the performance of LD students in secondary-level mainstream classes. *Learning Disability Quarterly, 11*, 3–16.

Bullock, J., Pierce, S., McClellan, L. (1991). *Touch Math: The touchpoint approach for teaching basic math computations*. Colorado Springs: Innovative Learning Concepts.

Bursuck, W. (1989). A comparison of students with learning disabilities to low achieving and higher achieving students on three dimensions of social competence. *Journal of Learning Disabilities, 22*, 188–194.

Butler, A. (1987). *The elements of whole language*. Crystal Lake, IL: Rigby.

Carbo, M. (1983). Research in reading and learning style: Implications for exceptional children. *Exceptional Children, 49,* 486–494.

Carbo, M. (1987). Reading styles research: What works isn't always phonics. *Phi Delta Kappan, 68,* 431–445.

Carbo, M. (1988). Debunking the great phonics myth. *Phi Delta Kappan, 70,* 226–239.

Carbo, M., Dunn, R., & Dunn, K. (1986). *Teaching students to read through their individual learning styles*. Englewood Cliffs, NJ: Prentice-Hall.

Carnegie Council on Adolescent Development. (1989). *Turning points: Preparing American youth for the 21st century*. New York: Author.

Carnine, D.W., (1980). Preteaching versus concurrent teaching of the component skills of a multiplication algorithm. *Journal for Research in Mathematics Education, 11,* 375–379.

Carnine, D.W., (1989). Teaching complex content to learning disabled students: The role of technology. *Exceptional Children, 55,* 524–533.

Carnine, D.W., (1991). Curricular interventions for teaching higher order thinking to all students: Introduction to the special series. *Journal of Learning Disabilities, 24,* 261–269.

Carnine, D.W., & Engleman, S. (1981). *Corrective mathematics*. Chicago: Science Research Associates.

Carnine, D.W., & Kinder, B.D. (1985). Teaching low-performing students to apply generative and schema strategies to narrative and expository material. *Remedial and Special Education, 6,* 20–30.

Carnine, D.W., & Silbert, J. (1979). *Direct instruction reading*. Columbus, OH: Merrill.

Carnine, D.W., Silbert, J., & Kameenui, E.J. (1990). *Direct instruction reading* (2nd ed.). Columbus, OH: Merrill.

Carpenter, D. (1983). Spelling error profiles of able and disabled readers. *Journal of Learning Disabilities, 16,* 102–104.

Carpenter, D., & Miller, L.J. (1982). Spelling ability of reading disabled LD students and able readers. *Learning Disability Quarterly, 5,* 65–70.

Carter, J., & Sugai, G. (1989). Social skills curriculum analysis. *Teaching Exceptional Children, 22,* 36–39.

Cawley, J.F., Baker-Kroczynski, S., & Urban, A. (1992). Seeking excellence in mathematics education for students with mild disabilities. *Teaching Exceptional Children, 24,* 40–43.

Cawley, J.F., Fitzmaurice, A.M., Goodstein, H.A., Lepore, A.V., Sedlak, R., & Althaus, V. (1976). *Project MATH*. Tulsa, OK: Educational Development Corporation.

Cawley, J.F., Fitzmaurice-Hayes, A.M., & Shaw, R. (1988). *Mathematics for the mildly handicapped: A guide to curriculum and instruction*. Boston: Allyn & Bacon.

Cawley, J.F., Kahn, H., & Tedesco, A. (1989). Vocational education and students with learning disabilities. *Journal of Learning Disabilities, 22,* 630–634.

Cawley, J.F., & Miller, J.H. (1986). Selected views on metacognition, arithmetic problem solving, and learning disabilities. *Learning Disabilities Focus, 2,* 36–48.

Cawley, J.F., Miller, J.H., & School, B.A. (1987). A brief inquiry of arithmetic word-problem-solving among learning disabled secondary students. *Learning Disabilities Focus, 2,* 87–93.

Cawley, J.F., & Parmar, R.S. (1992). Arithmetic programming for students with disabilities: An alternative. *Remedial and Special Education, 13,* 6–18.

Center, D.B., & Wascom, A.M. (1987). Teacher perceptions of social behavior in behaviorally disordered and socially normal children and youth. *Behavioral Disorders, 12,* 200–206.

Center for Special Education Technology. (1990, September). *Computers and cooperative learning*. Reston, VA: Council for Exceptional Children.

Chalfant, J.C., Pysh, M.V., & Moultrie, R. (1979). Teacher assistance teams: A model for within-building problem solving. *Learning Disability Quarterly, 2,* 85–96.

Chall, J.S. (1967). *Learning to read: The great debate*. New York: McGraw-Hill.

Chall, J.S. (1983). *Stages of reading development*. New York: McGraw-Hill.

Chall, J.S. (1989, March). "Learning to read: The great debate 20 years later—A response

to 'Debunking the great phonics myth.' "
Phi Delta Kappan, pp. 521–538.

Chan, S. (1987). Parents of exceptional Asian children. In M.K. Kitano & P.C. Chinn (Eds.). *Exceptional Asian children and youth* (pp. 36–53). Reston, VA: Council for Exceptional Children.

Chinn, P.C., & Hughes, S. (1987). Representation of minority students in special education classes. *Remedial and Special Education, 8*(4), 41–46.

Choate, J.S. (1990). Study the problem. *Teaching Exceptional Children, 22,* 44–46.

Choate, J.S., Enright, B.E., Miller, L.J., Poteet, J.A., & Rakes, T.A. (1992). *Curriculum-based assessment and programming* (2nd ed.). Boston: Allyn & Bacon.

Christensen, C.A., & Gerber, M.M. (1990). Effectiveness of computerized drill and practice games in teaching basic math facts. *Exceptionality, 1,* 149–165.

Christenson, S.L., Thurlow, M.L., & Ysseldyke, J.E. (1987). *Instructional effectiveness research: Implications for effective instruction of handicapped students* (Monograph No. 4). Minneapolis: University of Minnesota Institute for Research on Learning Disabilities.

Christenson, S.L., Ysseldyke, J.E., & Thurlow, M.L. (1989). Critical instructional factors for students with mild handicaps: An integrative review. *Remedial and Special Education, 10,* 21–31.

Clark, F.L., Deshler, D.D., Schumaker, J.B., Alley, G.R., & Warner, M.M. (1984). Visual imagery and self-questioning: Strategies to improve comprehension of written material. *Journal of Learning Disabilities, 17,* 145–149.

Clark, G.M., & Kolstoe, O.P. (1990). *Career development and transition education for adolescents with disabilities.* Boston: Allyn & Bacon.

Clarke, L.K. (1988). Invented versus traditional spelling in first grader's writings: Effects on learning to spell and read. *Research in the Teaching of English, 22,* 281–309.

Coates, R.D. (1989). The regular education initiative and opinions of regular classroom teachers. *Journal of Learning Disabilities, 22,* 532–536.

Cohen, S.B., & deBettencourt, L.V. (1988). Teaching children to be independent learners: A step-by-step strategy. In E.L. Meyen, G.A. Vergason, & R.J. Whelan (Eds.), *Effective instructional strategies for exceptional children* (pp. 319–334). Denver, CO: Love.

Cohen, S.B., & deBettencourt, L.V. (1991). Dropout: Intervening with the reluctant learner. *Intervention in School and Clinic, 26*(5), 263–271.

Cohen, S.B., & Hart-Hester, S. (1987). Time management strategies. *Teaching Exceptional Children, 20*(1), 56–57.

Cohen, S.B., & Hearn, D. (1988). Reinforcement. In R. McNergney (Ed.), *Guide to Classroom Teaching.* Boston: Allyn & Bacon.

Cohen, S.B., & Lynch, D.K. (1991). An instructional modification process. *Teaching Exceptional Children, 23,* 12–18.

Connolly, A.J. (1988). *KeyMath—Revised: A diagnostic battery of essential math skills.* Circle Pines, MN: American Guidance Service.

Coutinho, M.J. (1986). Reading achievement of students identified as behaviorally disordered at the secondary level. *Behavioral Disorders, 11,* 200–207.

Crabtree, C. (1989). Improving history in the schools. *Educational Leadership, 47*(3), 25–28.

Cronin, M.E. (1988). Applying curriculum for the instruction of life skills. In G.A. Robinson, J.R. Patton, E.A. Polloway, & L.R. Sargent (Eds.), *Best practices in mental disabilities* (Vol. 2, pp. 41–52). Des Moines: Iowa Department of Education, Bureau of Special Education.

Cruickshank, W.M. (1975). The learning environment. In W.M. Cruickshank & D.P. Hallahan (Eds.), *Perceptual and learning disabilities in children: Vol. 1. Psychoeducational practices.* Syracuse, NY: Syracuse University Press.

Cruickshank, W.M., Bentzen, F.A., Ratzeburg, F.H., & Tannhauser, M.T. (1961). *A teaching method for brain-injured and hyperactive children.* Syracuse, NY: Syracuse University Press.

Cullinan, B.E. (1987). Inviting readers to literature. In B.E. Cullinan (Ed.), *Children's literature in the reading program* (pp. 2–14). Newark, DE: International Reading Association.

Cullinan, D., Lloyd, J., & Epstein, M.H. (1981). Strategy training: A structured approach to arithmetic instruction. *Exceptional Education Quarterly, 2,* 41–49.

Cybriwsky, C.A., & Schuster, J.W. (1990). Using constant time delay procedures to teach multiplication facts. *Remedial and Special Education, 11,* 54–59.

Dangel, H.L. (1987). The coach's spelling approach. *Teaching Exceptional Children, 19,* 20–22.

Davidson, J. (1969). *Using the Cuisenaire rods.* New Rochelle, NY: Cuisenaire Company of America.

Davis, R.W., & Hajicek, J.O. (1985). Effects of self-instructional training and strategy training on a mathematics task with severely behaviorally disordered students. *Behavioral Disorders, 10,* 275–282.

Davis, W.D. (1988). The regular education initiative debate: Its promises and problems. *Exceptional Children, 55,* 440–446.

deBettencourt, L.U. (1987). How to develop parent relationships. *Teaching Exceptional Children, 19*(2), 26–27.

Deluke, S.V., & Knoblock, P. (1987). Teacher behavior as preventive discipline. *Teaching Exceptional Children, 19*(4), 18–24.

DeMaster, V.K., Crossland, C.L., & Hasselbring, T.S. (1986). Consistency of learning disabled students' spelling performance. *Learning Disability Quarterly, 9,* 89–96.

Deno, S.L. (1985). Curriculum-based measurement: The emerging alternative. *Exceptional Children, 52,* 219–231.

Deshler, D.D., Alley, G.R., Warner, M.N., & Schumaker, J.B. (1981). Instructional practices for promoting skill acquisition and generalization in severely learning disabled adolescents. *Learning Disability Quarterly, 4,* 415–421.

Deshler, D.D., & Schumaker, J.B. (1986). Learning strategies: An instructional alternative for low-achieving adolescents. *Exceptional Children, 52,* 583–590.

Deshler, D.D., & Schumaker, J.B. (1988). An instructional model for teaching students

how to learn. In J.L. Graden, J.E. Zins, & M.J. Curtis (Eds.), *Alternative educational delivery systems: Enhancing instructional options for all students* (pp. 391–411). Washington, DC: National Association of School Psychologists.

Deshler, D.D., Schumaker, J.B., Alley, G.R., Warner, M.M., & Clark, F.L. (1982). Learning disabilities in adolescent and young adult populations: Research implications. *Focus on Exceptional Children, 15,*(1), 1–12.

Devine, T.G. (1987). *Teaching study skills: A guide for teachers* (2nd ed.). Boston: Allyn & Bacon.

Dickinson, D.J. (1980). The direct assessment: An alternative to psychometric testing. *Journal of Learning Disabilities, 13*(9), 8–12.

Dixon, R.C. (1987). Strategies for vocabulary instruction. *Teaching Exceptional Children, 19,* 61–63.

Dixon, R.C. (1991). The application of sameness analysis to spelling. *Journal of Learning Disabilities, 24,* 285–291.

D'Nealian Home/School Activities: Manuscript Practice for Grades 1–3. (1986). Glenview, IL: Scott, Foresman.

Donahoe, K., & Zigmond, N. (1990). Academic grades of ninth-grade urban learning-disabled students and low-achieving peers. *Exceptionality, 1,* 17–27.

Donaldson, R., & Christiansen, J. (1990). Consultation and collaboration: A decision-making model. *Teaching Exceptional Children, 22,* 22–25.

Dowis, C.L., & Schloss, P. (1992). The impact of mini-lessons on writing skills. *Remedial and Special Education, 13*(5), 34–42.

Downing, J. (1965). *The initial teaching alphabet reading experiment.* Chicago: Scott, Foresman.

Downing J.A., Simpson, R.L., & Myles, B.S. (1990). Regular and special educator perceptions of nonacademic skills needed by mainstreamed students with behavioral disorders and learning disabilities. *Behavioral Disorders, 15,* 217–226.

Dunn, R. (1988). Teaching students through their perceptual strengths or preferences. *Journal of Reading, 31,* 304–309.

DuPaul, G.J., Rapport, M.D., & Perriello, L.M. (1991). Teacher ratings of academic skills: The development of the academic performance rating scale. *School Psychology Review, 20,* 284–300.

Dyck, N., & Sundbye, N. (1988). The effects of text explicitness on story understanding and recall by learning disabled children. *Learning Disabilities Research, 3,* 68–77.

Edgar, E. (1987). Secondary programs in special education: Are any of them justifiable? *Exceptional Children, 53,* 555–561.

Edmark Reading Program. (1972). Bellevue, WA: The Edmark Corporation.

Ehri, L.C. (1989). The development of spelling knowledge and its role in reading acquisition and reading disability. *Journal of Learning Disabilities, 22,* 356–365.

Eiserman, W.D. (1988). Three types of peer tutoring: Effects on the attitudes of students with learning disabilities and their regular class peers. *Journal of Learning Disabilities, 21*(4), 249–252.

Eitzen, D.S. (1992). Problem students: The sociocultural roots. *Phi Delta Kappan, 73,* 584–590.

Ekwall, E.E. (1989). *Locating and correcting reading difficulties* (5th ed). Columbus, OH: Merrill.

Ellis, E.S. (1986). The role of motivation and pedagogy on the generalization of cognitive training by the mildly handicapped. *Journal of Learning Disabilities, 19,* 66–70.

Ellis, E.S. (1989). A metacognitive intervention for increasing class participation. *Learning Disabilities Focus, 5,* 36–46.

Ellis, E.S., Deshler, D.D., Lenz, B.K., Schumaker, J.B., & Clark, F.L. (1991). An instructional model for teaching learning strategies. *Focus on Exceptional Children, 24*(1), 1–14.

Ellis, E.S., Deshler, D.D., & Schumaker, J.B. (1989). Teaching adolescents with learning disabilities to generate and use task-specific strategies. *Journal of Learning Disabilities, 22,* 108–119.

Ellis, E.S., & Lenz, B.K. (1987). A component analysis of effective learning strategies for LD students. *Learning Disabilities Focus, 2,* 94–107.

Engelmann, S., Becker, W., Hanner, S., & Johnson, G. (1980). *Corrective reading program.* Chicago: Science Research Associates.

Engelmann, S., & Bruner, E. (1984). *Reading Mastery: DISTAR Reading.* Chicago: Science Research Associates.

Engelmann, S., & Carnine, D. (1972, 1975, 1976). *DISTAR Arithmetic: DISTAR I, DISTAR II, and DISTAR III.* Chicago: Science Research Associates.

Engelmann, S., & Carnine, D. (1982). *Corrective mathematics program.* Chicago: Science Research Associates.

Engelmann, S., Carnine, L., Johnson, G., & Meyers, L. (1988). *Corrective reading: Decoding.* Chicago: Science Research Associates.

Engelmann, S., Carnine, D., & Steely, D.G. (1991). Making connections in mathematics. *Journal of Learning Disabilities, 24,* 292–303.

Englert, C.S. (1983). Measuring special education teacher effectiveness. *Exceptional Children, 50,* 247–254.

Englert, C.S. (1984). Effective direct instruction practices in special education settings. *Remedial and Special Education, 5*(2), 38–47.

Englert, C.S. (1992). Writing instruction from a sociocultural perspective: The holistic, dialogic, and social enterprise of writing. *Journal of Learning Disabilities, 25,* 153–172.

Englert, C.S., & Mariage, T.V. (1991). Shared understandings: Structuring the writing experience through dialogue. *Journal of Learning Disabilities, 24,* 330–342.

Englert, C.S., & Raphael, T.E. (1990). Developing successful writers through cognitive strategy instruction. In J. Brophy (Ed.), *Advances in research on teaching* (pp. 105–151). Greenwich, CT: JAI Press.

Englert, C.S., Raphael, T.E., Anderson, L.M., Anthony, H.M., Fear, K.L., & Gregg, S.L. (1988). A case for writing intervention: Strategies for writing informational text. *Learning Disabilities Focus, 3,* 98–113.

Enright, B., & Beattie, J. (1989). Problem solving step by step in math. *Teaching Exceptional Children, 22,* 58–59.

Epstein, M.H., Kinder, D., & Bursuck, B. (1989). The academic status of adolescents with behavioral disorders. *Behavioral Disorders, 14,* 157–165.

Everson, J.M. (1990). A local team approach. *Teaching Exceptional Children, 23,* 44–46.

Fad, K.S. (1990). The fast track to success: Social-behavioral skills. *Intervention in School and Clinic, 26*(1), 39–43.

Fagley, N.S. (1984). Behavioral assessment in the schools: Obtaining and evaluating information for individualized programming. *Special Services in the Schools, 1*(2), 45–57.

Feingold, B.F. (1976). Hyperkinesis and learning disabilities linked to the ingestion of artificial food color and flavors. *Journal of Learning Disabilities, 9,* 551–559.

Fernald, G.M. (1943). *Remedial techniques in basic school subjects.* New York: McGraw-Hill.

Fessler, M.A., Rosenberg, M.S., & Rosenberg, L.A. (1991). Concomitant learning disabilities and learning problems among students with behavioral/emotional disorders. *Behavioral Disorders, 16,* 97–106.

Fimian, M., Fafard, M.B., & Howell, K. (1984). *A teacher's guide to human resources in special education: Paraprofessionals, volunteers, and peer tutors.* Boston: Allyn & Bacon.

Flavell, J.H. (1979). Metacognition and cognitive monitoring: A new area of cognitive-developmental inquiry. *American Psychologist, 34,* 906–911.

Fleischner, J.E., Nuzum, M.B., & Marzola, E.S. (1987). Devising an instructional program to teach arithmetic problem-solving skills to students with learning disabilities. *Journal of Learning Disabilities, 20,* 214–217.

Flexer, R.J. (1989). Conceptualizing addition. *Teaching Exceptional Children, 21,* 20–25.

Foorman, B.R., & Liberman, D. (1989). Visual and phonological processing of words: A comparison of good and poor readers. *Journal of Learning Disabilities, 22,* 349–355.

Forness, S.R., & Kavale, K.A. (1988). Psychopharmacologic treatment: A note on classroom effects. *Journal of Learning Disabilities, 21,* 144–147.

Frankenberger, W., & Fronzaglio, K. (1991). A review of states' criteria and procedures for identifying children with learning disabilities. *Journal of Learning Disabilities, 24,* 495–500.

Freyd, P., & Lytle, J.H. (1990). A corporate approach to the 2 R's: A critique of IBM's Writing to Read program. *Educational Leadership, 47,* 83–89.

Fuchs, D., Fuchs, L.S., & Bahr, M.W. (1990). Mainstream assistance teams: A scientific basis for the art of consultation. *Exceptional Children, 57,* 128–139.

Fuchs, L.S. (1986). Monitoring progress among mildly handicapped pupils: Review of current practice and research. *Remedial and Special Education, 7*(5), 5–12.

Fuchs, L.S., Allinder, R.M., Hamlett, C.L., & Fuchs, D. (1990). An analysis of spelling curricula and teachers' skills in identifying error types. *Remedial and Special Education, 11,* 42–52.

Fuchs, L.S., Bahr, C.M., & Rieth, H.J. (1989). Effects of goal structures and performance contingencies on math performance of adolescents with learning disabilities. *Journal of Learning Disabilities, 22,* 554–560.

Fuchs, L.S., Fuchs, D., & Bishop, N. (1992). Teacher planning for students with learning disabilities: Differences between general and special educators. *Learning Disabilities Research and Practice, 7,* 120–128.

Fuchs, L.S., Fuchs, D., & Hamlett, C.L. (1989). Effects of alternative goal structures within curriculum-based measurement. *Exceptional Children, 55,* 429–438.

Fuchs, L.S., Fuchs, D., Hamlett, C.L., & Allinder, R.M. (1991). The contribution of skills analysis to curriculum-based measurement in spelling. *Exceptional Children, 57,* 443–452.

Fuchs, L.S., Fuchs, D., & Stecker, P. (1989). Effects of curriculum-based measurement on teachers' instructional planning. *Journal of Learning Disabilities, 22*(1), 51–59.

Gallagher, P.A. (1979). *Teaching students with behavior disorders: Techniques for classroom instruction.* Denver, CO: Love.

Gallegos, A.Y., & Gallegos, M.L. (1990). A student's perspective on good teaching: Michael. *Intervention in School and Clinic, 26,* 14–15.

Gardner, W. (1982). Why do we persist? *Education and Treatment of Children, 5,* 369–378.

Gartland, D. (1990). Classroom management: Preventive discipline. *LD Forum, 15*(3), 24–25.

Gartland, D., & Rosenberg, M.S. (1987). Managing time in the LD classroom. *LD Forum, 12*(2), 8–10.

Gast, D.L., Wolery, M., Morris, L.L., Doyle, P.M., & Meyer, S. (1990). Teaching sight word reading in a group instructional arrangement using constant time delay. *Exceptionality, 1,* 81–96.

Gerber, M.M. (1984). Orthographic problem-solving ability of learning-disabled and normally achieving students. *Learning Disability Quarterly, 17,* 157–164.

Gerber, M.M. (1988). Cognitive-behavioral training in the curriculum: Time, slow learners, and basic skills. In E.L. Meyen, G.A. Vergason, & R.J. Whelan (Eds.), *Effective instructional strategies for exceptional children* (pp. 45–64). Denver, CO: Love.

Gersten, R., & Diminio, J. (1990). *Reading instruction for at-risk students: Implications of current research* (OSSC Bulletin Vol. 33, No. 5). Eugene: Oregon School Study Council.

Gersten, R., & Keating, T. (1987). Long-term benefits from direct instruction. *Educational Leadership, 44,* 28–31.

Giek, K.A. (1992). Monitoring student progress through efficient record keeping. *Teaching Exceptional Children, 24*(3), 22–26.

Gilliam, H.V., & Van Den Berg, S. (1980). Different levels of eye contact: Effects on black and white college students. *Urban Education, 15,* 83–92.

Gillingham, A., & Stillman, B.W., (1956). *Remedial training for children with special disability in reading, spelling, and penmanship.* Cambridge, MA: Educator's Publishing Service.

Gillingham, A., & Stillman, B.W. (1973). *Remedial training for children with specific disability in reading, spelling, and penmanship.* Cambridge, MA: Educators Publishing Service.

Glickman, C.D. (1990). *Supervision of instruction: A developmental approach* (3rd ed.). Boston: Allyn & Bacon.

Glomb, N., & West, R.P. (1990). Teaching behaviorally disordered adolescents to use self-management skills for improving the completeness, accuracy, and neatness of creative writing homework assignments. *Behavioral Disorders, 15,* 233–242.

Goldstein, A.P. (1981). Social skills training. In A.P. Goldstein, E.G. Carr, W.S. Davidson, & P. Weher (Eds.), *In response to aggression: Methods of control and prosocial alternatives.* New York: Pergamon Press.

Goldstein, A.P., Sprafkin, R.P., Gershaw, N.J., & Klein, P. (1980). *Skillstreaming the adolescent.* Champaign, IL: Research Press.

Good, R.H., & Salvia, J. (1988). Curriculum bias in published norm-referenced reading tests: Demonstrable effects. *School Psychology Review, 17*(1), 51–60.

Good, T.L., Grouws, D.A., & Backerman, T. (1978). Curriculum pacing: Some empirical data in mathematics. *Journal of Curriculum Studies, 10,* 75–82.

Goodman, K.S. (1970). Behind the eye: What happens in reading. In K.S. Goodman & O.S. Niles (Eds.), *Reading process and program* (pp. 3–38). Urbana, IL: National Council of Teachers of Reading.

Goodman, K.S. (1986). *What's whole in whole language?* Portsmouth, NH: Heineman.

Gorton, C.E. (1972). The effects of various classroom environments on performance of a mental task by mentally retarded and normal children. *Education and Training of the Mentally Retarded, 7,* 32–38.

Graden, J., Casey, A., & Bonstrom, O. (1985). Implementing a prereferral intervention system: Part II. The data. *Exceptional Children, 51,* 487–496.

Graham, S., & Harris, K.R. (1988). Instructional recommendations for teaching writing to exceptional students. *Exceptional Children, 54,* 506–512.

Graham, S., & Harris, K.R. (1989a). Components analysis of cognitive strategy instruction: Effects on learning disabled students' compositions and self-efficacy. *Journal of Educational Psychology, 81,* 353–361.

Graham, S., & Harris, K.R. (1989b). Improving learning disabled students' skills at composing essays: Self-instructional strategy training. *Exceptional Children, 56,* 201–214.

Graham, S., Harris, K.R., & Sawyer, R. (1987). Composition instruction with learning disabled students: Self-instructional strategy training. *Focus on Exceptional Children, 20*(4), 1–11.

Graham, S., & MacArthur, C. (1988). Improving learning disabled students' skills at revising essays produced on a word processor: Self-instructional strategy training. *Journal of Special Education, 22,* 133–152.

Graham, S., & Miller, L. (1979). Spelling research and practice: A unified approach. *Focus on Exceptional Children, 12*(2), 1–16.

Graves, A.W. (1986). Effects of direct instruction and metacomprehension training on finding main ideas. *Learning Disabilities Research, 1,* 90–100.

Graves, A.W. (1987). Improving comprehension skills. *Teaching Exceptional Children, 19,* 63–65.

Graves, D.H. (1985). All children can write. *Learning Disability Focus, 1,* 36–43.

Greenwood, C.R., Delquadri, J.C., & Hall, R.V. (1984). Opportunity to respond and student academic performance. In W.L. Heward, T.E. Heron, D.S. Hill, & J. Trap-Porter (Eds.), *Focus on behavior analysis in education* (pp. 58–88). Columbus, OH: Merrill.

Gresham, F.M., & Elliott, S.N. (1990). *Social Skills Rating System (SSRS).* Circle Pines, MN: American Guidance Service.

Gresham, F.M., Elliott, S.N., & Black, F.L. (1987). Teacher-rated social skills of mainstreamed mildly handicapped and nonhandicapped children. *School Psychology Review, 16,* 78–88.

Griffey, Q.L., Zigmond, N., & Leinhardt, G. (1988). The effects of self-questioning and story structure training on the reading comprehension of poor readers. *Learning Disabilities Research, 4,* 45–51.

Grossman, H.J. (Ed.). (1983). *Classification in mental retardation.* Washington, DC: American Association on Mental Deficiency.

Guerin, G., & Maier, A. (1983). *Informal assessment in education.* Palo Alto, CA: Mayfield.

Guernsey, M.A. (1989). Classroom organization: A key to successful management. *Academic Therapy, 25*(1), 55–58.

Gurney, D., Gersten, R., Dimino, J., & Carnine, D. (1990). Story grammar: Effective literature instruction for high school students with learning disabilities. *Journal of Learning Disabilities, 23,* 335–342.

Guszak, F.J. (1972). *Diagnostic reading instruction in the elementary school.* New York: Harper & Row.

Gutkin, T.B., & Curtis, J.M. (1990). School-based consultation: Theory, techniques and research. In T.B. Gutkin & C.R. Reynolds (Eds.), *The Handbook of School Psychology* (2nd ed.), pp. 577–611. New York: Wiley.

Guyer, B.P., & Sabatino, D. (1989). The effectiveness of a multisensory alphabetic phonetic approach with college students who are learning disabled. *Journal of Learning Disabilities, 22,* 430–434.

Hallahan, D.P., & Cruickshank, W.M. (1973). *Psychoeducational foundations of learning disabilities.* Englewood Cliffs, NJ: Prentice-Hall.

Hallahan, D.P., & Kauffman, J.M. (1975). Research on the education of distractible and hyperactive children. In W.M. Cruickshank & D.P. Hallahan (Eds.), *Perceptual and learning disabilities in children, Vol. 2. Research and theory* (pp. 221–258). Syracuse, NY: Syracuse University Press.

Hallahan, D.P., & Kauffman, J.M. (1977). Labels, categories, behaviors: ED, LD, and EMR reconsidered. *Journal of Special Education, 11,* 139–149.

Hallahan, D.P., & Kauffman, J.M. (1991). *Exceptional children: Introduction to special education* (5th ed.). Englewood Cliffs, NJ: Prentice-Hall.

Hallahan, D.P., Kauffman, J.M., & Lloyd, J.W. (1985). *Introduction to learning disabilities.* Englewood Cliffs, NJ: Prentice-Hall.

Hallahan, D.P., Keller, C.E., McKinney, J.D., Lloyd, J.W., & Bryan, T. (1988). Examining the research base of the regular education initiative: Efficacy studies and the adaptive learning environments model. *Journal of Learning Disabilities, 21,* 29–35.

Hallahan, D.P., Lloyd, J.W., & Stoller, L. (1982). *Improving attention with self-monitoring: A manual for teachers.* Charlottesville: University of Virginia Learning Disabilities Research Institute.

Halpern, A.S. (1992). Transition: Old wine in new bottles. *Exceptional Children, 58,* 202–211.

Hammill, D.D. (1990). On defining Learning Disabilities: An emerging consensus. *Journal of Learning Disabilities 23,* 74–84.

Hammill, D.D., Brown, L.L., Larsen, S.C., & Wiederholt, J.L. (1987). *Test of adolescent language—2.* Austin, TX: Pro-Ed.

Hammill, D.D., Leigh, J.E., McNutt, G., & Larsen, S.C. (1981). A new definition of learning disabilities. *Learning Disability Quarterly, 4,* 336–342.

Hammill, D.D., & Newcomer, P.L. (1988). *Test of language development—2: Intermediate.* Austin, TX: Pro-Ed.

Hanau, L. (1974). *The study game: How to play and win with Statement-Pie.* New York: Barnes & Noble.

Hanover, S. (1983). Handwriting comes naturally? *Academic Therapy, 18,* 407–412.

Hargis, C.H. (1982). Word recognition development. *Focus on Exceptional Children, 14*(9), 1–8.

Harris, L. & Associates, Inc. (1989). *The metropolitan life survey of the American teacher 1989: Preparing schools for the 1990's.* New York: Author.

Harris, T., Creekmore, M., & Greenman, M. (1967). *Phonetic keys to reading.* Oklahoma City: Economy Company.

Harris, K.R., & Pressley, M. (1991). The nature of cognitive strategy instruction: Interactive strategy construction. *Exceptional Children, 57,* 392–404.

Hasselbring, T.S., Goin, L.I., & Bransford, J.D. (1987). Developing automaticity. *Teaching Exceptional Children, 19,* 30–33.

Hayes, J., & Flower, L. (1986). Writing research and the writer. *American Psychologist, 41,* 1106–1113.

Haynes, M.C., & Jenkins, J.R. (1986). Reading instruction in special education resource rooms. *American Educational Research Journal, 23,* 161–190.

Hembree, R. (1986). Research gives calculators a green light. *Arithmetic Teacher, 34,* 18–21.

Henk, W.A., Helfeldt, J.P., & Platt, J.M. (1986). Developing reading fluency in learning disabled students. *Teaching Exceptional Children, 18,* 202–206.

Henrico County Public Schools. (1989). *Tutoring: Lending a helping hand.* Richmond, VA: Author.

Herman, R. (1975). *The Herman Method for Reversing Reading Failure.* Sherman Oaks, CA: Romar Publications.

Heron, T.E., & Harris, K.C. (1987). *The educational consultant* (2nd ed.). Austin, TX: Pro-Ed.

Higgins, K., & Boone, R. (1990a). Hypertext: A new vehicle for computer use in reading instruction. *Intervention in School and Clinic, 26,* 26–31.

Higgins, K., & Boone, R. (1990b). Hypertext computer study guides and the social studies achievement of students with learning disabilities, remedial students, and regular education students. *Journal of Learning Disabilities, 23,* 529–540.

Hightower, A.D., Work, W.C., Cowen, E.L., Lotyczewski, B.S., Spinell, A.P., Guare, J.C., & Rohrbeck, C.A. (1986). The teacher-child rating scale: A brief objective measure of elementary children's school problem behaviors and competencies. *School Psychology Review, 15,* 393–409.

Hoffman, E. (1988). Time management from the kitchen. *Academic Therapy, 23*(3), 275–277.

Hoffmeister, A.M. (1981). *Handwriting resource book: Manuscript/cursive.* Allen, TX: DLM Teaching Resources.

Horton, S.V., & Lovitt, T.C. (1989). Using study guides with three classifications of secondary students. *Journal of Special Education, 22,* 447–462.

Horton, S.V., Lovitt, T.C., & Christensen, C.C. (1991). Notetaking from textbooks: Effects of a columnar format on three categories of secondary students. *Exceptionality, 2,* 19–40.

Horton, S.V., Lovitt, T.C., & White, O.R. (1992). Teaching mathematics to adolescents classified as educable mentally handicapped: Using calculators to remove the computational onus. *Remedial and Special Education, 13*, 36–46.

Howell, K.W. (1985). Task analysis and the characteristics of tasks. *Journal of Special Education Technology, 6*, 5–14.

Howell, K.W. (1986). Direct assessment of academic performance. *School Psychology Review, 15*, 324–335.

Howell, R., Sidorenko, E., & Jurica, J. (1987). The effects of computer use on the acquisition of multiplication facts by a student with learning disabilities. *Journal of Learning Disabilities, 20*, 336–341.

Hughes, C.A., Schumaker, J.B., Deshler, D.D., & Mercer, C. (1987). *The test-taking strategy*. Lawrence, KS: Excel Enterprises.

Hunter, M. (1982). *Mastery teaching*. El Segundo, CA: TIP Publications.

Idol, L. (1987). Group story mapping: A comprehension strategy for both skilled and unskilled readers. *Journal of Learning Disabilities, 20*, 196–205.

Idol-Maestas, L., & Ritter, S. (1985). A follow-up study of resource/consulting teachers. *Teacher Education and Special Education, 8*, 121–131.

Isaacson, S.L. (1988). Effective instruction in written language. In E.L. Meyen, G.A. Vergason, & R.J. Whelan (Eds.), *Effective instructional strategies for exceptional children* (pp. 288–306). Denver, CO: Love.

Isaacson, S.L. (1992). Volleyball and other analogies: A response to Englert. *Journal of Learning Disabilities, 25*, 173–177.

Jackson, N.F., Jackson, D.A., & Monroe, C. (1983). *Getting along with others: Teaching social effectiveness to children*. Champaign, IL: Research Press.

Jenkins, J.R., Gorrafa, Q., & Griffiths, S. (1972). Another look at isolation effects. *American Journal of Mental Deficiency, 76*, 591–593.

Jenkins, J., & Jenkins, L. (1988). Peer tutoring in elementary and secondary programs. In E.L. Meyen, G.A. Vergason, & R.J. Whelan (Eds.), *Effective instructional strategies for exceptional children* (pp. 335–354). Denver, CO: Love.

Jenkins, J.R., Stein, M.L., & Osborn, J.R. (1981). What next after decoding?

Instruction and research in reading comprehension. *Exceptional Education Quarterly, 2*, 27–39.

Jenson, W.R., Sloane, H.N., & Young, K.R. (1988). *Applied behavior analysis in education: A structured teaching approach*. Englewood Cliffs, NJ: Prentice-Hall.

Johnson, D.D. (1971). The Dolch list reexamined. *The Reading Teacher, 24*, 455–456.

Johnson, D.J., & Myklebust, H.R. (1967). *Learning disabilities: Educational principles and practices*. New York: Grune & Stratton.

Johnson, D.W., & Johnson, R.T. (1986). Mainstreaming and cooperative learning strategies. *Exceptional Children, 52*, 553–562.

Johnson, D.W., & Johnson, R.T. (1987). *Learning together and alone: Cooperative, competitive, and individualistic learning* (2nd ed.). Englewood Cliffs, NJ: Prentice-Hall.

Johnson, L.J., Pugach, M.C., & Hammitte, D.J. (1988). Barriers to effective special education consultation. *Remedial and Special Education, 9*, 41–47.

Johnson, L.J., Pugach, M.C., & Devlin, S. (1990). Professional collaboration. *Teaching Exceptional Children, 22*, 9–11.

Jones, G.A., Thornton, C.A., & Toohey, M.A. (1985). A multi-option program for learning basic addition facts: Case studies and an experimental report. *Journal of Learning Disabilities, 18*, 319–325.

Jones, K.H., & Bender, W.N. (1993). Utilization of paraprofessionals in special education: A review of the literature. *Remedial and Special Education, 14*(1), 7–14.

Kagan, S. (1990). *Cooperative learning: Resources for teachers*. San Juan Capistrano, CA: Spencer Kagan, Ph.D.

Kameenui, E.J., & Simmons, D.C. (1990). *Designing instructional strategies: The prevention of academic learning problems*. Columbus, OH: Merrill.

Kane, B.J., & Alley, G.R. (1980). A peer tutored instructional management program in computational mathematics for incarcerated learning disabled juvenile delinquents. *Journal of Learning Disabilities, 13*, 39–42.

Kauffman, J.M. (1989a). *Characteristics of behavior disorders of children and youth* (4th ed.). Columbus, OH: Merrill.

Kauffman, J.M. (1989b). The regular education initiative as Reagan-Bush education policy: A trickle-down theory of education of the hard-to-teach. *Journal of Special Education, 23,* 256–278.

Kauffman, J.M., Gerber, M.M., & Semmel, M.I. (1988). Arguable assumptions underlying the regular education initiative. *Journal of Learning Disabilities, 21,* 6–11.

Kauffman, J.M., Hallahan, D.P., Haas, K., Brame, T., & Boren, R. (1978). Imitating children's errors to improve their spelling performance. *Journal of Learning Disabilities, 11,* 217–222.

Kauffman, J.M., Wong, K.L.H., Lloyd, J.W., Hung, L., & Pullen, P.L. (1991). What puts pupils at risk? An analysis of classroom teachers' judgments of pupils' behavior. *Remedial and Special Education, 12,* 7–16.

Kaufman, A.S., & Kaufman, N.L. (1985). *Kaufman tests of educational achievement.* Circle Pines, MN: American Guidance Service.

Kavale, K.A., & Forness, S.R. (1987). Substance over style: Assessing the efficacy of modality testing and teaching. *Exceptional Children, 54,* 228–239.

Keel, M.C., & Gast, D.L. (1992). Small-group instruction for students with learning disabilities: Observational and incidental learning. *Exceptional Children, 58*(4), 357–368.

Kelly, B., Gersten, R., & Carnine, D. (1990). Student error patterns as a function of curriculum design: Teaching fractions to remedial high school students and high school students with learning disabilities. *Journal of Learning Disabilities, 23,* 23–29.

Kerr, M.M., Zigmond, N., Schaeffer, A.L., & Brown, G. (1986). An observational follow-up study of successful and unsuccessful high school students. *High School Journal, 71,* 20–32.

Kinder, D., & Bursuck, W. (1991). The search for a unified social studies curriculum: Does history really repeat itself? *Journal of Learning Disabilities, 24,* 270–275.

King-Sears, M.E., Mercer, C.D., & Sindelar, P.T. (1992). Toward independence with keyword mnemonics: A strategy for science vocabulary instruction. *Remedial and Special Education, 13*(5), 22–33.

Kirby, J.R., & Becker, L.D. (1988). Cognitive components of learning problems in arithmetic. *Remedial and Special Education, 9,* 7–16.

Kirk, S.A., Kirk, W.D., & Minskoff, E.H. (1985). *Phonic remedial reading lessons.* Novato, CA: Academic Therapy Publications.

Kleinert, H.L., & Gast, D.L. (1982). Teaching a multihandicapped adult manual signs using a constant time delay procedure. *Journal of the Association of the Severely Handicapped, 6*(4), 25–32.

Kline, F.M., Schumaker, J.B., & Deshler, D.D. (1991). Development and validation of feedback routines for instructing students with learning disabilities. *Learning Disability Quarterly, 14,* 191–207.

Knapczyk, D. (1991). Effects of modeling in promoting generalization of student question asking and question answering. *Learning Disabilities Research and Practice, 6,* 75–82.

Knoff, H.M., McKenna, A.F., & Riser, K. (1991). Toward a consultant effectiveness scale: Investigating the characteristics of effective consultants. *School Psychology Review, 20,* 81–96.

Kuder, S.J. (1990). Effectiveness of the DISTAR Reading Program for children with learning disabilities. *Journal of Learning Disabilities, 23,* 69–71.

Kuder, S.J. (1991). Language abilities and progress in a direct instruction reading program for students with learning disabilities. *Journal of Learning Disabilities, 24,* 124–127.

LaBerge, D., & Samuels, S.J. (1974). Toward a theory of automatic information processing in reading. *Cognitive Psychology, 6,* 293–323.

Lapadat, J.C. (1991). Pragmatic language skills of students with language and/or learning disabilities: A quantitative synthesis. *Journal of Learning Disabilities, 24,* 147–158.

Laughton, J., & Morris, N.T. (1989). Story grammar knowledge of learning disabled students. *Learning Disabilities Research, 4,* 87–95.

Lenchner, O., Gerber, M.M., & Routh, D.K. (1990). Phonological awareness tasks as predictors of decoding ability: Beyond segmentation. *Journal of Learning Disabilities, 23,* 240–247.

Lenz, B.K., Alley, G.R., & Schumaker, J.B. (1987). Activating the inactive learner: Advance organizers in the secondary content classroom. *Learning Disability Quarterly, 10,* 53–68.

Lenz, B.K., & Hughes, C.A. (1990). A word identification strategy for adolescents with learning disabilities. *Journal of Learning Disabilities, 23,* 149–158.

Lenz, B.K., Schumaker, J.B., Deshler, D.D., & Beals, V.L. (1984). *Learning strategies curriculum: The word identification strategy.* Lawrence: University of Kansas Institute for Research on Learning Disabilities.

Lewis, E.R., & Lewis, H.P. (1965). An analysis of errors in the formation of manuscript letters by first grade children. *American Educational Research Journal, 2,* 25–35.

Liberman, I.Y., & Shankweiler, D. (1985). Phonology and the problems of learning to read and write. *Remedial and Special Education, 6,* 8–17.

Licht, B.G. (1984). Cognitive-motivational factors that contribute to the achievement of learning-disabled children. *Annual Review of Learning Disabilities, 2,* 119–126.

Lipstreu, B.L., & Johnson, M.K. (1988). Teaching time using the whole clock method. *Teaching Exceptional Children, 20,* 10–12.

Lloyd, J.W. (1984). How shall we individualize instruction: Or should we? *Remedial and Special Education, 5,* 7–15.

Lloyd, J.W. (1988). Direct academic interventions in learning disabilities. In M.C. Wang, M.C. Reynolds, & H.J. Walberg (Eds.), *Handbook of special education: Research and practice: Vol. 2. Mildly handicapped conditions.* (pp. 345–366). New York: Pergamon Press.

Lloyd, J.W., & Keller, C.E. (1989). Effective mathematics instruction: Development, instruction, and programs. *Focus on Exceptional Children, 21*(7), 1–10.

Lovitt, T.C., & Curtiss, K. (1968). Effects of manipulating an antecedent event on mathematics response rate. *Journal of Applied Behavior Analysis, 1,* 329–333.

Lubke, M.M., Rogers, B., & Evans, K.T. (1989). Teaching fractions with videodiscs. *Teaching Exceptional Children, 21,* 55–56.

Maag, J.W. (1989). Assessment in social skills training: Methodological and conceptual issues for research and practice. *Remedial and Special Education, 10,* 6–17.

Madge, S., Affleck, J., & Lowenbraun, S. (1990). Social effects of integrated classrooms and resource room/regular class placements on elementary students with learning disabilities. *Journal of Learning Disabilities, 23,* 439–445.

Maheady, L., & Harper, G.F. (1987). A classwide peer tutoring program to improve the spelling test performance of low income, third and fourth grade students. *Education and Treatment of Children, 10,* 120–133.

Maheady, L., Mallett, B., Harper, G.F., & Sacca, K. (1991). Heads Together: A peer-mediated option for improving the academic achievement of heterogeneous learning groups. *Remedial and Special Education, 12*(2), 25–33.

Maheady, L., Sacca, M.K., & Harper, G.F. (1987). Classwide student tutoring teams: The effects of peer mediated instruction on the academic performance of secondary mainstreamed students. *Journal of Special Education, 21,* 107–121.

Maheady, L., Sacca, M.K., & Harper, G.F. (1988). Classwide peer tutoring with mildly handicapped high school students. *Exceptional Children, 55*(1), 52–59.

Maher, G.B. (1989). ''Punch Out'': A behavior management technique. *Teaching Exceptional Children, 21*(2), 74.

Malouf, D.B., Jamison, P.J., Kercher, M.H., & Carlucci, C.M. (1991). Integrating computer software into effective instruction. *Teaching Exceptional Children, 23,* 54–56.

Mann, V.A., Cowin, E., & Schoenheimer, J. (1989). Phonological processing, language comprehension, and reading ability. *Journal of Learning Disabilities, 22,* 76–89.

Mann, V., & Liberman, I. (1984). Phonological awareness and verbal short-term memory. *Journal of Learning Disabilities, 17,* 592–599.

Margolis, H., & McGettigan, J. (1988). Managing resistance to instructional modifications in mainstreamed environments. *Remedial and Special Education, 9*, 15–21.

Marion, R. (1979). Minority parent involvement in the IEP process: A systematic model approach. *Focus on Exceptional Children, 10*(8), 1–15.

Marozas, D.S., & May, D.C. (1986). *Issues and practices in special education.* New York: Longman.

Marston, D., & Magnusson, D. (1985). Implementing curriculum-based measurement in special and regular education settings. *Exceptional Children, 52*, 266–276.

Marston, D., & Magnusson, D. (1988). Curriculum-based measurement: District level implementation. In J.Z. Graden & M. Curtis (Eds.), *Alternative education delivery systems: Enhancing instructional options for all students* (pp. 137–172). Washington, DC: National Association of School Psychologists.

Martens, B.K., Peterson, R.L., Witt, J.C., & Cirone, S. (1986). Teacher perceptions of school-based interventions. *Exceptional Children, 53*, 213–223.

Mastropieri, M.A., Emerick, K., & Scruggs, T.E. (1988). Mnemonic instruction of science concepts. *Behavioral Disorders, 14*, 48–56.

Mastropieri, M.A., & Scruggs, T.E. (1987). *Effective instruction for special education.* Boston: College-Hill Press.

Mastropieri, M.A., & Scruggs, T.E. (1988). Increasing content area learning of learning disabled students: Research implementation. *Learning Disabilities Research, 4*, 17–25.

Mastropieri, M.A., & Scruggs, T.E. (1989a). Constructing more meaningful relationships: Mnemonic instruction for special populations. *Educational Psychology Review, 1*, 83–111.

Mastropieri, M.A., & Scruggs, T.E. (1989b). Mnemonic social studies instruction: Classroom applications. *Remedial and Special Education, 10*, 40–46.

Mastropieri, M.A., & Scruggs, T.E. (1989c). Reconstructive elaborations: Strategies that facilitate content learning. *Learning Disabilities Focus, 4*, 73–77.

Mastropieri, M.A., Scruggs, T.E., & Shiah, S. (1991). Mathematics instruction for learning disabled students: A review of research. *Learning Disabilities Research and Practice, 6*, 89–98.

Mattingly, J.C., & Bott, D.A. (1990). Teaching multiplication facts to students with learning problems. *Exceptional Children, 56*, 438–449.

McDonough, K.M. (1989). Analysis of the expressive language characteristics of emotionally handicapped students in social interactions. *Behavior Disorders, 14*, 127–139.

McGill-Franzen, A., & Allington, R.L. (1991). The gridlock of low reading achievement: Perspectives on practice and policy. *Remedial and Special Education, 12*, 20–30.

McGinnis, E., & Goldstein, A.P. (1984). *Skillstreaming the elementary school child.* Champaign, IL: Research Press.

McKenzie, R.G., & Houk, C.S. (1986). The paraprofessional in special education. *Teaching Exceptional Children, 19*, 246–252.

McKeown, M.G., & Beck, I.L. (1988). Learning vocabulary. Different ways for different goals. *Remedial and Special Education, 9*, 42–52.

McKinney, J.D. (1987). Research on conceptually and empirically derived subtypes of specific learning disabilities. In M.C. Wang, M.C. Reynolds, & H.J. Walberg (Eds.), *Handbook of special education: Research and practice* (pp. 253–282). Elmsford, NY: Pergamon Press.

McKinney, J.D. (1989). Longitudinal research on the behavioral characteristics of children with learning disabilities. *Journal of Learning Disabilities, 22*, 141–150.

McLeod, T., & Armstrong, S. (1982). Learning disabilities in mathematics-skills deficits and remedial approaches at the intermediate and secondary grades. *Learning Disability Quarterly, 5*, 305–311.

Meadows, N., Neel, R.S., Parker, G., & Timo, K. (1991). A validation of social skills for students with behavioral disorders. *Behavioral Disorders, 16*, 200–210.

Meichenbaum, D. (1977). *Cognitive behavior*

modification: An integrative approach. New York: Plenum.

Meichenbaum, D. (1980). Cognitive behavior modification with exceptional children: A promise yet unfulfilled. *Exceptional Education Quarterly, 1*, 83–88.

Mercer, C.E., & Mercer, A.R. (1989). *Teaching students with learning problems* (3rd ed.). Columbus, OH: Merrill.

Mercer, C.D., & Miller, S.P. (1992a). *Strategic math series*. Lawrence, KS: Edge Enterprises.

Mercer, C.D., & Miller, S.P. (1992b). Teaching students with learning problems in math to acquire, understand, and apply basic math facts. *Remedial and Special Education, 13*, 19–35, 61.

Merrill Linguistic Reading Program (4th ed.). (1986). Columbus, OH: Merrill.

Meyers, J., Gelzheiser, L.M., & Yelich, G. (1991). Do pull-in programs foster teacher collaboration? *Remedial and Special Education, 12*(2), 7–15.

Minner, S., & Prater, G. (1989). Arranging the physical environment of special education classrooms. *Academic Therapy, 25*(1), 91–96.

Miramontes, O.B. (1990). Organizing for effective paraprofessional services in special education: A multilingual/multiethnic instructional service team model. *Remedial and Special Education, 12*(1), 29–36.

Montague, M., Bos, C., & Doucette, M. (1991). Affective, cognitive, and metacognitive attributes of eighth-grade mathematical problem solvers. *Learning Disabilities Research & Practice, 6*, 145–151.

Moran, M.R. (1980). *An investigation of the demands on oral language skills of learning disabled students in secondary classrooms* (Research Report No. 1). Lawrence: University of Kansas Institute for Research in Learning Disabilities.

Morgan, D.P., & Jenson, W.R. (1988). *Teaching behaviorally disordered students: Preferred practices*. Columbus, OH: Merrill.

Morsink, C.V., Thomas, C.C., & Correa, V.I. (1991). *Interactive teaming: Consultation and collaboration in special programs*. New York: Merrill/Macmillan.

Myles, B.S., & Hronek, L.J. (1990). Transition

activities: A classroom management tool. *LD Forum, 15*(3), 20–22.

National Assessment of Educational Progress. (1985). *The reading report card: Progress toward excellence in our schools; trends in reading over four national assessments, 1971–1984*. Princeton, NJ: Author.

National Center for Education Statistics. (1990). *The condition of education: Vol. 1. Elementary and secondary education*. Washington, DC: Author.

National Center for Education Statistics. (1991). *Dropout rates in the United States; 1990*. Washington, DC: Author.

National Commission on Children. (1991). *Speaking of kids: A national survey of children and parents*. Washington, DC: Author.

National Commission on Excellence in Education. (1983). *A nation at risk: The imperative for educational reform*. Washington, DC: U.S. Government Printing Office.

National Council of Teachers of Mathematics. (1989). *Curriculum and evaluation standards for school mathematics*. Reston, VA: Author.

National Governor's Association. (1986). *Time for results: The governors' report on education*. Washington, DC: Author.

National Joint Committee on Learning Disabilities. (1988). Unpublished letter to member organizations.

National Law Center on Homelessness and Poverty. (1990). *Shut out: Denial of education to homeless children*. Washington, DC: Author.

Nelson, J.R., Smith, D.J., Dodd, J.M., & Gilbert, C. (1991). The time estimation skills of students with emotional handicaps: A comparison. *Behavioral Disorders, 16*, 116–119.

Newcomer, P.L., & Barenbaum, E.M. (1991). The written composing ability of children with learning disabilities: A review of the literature from 1980–1990. *Journal of Learning Disabilities, 24*, 578–593.

Newcomer, P.L., & Hammill, D.D. (1988). *Test of language development—2: Primary*. Austin, TX: Pro-Ed.

Newland, T.E. (1932). An analytical study of the development of illegibilities in handwriting from the lower grades to adulthood. *Journal of Educational Research, 26,* 249–258.

Nihira, K., Foster, R., Shellhaas, M., & Leland, H. (1981). *AAMD adaptive behavior scale—School edition.* Washington, DC: American Association on Mental Deficiency.

Northwest Regional Educational Laboratory. (1990). *Effective schooling practices: A research synthesis 1990 update.* Portland, OR: Author.

O'Connor, S. (1988). Affective climate. In R. McNergney (Ed.), *Guide to classroom teaching* (pp. 247–261). Boston: Allyn & Bacon.

O'Melia, M.C., & Rosenberg, M.S. (1989). Classroom management: Preventing behavior problems in classrooms for students with learning disabilities. *LD Forum, 15*(1), 23–26.

O'Shea, L.J., Sindelar, P.T., & O'Shea, D.J. (1985). The effects of repeated readings and attentional cues on reading fluency and comprehension. *Journal of Reading Behavior, 17,* 129–141.

Olson, J. (1989). Managing life in the classroom: Dealing with the nitty gritty. *Academic Therapy, 24*(5), 545–553.

Osborne, S.S., Schulte, A.C., & McKinney, J.D. (1991). A longitudinal study of students with learning disabilities in mainstream and resource programs. *Exceptionality, 2,* 81–95.

Paddock, C. (1992). Ice cream stick math. *Teaching Exceptional Children, 24,* 50–51.

Palincsar, A.S. (1986). Metacognitive strategy instruction. *Exceptional Children, 53,* 118–124.

Palincsar, A.S., & Brown, A.L. (1984). Reciprocal teaching of comprehension fostering and comprehension monitoring activities. *Cognition and Instruction, 1,* 117–175.

Patton, J.R., Beirne-Smith, M., & Payne, J.S. (1990). *Mental retardation* (3rd ed.). Columbus, OH: Merrill.

Patton, J.R., Polloway, E.A., & Cronin, M.E. (1987). Social studies instruction for mildly handicapped students: A status report. *The Social Studies, 71,* 131–135.

Paul, P.V., & O'Rourke, J.P. (1988). Multimeaning words and reading comprehension: Implications for special education students. *Remedial and Special Education, 9,* 42–52.

Pearson, P.D., & Johnson, D.D. (1978). *Teaching reading comprehension.* New York: Holt, Rinehart, & Winston.

Peck, D.M., & Connell, M. (1990). *Peatmoss math: The fraction books.* Salt Lake City: Wild Goose.

Peck, G. (1989). Facilitating cooperative learning: A forgotten tool gets it started. *Academic Therapy 25*(2), 145–150.

Peterson, S.K., Mercer, C.D., & O'Shea, L. (1988). Teaching learning disabled students place value using the concrete to abstract sequence. *Learning Disabilities Research 4,* 52–56.

Peterson, S.K., Scott, J., & Sroka, K. (1990). Using the language experience approach with precision. *Teaching Exceptional Children, 22,* 28–31.

Phillips, V., & McCullough, L. (1990). Consultation-based programming: Instituting the collaborative ethic in schools. *Exceptional Children, 56,* 291–304.

Pianta, R.C. (1990). Widening the debate on educational reform: Prevention as a viable alternative. *Exceptional Children, 56,* 306–313.

Pinnell, G.S. (1990). Success for low achievers through reading recovery. *Educational Leadership, 48,* 17–21.

Polloway, E.A., Epstein, M.H., Polloway, C., Patton, J.R., & Ball, D.W. (1986). Corrective reading program: An analysis of effectiveness with learning disabled and mentally retarded students. *Remedial and Special Education, 7,* 41–47.

Polloway, E.A., Patton, J.R., Payne, J.S., & Payne, R.A. (1989). *Strategies for teaching learners with special needs* (4th ed.). Columbus, OH: Merrill.

Polsgrove, L., & McNeil, M. (1989). The consultation process: Research and practice. *Remedial and Special Education, 10*(1), 6–13.

Poplin, M.S. (1988). The reductionist fallacy in learning disabilities: Replicating the past by reducing the present. *Journal of Learning Disabilities, 21,* 389–400.

Porter, A. (1989). A curriculum out of balance: The case of elementary school mathematics. *Educational Researcher, 18,* 9–15.

Prawat, R.S. (1989). Promoting access to knowledge, strategy, and disposition in students: A research synthesis. *Review of Educational Research, 59,* 1–42.

Pressley, M., Burkell, J., Cariglia-Bull, T., Lysynchuk, L., McGoldrick, J.A., Schneider, B., Snyder, B.L., Symons, S., & Woloshyn, V.E. (1990). *Cognitive strategy instruction that really improves children's academic performance.* Cambridge, MA: Brookline Books.

Pressley, M., Scruggs, T.E., & Mastropieri, M.A. (1989). Memory strategy research in learning disabilities: Present and future directions. *Learning Disabilities Research, 4,* 68–77.

Public Law 101–476 (Individuals with Disabilities Education Act [IDEA]) 20 U.S.C., Chapter 33, 1990.

Pugach, M.C., & Johnson, L.J. (1988). Peer collaboration. *Teaching Exceptional Children, 20,* 75–77.

Pugach, M.C., & Johnson, L.J. (1989). The challenge of implementing collaboration between general and special education. *Exceptional Children, 56,* 232–235.

Putnam, M.L. (1992a). Characteristics of questions on tests administered by mainstream secondary classroom teachers. *Learning Disabilities Research and Practice, 7,* 129–136.

Putnam, M.L. (1992b). The testing practices of mainstream secondary classroom teachers. *Remedial and Special Education, 13*(5), 11–21.

Ramey, P., & Robbins, P. (1989). Professional growth and support through peer coaching. *Educational Leadership, 46*(8), 35–38.

Ramirez, B.A. (1988). Culturally and linguistically diverse children. *Teaching Exceptional Children, 20,* 45.

Rappaport, S.R. (1991). Diagnostic-prescriptive teaming: The road less traveled. *Reading, Writing, and Learning Disabilities, 7,* 183–199.

Rathjen, D.P. (1984). Social skills training for children: Innovations and consumer guidelines. *School Psychology Review, 13,* 292–301.

Reisberg, L., & Wolf, R. (1988). Instructional strategies for special education consultants. *Remedial and Special Education, 9,* 29–40.

Reith, H.J., Polsgrove, L., McLeskey, J., Payne, K., & Anderson, R. (1978). The use of self-recording to increase the arithmetic performance of severely behaviorally disordered students. In R.B. Rutherford & A.G. Prieto (Eds.), *Severe behavior disorders of children and youth* (pp. 50–58). Monograph in behavioral disorders, Arizona State University, Tempe.

Reschly, D.J. (1987). Learning characteristics of mildly handicapped students: Implications for classification, placement, and programming. In M.C. Wang, M.C. Reynolds, & H.J. Walberg (Eds.), *Handbook of special education: Research and practice: Vol. 1. Learner characteristics and adaptive education* (pp. 35–38). New York: Pergamon Press.

Reynolds, C.J., Salend, S.J., & Beahan, C.L. (1989). Motivating secondary students: Bringing in the reinforcements. *Academic Therapy, 25*(1), 81–89.

Reynolds, M.C., Wang, M.C., & Walberg, H.J. (1987). The necessary restructuring of special and regular education. *Exceptional Children, 53,* 391–398.

Roberts, C., & Zubrick, S. (1992). Factors influencing the social status of children with mild academic disabilities in regular classrooms. *Exceptional Children, 59,* 192–202.

Robinson, F.P. (1961). *Effective study.* New York, NY: Harper & Row.

Rooney, K.J. (1988). *Independent strategies for efficient study.* Richmond, VA: J.R. Enterprises.

Rooney, K.J. (1990). *Independent strategies for efficient study.* Richmond, VA: J.R. Enterprises.

Rooney, K.J., & Hallahan, D.P. (1985). Future directions for cognitive behavior modification research: The quest for cognitive change. *Remedial and Special Education, 6,* 46–51.

Rose, T.L. (1984). Effects of previewing on the oral reading of mainstreamed behaviorally disordered students. *Behavioral Disorders, 10,* 33–39.

Rose, T.L., & Sherry, L. (1984). Relative effects of two previewing procedures on the oral reading performance of learning disabled adolescents. *Learning Disability Quarterly, 7,* 39–44.

Rosenshine, B.V. (1976). Classroom instruction. In N.L. Gage (Ed.), *The psychology of teaching methods: Seventy-seventh yearbook of the National Society for the Study of Education,* (pp. 335–371). Chicago: University of Chicago Press.

Rosenshine, B.V. (1983). Teaching functions in instructional programs. *Elementary School Journal, 83,* 335–352.

Rosenshine, B.V. (1986). Synthesis of research on explicit teaching. *Educational Leadership, 43*(7), 60–69.

Rost, K.J., & Charles, D.C. (1967). Academic achievement of brain injured and hyperactive children in isolation. *Exceptional Children, 34,* 125–126.

Routman, R. (1988). *Transitions: From literature to literacy.* Portsmouth, NH: Heineman.

Ruhl, K.L., Hughes, C.A., & Schloss, P.J. (1987). Using the pause procedure to enhance lecture recall. *Teacher Education and Special Education, 10*(1), 14–18.

Runge, A., Walker, J., & Shea, T.M. (1975). A passport to positive parent-teacher communications. *Teaching Exceptional Children, 7,* 91–92.

Sabatino, D.A. (1987). Preventive discipline as a practice in special education. *Teaching Exceptional Children, 19*(4), 8–11.

Sabornie, E.J. (1985). Social mainstreaming of handicapped students: Facing an unpleasant reality. *Remedial and Special Education, 6,* 12–16.

Sabornie, E.J. (1987). Bi-directional social status of behaviorally disordered and nonhandicapped elementary school pupils. *Behavioral Disorders, 13,* 45–57.

Sabornie, E.J., Kauffman, J.M., & Cullinan, D.A. (1990). Extended sociometric status of adolescents with mild handicaps: A cross-categorical perspective. *Exceptionality, 1,* 197–209.

Salvia, J., & Hughes, C. (1990). *Curriculum-based assessment: Testing what is taught.* New York: Macmillan.

Salvia, J., & Ysseldyke, J. (1988). *Assessment in special and remedial education* (4th ed.). Boston: Houghton Mifflin.

Samuels, S.J. (1979). The method of repeated readings. *Reading Teacher, 32,* 403–408.

Samuels, S.J. (1981). Some essentials of decoding. *Exceptional Education Quarterly, 2,* 11–25.

Samuels, S.J. (1987). Information processing abilities and reading. *Journal of Learning Disabilities, 20,* 18–22.

Samuels, S.J. (1988). Decoding and automaticity: Helping poor readers become automatic at word recognition. *Reading Teacher, 41,* 756–760.

Sasso, G.M., Melloy, K.J., & Kavale, K.A. (1990). Generalization, maintenance, and behavioral covariation associated with social skills training through structured learning. *Behavioral Disorders, 16,* 9–22.

Schaeffer, A.L., Zigmond, N., Kerr, M.M., & Farra, H.E. (1990). Helping teenagers develop school survival skills. *Teaching Exceptional Children, 23,* 6–9.

Schloss, P.J., Schloss, C.N., Wood, C.E., & Kiehl, W.S. (1986). A critical review of social skills research with behaviorally disordered students. *Behavioral Disorders, 12,* 1–14.

Schoolfield, L.D., & Timberlake, J.B. (1974). *The phonovisual method* (rev. ed.). Rockville, MD: Phonovisual Products.

Schrader, B., & Valus, A. (1990). Disabled learners as able teachers: A cross-age tutoring project. *Academic Therapy 25*(5), 589–597.

Schumaker, J.B., Denton, P.H., & Deshler, D.D. (1984). *The paraphrasing strategy (Learning Strategies Curriculum).* Lawrence: University of Kansas Institute for Research on Learning Disabilities.

Schumaker, J.B., & Deshler, D.D. (1988). Implementing the regular education initiative in secondary schools: A different ball game. *Journal of Learning Disabilities, 21,* 36–41.

Schumaker, J.B., Deshler, D.D., Alley, G.R., & Warner, M.M. (1983). Toward the development of an intervention model for learning disabled adolescents: University of Kansas Institute. *Exceptional Education Quarterly, 4,* 45–74.

Schumaker, J.B., Deshler, D.D., Alley, G.R., Warner, M.M., & Denton, P.H. (1982). Multipass: A learning strategy for improving reading comprehension. *Learning Disability Quarterly, 5,* 295–304.

Schumaker, J.B., Nolan, S.M., & Deshler, D.D. (1985). *Learning strategies curriculum: The error monitoring strategy.* Lawrence:

University of Kansas Institute for Research on Learning Disabilities.

Schumm, J.S., & Vaughn, S. (1991). Making adaptations for mainstreamed students: General classroom teachers' perspectives. *Remedial and Special Education, 12,* 18–27.

Schumm, J.S., & Vaughn, S. (1992). Planning for mainstreamed special education students: Perceptions of general classroom teachers. *Exceptionality, 3,* 81–98.

Schunk, D.H. (1985). Participation in goal setting: Effects on self-efficacy and skills of learning disabled children. *Journal of Special Education, 19,* 307–317.

Schwartz, S.E. (1977). *Real life math program.* Chicago: Hubbard.

Schworm, R.W. (1988). Look in the middle of the word. *Teaching Exceptional Children, 20,* 13–17.

Scruggs, T.E., & Marsing, L. (1987). Teaching test-taking skills to behaviorally disordered students. *Behavioral Disorders, 13,* 240–244.

Scruggs, T.E., & Mastropieri, M.A. (1986). Academic characteristics of behaviorally disordered and learning disabled students. *Behavioral Disorders, 11,* 184–190.

Scruggs, T.E., & Mastropieri, M.A. (1990). Mnemonic instruction for students with learning disabilities: What it is and what it does. *Learning Disability Quarterly, 13,* 271–280.

Scruggs, T.E., Mastropieri, M.A., Levin, J.R., & Gaffney, J.S. (1985). Facilitating the acquisition of science facts in learning disabled students. *American Educational Research Journal, 22,* 575–586.

Scruggs, T.E., Mastropieri, M.A., Levin, J.R., McLoone, B., Gaffney, J.S., & Prater, M.A. (1985). Increasing content-area learning: A comparison of mnemonic and visual-spatial direct instruction. *Learning Disabilities Research, 1*(1), 18–31.

Scruggs, T.E., & Richter, L. (1985). Tutoring learning disabled students: A critical review. *Learning Disability Quarterly, 8,* 286–298.

Seidel, J.F., & Vaughn, S. (1991). Social alienation and the learning disabled school dropout. *Learning Disabilities Research & Practice, 6,* 152–157.

Seidenberg, P.L. (1989). Relating text-processing research to reading and writing instruction for learning disabled students. *Learning Disabilities Focus, 5,* 4–12.

Self, H., Benning, A., Marston, D., & Magnusson, D. (1991). Cooperative teaching project: A model for students at risk. *Exceptional Children, 58,* 26–34.

Semmel, M.I., Abernathy, T.V., Butera, G., & Lesar, S. (1991). Teacher perceptions of the regular education initiative. *Exceptional Children, 58,* 9–24.

Shake, M.C., Allington, R.L., Gaskins, R., & Marr, M.B. (1989). How remedial teachers teach vocabulary. *Remedial and Special Education, 10,* 51–57.

Shea, T.M., & Bauer, A.M. (1985). *Parents and teachers of exceptional students: A handbook for involvement.* Boston: Allyn & Bacon.

Shea, T.M., & Bauer, A.M. (1991). *Parents and teachers of children with exceptionalities.* Boston: Allyn & Bacon.

Shields, J.M., & Heron, T.E. (1989). Teaching organizational skills to students with learning disabilities. *Teaching Exceptional Children, 21,* 8–13.

Shinn, M.R. (1988). Development of curriculum-based local norms for use in special education decision-making. *School Psychology Review, 17*(1), 61–80.

Shinn, M.R., Tindal, G.A., & Stein, S. (1988). Curriculum-based measurement and the identification of mildly handicapped students: A research review. *Professional School Psychology, 3*(1), 69–85.

Shores, R.E., & Haubrich, P.A. (1969). Effects of cubicles in educating emotionally disturbed children. *Exceptional Children, 36,* 21–26.

Shrung-Schaffner, L., & Sapona, R.H. (1990). May the FORCE be with you: A test preparation strategy for learning disabled adolescents. *Academic Therapy, 25*(3), 291–300.

Silbert, J., Carnine, D., & Stein, M. (1990). *Direct instruction mathematics* (2nd ed.). Columbus, OH: Merrill.

Simmonds, E.P.M., Luchow, J.P., Kaminsky, S., & Cottone, V. (1989). Applying cognitive learning strategies in the classroom: A collaborative training institute. *Learning Disabilities Focus, 4,* 96–105.

Simmons, D.C., Fuchs, D., & Fuchs, L.S.

(1991). Instructional and curricular requisites of mainstreamed students with learning disabilities. *Journal of Learning Disabilities 24*, 354–360.

Simmons, D.C., & Kameenui, E.J. (1990). The effect of task alternatives on vocabulary knowledge: A comparison of students with and without learning disabilities. *Journal of Learning Disabilities, 23*, 291–297.

Simms, R.B., & Falcon, S.C. (1987). Teaching sight words. *Teaching Exceptional Children, 20*, 30–33.

Simpson, R.L. (1982). *Conferencing parents of exceptional children*. Rockville, MD: Aspen.

Sindelar, P.T. (1982). The effects of cross-aged tutoring on the comprehension skills of remedial reading students. *Journal of Special Education, 16*, 199–206.

Sindelar, P.T., Smith, M.A., Harriman, N.E., Hale, R.L., & Wilson, R.J. (1986). Teacher effectiveness in special education programs. *Journal of Special Education, 20*, 195–207.

Sindelar, P.T., Watanabe, A.K., McCray, A.D., & Hornsby, P.J. (1992). Special education's role in literacy and educational reform. *Teaching Exceptional Children, 24*, 38–40.

Slavin, R.E. (1987). *Cooperative learning: Student teams* (2nd ed.). Washington, DC: National Education Association.

Slavin, R.E. (1988). *Educational psychology: Theory into practice*. Englewood Cliffs, NJ: Prentice-Hall.

Slavin, R.E. (1990). *Cooperative learning: Theory, research and practice*. Englewood Cliffs, NJ: Prentice-Hall.

Slavin, R.E. (1991a). *Educational psychology* (3rd ed.). Englewood Cliffs, NJ: Prentice-Hall.

Slavin, R.E. (1991b). Synthesis of research on cooperative learning. *Educational Leadership, 48*(6), 71–82.

Slavin, R.E., Karweit, N.L., & Madden, N.A. (1989). *Effective programs for students at risk*. Boston: Allyn & Bacon.

Slavin, R., & Madden, N. (1989). What works for students at risk: A research synthesis. *Educational Leadership, 46*, 4–13.

Smith, D.D., & Lovitt, T.C. (1975). The use of modeling techniques to influence the acquisition of computational arithmetic skills in learning-disabled children. In E. Ramp &

G. Semb (Eds.), *Behavior analysis: Areas of research and application* (pp. 283–308). Englewood Cliffs, NJ: Prentice-Hall.

Smith, F. (1971). *Understanding reading*. New York: Holt, Rinehart, & Winston.

Smith, J.O. (1992). Falling through the cracks: Rehabilitation services for adults with learning disabilities. *Exceptional Children, 58*, 451–460.

Smith, S.W. (1990). Individualized education programs (IEP's) in special education: From intent to acquiescence. *Exceptional Children, 57*, 6–14.

Sommerville, J.W., Warnberg, L.S., & Bost, D.E. (1973). Effects of cubicles versus increased stimulation on task performance by first-grade males perceived as distractible and nondistractible. *Journal of Special Education, 7*, 169–185.

Sonnenschein, P. (1981). Parents and professionals: An uneasy relationship. *Teaching Exceptional Children, 14*, 62–65.

Spalding, R.B., & Spalding, W.T. (1962). *The writing road to reading*. New York: Morrow.

Sparrow, S.S., Balla, D.A., & Cichetti, D.V. (1984). *Vineland adaptive behavior scales*. Circle Pines, MN: American Guidance Service.

Spear, L.D., & Sternberg, R.J. (1986). An information processing framework for understanding reading disability. In S. Ceci (Ed.), *Handbook of cognitive, social, and neuropsychological aspects of learning disabilities* (pp. 3–31). Hillsdale, NJ: Erlbaum.

Spiro, R. & Myers, A. (1984). Individual differences and underlying cognitive processes. In P.D. Pearson (Ed.), *Handbook of reading research* (pp. 471–504). New York: Longman.

Stahl, S.L., & Miller, P.D. (1989). Whole language and language experience approaches for beginning reading: A quantitative research synthesis. *Review of Educational Research, 59*, 87–116.

Stainback, W., Stainback, S., & Bunch, G. (1989). Introduction and historical background. In S. Stainback, W. Stainback, & M. Forest (Eds.), *Educating all students in the mainstream of regular education* (pp. 3–14). Baltimore, MD: Paul Brookes.

Stainback, W., Stainback, S., & Froyen, L. (1987). Structuring the classroom to prevent disruptive behaviors. *Teaching Exceptional Children, 19*(4), 12–16.

Stallings, J.A. (1974). *Follow through classroom observation evaluation 1972–1973* (Executive Summary SRI Project URU-7370). Menlo Park, CA: Stanford Research Institute.

Stallings, J.A. (1985). A study of implementation of Madeline Hunter's model and its effects on students. *Journal of Educational Research, 78*, 325–337.

Stanovich, K. (1980). Toward an interactive-compensatory model of individual differences in the development of reading fluency. *Reading Research Quarterly, 16*, 32–71.

Stanovich, K. (1986a). Explaining the variance in reading ability in terms of psychological processes: What have we learned? *Annals of Dyslexia, 35*, 967–996.

Stanovich, K. (1986b). Matthew effects in reading: Some consequences of individual differences in the acquisition of literacy. *Reading Research Quarterly, 31*, 360–406.

Stauffer, R.G. (1970). *The language-experience approach to the teaching of reading.* New York: Harper & Row.

Stein, N.L., & Trabasso, T. (1982). What's in a story?: An approach to comprehension and instruction. In R. Glaser (Ed.), *Advances in instructional psychology* (Vol. 2, pp. 213–267). Hillsdale, NJ: Erlbaum.

Stein, M. (1987). Arithmetic word problems. *Teaching Exceptional Children, 19*, 33–35.

Stevens, K.B., & Schuster, J.W. (1987). Effects of a constant time delay procedure on the written spelling performance of a learning disabled student. *Learning Disability Quarterly, 10*, 9–16.

Stevens, K.B., & Schuster, J.W. (1988). Time delay: Systematic instruction for academic tasks. *Remedial and Special Education, 9*, 16–21.

Stevens, R., & Rosenshine, B. (1981). Advances in research on teaching. *Exceptional Education Quarterly, 2*(1), 1–9.

Stinson, D.M., Gast, D.L., Wolery, M., & Collins, B.C. (1991). Acquisition of nontargeted information during small-group instruction. *Exceptionality, 2*(2), 65–80.

Stokes, T.F., & Baer, D.M. (1977). An implicit technology of generalization. *Journal of Applied Behavior Analysis, 10*, 349–367.

Stone, W.L., & La Greca, A.M. (1990). The social status of children with learning disabilities: A reexamination. *Journal of Learning Disabilities, 23*, 32–37.

Stowitschek, J.J., & Salzberg, C.L. (1987). *Job success for handicapped youth: A social protocol curriculum.* Reston, VA: Council for Exceptional Children.

Strain, P.S., & Odom, S.L. (1986). Peer social initiations: Effective intervention for social skills development of exceptional children. *Exceptional Children, 52*, 543–551.

Strauss, A.A., & Lehtinen, L.E. (1947). *Psychopathology and education of the brain-injured child.* New York: Grune & Stratton.

Sugai, G., & Fuller, M. (1991). A decision model for social skills curriculum analysis. *Remedial and Special Education, 12*, 33–42.

Swanson, H.L., & Rhine, B. (1985). Strategy transformations in learning disabled children's math performance: Clues to the development of expertise. *Journal of Learning Disabilities, 18*, 596–603.

Systems Impact, Inc. (1985). *Mastering fractions.* Washington, DC: Author.

Telzrow, C. (1988). Debate over usefulness of IQ. *Communique, 17*, 4–6.

Templeton, S. (1986). Synthesis of research on the learning and teaching of spelling. *Educational Leadership, 43*, 73–78.

Thomas, C.C., Englert, C.S., & Gregg, S. (1987). An analysis of errors and strategies in the expository writing of learning disabled students. *Remedial and Special Education, 8*, 21–30.

Thornton, C.A., & Toohey, M.A. (1985). Basic math facts: Guidelines for teaching and learning. *Learning Disabilities Focus, 1*, 44–57.

Thornton, C.A., & Toohey, M.A. (1986). Subtraction hide and seek cards can help. *Teaching Exceptional Children, 19*, 10–14.

Thousand, J.S., & Villa, R.A. (1989). Enhancing success in heterogeneous schools. In S. Stainback, W. Stainback, & M. Forest (Eds.), *Educating all students in the mainstream of regular education* (pp. 89–103). Baltimore, MD: Paul Brookes.

Thurber, D.N., & Jordan, D.R. (1981). *D'Nealian handwriting*. Glenview, IL: Scott, Foresman.

Torgesen, J.K. (1982). The learning disabled child as an inactive learner: Educational implications. *Topics in Learning and Learning Disabilities, 2*(1), 45–52.

Torgesen, J.K. (1986). Using computers to help learning disabled children practice reading: A research-based perspective. *Learning Disabilities Focus, 1,* 72–81.

Torgesen, J.K., & Kail, R.V. (1980). Memory processes in exceptional children. In B. Keogh (Ed.), *Advances in special education: Vol. 1. Basic constructs and theoretical orientations* (pp. 59–99). Greenwich, CT: JAI Press.

Touchette, P.E. (1971). Transfer of stimulus control: Measuring the moment of transfer. *Journal of Experimental Analysis of Behavior, 15,* 347–354.

Touchette, P.E., & Howard, J.S. (1984). Errorless learning: Reinforcement contingencies and stimulus control transfer in delayed prompting. *Journal of Applied Behavior Analysis, 17,* 175–188.

Tovey, D. (1978). Sound-it-out: A reasonable approach to spelling? *Reading World, 17,* 220–233.

Trifiletti, J.J., Frith, G.H., & Armstrong, S. (1984). Microcomputers versus resource rooms for LD students: A preliminary investigation of the effects on math skills. *Learning Disability Quarterly, 7,* 69–76.

Turnbull, A.P., & Turnbull, H.R. (1986). *Families, professionals, and exceptionality: A special partnership*. Columbus, OH: Merrill.

Tyson, H., & Woodward, A. (1989). Why students aren't learning very much from textbooks. *Educational Leadership, 47*(3), 14–17.

U.S. Department of Education. (1991a). *America 2000: An education strategy sourcebook*. Washington, DC: U.S. Department of Education.

U.S. Department of Education. (1991b). *Thirteenth annual report to Congress on the implementation of the Individuals with Disabilities Education Act*. Washington, DC: U.S. Department of Education.

Vacc, N.N. (1987). Word processor versus handwriting: A comparative study of writing samples produced by mildly mentally handicapped students. *Exceptional Children, 54,* 156–165.

Vallecorsa, A.L., & Garriss, E. (1990). Story composition skills of middle-grade students with learning disabilities. *Exceptional Children, 57,* 48–54.

Vallecorsa, A.L., Ledford, R.R., & Parnell, G.G. (1991). Strategies for teaching composition skills to students with learning disabilities. *Teaching Exceptional Children, 23,* 52–55.

Vaughn, S., Bos, C., Harrell, J., & Lasky, B. (1988). Parent participation in the initial IEP conference ten years after mandated involvement. *Journal of Learning Disabilities, 21,* 82–89.

Villa, R.A., Thousand, J.S., Paolucci-Whitcomb, P., & Nevin, A. (1990). In search of new paradigms for collaborative consultation. *Journal of Educational and Psychological Consultation, 1,* 279–292.

Wagner, M. (1989). *The transition experience of youth with disabilities: A report from the national longitudinal transition study*. Menlo Park, CA: SRI International.

Walker, H.M., McConnell, S., Holmes, D., Todis, B., Walker, J., & Golden, N. (1983). *The Walker social skills curriculum: The ACCEPTS program*. Austin, TX: Pro-Ed.

Walker, H.M., Todis, B., Holmes, D., & Horton, G. (1988). *The Walker social skills curriculum: The ACCESS program*. Austin, TX: Pro-Ed.

Wallace, G.W., & Bott, D.A. (1989). Statement-Pie: A strategy to improve the paragraph writing skills of adolescents with learning disabilities. *Journal of Learning Disabilities, 22,* 541–543.

Wallace, G.W., & McLoughlin, J.A. (1988). *Learning disabilities: Concepts and characteristics* (3rd ed.). Columbus, OH: Merrill.

Wang, M.C., & Birch, J.W. (1984). Effective special education in regular classes. *Exceptional Children, 50,* 391–398.

Warner, M.M., Schumaker, J.B., Alley, G.R., & Deshler, D.D. (1980). Learning disabled adolescents in public schools: Are they different from other low achievers?

Exceptional Education Quarterly, 1(2), 27–36.

Wechsler, D. (1991). *Wechsler intelligence scale for children, 3rd edition*. San Antonio, TX: Psychological Corporation.

Wehrung-Schaffner, L., & Sapona, R.H. (1990). May the FORCE be with you: A test preparation strategy for learning disabled adolescents. *Academic Therapy, 25*(3), 291–300.

Weiss, E. (1984). Learning disabled children's understanding of social interactions of peers. *Journal of Learning Disabilities, 17,* 612–615.

Welch, M., & Jensen, J.B. (1990). Write, P.L.E.A.S.E.: A video-assisted strategic intervention to improve written expression of inefficient learners. *Remedial and Special Education, 12,* 37–47.

Wesson, C., Wilson, R., & Mandlebaum, L.H. (1988). Learning games for active student responding. *Teaching Exceptional Children, 20,* 12–14.

West, J.F. (1990). Educational collaboration in the restructuring of schools. *Journal of Educational and Psychological Consultation, 1*(1), 23–40.

Whalen, C.K. (1989). Attention deficit and hyperactivity disorders. In T. Ollendick & M. Hersen (Eds.), *Handbook of child psychopathology* (pp. 131–169). New York: Plenum.

Whinnery, K.W., Fuchs, L.S., & Fuchs, D. (1991). General, special, and remedial teachers' acceptance of behavioral and instructional strategies for mainstreaming students with mild handicaps. *Remedial and Special Education, 12,* 6–17.

White, W.A.T. (1988). A meta-analysis of effects of direct instruction in special education. *Education and Treatment of Children, 11,* 364–373.

Whitt, J., Paul, P.V., & Reynolds, C.J. (1988). Motivate reluctant learning disabled writers. *Teaching Exceptional Children, 20,* 37–39.

Wiedmeyer, D., & Lehman, J. (1991). Approach to collaborative teaching and consultation. *Teaching Exceptional Children, 23*(3), 6–10.

Wiener, J. (1991). Alternatives in the assessment of the learning disabled

adolescent: A learning strategies approach. *Learning Disabilities Focus, 1,* 97–107.

Wiig, E.H. (1990). Language disabilities in school-age children and youth. In G.H. Shames & E.H. Wiig (Eds.), *Human communication disorders*. Columbus, OH: Merrill.

Wiig, E.H., & Semel, E.M. (1984). *Language assessment and intervention for the learning disabled* (2nd ed.). Columbus, OH: Merrill.

Will, M.C., (1984). *OSERS programming for the transition of youth with disabilities: Bridges from school to working life*. Washington, DC: Office of Special Education and Rehabilitative Services.

Will, M.C. (1986). Educating children with learning problems: A shared responsibility. *Exceptional Children, 52,* 411–415.

Williams, R.M., & Rooney, K.J. (1986). *A handbook of cognitive behavior modification procedures for teachers*. Charlottesville: University of Virginia Learning Disabilities Research Institute.

Wilson, M.S. (1991). Support services professionals' evaluation of current services for students with learning disabilities and low achieving students without learning disabilities: More grist for the reform mill. *School Psychology Review, 20,* 67–80.

Wilson, R., & Wesson, C. (1991). Increasing achievement of learning disabled students by measuring and controlling task difficulty. *Learning Disabilities Research and Practice, 6,* 34–39.

Winterling, V. (1990). The effects of constant time delay, practice in writing or spelling, and reinforcement on sight word recognition in a small group. *Journal of Special Education, 24,* 101–116.

Winton, P.J., & Turnbull, A.P. (1981). Parent involvement as viewed by parents of preschool handicapped children. *Topics in Early Childhood Special Education, 1*(3), 11–19.

Wittrock, M.C. (Ed.). (1986). *Handbook of research on teaching* (3rd ed.). New York: Macmillan.

Wolery, M., Ault, M.J., Gast, D.L., Doyle, P.M., & Mills, B.M. (1990). Use of choral and individual attentional responses with constant time delay when teaching sight word reading. *Remedial and Special Education, 11,* 47–58.

Wolery, M., Bailey, D.B., & Sugai, G.M. (1988). *Effective teaching: Principles and procedures of applied behavior analysis with exceptional students.* Boston: Allyn & Bacon.

Wong, B., & Jones, W. (1982). Increasing metacomprehension in learning disabled and normally achieving students through self-questioning training. *Learning Disability Quarterly, 5,* 228–240.

Wong, B.Y.L., Wong, R., Darlington, D., & Jones, W. (1991). Interactive teaching: An effective way to teach revision skills to adolescents with learning disabilities. *Learning Disabilities Research and Practice, 6,* 117–127.

Wong, B.Y.L., Wong, R., Perry, N., & Sawatsky, D. (1986). The efficacy of a self-questioning summarization strategy for use by underachievers and learning disabled adolescents in social studies. *Learning Disabilities Focus, 2*(2), 20–35.

Wood, P.C. (1987). A game to prevent disciplinary problems. *Teaching Exceptional Children, 19*(4), 52–53.

Woodcock, R. (1987). *Woodcock reading mastery tests—revised.* Circle Pines, MN: American Guidance Service.

Woodcock, R., & Johnson, M.B. (1989a). *Woodcock–Johnson tests of achievement.* Allen, TX: DLM Teaching Resources.

Woodcock, R., & Johnson, M.B. (1989b). *Woodcock–Johnson tests of cognitive ability.* Allen, TX: DLM Teaching Resources.

Woodward, J. (1991). Procedural knowledge in mathematics: The role of the curriculum. *Journal of Learning Disabilities, 24,* 242–251.

Woodward, J., & Noell, J. (1991). Science instruction at the secondary level: Implications for students with learning disabilities. *Journal of Learning Disabilities, 24,* 277–284.

Ysseldyke, J.E. (1987). Classification of handicapped students. In M.C. Wang, M.C. Reynolds, & H.J. Walberg (Eds.), *Handbook of special education: Research and practice* (pp. 253–271). Elmsford, NY: Pergamon Press.

Ysseldyke, J.E., & Algozzine, B. (1982). *Critical issues in special and remedial education.* Boston: Houghton Mifflin.

Yssledyke, J.E., Algozzine, B., & Thurlow, M.L. (1992). *Critical issues in special education* (2nd ed.). Boston: Houghton Mifflin.

Ysseldyke, J.E., Christenson, S.L., & Thurlow, M.L. (1987). *Instructional factors that influence student achievement: An integrative review* (Monograph No. 7). Minneapolis: University of Minnesota.

Zaragoza, N., Vaughn, S., & McIntosh, R. (1991). Social skills interventions and children with behavior problems: A review. *Behavioral Disorders, 16,* 260–275.

Zigmond, N., Kerr, M.M., Schaeffer, A., Brown, G., & Farra, H. (1986). *The school survival skills curriculum.* Pittsburgh: University of Pittsburgh.

Photo Credits

Name Index

Subject Index